THE PSYCHOLOGY OF THE CHINESE PEOPLE

D1069964

The Psychology of the Chinese People

- **EDITOR**

Michael Harris Bond

- **CONTRIBUTORS**

Michael Harris Bond   Fanny M.C. Cheung

David Y.F. Ho   Rumjahn Hoosain

Kwang-kuo Hwang   In-mao Liu

Gordon Redding   Gilbert Y.Y. Wong

Kuo-shu Yang

The Chinese University Press

First published by Oxford University Press 1986.

Grateful acknowledgement is made to Oxford University Press for permission to use the typographical arrangement of the original edition of the title, *The Psychology of the Chinese People*.

The Psychology of the Chinese People
  Edited by Michael Harris Bond

© **The Chinese University of Hong Kong**, 2008

All rights reserved. No part of this publication may be reproduced or transmitted in any form or by any means, electronic or mechanical, including photocopying, recording, or any information storage and retrieval system, without permission in writing from The Chinese University of Hong Kong.

ISBN: 978–962–996–353–8

THE CHINESE UNIVERSITY PRESS
The Chinese University of Hong Kong
SHA TIN, N.T., HONG KONG
Fax: +852 2603 6692
     +852 2603 7355
E-mail: cup@cuhk.edu.hk
Web-site: www.chineseupress.com

Printed in Hong Kong

The East hath ever been
the dawning-place of
the Sun of Truth

(Abdu'l-Baha, 1911)

Contributors

Dr Michael Harris Bond
Senior Lecturer in the Department of Psychology at The Chinese University of Hong Kong

Dr Fanny M.C. Cheung
Senior Lecturer in the Department of Psychology at The Chinese University of Hong Kong

Dr David Y.F. Ho
Reader in the Department of Psychology at the University of Hong Kong

Dr Rumjahn Hoosain
Senior Lecturer in the Department of Psychology at the University of Hong Kong

Dr Kwang-kuo Hwang
Associate Professor in the Department of Psychology at the National Taiwan University

Professor In-mao Liu
Professor and Chairman of the Department of Psychology at The Chinese University of Hong Kong

Professor Gordon Redding
Professor and Chairman of the Department of Management Studies at the University of Hong Kong

Mr Gilbert Y.Y. Wong
Lecturer in the Department of Management Studies at the University of Hong Kong

Dr Kuo-shu Yang
Professor and Chairman of the Department of Psychology at National Taiwan University

Editor's Preface

A journey of a thousand miles begins with a single step.

(Traditional Chinese proverb.)

This collection attempts to fill a vacuum. At present, there is no book available that summarizes and integrates the empirical data on the psychological functioning of Chinese people. This is a lamentable state of affairs, given that Chinese people constitute more than one-quarter of the world's population.

There is a wealth, or perhaps one should say an excess, of speculation about what Chinese people are like. Although often perceptive, these speculations are bounded by the experiences and attitudes of their authors. Data collected under the constraints of scientific methodology are freed from many of these limitations, and may provide an antidote to the effusion, ethnocentrism, and axe-grinding which characterize much of the speculation.

In sharp contrast to the vast numbers of Chinese people is the malnourished base of empirical data about their behaviour. The science of psychology is a recent immigrant to Chinese intellectual communities. Furthermore, it has occasionally suffered from association with its origins in the West. Only recently has it emerged as an acceptable academic discipline in the People's Republic of China following the Cultural Revolution. This edited volume is offered in the hope of stimulating the accumulation of empirical data and directing future psychological research into productive channels.

In choosing the authors for each chapter, I was first concerned with selecting those who were actively creating scientific knowledge about Chinese psychology in those areas to be covered. An additional consideration was to ensure that a Chinese-reading author was associated with each chapter, so that no published research would be overlooked. Beyond these basic criteria, I naturally wanted the most competent scholars in their chosen fields to participate in the project. It seemed a harbinger of success that my first choices all agreed to contribute.

The authors were given the task of summarizing and integrating the major strands of research in their designated areas. They were also asked to build a comparative perspective into their treatment of the data, so that the Chinese could be located as a group with respect to other cultural groups. And, finally, all were requested to specify topics where future research seemed to be required.

My job as editor was made easier by the good cheer of the chapter authors in responding to my prodding about deadlines and by their gracious professionalism in thoughtfully considering my various suggestions about content, organization, and style. Our happy association reminds me of the Chinese proverb, 'When a family is united, everything succeeds'. I believe that we have, together, taken a successful first step towards understanding the Chinese psychologically; I hope that you, the reader, will agree.

MICHAEL HARRIS BOND
Hong Kong

Contents

1 Chinese Patterns of Socialization: a Critical Review

DAVID Y.F. HO

INTRODUCTION

The literature on Chinese socialization processes derives from very diverse sources, with great variations in theoretical perspective and methodological approach, as well as in the scope, depth, and quality of analysis. Furthermore, it is scattered in books and journals addressed to different groups of readers. A major aim of the present review is to bring together these diverse sources of material published in both English and Chinese, in order to assess the current state of knowledge in the field, note the conceptual and methodological issues involved, reveal serious gaps in knowledge, integrate and distil the findings and insights of previous investigators, and point out areas where further research is needed. The emphasis is on reviewing empirical investigations, an emphasis urgently needed at the present state of our knowledge (in a previous article, Ho, 1981a, the emphasis was put on traditional patterns). It is hoped that this review will encourage and enable greater co-ordination of efforts among different investigators in the field, so that a body of scientific knowledge built upon hierarchically ordered investigations will be more readily realized in the future.

CONTRIBUTIONS TO THE LITERATURE

Authors who have contributed to the literature on Chinese patterns of socialization appear to fall primarily into four groups, each identifiable by the intellectual discipline with which they are associated and consequently by the perspectives, approaches, and focus of interests germane to that discipline. The first of these is comprised of cultural anthropologists and, to a lesser extent, sociologists who rely on informants, biographical and autobiographical materials (notable examples of which are Chiang, 1940; Pruitt, 1945; J.S. Wong, 1950), content analysis of cultural productions, observations, and field studies of specific subcultural groups in various localities. Such sources have given detailed accounts of child-rearing practices; typically, however, the data obtained do not lend themselves easily to quantified presentation or analysis. The work of the Chinese group under the direction of Ruth Bunzel in the Columbia University Research in Contemporary Cultures project marked a milestone in anthropological investigations, and represented an early effort through which information on Chinese child-rearing practices was systematically gathered. The project yielded a large number of documents, most of which are unpublished. It may be noted that, judging from publications by authors who were participants in the project (such as Heyer, 1953; Muensterberger, 1951; Weakland, 1956; and Wolfenstein, 1955) psychoanalytic theory exerted a strong influence in guiding the work of the Chinese group. Despite the contributions of psychoanalytic theory, the information on Chinese socialization was limited in that it was derived from informants (see Bunzel, 1950), content analysis of children's stories (see Hu, 1950; Mead and Wolfenstein, 1955, the chapter on 'Monkey') and other cultural productions (for example, literary and artistic materials, films, games, and slang). The Columbia project was, indeed, 'The Study of Culture at a Distance' (Mead and Metraux, 1953). Other investigations (Hsu, 1967; Li, 1970; Osgood, 1975; Ward, 1970; Wolf, 1964; Wolf, 1970; Wu, 1966; and Yang, 1945) were, however, based on direct observations in specific Chinese communities.

The second group is represented by political scientists who have attempted to apply the political-culture approach to the study of China. A central thesis underlying this approach is that political processes and institutions characteristic of a nation over a period of time are under the pervasive influence of certain deeply rooted and enduring predispositions of the culture in which members of that nation are immersed. In particular, a focus on childhood political socialization promises to relate adult political behaviour to its antecedent conditions, that is, childhood experiences in authority relationships, styles of leadership, peer-group pressures towards conformity, and the like. The assumption is that a child, accustomed to these experiences, will be predisposed to feel and act in predictable ways in his political behaviour during adulthood. It is beyond the scope of this review to examine the validity of this assumption, or of the wider issues entailed in the notion of political culture. Nevertheless, the writings of political scientists who have used this approach add a new dimension to the understanding of childhood socialization in Chinese society. Notable among these are Solomon (1969; 1971) and Wilson (1970; 1974; 1977; 1981).

The third group is represented by Chinese psychologists or foreign psychologists with cross-cultural interests. Their entrance into the field is later than that of anthropologists or sociologists, with most of their studies reported only within the last two decades. A large proportion of these studies has been done in the United States, using samples of Chinese students (Scofield and Sun, 1960), immigrants, or Chinese Americans (Kriger and Kroes, 1972; Kurokawa, 1969 — including both Chinese and Japanese Americans; Niem and Collard, 1972; Sollenberger, 1968). Investigations in Taiwan are also becoming more frequent. Typically, the psychologists have used techniques of measurement capable of yielding data for quantitative analysis and presentation.

Finally, the fourth group is comprised of psychiatrists and other professional workers who have come into contact with Chinese individuals or families in psychological distress, where a sound knowledge of childhood experiences, parent-child relationships, and family dynamics in the Chinese cultural context would be indispensable to a fuller assessment and effective therapeutic intervention. Insight into and knowledge about subtleties in complex socialization processes, which are missing from quantitative approaches in the study of groups, may be gained through clinical work. Examples of contributions to the literature with a clinical flavour are Ho (1979d; 1981b), Hsu (1972), Hsu and Tseng (1974), W.S. Tseng (1972), Tseng and Hsu (1969–70; 1972).

Most studies reported in the literature relate to one of two major themes, namely, impulse control and achievement. These are also, as we shall see, two areas of primary concern to Chinese parents. Accordingly, they provide a convenient framework for the organization of this literature review.

IMPULSE CONTROL

Leniency versus Harshness

One important assertion regarding Chinese socialization is that the pattern changes as a function of the child's age (Lazure, 1962, p. 181; Li, 1970; Muensterberger, 1951, pp. 42–50; Tseng and Hsu, 1969–70, p. 8; Wolf, 1970, pp. 40–6; Wu, 1966, pp. 5–6). Parents tend to be highly lenient, perhaps even indulgent, towards the infant and young child (below approximately 6 years of age), in marked contrast to the strict, perhaps even harsh, discipline they impose upon the older child. Furthermore, these disciplinary demands are introduced rather abruptly and are not marked by any ceremony, other than that of beginning primary school, to signify that the child is passing into a new period of life. The result is that the child may find the sudden change in parental attitudes quite drastic and bewildering (Wolf, 1970).

The reason for leniency toward the younger child is that he or she is considered to be not yet capable of 'understanding things', and therefore should not be held responsible for his or her wrongdoings or failures to meet expectations (Bunzel, 1950; Li, 1970; Wolf, 1970). It is thought that training cannot be expected to accomplish much for infants or young children; they are viewed as passive dependent creatures who are to be cared for, and whose needs are to be met with little delay or interference. The mother seems to assume almost total responsibility for their physical well-being, making sure that they are well fed, fully clothed, and protected from hazards. And if a mother is temporarily absent, there are other women available to take care of young children. Thus children receive multiple mothering from a very young age (see, for example, Parish and Whyte, 1978; Sidel, 1972, p. 99). Weaning and toilet training are mild; strict bedtimes are rarely enforced (see, for example, Bunzel, 1950; Hsu, 1967; Muensterberger, 1951; Sollenberger, 1968; Wolfenstein, 1955; Wu, 1966). Infants or young children are not put on a rigid schedule in regard to any biological function; they eat and sleep according to their needs and not according to the clock (Bunzel, 1950). Little or no emphasis is put on training for independence. On the whole, the period of infancy and early childhood can be said to be one of great leniency and indulgence. The only study which contradicts this conclusion is that by Scofield and Sun (1960), who reported that Chinese child-rearing practices from infancy, with the exception of toilet training, were more severe than American practices. It should be noted that this study was based on retrospective reports by Chinese students attending American universities, and this raises questions concerning both the representativeness and the validity of their reports.

It should be added that active or exploratory demands tend to be thwarted even during the period of infancy and early childhood, although passive oral needs are typically met without hesitation (see Bunzel, 1950; Muensterberger, 1951, p. 45; Tseng and Hsu, 1969–70, p. 7; Weakland, 1956, p. 246). In particular, sex and aggression are two areas in which prohibitive training is more severe (see Ho and Kang, 1984, Study 1; and the section below on attitudes toward aggression; compare also Hu, 1951; W.S. Tseng, 1972, pp. 236–7; Tseng and Hsu, 1969–70, pp. 8–9). Ho and Kang reported that sex training was the most severe of the various areas of child rearing. All of the 34 grandmothers and mothers interviewed were uniformly rated 'not at all permissive' on the scale 'Permissiveness for Going Without Clothes Indoors'. Anxiety over sex was high. Only one of the 34 interviewees admitted having observed masturbation in her children. Similarly, in a mental health survey covering 8,329 schoolchildren in Taipei (Hsu, 1966), no problems related to sex, toilet habits or obsessive-compulsive behaviour were reported by teachers. I am inclined to interpret these results as indicative of a lack of awareness or a reluctance to discuss such matters among Chinese. Traditionally, Chinese have regarded masturbation as a shameful bad habit which is harmful to the body and is to be stopped — but the notion that it is sinful is alien to Chinese culture. The belief that it is harmful to the body continues to be officially upheld in the People's Republic of China, as reflected in hygiene manuals written for childcare workers and teachers by health authorities. Mitchell and Lo (1968, p. 317) reported that mothers in Hong Kong would punish their children or tell them that such behaviour was 'dirty' if they found them 'playing with themselves'.

Another important point is that, although the mother stays very close to the young child, it is possible that she does so more out of protectiveness and physical caring than out of consideration for the child's affective needs (see Kagan, Kearsley, and Zelazo, 1978; Ryback, Sanders, Lorentz, and Koestenblatt, 1980). Ryback *et al.* reported that, among six cultural groups, Chinese responses to a questionnaire ranked first on whether the mother was near the young child most of the time, but last on whether the child was made to feel loved and on whether the father and mother were usually sensitive to the child's needs. Thus leniency, indulgence, and physical proximity do not necessarily entail a high degree of sensitivity to all of the child's needs or of overt affective expressiveness.

Despite the general agreement among observers on the sharp contrast between disciplinary attitudes towards the young child and those towards the older child, questions may be raised concerning the abruptness of this change, as well as the age at which parental demands are introduced. According to Lang (1946): 'Children under two years of age are the only family members not subjected to any discipline. At the age of two, and sometimes before, the children hear the first "don'ts", as their education begins' (p. 239). Levy (1949, Chapter 3) stated that, in the traditional pattern, the general position of the child during the *ying-erh shih-ch'i* (infant period, lasting from birth to about 4 years of age) was one which demanded kindly attention and care and in which the child's general security was not seriously threatened at any point. It was a period of freedom and indulgence. Particularly during the first two years of life, no systematic training or discipline was attempted at all. Only in the latter part of the *ying-erh shih-ch'i* were discipline and teaching introduced, and even then they remained very mild. It was during the *yu-nien shih-ch'i* (period of young or tender age, ranging from about 4 years to 15 or 16 years) that the real discipline of Chinese life made itself felt upon the child. Children in this period were considered to be *nien yu wu chih* (young in years and without knowledge) — which did not imply, however, that they were incapable of 'understanding things' or being taught.

More recently Kvan (1969, pp. 338–9) argued that the introduction of disciplinary impulse control begins even earlier — by the age of 2 years, the Chinese child is already expected to behave like a 'miniature adult'. It is not clear how this conclusion was reached. There are, however, some data directly relevant to the issue under discussion (Ho and Kang, 1984, Study 2), which are based on interviews of 20 pairs of grandfathers and fathers in Hong Kong. The fathers judged the 'age of understanding' as significantly younger (the median was 3.5 years) than did the grandfathers (the median was 6.5 years). This suggests that younger parents are becoming more aware of the young child's potential for learning — in line with the proposition that, as parents become more psychologically sophisticated, they discover more about the child's competence. For both generations, however, there was great variation in what was thought to be the 'age of understanding' and, to a lesser extent, the age at which discipline (scolding and beating) needs to be introduced. Clearly there is no uniformity of belief among Chinese parents concerning the 'age of understanding', contrary to claims made by previous observers. More systematic observations, particularly within a cross-cultural framework, are needed to delineate more precisely changes in parental attitudes as a function of the child's age.

It would appear, however, that radical changes in the treatment that the child receives as he or she grows older are very real, whether they are gradual or abrupt, and regardless of the age at which they are introduced. These changes stem from a fundamental contrast in cultural expectations. During the early years of the child's life, it is the parents (especially the mother) who are expected to meet the child's needs; from then on, it is the child who must be taught to obey the parents and be prepared for the fulfilment of social, especially filial, obligations in adulthood (see Ho, 1981a).

We now turn to some of the implications for adjustment of the leniency or otherwise of children's socialization. Research has not dealt with the effects of early parental leniency, contrasted with later strictness, on the personality formation of children, or with how they manage to cope with such a change in parental attitudes as they experience it. It has been stated that among Chinese children, particularly boys, the age period of 6 to 10 years is one of special difficulty, during which conflict with parental authority is more likely to be acute:

It is the time when, following the comparatively great permissiveness and constant attention of the early years of his life, the child is suddenly weaned from the care of his mother, or mother-surrogate, and placed under the tutelage of his father or a father-surrogate. Usually, the father-surrogate (e.g., a teacher) is preferred because it reduces the possibility of conflict with the father (Mead and Wolfenstein, 1955, p. 248).

Ward (1970, p. 115) stated that the period of greatest emotional strain, for boys at least, appeared to be in the tantrum years from about 5 to 10. Levy (1949, Chapters 3 and 9) also stated that in traditional Chinese society (represented by the Ch'ing Dynasty) the *yu-nien* period tended to be a difficult one for the male child; the 'worst of his discipline' was directly applied by the father. For sons of gentry families, the severest discipline was met in their schooling; their teachers were absolute masters. In more recent years, however, there has been a growing trend for the male *yu-nien* to come under the direct domination of females (his mother and female teachers; see Yuan, 1972). In contrast to Levy, Hsu (1967, p. 227) stated that parental discipline in a town in south-west China (identified only as 'West Town') was more severe on girls than on boys. Mothers, who had complete control of their children before the age of 10, were more severe with their daughters than with their sons.

Some quantitative data relevant to the question under discussion are available. Salili and Hoosain (1985) reported that mean ratings by teachers on hyperactivity in Hong Kong schoolchildren reach their peak at about 9 to 10 years of age for boys and at about 7 to 8 for girls; for both sexes, mean ratings drop quite rapidly after the age of 10. The extent to which adults feel the need to exercise control over the children under their supervision may be proportional to the level of the children's hyperactivity. In this connection, results from a large-scale mental health survey based on teacher evaluations conducted by Hsu (1966) in Taiwan are instructive. It was found that the number of problem children reached its peak in grade 4 for boys and in grade 5 for girls (corresponding to approximately 10 and 11 years respectively), resulting primarily from a marked increase in problems associated with acting out or learning attitudes. This resembles the results of the Mental Health Survey of Los Angeles County (cited in Anthony, 1970), also based on teacher evaluations, and those reported by Rosen, Bahn, and Kramer (1964), which are based on clinic termination rates in the United States. In another large-scale survey, pertaining to urban family life in Hong Kong, Mitchell (1972a) reported that 'Scolding [over schoolwork] reaches its peak when the oldest child is between nine and eleven years old. The age of the youngest child is not related to spanking' (p. 301). In conclusion, the evidence supports the contention that, in terms of disciplinary problems, the period around 10 years of age is one of special difficulty for Chinese children.

Solomon (1971, Chapter 3) asserts that there is a tendency to idealize childhood as 'life's golden age' in Chinese culture. He found that approximately 65 per cent of his Chinese adult interviewees saw childhood as a happier time of life than adulthood; 15 to 20 per cent saw adulthood as the happier time; and the remainder were undecided. In contrast, more Americans saw adulthood as the happier time of life. Ripple, Jaquish, Lee, and Spinks (1983) reported that, among Hong Kong Chinese, there was an overall decrease in perceived positiveness (for example, 'happy', 'energetic', and 'achievement') from younger to older ages, more noticeably after the age-decade 30–9. Similar results were obtained in previous research in the United States and South Africa, using the same data-gathering instrument and procedure (Jaquish, Ripple, and Arndt, under review). These results appear to be at variance with Solomon's data on Americans.

One feature of the results obtained by Ripple et al. (1983) deserves particular attention. There was a noticeable dip in perceived positiveness in the 10–19 age-decade, suggesting that the teenage period is one which presents special difficulties in adjustment. This would represent a departure from the traditional pattern of continuity in the transition from childhood through adolescence to adulthood. Further evidence for this departure is manifest in an intergenerational gap (see Tsao, 1981) and an increase in rates of juvenile delinquency in modern Taiwan (R.Y. Lin, 1983; Ma, 1984).

Parental Attitudes

There is general agreement among observers that traditionally Chinese parents have been more concerned with impulse control and less tolerant of aggressive behaviour in their children than Western parents. Children tend to be discouraged from independent, active, or exploratory activities, especially when these entail risks of physical injury to themselves or others. Bunzel (1950), Muensterberger (1951, p. 45), Weakland (1956, p. 246), and Tseng and Hsu (1969-70, p. 7) have expressed the view that these activities are subjected to severe restrictions almost from birth. Kriger and Kroes (1972) found that, while Chinese mothers did not differ significantly from Jewish or Protestant mothers on the Rejection scale of the Parental Attitude Research Instrument (Schaefer, Bell, and Bayley, 1959; mean scores were 56, 55, and 56 respectively), they were significantly more restrictive in their child-rearing attitudes than the other two groups, as measured by the Control scale (mean scores were 212 for Chinese, 152 for Jewish, and 150 for Protestant mothers). These results are in agreement with those of Chu (1974; but see the section 'Implications for Research' towards the end of this chapter). That the concern with impulse control is grounded in the Confucian ethic of filial piety is supported by results obtained by Ho and Kang (1984, Study 2), showing that attitudes toward filial piety were correlated with the placing of great emphasis on strictness of discipline and proper behaviour, and less emphasis on the child's expression of opinions, independence, self-mastery, creativity, and all-round personal development. In this connection, results obtained by Mitchell and Lo (1968) are instructive. They suggest that independent and assertive Chinese children tend to have mothers who are permissive (for example, allowing the child to participate in adult conversation), less harsh or punitive in the disciplinary techniques they use, setting high standards of achievement for their children, and also encouraging them to compete with other children.

Chinese parental attitudes toward aggression are usually unambiguous. The expression of aggression, especially physical, is prohibited. Instead, positive values of sharing and non-competitiveness are stressed; older children are encouraged to set an example for their younger siblings in gentleness, good manners, unselfishness, and willingness to concede during a quarrel (see, for example, Columbia University Research in Contemporary Cultures — Chinese Series, 1950; M.C. Yang, 1967). Wolf (1970) made the point that adults in Taiwan were concerned with quarrels and fighting among children, particularly because of their disruptive influence within the family and the potential danger that adults might be drawn into the conflict, thus endangering good relations between relatives. A child guilty of aggression might therefore be severely punished by his mother, who was very concerned to let the family and the larger world know that she would not permit such behaviour by her children. Parish and Whyte (1978, pp. 225–6) also noted that, in rural Kwangtung in China, fighting and stealing were the kinds of misbehaviour that were most feared, mainly because they could lead to conflicts between families and threaten harmonious relations among adults. In general, Chinese parents tend to be severe in controlling the child's aggression, whereas their attitudes in other areas of child rearing are more permissive (see Ho and Kang, 1984, Study 1; Li, 1970; Ryback et al., 1980; Sollenberger, 1968; Ward, 1970, pp. 118–20).

Both Sollenberger (1968) and Ho and Kang (1984) made use of the interview schedule developed by Sears, Maccoby, and Levin (1957), and their results pertaining to aggression training are in close agreement. Sollenberger presented data on the American sample studied by Sears et al., for the purpose of making comparisons. Obviously, such a comparison should be interpreted with great caution, in view of the methodological problems involved: observer and response biases, problems of cross-language translation, and the control of relevant variables such as age, sex, and socio-economic class. Nevertheless, the dramatic differences between the Chinese American and the American mothers do not appear to be accounted for solely by these problems. To illustrate, the majority of Chinese American mothers (74 per cent) made no demands whatsoever on the child to be aggressive, even in appropriate situations, and never put pressure on the child to fight back under any circumstances; by contrast, most American mothers made demands on the child to be aggressive in appropriate situations and to fight back — as many as 15 per cent had punished a child who had run home for help rather than fighting back.

It might be noted, however, that, in terms of world-wide comparisons, such a dramatic difference in parental attitudes reflects an extreme in the permissiveness towards, or even the expectation of, aggressiveness in American culture rather than in the intolerance of aggressiveness in Chinese culture. Unfortunately, systematic cross-cultural data for such comparisons are lacking. Some relevant data, however, based on university students' responses to a questionnaire in six cultures (Ethiopia, Taiwan, Thailand, Israel, India, and the United States) are available (Ryback et al., 1980). The Chinese ranked third on not allowing children to express aggression and on not encouraging aggressive behaviour. On the whole, they were also consistently the least tolerant of specific forms of aggressive behaviour (fighting with other children, throwing temper tantrums, saying bad words, damaging property, and disobeying parents or other authority figures); data on these items were not, however, available for the Thai group.

Techniques of Control and Discipline

On the basis of his observations of aggressive behaviour in a Hokkien village in Taiwan, Wolf (1964, p. 7) stated: 'Rather than rewarding their children for the absence of aggression, or shaming them with reference to cultural models, the Chinese parents choose to use harsh physical punishments'. Likewise, Parish and Whyte (1978, p. 225) stated:

Spanking (ta) and scolding (ma) are the mainstays of discipline, and some informants even claim these are the only techniques used to discipline children. A naughty child is yelled at, cuffed on the ear or rear, or beaten with a bamboo rod. There seems to be little reliance on the techniques of persuasion, praise, or withdrawal of love which are favored by child-care authorities in both China and America. The Chinese government's campaign since the early 1950s against corporal punishment of children may have reduced reliance on this tactic in urban areas and even in rural schools, but apparently not in homes in rural Kwangtung. The sent-down urban youths among our informants were surprised and even shocked by the heavy reliance on physical punishment in rural homes.

It would appear that the official position advocated, that patient persuasion through reasoning, rather than coercion or punishment, be used to educate children (Ho, 1974a; Baum and Baum, 1979; Kessen, 1975), was by no means fully accepted. The continued use of physical punishments has been reflected in children's books published since the Cultural Revolution (see Blumenthal, 1977). A content analysis of 30 stories revealed that physical punishment was the most common form of punishment, though social disapproval and rejection also ranked high. Social rewards were the most frequent kind of reward. The main characters in the stories were consistently and immediately rewarded for socially desirable acts, and negative characters were punished for evil deeds.

In a large-scale survey of urban family life in Hong Kong (Mitchell, 1972a, Chapter 13), it was found that 61 per cent of mothers and 42 per cent of fathers spanked then children sometimes or many times 'because they did something wrong' (p. 300). Only 18 per cent never spanked at all. Also, 70 per cent of mothers and 65 per cent of fathers scolded their children about homework sometimes or many times. A survey in Hong Kong of working mothers with at least one child of 6 years old or under (Hong Kong Young Women's Christian Association and Hong Kong Shue Yan College, 1982, Tables 3.31, 3.32) also found that scolding (53.5 per cent) and beating (26.9 per cent) were the most frequent maternal reactions to their children's misbehaviour; 'reasoning out with them' (9.4 per cent) was less frequent. Maternal reactions to good behaviour were: verbal praise (45.9 per cent), kissing (15.5 per cent), giving material rewards (26.2 per cent), and doing nothing (8.4 per cent).

Solomon (1971, pp. 51, 68, 559–60) reported that, of 79 interviewed adults who provided information on how they had been punished in childhood, 79 per cent recalled receiving frequent physical punishments and 21 per cent asserted that they had received only non-physical punishments from their parents. The major causes of parental punishments were: quarreiling or fighting (44.5 per cent), doing poorly in school (33.4 per cent), and disobeying parental instructions (30.6 per cent). Similarly, among a sample of 167 university students in Taiwan, 90 per cent stated that physical punishment was used by parents, but only 29 per cent of the students believed that it was effective in correcting behaviour; 62 per cent stated that parents set definite regulations for their children (Ryback et al., 1980). Among the six cultural groups studied, the Taiwanese ranked second on the use of physical punishment; Americans ranked third, with 84 per cent affirmative responses.

In contrast to these reports, Sollenberger (1968) found from informants and participant observations that the punishment generally used was withdrawal from the social life of the family or deprivation of special privileges or objects, rather than physical punishment;

and very rarely, if ever, was the child ridiculed. More systematic data obtained by Niem and Collard (1972) showed that mothers in Taiwan reported a significantly higher use of love-oriented methods (withdrawal or threat of withdrawal of love, reasoning, coaxing, soothing, meeting the child's needs, and promise of future gratification) than American mothers: 421 times over a 30-day period compared with 187 times respectively; and a lower use of non-love-oriented methods (physical punishment or control, material reward, scolding or shouting at, deprivation of privilege, and threat of punishment): 55 as compared with 117 times respectively; furthermore, under love-oriented methods, Chinese parents used less withdrawal of love (isolation), but more reasoning, meeting the child's needs, and appeals to conscience or empathy. It should be noted, however, that the children in question were rather young, being between the ages of 4 years and 2 months and 4 years and 6 months — very likely to be still within the period when the parents were disposed towards leniency in treating them. The same remarks also apply in part to Sollenberger's study, since the mean age of the children was 6.2 years. (The ages of children observed to be disciplined were not explicitly stated.) And it is likely that the high percentages of physical punishment reported by Solomon (1971) and Ryback et al. (1980) were applicable to the respondents when they were older children. Furthermore, these respondents were already adults when serving as informants, and this means that they were describing parental discipline in an earlier period, when attitudes may have been different from present attitudes.

Several researchers from Taiwan have relied heavily on the Parent-Child Relations Questionnaire, originally developed by Roe and Siegelman (1963) and revised for use with Chinese children by Chu (1975), to investigate child training and its effects on aggressive behaviour (Su, 1975a), moral development (Su, 1975b), academic achievement (Su, 1976), adjustment of adolescents (Chen and Su, 1977), and personality development (Su, Hwang, Lu, and Chen, 1979). In the study of moral development, children in grade 7 reported that both fathers and mothers relied far more on induction (explaining why the unwanted behaviour is wrong and what consequences it would have) than on love withdrawal or power assertion in disciplining their children (in contrast, however, see Chu, 1974, and Kriger and Kroes, 1972, reporting that Chinese parents were stronger in authoritarian control than American parents). My own inspection of the data reported (see the section 'Implications for Research' below) reveals that there was a tendency for both parents to rely more on induction when disciplining daughters than when disciplining sons, and more on power assertion and love withdrawal when disciplining sons than when disciplining daughters.

Finally, some systematic data have been gathered by Olsen (1975) on social class (determined on the basis of the occupation of the family's main wage earner) and rural-urban patterning of socialization. A structured interview schedule was given to 107 mothers in Taiwan. The results showed that high-status urban mothers placed more emphasis on self-reliance, and less emphasis on conformity to authority and control of aggression, than low-status urbanites. They were also more affectionate and rewarding with their children, and were more inclined to use love-oriented than power-assertive modes of discipline. Rural mothers were at the opposite extreme on all of these dimensions. Maternal educational level was found to be more important than social class as a determinant of affection, the use of love-oriented discipline, conformity, and values of self-reliance. In contrast, social class had a greater impact on aggression control and power-assertive discipline. Olsen felt that the social class and rural-urban pattern of socialization was very similar to that observed in other countries (see also Li, 1970, for maternal child training in rural Taiwan; Chen and Su, 1977; Su, 1975a; and 1975b, for data on social class differences in parental attitudes).

Olsen (1975) discounted the importance of family modernism, since a partial correlation analysis demonstrated that controlling for this factor did little to reduce the association between social class and socialization variables. Controlling for social class is, however, more appropriate for assessing the contribution of modernism to socialization variances. My own computations show that, as expected, the strength of the association between modernism and socialization was much reduced, but not completely removed, when social class was held constant. In all instances, the absolute magnitude of the partial correlation coefficient was smaller than that computed with modernism held constant. Even so, one is not justified in concluding that modernism is of no real significance to socialization. Because modernism is associated with social class, if one controls for social class, one removes a large portion of the very source of variation one is interested in.

Some of the theoretical implications of the control techniques discussed above are now outlined. Wilson (1970, Chapter 1; 1973) found shaming, together with the threat of ostracism or abandonment by the group, to be dominant in the socialization of Chinese children. In a later work (Wilson, 1974, p. 75; see also 1977; and 1981), he stated:

Although physical punishment is observed in the dealings of Chinese mothers with their children, techniques of love withdrawal [strictness] combined with warmth and induction training [where authority figures focus on the consequences of an act for others and where both the child's need for love and his empathy are enlisted] are by far the most common forms of maternal behavior.

On the basis of the literature on socialization, Wilson argued that such a combination of maternal behaviour leads to a strong development of dependency, a moral orientation with a high internalization of values related to standards of behaviour, a conformity to explicit parental example, and an extreme reluctance to express hostility, especially towards authority, unless it is legitimized by specific violations of behaviour codes by others. Internalized control is further strengthened in the school learning environment through moral training and shaming punishments.

Wilson's argument has received some empirical support. He found that Chinese children (especially those in Taiwan) were more autocentric (oriented to rules or principles) and less heterocentric (oriented to particular others as the authority for behaviour) than American children. This implies that they had a greater internalized set of learned dispositions invested with value orientations and relied on this rather than on the external cues provided by others for expected ideal behaviour. A study by Bloom (1977a; see also Bloom, 1977b), however, found that Hong Kong Chinese scored markedly lower than Americans and French on a cognitive dimension of social control, social principledness (the means were 0.18, 0.43, and 0.47 respectively, on a range from zero to one). Bloom (1977a, p. 69) explained that:

A low level along such a dimension ... would be marked by a capacity for understanding the abstract notion of sociopolitical responsibility at the societal level, but be limited to the view that sociopolitical responsibility consists in unanalytic adherence to the demands of existing political authority, i.e., in placing obedience to that authority above any individual intuition as to what might constitute proper action. By contrast, a high level ... would be marked by the development of a personal, analytically derived conception of what values. a sociopolitical system should seek to maximize and by continuing critical evaluation of the degree to which the institutions and policies of the existing system are successful in realizing that goal.

One would expect that a person who is high in social principledness is more likely to be autocentric, and that a person who is low is more likely to be heterocentric. Thus the findings of Bloom and Wilson do not appear to be consistent with each other. Moreover, in view of the lack of agreement on the disciplinary techniques used by Chinese parents, Wilson's argument appears to rest on rather uncertain empirical grounds.

Conflicting claims have been made about the training and disciplinary techniques characteristically used by Chinese parents. The evidence does not allow unequivocal generalizations to be made about a single Chinese pattern of disciplining children. Rather, it serves to guard against assertions that any particular technique or pattern predominates or that it is peculiarly Chinese. Theoretical positions on political socialization in Chinese society based on such assertions therefore rest upon shaky empirical grounds. Threatening, scolding, shaming, and punishment have indubitably been acceptable and frequently used techniques, in so far as they are applied to older children. However, these are by no means the only techniques used, and are being emphasized less by modern Chinese parents. It is more correct to say that, as elsewhere, a variety of training and disciplinary techniques is used. The major factors underlying the observed variations appear to be the child's sex and age, parent-child relationships (same sex or opposite sex), parental education and occupation, and geographic location (rural or urban). To the extent that social class, parental education, and rural-urban patterning have been systematically investigated, the study by Olsen (1975) deserves to be given special attention and more weight than the other studies reviewed.

The Child's Perception of Parents

A study by Chan (1981b) has provided some data on parental treatment, teaching, and discipline from the viewpoint of the child. This study is noteworthy as it was based on a rather large stratified random sample of 1,408 secondary-school students from 14 schools in Hong Kong. Using the Parent Image Differential developed by Ginsburg, McGinn, and Harburg (1970), three favourable factors, Concerned, Democratic, and Rational, and three unfavourable factors, Restrictive (inappropriately named Restricted by the author), Demanding, and Autocratic, were identified for both the father and the mother. Some evidence for the cross-cultural stability of these parental factors has been provided, in that similar factor patterns were found in four cultures (Chan, 1976b). The Hong Kong pattern was found to be, as expected, more congruent with that of Singapore than with the American or Mexican patterns. The results of Chan's (1981b) study clearly showed that generally mothers were viewed more favourably than fathers. Boys experienced stronger restrictive treatment and demanding teaching by the father, as well as stronger autocratic discipline by both parents, than did the girls. On the whole, the data showed that the child's attitudes towards home were, as expected, positively related to the favourable factors and negatively to the unfavourable factors. The child's social interests (affiliation) were also positively related to the favourable factors, but showed little relation to the unfavourable factors. The child's popularity in class, assessed by a sociometric technique, was positively related to the Concerned factor and negatively to the Restrictive factor. The author felt that most of these findings were in accord with those of previous investigations. In a similar vein Huang (1976) found that rejecting, harsh, and inconsistent parental attitudes (both within and between parents) were associated with poorer personal and social adjustment in secondary-school students in Taiwan.

Su (1968) studied the child's perception of parental roles, using a questionnaire distributed to 708 pupils in grades 4, 5, and 6 in Taiwan. The data showed that either the father (25.42 per cent) or the mother (26.84 per cent) could function as the main disciplinarian; 43.64 per cent of the children reported that they were disciplined by both parents. There was no appreciable difference between parents in the frequency of giving punishments, even though in most cases (69.63 per cent) it was the mother who spent more time in disciplining the child. In a majority of cases, the father was perceived to be the harsher disciplinarian (65.54 per cent) and the authority figure in the home (66.81 per cent), and was the parent of whom the child was more afraid (61.16 per cent). In contrast, the mother was more likely than the father to be perceived as the more forgiving parent (52.82 per cent, as compared with 39.55 per cent) and to be better liked by the child (35.03 per cent, as compared with 22.6 per cent). The data also revealed a contrasting pattern between same-sex and opposite-sex relationships. More boys than girls reported that the father spent more time in disciplining them, administered more punishments, and was a harsher disciplinarian than the mother, and that the mother was the more forgiving and the better-liked parent. The pattern for girls was a complete reversal of that for boys. Taken together, the data suggest that father-child affectional distance is greater than that between the child and the mother; at the same time, and superimposed on this difference, a greater affectional distance is present in parent-child relations of the same sex than in those of the opposite sex. In addition, it appears that there is a direct association between the amount and severity of discipline and affectional distance.

Similar results were obtained in a study conducted by the Boys' and Girls' Clubs Association (1980), in which a modified version of Su's questionnaire was given to 494 children in Hong Kong. It was found that mothers were more likely to be better liked by children than fathers. Again, this result is hardly surprising, and is consistent with those obtained by Su (1968), Mitchell (1972b, Chapter 9), and Chan (1981b). Another salient finding is that most parents typically did not spend time playing together with their children. Considerable parent-child distance in communication is suggested by the result that as many as 56.1 per cent of the children kept unhappy feelings to themselves. Similar results were obtained in a survey of 3,694 Form 5 secondary-school pupils in Hong Kong (Mitchell, 1972b, Chapter 9), in which 68 per cent responded that they 'only occasionally' told their parents what had happened or that they 'hardly [told] them anything' (p. 149); 27 per cent of the males and 33 per cent of the females responded that 'nobody understands' them (p. 163). Corroborative data were also obtained in Mitchell (1972a Chapter 13): 34 per cent of parents with children aged 18 or under at home stated that their children never told them 'their worries and problems', and 24 per cent stated that their children never told them 'things that happened to them at work or at school'.

The contrasting pattern of paternal and maternal roles found by Su (1968) bears a remarkable resemblance to that of rural Kwangtung in China, described by Parish and Whyte (1978). However, some of Su's results are not consistent with those reported in other studies. Tsai (1966) found that, among secondary-school students in Taiwan, both boys and girls related more closely with the mother than the father; father-daughter relations were clearly not as close as mother-daughter relations, but father-son relations were nearly equal to mother-son relations in closeness (compare this with Mitchell, 1972b, Table 9.1, p. 152, which shows no appreciable difference in the closeness of relations between parents and children of the same or opposite sex among secondary-school students in Hong Kong). It is possible that the difference in age between the respondents in Su's and Tsai's studies accounted for the inconsistency. At present, conclusions about the closeness or affectional distance of relations between parents and children of the same or opposite sex are premature.

It is also instructive to compare Su's (1968) results with those reported by Niem and Collard (1972) and Yuan (1972). Niem and Collard reported that Chinese fathers were more often involved than American fathers in the discipline of their sons. They also reported that Chinese children were disciplined far more frequently by relatives and persons other than their parents than American children. These findings support the contention that Chinese children are subject to more generalized adult controls than their counterparts in cultures where age and generational rank are not such important determinants of authority, and where parents assume a more exclusive role as the agents of socialization. Data presented in Yuan (1972) suggested that mothers in Taiwan, at least those from nuclear families, were assuming a more important role as the disciplinary agent in the home. A clear majority (82.08 per cent) of the primary-school children who served as subjects mentioned both the father and the mother as the person(s) 'whose instructions must be obeyed'. Among secondary-school children, 30.39 per cent mentioned the father, 43.65 per cent mentioned the mother, and 25.96 per cent mentioned both parents; furthermore, there was a tendency for the father to be perceived as more lenient than the mother. To the extent that these results represent a departure from the traditional pattern, they are symptomatic of the social changes that are taking place in Taiwan.

The Child's Behaviour

What effects do the parental attitudes and training patterns described above have on the behaviour of the child? In a study of children's behaviour at a public school in New York, Liu (1950) reported that all the teachers remarked that Chinese children were better behaved, more obedient, and more responsible than Caucasian children. Green (1969) observed in two Chicago pre-school nurseries that Chinese American pre-school children were more emotionally controlled than the Caucasians (see also Bronson, 1972, who noted less motor reactivity to novel events among infants of Asian ancestry than among Caucasian infants). Furthermore, differences between Chinese and Caucasians, mainly in the areas of temperament and excitability, appear to have their beginnings very early in life. Freedman and Freedman (1969; see also Freedman, 1971) found that Chinese American newborns were less changeable, less perturbable, tended to habituate more readily, and tended to calm themselves or to be consoled more readily when upset. The two groups were essentially equal in the other areas studied: sensory development, central nervous system maturation, motor development, and social responsivity. Since no potentially important covariables could be found to account for the differences, a genetic interpretation is strongly suggested. Freedman (1974) also summarized observations made in the homes of upper-middle-class Chinese American and Caucasian infants during their first 5 months: the Chinese infants were less labile, active, and irritable than the Caucasians.

By far the most detailed data on the behaviour of Chinese infants were obtained in the study by Kagan, Kearsley, and Zelazo (1978). A sample of 116 infants (53 Chinese and 63 Caucasian) from working- and middle-class families in the Boston area was studied for a period of over two years, beginning from the time when the infants were between 3.5 and 5.5 months, and continuing until they had reached 29 months of age. Of these infants, 67 were cared for at home, 33 attended a day-care centre, and 16 had mixed care experiences. The results showed that ethnic differences, again mostly in situations involving excitability and temperament, were the least equivocal and the most coherent. The Chinese infants, both those from the day-care centre and those brought up at home, were less vocal, less active, less likely to smile to many (but not all) of the laboratory episodes, and more apprehensive in social and separation situations; they were quieter, stayed closer to the mother, played less when they were with unfamiliar children or adults, and cried more often following maternal departure; finally, they showed consistently more stable heart rates during laboratory episodes. The authors suggested that this cluster of qualities implied a disposition toward inhibition among Chinese children. With the exception of heart-rate range, significant differences between the two ethnic groups were not found until the last half of the first year of life and were more pronounced among infants from the working class than the middle class. Thus, there is good reason to believe that familial experiences contributed to these differences, in contradiction to the genetic interpretation favoured by Freedman and Freedman (1969). It appears that the issue of nature versus nurture pertaining to ethnic differences in the behaviour of infants is by no means resolved. Kagan, Kearsley, and Zelazo (1978) obtained additional data from the mother's description of the child at 29 months of age. Ethnicity was found to be moderately associated with apprehension and affectivity. Mothers were asked to rank traits on a scale from most to least characteristic of their child. A greater percentage of Caucasian than Chinese mothers gave the top three ranks to laughing easily, being active, and being talkative, and the bottom three ranks to dislike of the dark, fighting with peers, and fusses when mother leaves. (A mistake was made in the text, on p. 255, in including being patient among the traits given the bottom three ranks by more Caucasians than Chinese mothers. An inspection of Table 5.12, on p. 257, indicates that quite the contrary was true.) For Chinese mothers, staying close to mother was the trait most characteristic of their child. The mothers' reports were in accord with the observations in the laboratory 'indicating that the Chinese children were more fearful and less affective than the Caucasians' (Kagan et al., 1978, p. 255).

The area of aggressive behaviour requires special attention. Observations of different subcultural groups in diverse geopolitical localities (Kessen, 1975; Sollenberger, 1968; Wu, 1966) agree that aggressive expressions in daily life, such as bickering, scuffling, and fighting, are rather infrequent among Chinese children. More systematic observations were reported in two studies (Su, 1969; Niem and Collard, 1972). Su obtained time samples of aggressive behaviour in pre-school children of 3 to 5 years of age in Taiwan during free play and during standardized doll-play sessions (see Sears, 1951). The main findings were as follows.

1. The frequency of aggressive responses, particularly for girls during doll play, increased with age. This result is consistent with Wolf's (1964) observation. After contrasting his data with those from the Six Cultures Study, Wolf made the assertion: 'The Chinese appear to be the *rare* case in which aggression and age are positively correlated' (p. 15, emphasis added). One must question this assertion, however. Earlier studies (Muste and Sharpe, 1947; Walters, Pearce, and Dahms, 1957) found that aggression also increased with age for American children.

2. Boys showed more aggressive responses than girls during free play, but there was no significant sex difference during doll play.

3. During free play, boys showed more physical than verbal aggressive responses, but girls showed a nearly equal number of physical and verbal aggressive responses. This differs from the American finding that, whereas Americans boys showed more physical aggression, American girls showed more verbal aggression (Muste and Sharpe, 1947).

4. During free play, there was not a single aggressive response directed against the teachers, although there were some directed against other adults (observers who took part in the study). Most of the aggressive responses were directed against other children. In contrast, Body (1955) observed that aggression was directed against teachers by American nursery-school children.

5. There was no correlation between the frequencies of aggression during free play and during doll-play sessions. The children were rather inhibited in the doll-play situation, with which they were unfamiliar. Thus the doll-play technique was probably not a suitable research technique to have used for these children.

6. A comparison with Sears' (1951) study reveals that, regardless of age, both American boys and American girls showed considerably more aggression during doll play than either Chinese boys or Chinese girls (except 5-year-old Chinese girls who showed more aggression than both Chinese boys and American girls). This comparison should, however, be made with great caution, in view of the lack of controls and the unsuitability of the doll-play technique for Chinese children.

7. A clear majority of the mothers of the Chinese children (60.78 per cent) responded in interviews that they would 'absolutely not tolerate' aggressive behaviour directed against parents; the percentages were much lower if the behaviour was directed against siblings (15.69 per cent) or against children in the neighbourhood (19.61 per cent).

In the other study, Niem and Collard (1972) compared the aggressive behaviour of children in Taipei and in two university towns in Massachusetts, as recorded by their mothers over a 30-day period. It was found that the Chinese children had more aggressive incidents than the American children (408 as compared with 304); there was, however, little difference between the two groups in the total number of aggressive responses within the incidents (559 as opposed to 519). A more important finding was that the Chinese children showed significantly less physical aggression (125 compared with 162 responses), but significantly more verbal aggression (329 instances, compared with 238) than the American children. The Chinese children also used physical attack less often (86 times as compared with 132), but showed more diffuse discharge of aggression (41 instances, compared with 25). As expected, they were subjected to more parental control over their aggressive behaviour than the American children (597 occurrences as compared with 416). Two considerations are pertinent to the interpretation of these results. First, the children under study were rather young, at an age when, in the Chinese case, the mother may still be lenient and the father's discipline, which the child fears, has not yet been fully felt. Second, it is not unusual to find Chinese children behaving aggressively — like 'little tyrants' — at home, and yet being quiet and well behaved at school. Empirical support for this interpretation may be found in Su (1975a, Table 3), showing that children's aggressiveness in school was poorly correlated with their aggressiveness at home. Both of these considerations suggest that, if a study of older children's aggressive behaviour at school were to be conducted (see, for example, Liu, 1950), a greater reduction in the level of aggressiveness among Chinese children than among American children would be found.

A comparison of the two studies summarized above reveals that there is an apparent inconsistency on one rather important point, which concerns the relative frequency of physical and verbal expressions of aggression in Chinese children. Niem and Collard found that there were more verbal (329) than physical (125) aggressive responses, and this is in line with Wolf's (1964) observation that Chinese children rarely received punishment for verbal attacks. On the other hand, Su found that boys showed more physical than verbal aggressive responses, but that girls did not. Since the children in both studies fell within the pre-school age level (from 3 to 5 years), the inconsistency cannot have been affected by age. However, sex and socio-economic class might have been contributory factors. The frequency of aggressive responses was not broken down according to sex in the study by Niem and Collard (there were 10 boys and 7 girls in both samples from Taipei and Massachusetts); as reported by the authors, the children in Su's study came from families of uniformly lower-middle-class backgrounds, whereas those in Niem and Collard's study were all from middle-class families. This interpretation receives support from some of the data reported by Su (1975a, Table 8), showing that there was an interaction effect between sex and paternal education on aggressiveness in school: it was striking that there was a substantial negative correlation between paternal education and boys' aggressiveness, and a positive correlation with girls' aggressiveness. (Correlations for aggressiveness at home were, however, not statistically significant.) Other factors which might have contributed to the inconsistency were the situational context (school or home) and the technique of observation (direct observation during time samples or mothers' reports).

From a methodological point of view, this inconsistency highlights the need for much more sophistication in future research on aggression (see Bond and Wang, 1983, pp. 62–3; Wong, 1982). It is simply not sufficient to treat aggression as an isolated phenomenon, unidimensional or undifferentiated. Experimental-contextual variables such as direction (agent as compared with object), types and modes of expression, situational and interpersonal contexts, antecedent conditions and consequences following the display of aggression, and techniques of observation, recording, and coding should be considered.

A study by Kurokawa (1969) dealt with the effects of acculturation, in both the mother and child, on childhood behaviour and accident rates. Both Chinese and Japanese Americans were included in the sample studied, without separate analyses, although an effort was made to draw equal numbers of children from both groups. However, the study is relevant to the present review, and has provided some interesting data in answer to the question of what happens to parents and their children when they are exposed to a new culture with vastly different expectations regarding impulse control and aggression. Kurokawa divided the children studied into three types: the acculturated child whose mother was also acculturated (Type 1), the acculturated child whose mother was not acculturated (Type 2), and the non-acculturated child whose mother was also non-acculturated (Type 3). It was found that acculturated mothers were significantly more independent of the Oriental tradition of submissiveness, more egalitarian, and more permissive towards the child's activities than non-acculturated mothers (of both Type 2 and Type 3 children). As reported by their mothers, acculturated children (both Type 1 and Type 2) were significantly more independent and adventurous than the non-acculturated; they were also much more likely to have accidents (defined as injuries which received medical attention), particularly when Type 2 and Type 3 girls were compared. Mothers of Type 1 and Type 3 boys were significantly less likely to prohibit aggression than the mothers of Type 2 boys; mothers of

Type 1 girls were significantly less prohibitive of aggression than mothers of Type 2 and Type 3 girls. Acculturated children (Type 1) were significantly more aggressive and disobedient than non-acculturated children. In covert expression, however, Type 2 children were significantly more aggressive than Type 1 or Type 3 children; Type 2 children experienced the most conflict with their mothers, tended to pout or sulk frequently, and to hurt themselves when angry, and were more likely to be reported by their mother to be maladjusted.

It should be added that Oriental American children are in general much less frequently injured in accidents than Caucasians or Negroes, according to a study by the California Department of Public Health (1962–7); furthermore, within each racial group, differences by occupation are insignificant. This study suggests, as does Kurokawa's, that cultural factors which relate to the inhibition of exploratory, risk-taking, or aggressive behaviour are important in determining childhood accident rates. In the Chinese case, such inhibition is rooted in the ethic of filial piety (which applies also to the Japanese — see also Hsu, 1971c), because exposing oneself to physical danger is regarded as being unfilial. It appears that the Confucian injunction, 'The body with its hair and skin is received from parents; do not cause it harm', continues to exercise its influence on Chinese parents and their children living on American soil.

ACHIEVEMENT

Achievement Motivation

It is generally recognized that modern Chinese parents place great emphasis on the achievement of their children. In the study of child-rearing attitudes and practices in Hong Kong by Ho and Kang (1984, Study 2), the most frequently mentioned personal characteristics expected of the child when grown up were those concerned with competence and achievement, followed by those concerned with moral character, sociability, and controlled temperament. Furthermore, this ranking held for both grandfathers and fathers.

Studies on Chinese achievement motivation have obviously been strongly influenced by the work of McClelland and his associates, and have been modelled upon the methodology they developed. Three related studies (Lewis, 1965; McClelland, 1963; Solomon,

1965; see also Chang, 1979; Ridley, Godwin, and Doolin, 1971), relying on content analysis of educational materials, examined efforts to foster the development of independence and achievement motivation in children in mainland China.

Lewis selected for analysis teachers' manuals for kindergartens in Kiangsu province, which included teaching materials, prescribed physical games, play situations, and stories. He found that 'the Kiangsu manuals reveal a highly sophisticated program of training conducive to individual achievement motivation' (Lewis, 1965, p. 425). Teachers emphasized games which were competitive and individualistic. It is clear that strong efforts were directed towards training children to become active, self-reliant, competent, intellectually critical, and achievement oriented. Lewis suggested that there might be a discontinuity between the socialization of children, which stressed individualistic achievement, and that of political cadres, which stressed non-competitive and collectivist orientations (see also Chin, 1964). It might be added that a discontinuity with both the traditional protectiveness and the emphasis on obedience at home would also be observed.

McClelland (1963) compared three sets of Chinese stories used to teach children in public schools: one from Republican China (1920-9), one from Taiwan (1950-9), and one from mainland China (1950-9). The stories were objectively scored for need for achievement (nAch), need for affiliation (nAff), and need for power (nPow). The results showed that the pattern of scores for Republican China corresponded to that found very frequently in static, tradition-oriented societies governed by an authoritarian regime — low nAch, very low nAff, and very high nPow. Both Taiwan and mainland China, however, showed an increase in nAch and nAff, but the increases were much greater in mainland China than in Taiwan. For mainland China, nAch rose above the world average (based on comparative sets of stories from studies of over 40 countries for the period 1950-9), whereas that for Taiwan was still below the average. McClelland interpreted an increase in nAff as indicating movement in the 'modern' direction, since nAff tends to rise in the contractual type of society which he believed is necessary for a modern economic order, whereas in a tradition-oriented society affiliative relationships do not require special effort or concern over their maintenance. With regard to nPow, there was a decrease for Taiwan but a dramatic increase for mainland China in comparison with Republican China. Stories from mainland China dealing with authority or power relationships were, however, of a different sort from those of the past. McClelland (1963, p. 17) stated:

In contrast to the Chinese stories of the 1920's, the emphasis here is clearly on everyone assuming responsibility insofar as he can for the welfare of others. The power to help, to guide, and control others is not now way off somewhere else, as a kind of dangerous impersonal force, but resides in every person at least in some degree.... So the motivational concerns which favor economic and social modernization are more prominent in the Communist Chinese stories than in the China-Taiwan stories at nearly every point.

Similarly, Solomon (1965) analysed two sets of Chinese children's texts, one from Shanghai between 1922 and 1929, and the other from Beijing in 1960. He concluded that there had been an increase in the salience of achievement-oriented activities, in agreement with Lewis and McClelland. More recently, Blumenthal (1977) analysed a set of 252 children's stories published since the Cultural Revolution in the People's Republic of China. She found that:

Achievement appeared as the central behavior in half the stories. The next most frequent behavior was altruism, and the third was social and personal responsibility. Since achievement was almost always for the group, rather than personal goals, the three behaviors together indicate a strong emphasis on actions which further the interests of society as a whole. (p. 6357A)

Yu (1974) replicated McClelland's procedures in a study of achievement motivation and its relations with filial piety and familism in Chinese teenagers. It was found that: (a) teenagers upheld filial piety; (b) verbal statements on achievement were uncorrelated with nAch as measured by Thematic Apperception Test (TAT) stimuli; (c) nAch was not significantly correlated with filial piety, the Familism scale, or with either the Extended Familism or the Nuclear Familism subscales; (d) verbal statements on achievement were, however, significantly correlated with both filial piety and the Familism scale: the correlation was higher with the Extended Familism subscale than with the Nuclear Familism subscale, with or without any control variable. Yu interpreted the findings as support for the argument about the saliency of the collectivist orientation among Chinese, on the basis of the presupposition that nAch is rooted in the individual-istic perspective, whereas filial piety and familism encompass a non-individualistic collectivist orientation. The logic of this presupposition may be questioned, however. For, although the verbal statements and the TAT stimuli appeared to measure different aspects of achievement motivation (as indicated by the lack of correlation between the two), both types of measure should be capable of reflecting achievement strivings which are rooted in either the individualistic or the collectivist orientation. Nevertheless, the finding that verbal statements on achievement correlated more highly with the Extended Familism subscale than with the Nuclear Familism subscale suggests that Chinese achievement motivation is rooted more firmly in the collectivist than in the individualistic orientation.

Further support for this contention is provided by Abbott (1970; 1974), whose data showed greater differences between Americans and Chinese on the Achievement via Independence scale than on the Achievement via Conformance scale in the California Psychological Inventory; by Wilson (1970, pp. 42–3), in an analysis of textbook stories for primary-school children in Taiwan; by Blumenthal (1977), in an analysis of children's stories in the People's Republic of China; and by Li, Cheung, and Kau (1979), in an experimental study indicating that Chinese children in both Hong Kong and Taiwan showed greater co-operation with increasing age, even when the co-operative reward condition was changed to the competitive reward condition, in contrast to a similar American study (Madsen, 1971) which showed more non-adaptive competition with increasing age.

Other studies have dealt with differences between boys and girls in achievement motivation. In a study of 36 children aged from 6 to 10 years from an agricultural village in northern Taiwan, Olsen (1971) found that low rewards for dependent overtures and early training in self-reliance (regarding feeding and dressing), as reported by their mothers, were significantly related to achievement motivation in boys; independence training, however, was unrelated to achievement motivation in girls. Li (1974) constructed a 20-item Parental Attitude Scale and, with the use of principal component analysis, derived three parental attitude scores, Dominance and Harshness, Obedience, Strictness, and Fostering Dependency, and Communication, Comradeship, and Sharing. Among grade 5 and 6 children in Hong Kong, test anxiety in boys was related to high parental demands for obedience, strictness, and fostering dependency, and to low parental communication, comradeship, and sharing. This is consistent with findings reported by Sarason, Davidson, Lighthall, Waite, and Ruebush (1960). For girls, test anxiety was related to low parental dominance and harshness. It was also found that achievement motivation in boys was related to low parental dominance and harshness. This finding is consistent with those reported in several national samples (Bradburn, 1963; McClelland, 1961; Rosen and D'Andrade, 1959). In the case of girls, however, high achievement motivation was related to low parental communication, comradeship, and sharing. It would be instructive to view this result in the light of findings that mothers of achieving girls tend to be hostile towards their daughters (Kagan and Moss, 1962), strict, authoritarian, and controlling (Pierce, 1961), and less affectionate and less nurturant (Crandall, Dewey, Katkovsky, and Preston, 1964). Kagan and Moss found that one of the best predictors of child and adult intellectual achievement in girls was early maternal hostility during their first three years of life. The mothers tended to be aggressive and competitive women who were critical of their daughters. For boys, on the other hand, maternal protectiveness predicted achievement.

Olsen's (1971) and Li's (1974) results suggested that achievement motivation in Chinese girls was influenced by a very different pattern of parental attitudes from that in the case of Chinese boys. This finding adds to the evidence suggesting the presence of differential effects of parental attitudes on the development of achievement motivation between the sexes in diverse cultural settings. Results reported by Huang (1976), however, were not consistent with those of Olsen and Li. My inspection of the data presented by Huang revealed no clear-cut contrast between boys and girls in the pattern of correlations between parental attitudes (both father's and mother's) and measures of personal and social adjustment, learning attitudes, achievement motivation, and occupational interests. For both boys and girls, rejecting and inconsistent parental attitudes tended to be associated with low achievement motivation and poor learning attitudes; placing expectations on children tended to enhance their achievement motivation; occupational interests were mostly uncorrelated with parental attitudes. It would thus appear that conclusions about sexual differences in achievement motivation in relation to parental attitudes are premature.

Academic and Cognitive Abilities

Given that Chinese parents attach great importance to education and academic achievement (see, for example, Sollenberger, 1968), research related to this area should be of particular interest. Ho (1979a) reported that, in a sample of 1,945 students attending primary and secondary schools in Hong Kong, near-zero correlations were obtained between father's and mother's level of education and measures of verbal intelligence and academic performance. Two plausible possibilities may be suggested to account for the near-zero correlations pertaining to academic performance. First, the pressure on students to study hard and to do well in examinations, which is notorious in Hong Kong, may be present regardless of the educational level of parents. Second, the relation between parental education and academic performance may be curvilinear, and is therefore not properly reflected by the Pearson correlation coefficients reported in the study. Nevertheless, the explanation for the absence of association between parental education and verbal intelligence must await further research.

Ho (1979c) reported two other main findings. First, a quadratic relation was found between sibship size (the number of children in a family) and measures of verbal intelligence and academic performance. Optimal sibship sizes appeared to be from three to six, above which number group means in verbal intelligence began to drop quite markedly. The mean of the group with a sibship size of ten or more was lower than that of the group with a sibship size of four, by as much as approximately one-half of a standard deviation. Second, children born last were inferior in verbal intelligence to first-born children or children born in between. This result is in agreement with that reported by Belmont and Marolla (1973). Further research is needed, however, to investigate how sibship size and birth order give rise to differences in the child's psychological experience in the familial environment, and how these differences, in turn, affect cognitive development.

Su (1976) reported that, in comparison with under-achievers with whom they were matched on the basis of intelligence, achieving students in Taiwan perceived their parents as more loving, more accepting (less rejecting), more concerned (less neglecting), using symbolic-love rewards more often, and using symbolic-love punishments less often. No significant difference was found, however, on measures of parental protection, demand, casualness, and use of direct-object rewards or direct-object punishments. Data reported by Hung and Yang (1979, Tables 19 and 20) showed that boys' academic performance was positively correlated with both paternal and maternal positive attitudes (loving), and negatively correlated with all of the negative attitudes (inconsistency, rejecting, neglecting, demanding, and use of symbolic-love or direct-object punishments); thus there were more significant correlations with the negative than with the positive attitudes. For girls, however, most of the correlations with either positive or negative paternal and maternal attitudes did not reach statistical significance.

Chan (1981b) reported that academic motivation was positively correlated with favourable parental factors (Concerned, Democratic, and Rational), but correlations with unfavourable factors (Restrictive, Demanding, and Autocratic) were mostly not significant. Adolescents with higher intellectual abilities tended to have fathers who were more concerned and less restrictive, and mothers who were less restrictive but more autocratic. With regard to the non-verbal and general intelligence of boys, the paternal Concerned and Democratic factors appeared to be more important than the maternal Restrictive and Autocratic factors. Boys were superior to girls on all ability measures, except verbal. Maternal factors appeared to have played an important part in contributing to these sex differences, while unfavourable paternal factors appeared to be more important in reducing the size of these differences.

Chu (1975) investigated parent-child relations and the cognitive abilities of children in Taiwan. For the girls, but not for the boys, significant positive correlations, with a few exceptions, were obtained between positive parental attitudes (protecting, loving, rewarding, and being casual — as perceived by the child) and both verbal and non-verbal aspects of convergent and divergent thinking abilities. Significant negative correlations were obtained between negative parental attitudes (rejecting, demanding, neglecting, and punitive — as perceived by the child) and these abilities; these negative correlations were more often found between opposite-sex parents and children than between same-sex parents and children.

Boey (1976) developed a Parental Attitude Scale and identified three paternal attitude factors (Overcontrol and Harshness, Rigid Orientation and Discouragement of Contradictory Opinions, and Hardship and Repayment of Parent's Kindness) and two maternal attitude factors (Harshness and Discouragement of Contradictory Opinions, and Overprotection and Overcontrol). Among college students in Hong Kong, some measures of cognitive complexity, especially those related to interpersonal relations, were negatively correlated with the three paternal factors and the maternal factor of Overprotection and Overcontrol; some measures of cognitive rigidity were positively correlated with the paternal factor of Rigid Orientation and Discouragement of Contradictory Opinions. The students' own attitudes towards filial piety were not significantly correlated with any of the cognitive complexity or rigidity measures. Father's attitude toward filial piety, however, was positively correlated with some of the measures of cognitive rigidity; and mother's attitude toward filial piety was negatively correlated with some of the measures of cognitive complexity.

Confronted by the plethora of empirical findings reported above, this reviewer is hard put to discern an unequivocal pattern of relations between parental attitudes and academic or cognitive abilities. In general, positive parental attitudes (such as loving, concerned, and undemanding) promote these abilities, and negative parental attitudes (for example, rejecting, neglecting, and punitive) retard them. But even this generalization, reasonable as it is, has not been uniformly confirmed by the data. Boys and girls may be influenced by different patterns of parental attitudes, but these patterns are far from simple, and the evidence in support of them is far from unequivocal. With regard to family-structure variables, the evidence is that last-born children or those from very large families tend to have lower verbal intelligence (Ho, 1979c).

IMPLICATIONS FOR RESEARCH

Several observations may be made from the above review of the literature regarding the current status of research on Chinese patterns of socialization. First, individual investigators or groups of investigators often work quite independently, each apparently uninformed about the work of others. Furthermore, published studies are too often the result of piecemeal efforts. Thus, despite a sizeable amount of published work, collectively these studies do not comprise a coherent body of knowledge, with later investigations being built upon the refinement of earlier ones and the avoidance of their failures. This is obviously not the ideal fashion in which to advance scientific knowledge. Interdisciplinary and language barriers have largely contributed to the lack of co-ordinated efforts. The first of these may be overcome if investigators take the time to become acquainted with research conducted by those outside their own discipline. The second is unidirectional, in that Chinese investigators normally read publications in foreign languages, whereas foreign investigators do not normally read publications in Chinese. One provisional solution to this formidable problem is for Chinese scholars to exert a greater effort to make their research known, through translating selected publications in Chinese into foreign languages. The second observation relates to the interdisciplinary and language barriers just mentioned. In many instances foreign investigators — particularly psychologists — are handicapped by their lack of knowledge of Chinese society and culture. The study by Kriger and Kroes (1972) may be cited as a case in point. These investigators predicted that Chinese mothers would have higher scores than Jewish and Protestant mothers on the Rejection scale of the Parental Attitude Research Instrument:

Because of the fact that she places a higher value on strictness and control of behavior, [the Chinese mother] is likely to approve the expression of hostility and rejection towards the child. The Chinese mother is likely to use verbal or gestural rejection, since these are considered effective for the purpose of disciplining the child and training him to bring honor to his family and to himself. (p. 206)

A number of dubious assertions as well as unstated assumptions are embodied in this quotation, amounting to a wild logical jump in making the prediction. Not surprisingly, the results obtained did not confirm the prediction. Unfortunately, it remains a fact that there are few psychologists who are both interested in, and knowledgeable about, Chinese society and culture.

Third, methodological weaknesses abound in published studies, and they may account for the conflicting results obtained. At the very least, it is essential to consider personal characteristics (age and sex), social background, and geographical location (rural or urban) as variables — an obvious point, but one which has to be reiterated. In addition, the results obtained in the various studies reviewed suggest that it is important to include relational variables such as same-sex versus opposite-sex relationships in research on parent-child interactions. Unfortunately, the problem sometimes goes deeper. It concerns the very trustworthiness of the data presented, as well as the appropriateness and accuracy of the statistical analyses performed. This problem was encountered, for instance, in my review of Su's (1975b) study. There were obvious inconsistencies in the data presented as well as computational errors, rendering the study as a whole suspect. An inspection of Table 6 revealed that, as measured by the Parent-Child Relations Questionnaire, parental techniques of child training were, in descending order: direct-object reward, symbolic-love punishment, direct-object punishment, and symbolic-love reward. But in a later study (Chen and Su, 1977), the order was: symbolic-love reward, direct-object reward, symbolic-love punishment, and direct-object punishment. Thus, symbolic-love reward ranked last in the earlier study, but first in the later study. Nothing was said by the authors to account for the inconsistency of the results obtained. Another example of carelessness in reporting was found in C.P. Chu (1973; 1974): a careful comparison of the two reports revealed that there were inconsistencies in the data (obtained from the same sample) presented. As in Su's study, interpretations of the data were extremely hard to follow and were questionable. After spending many hours examining such studies, I was finally forced either to exclude them in part or in whole from the body of scientifically admissible evidence, or to rely on my own analysis to discover just what acceptable findings did emerge.

Fourth, when cross-cultural comparisons are made, the group with which Chinese are compared is, more often than not, American. Not surprisingly, some dramatic differences have been found between the two groups in the ways in which children are socialized. It happens that Americans have been the most intensively studied national group — to the point where they have almost come to be taken as a standard reference group against which other national groups are compared. The point should be made, however, that the American pattern may be more atypical than typical in a world-wide perspective. This is yet another reason why other cultural or national groups should be included in cross-cultural studies.

Fifth, investigators need to face two issues which are of central concern: variance versus invariance across geopolitical locations, and continuity versus change over a period of time. Although conceptually these two issues are distinct, in practice it is quite impossible to discuss one without at the same time dealing with the other. For continuities with and departures from the traditional pattern of socialization in Chinese society differ radically, depending on the geopolitical location. There are undeniable variations in socialization between Chinese in mainland China, Taiwan, Hong Kong, and overseas, and these represent divergent departures from the traditional pattern. These variations stem from radical differences in the politico-cultural context in which Chinese find themselves — particularly in ideological objectives and in conceptions of what constitutes the desired end-product of the socialization process. For this reason, a clear delineation of the traditional socialization pattern is not only of interest in itself but also of strategic importance. It would provide us with a stable frame of reference against which the extent, momentum, and direction of change, as well as variations across geopolitical locations, can be gauged. The lack of research on socialization in mainland China remains a serious gap in our knowledge. It is hoped that research in this area will receive greater attention from researchers in the future.

There is a lack of comparative data to enable one to chart the course of change in Chinese socialization patterns over a period of time. It is only since the 1940s that the behavioural science approach has been applied to the study of these patterns. One possibility for comparative research is to use content analysis of cultural productions related to children. An example of this kind of research is the study of achievement motivation by McClelland (1963). Another possibility is to study intergenerational gaps (Tsao, 1981) or differences in child-rearing attitudes and practices (Ho and Kang, 1984). The use of grandfather-father or grandmother-mother pairs within families to serve as subjects in the study by Ho and Kang has methodological appeal. It is expected that, in societies undergoing rapid industrialization, younger generations will have higher levels of education, occupational status, and income than older generations. Control for these variables between generations may be achieved, rather economically, through the use of families, rather than individuals, as the units of investigation.

SUMMARY

A distillate of the literature reviewed may be summarized in the following propositions. At the present state of our knowledge, they represent permissible generalizations which have received relatively strong and consistent empirical support or on which there is overall agreement among observers.

1. Chinese parents tend to be highly lenient or even indulgent in their attitudes toward the infant and young child, in sharp contrast to the strict discipline they impose on older children. Many observers believe that the change in parental attitudes occurs when the child reaches the age of 'reason' or 'understanding', at around 4 to 6 years.

2. Traditionally, great emphasis was placed on obedience, proper conduct, moral training, and the acceptance of social obliga-

tions, in contrast to the lack of emphasis placed on independence, assertiveness, and creativity.

3. Chinese parents tend to be highly concerned with impulse control. The child's exploratory, adventurous, or risky activities tend to be discouraged. Compared with other areas of behaviour, sex training and the control of aggression tend to be severe; in particular, expressions of physical aggression are suppressed. Chinese children tend to be physically non-aggressive; in particular, aggression directed toward authority figures is rarely expressed.

4. Traditionally, the father has been perceived to be a harsher disciplinarian than the mother, and is the parent of whom the child is more afraid. Father-child affectional distance is greater than that between the mother and the child. However, contemporary mothers appear to be assuming a more important role as disciplinarians.

5. Variation rather than uniformity has been observed among Chinese parents in the control and disciplinary techniques they use. Important factors underlying variations in the use of these techniques are parental education, social class, geographical location (urban or rural), the sex and age of the child, and same-sex versus opposite-sex parent-child relationships. It appears that punitive and power-assertive techniques are receiving less emphasis.

6. In comparison with Caucasian infants, Chinese infants tend to be less vocal, less active, less likely to smile, and more apprehensive in social and separation situations — that is, disposed toward inhibition.

7. Educational programmes in mainland China place a stronger emphasis on achievement motivation than educational programmes in Republican China in the past, or in present-day Taiwan. Efforts are directed towards training children to become active, self-reliant, competent, intellectually critical, and achievement oriented.

8. Achievement motivation is more firmly rooted in the collectivist than in the individualistic orientation. Co-operative efforts by members of a group toward achieving collective goals are emphasized more than individual competitiveness.

9. Most results conform to the expectation that positive parental attitudes are conducive to desirable effects (higher achievement motivation, superior cognitive development and academic performance, and better personal and social adjustment) and that

negative parental attitudes have the opposite effects in Chinese children. A number of studies, however, suggest that boys and girls may be influenced differently by patterns of parenting (for example, the relationship with the father and that with the mother and the quality of these relationships). These differing patterns are far from simple and the evidence in support of them is far from unequivocal.

Note: The author gratefully acknowledges the financial support of the Centre of Asian Studies of the University of Hong Kong in the preparation of this chapter.

2 Perceptual Processes of the Chinese

RUMJAHN HOOSAIN

WHILE we will be looking in this chapter at some perceptual processes of the Chinese which have distinctive characteristics, it should be noted that the Chinese cannot be considered a homogeneous population. With a quarter of the people on earth and with the geographical, ethnic, and cultural variety found in the country, uniformity in any psychological domain, including perception, is not to be expected. This chapter will review some of these perceptual processes in relation to environmental and other variables that are pertinent to the Chinese. Such a combination of variables may be unique to the Chinese, but it is more likely that some of the variables are also shared by other groups elsewhere. What should emerge after a review of such factors and their related effects is a kind of picture of the various aspects of the perceptual processes of the Chinese. Such a picture will be by no means complete, but will nevertheless be reasonably informative and will, it is hoped, entice some of us to engage in further work in providing more details, if not a new angle of perspective.

A number of concepts are useful in reviewing these variables. One is biosocial psychology (Dawson, 1977a), which refers to the adaptation of different peoples to their biological environments. This results in different adaptive social systems which also influence the development of various cognitive processes, behavioural skills, attitudes, and values, which have survival values for their specific ecosystems. By its nature, biosocial psychology emphasizes 'sub-universals' and uniquenesses rather than human universals. 'Sub-universals' are characteristics that are shared by more than one homogeneous group, presumably as a result of commonly shared relevant variables. For example, different peoples sharing the same religion may exhibit similar behavioural patterns which are not shown by others of a different religion. Among other topics, biosocial psychology is concerned with cognitive styles of peoples as a result of their biological and social environments. In this regard, this chapter will also review the aspects of the Chinese environment which bring about cognitive styles found in other similar environments.

Another notion that is useful in considering Chinese perceptual processes is the distinction between what are referred to as data-driven or bottom-up processes, and conceptually driven or top-down processes (Lindsay and Norman, 1977). The former are initiated and largely determined by perceptual data, but the latter are dominated by knowledge of the possible interpretation and conceptualization of sensory experiences. For example, in reading a word, factors like the size and clarity of the print affect bottom-up processes. Knowledge of the language possessed by the reader, on the other hand, affects top-down processes. The two sets of processes interact to determine the ease with which the reader can identify words. A poor reader requires clear and distinctive print to be able to read, but a good reader, with his knowledge of the language, can possibly handle poorly printed words. In the present context, we would wish to examine the possibility that distinctive characteristics of Chinese perceptual processes are more likely to be found in bottom-up processes than in top-down processes. This means that it is in the more rudimentary processes that cross-cultural or cross-linguistic differences appear. In higher-order processes, which involve instead the conceptualization of what is seen, universal human characteristics override elementary perceptual differences.

Finally, some of the distinctive perceptual processes reviewed in this chapter might be viewed as a new aspect of linguistic determinism, first put forward by Sapir and Whorf (see, for example, Whorf, 1956). They proposed that language determines thought. The kinds of perceptual experience affected by language include such aspects as the ability or propensity to perceive different types within a category (of, for example, snow, camels, or rice), an ability which is commensurate with the richness of the indigenous vocabulary in each of these categories. Another side of Whorf's work concerned the effect of grammar on subtle distinctions in the speaker's 'world view', and this is illustrated by his studies of American Indian languages. As we shall see in this chapter, however, the effects of language or orthography differences tend to be in terms of cognitive processing which was not envisaged in the original proposal of Sapir and Whorf (see Tzeng and Hung, 1981).

In some areas of cognition, possible distinctive Chinese phenomena have not been fully investigated. When there are good theoretical or other indications that such distinctions do, or do not, exist, the following discussion will mention these, and their implications. This discussion will serve the purpose of providing completeness in treatment as well as suggesting needed research. We look first at some of the more basic aspects of visual perception, including acuity of vision, direction of scanning, and eye movements in reading. We then turn to the experience of colour, including how we feel about different colours. The latter is related to cultural factors. Of all the variables referred to in this chapter, cognitive style is perhaps the one that is most related to socialization and cultural factors. Subsumed under this notion are factors such as susceptibility to perceptual illusions, field dependence, and cognitive complexity. Handedness and its cognitive implications are then discussed, including cerebral-hemisphere lateralization of cognitive functions. We end with a review of the applied aspects of Chinese perceptual processes. This covers reading behaviour and reading disability, as well as mathematical abilities related to language factors.

VISUAL ACUITY, DIRECTIONAL SCANNING, AND EYE MOVEMENTS

Visual Acuity

According to Curran (1980), the first cross-cultural experimental study of cognition was done at the turn of the century to investigate the visual acuity of 'savages'. The visual field within which we can identify shapes or colours is usually of greater extent along the horizontal dimension than along the vertical dimension. This makes sense in terms of man's evolution since, as dwellers on the surface of the earth (or, more appropriately nowadays, on the surface of floors of buildings), more events of significance to us occur horizontally than vertically in relation to ourselves. However, when we consider the acuity of things at which we look directly, that is, not just items in our peripheral vision, it appears that there is still some difference between stimuli arranged horizontally and vertically. Freeman (1980) reported that his American subjects found it more difficult to identify random English letters arranged in vertical arrays than those arranged in horizontal arrays. However, when these subjects were tested with non-letter test stimuli such as Landolt rings, which contain a gap at the top, bottom, left, or right, no differences were found in the detection of vertical and horizontal displays. When Freeman tested bilingual Chinese subjects, he found that there was no significant acuity difference in the perception of Chinese characters, in rows and columns, or English letters.

The performance of the Chinese subjects was attributed to their experience of reading Chinese which can be in either columns or rows. (In fact, on the same page of some newspapers in Hong Kong, one can find some items of text printed in columns and others in rows.) But the absence of difference in acuity for horizontal and vertical arrays was not due to racial factors. Chinese American subjects who had never learned to read or write characters showed the same pattern of acuity difference for English letters as the other American subjects. Also, American children of 4 to 5 years old, who knew the alphabet but could not read, failed to show any consistent acuity differences in the perception of rows or columns of letters. It would seem that the existence of an acuity bias for horizontally arranged linguistic signs was related to learning to read a particular orthography. It would also seem that it is possible to carry over effects of a native language to situations involving a second language, as shown by the performance of Chinese/English bilinguals with letter arrays.

Directional Scanning

Directional scanning refers to the movement of the eyes in a path in certain directions over an area to be processed visually. There is a general finding that subjects prefer to scan from top to bottom and from left to right, and this has been found with very different types of stimuli scattered in various distributions in front of subjects (Braine, 1968; Aaron and Handley, 1975). There are suggestions that this preferred direction of scanning reflects some central scanning mechanism or neural organization. Hebrew is a language written and read horizontally from right to left, and with Hebrew readers it was found that younger subjects tended to scan stimuli from right to left, but this tendency was reversed as they grew older (Braine, 1968; Kugelmass and Lieblich, 1970). Some kind of maturational mechanism appears to override specific cognitive experience.

Chen (1981) studied the preferred directional scanning of two groups of Chinese subjects in Taiwan. One group comprised high-school students who had little experience with English and the other group university students with more English experience. Stimuli, including Chinese characters, English letters, geometrical shapes, and numbers, were displayed in front of the subjects in different configurations for their scanning and quick identification. Although the two groups differed in age and amount of experience with English, there was no significant difference in their direction of scan, irrespective of stimulus type. High-school students, with little experience of English, did not differ from older university subjects, and this was taken to mean that reading experience was not crucial in this aspect of behaviour. Chen's subjects had past experience with Chinese written or printed from top to bottom, left to right, or right to left. But it seems that, in spite of this, the preferred directions of scan were top to bottom and left to right.

Eye Movements

The eyes are moved around by three pairs of oculomotor muscles, and vertical eye movements entail more complicated co-ordination of the muscles than horizontal movements. While we may think that our eyes move around smoothly, the most common type of eye movement is actually the saccade, which is an abrupt and quick jump as our eyes move from one fixation to the next (see Schiffman, 1976). Smooth or pursuit movements are usually found only when one is tracking a moving stimulus. In reading, saccadic movements are typical, and reading speed is determined by how big a span can be covered by a saccade between one fixation and the next, the amount of time spent in each fixation before the next saccade, as well as the need for the occasional regression of eye movements to retrieve missed information. Quite some time ago, when Chinese was largely written from the top down, Shen (1927) reported differences in eye movement when subjects read vertical texts and horizontal texts. There were more smooth gliding movements in vertical reading and longer saccade spans, although fixation time was also longer. The opinion was expressed that small degrees of movement like gliding might be more suited to the processing of the more compact Chinese language (see next paragraph). More recently, as the writing of Chinese from left to right has become popular, there have also been occasional reports of pursuit movements in reading horizontal Chinese text (Stern, 1978). But saccadic movements appear to be the norm in reading Chinese or English.

The main distinction between eye movements in reading Chinese and eye movements in reading English seems to be the frequency of saccades. Peng, Orchard, and Stern (1983) reported that Chinese subjects reading horizontal left-to-right Chinese text required more saccades per line than American subjects reading the same text in English. Also, bilingual Chinese subjects reading English required significantly more saccades than American subjects. The greater frequency of saccades for Chinese is probably related to the greater compactness or density of Chinese text, which requires more attention. In comparing the translation of material in publications with bilingual sections, such as the Chinese *Reader's Digest*, it can be seen that lines of English text are usually 60 or 70 per cent longer than lines of Chinese text. Chinese syntax accounts for part of the density (for example, there are no inflections like '-ing'), but the non-alphabetical orthography is undoubtedly a cause of the higher visual density. We will review the relationship between the greater frequency of fixations for, and the density of, Chinese text, as well as other factors, later in this chapter. However, the difference between native English-speaking subjects and Chinese/English bilinguals reading English might not be entirely due to the latter group's weakness in English. These subjects were graduate students or visiting scholars at an American university, and a relative lack of proficiency in English might not have alone produced all of the discrepancy. It may be that such bilinguals could have applied the strategy that made them proficient readers of Chinese to the reading of English. In the case of acuity for vertical as compared with horizontal arrays, we have also seen that bilingual Chinese subjects extend the lack of acuity difference for Chinese characters to English letters. The practical implications of the acuity phenomenon is not immediately obvious, but that of eye fixation habits is clear. If a hypothesis suggesting transfer of habit is correct, Chinese students would be slowed down in their reading of English simply because of the habit of eye movement acquired in the mastery of their first language.

Overview

While there is no suggestion of any racially unique perceptual characteristics in acuity of perception (and Freeman, 1980, actually ruled this out), directional scanning, or eye movement, there is evidence that experience results in some distinctively Chinese characteristics. In this section we have unearthed some basic determinants of perception. The first is innate hardware, and the kind of neural mechanism suggested is one that prefers directional scanning from top to bottom and from left to right. We would expect that, irrespective of racial or cultural differences, human beings share this common endowment. Another determinant, that of the indigenous language or more specifically of how the language is written, may be appropriately included as part of the human environment. We have seen how Chinese orthography is related to acuity as well as eye movements in reading.

COLOUR CODING AND AFFECT

Colour Coding

The area of colour perception and colour coding is one in which there has been a cross-cultural interest in perceptual variations in relation to language or vocabulary differences, in line with the linguistic determinism hypothesis of Sapir and Whorf (see, for example, Berlin and Kay, 1969). To the extent that the actual perception of colour is physiologically determined, theories of colour vision themselves postulate universal processes as being responsible for our colour experience (see Hurvich and Jameson, 1974). In this regard, there are probably no distinctively Chinese characteristics of colour perception. There are studies of how colours are coded in memory, and although there are no specific data from Chinese subjects, we will draw some tentative conclusions from the data of others. In the case of affect for colours, we do have data for Hong Kong Chinese subjects.

Interest in cross-cultural colour coding started with the cross-linguistic study of Berlin and Kay (1969). They studied some 20 languages and discovered meaningful regularities in the use of basic colour terms. Basic colour terms are names of colour categories consisting of only one morpheme, which is the unit of meaning in language. In this regard, the Chinese for the colour pink, which can be translated into English literally as powder red, would not be a basic colour term. Basic colour terms also should not be applicable only to a small set of objects, thus excluding such colour names as blond. The number of such terms discovered in each of the languages investigated varied from 2 (as in the case of Dani in Papua New Guinea) to 11 (as in English, namely, black, white, red, yellow, green, blue, brown, purple, pink, orange, and grey). If it is possible to have any combination of 2, 3, 4, and up to 11, colours, there would be more than 2,000 permutations of possible colour terms in use in various languages. In reality, however, actual permutations found are limited and orderly. If there are only 2 basic colour terms, as in Dani, the 2 terms correspond to black and white. If there are 3, red is added. If there are 6, they would be black, white, red, green, blue, and yellow. The collection of 6 is particularly interesting, since the 6 colours correspond to those referred to in theories of colour vision (see, for example, Hurvich and Jameson, 1974). It is possible that these are the colours that produce the maximum neural response in human visual systems, and consequently became the first 6 to be described by basic colour terms.

Since there are languages with different basic colour terms, an opportunity exists for a Whorfian type of investigation of colour perception and coding. Subjects in the various language communities can be tested to see if they perceive colours differently. It has been reported that different languages cut up the colour spectrum into different packages, each with its own label or colour name. If we take the colour spectrum as being like the range of colours of a rainbow and ask subjects from different linguistic backgrounds to mark off the portions they consider blue or green (for example) in their own languages, they may cut up the spectrum differently. But their choice of focal colours coincides (see Berlin and Kay, 1969). In other words, they agree on which particular spot is the best example of blue or green and so on. Focal colours may be those with wavelengths that activate the human visual system to the greatest extent, and they therefore produce universal agreement.

In colour coding and memory studies, universal patterns of human experience are again suggested. Dani speakers seemed to remember colours and to make mistakes about them in the same ways as English speakers (Heider and Olivier, 1972). Also, irrespective of the native language of the subjects, focal colours are named more quickly and with shorter expressions than non-focal colours (Heider, 1972). The absence of cross-cultural differences in the perception and coding of colours, as contrasted with snow or camels, is probably because the perception and the coding of colours are physiologically determined. Human visual systems are activated by colours, independent of the language of the community, and there is less room for selective attention depending on language use, as in the case of snow or camels. (As a footnote to the saga of Eskimo words for snow, Arab words for camels, and others for rice, it might be noted that there were a dozen distinct characters for different kinds of cattle in classical Chinese. The modern Chinese person, of course, cannot be expected to know the characters or identify all the bovine varieties depicted in the field. Thus, as with snow or camel names, a case can be made for the relation between language usage and perceptual salience.)

Colour Affect

While colour vision is universal, what people feel about colours is definitely more subject to cultural variation. In a cross-cultural study of affective meaning, Osgood and his colleagues (Osgood, May, and Miron, 1975) compared semantic differential measurements of about 600 concepts in over 20 communities all over the world. Colour names were included in this probe into 'subjective culture' (as contrasted with more observable aspects of culture). Results were expressed in terms of three dimensions, evaluation — indicating whether subjects felt that concepts were something like good or bad, nice or awful, and so on; potency — indicating big or small, powerful or powerless, and so on; and activity — indicating fast or slow, young or old, and so on. Across the language communities tested, colour terms produced some universals of affect. These included the following: the feature brightness universally showed high evaluation, the colours black and grey showed low evaluation and activity, and red showed high potency as well as high activity. The Hong Kong Chinese subjects demonstrated some unique affective meanings: the colour red yielded a higher activity score than in all the other language communities, and yellow yielded the lowest evaluation, with the only negative affect score amongst all the sample communities. It is possible to explain these results, by relating them to cultural phenomena such as the use of red in many festivities in China and the connection of yellow with ill health and vice. Necessarily, however, each such explanation has to be *ad hoc*.

There is another aspect of these affective meanings. As the scores are expressed on three independent dimensions, each colour concept can be conceived of as being located somewhere in a three-dimensional space of affective meaning; and the semantic distance between any two colours can be computed, as can the mean distance for all possible pairs of colours in the semantic space. Countries or language communities that tend to have greater mean distances, that is, those that made greater semantic differentiations amongst colour concepts, can be identified, as can those that tended to be low differentiators. Hong Kong Chinese, Thais, and Japanese (East Asians) were among the high differentiators, but Middle Eastern people, West Asians, and Indians were among the low differentiators. These observations fit nicely into geographical and cultural sub-universals.

The high differentiation among the Chinese might be related to the constitution of colour names as bound morphemic components of Chinese words. In Chinese, words are often two- or three-character combinations, and colour names can be an element of these different words. The relatively more frequent occurrence of colour names with different concepts could enrich the feelings for colour concepts themselves. Furthermore, Chinese is a language with many homonyms — different characters with identical pronunciations but distinct meanings. A colour name could therefore elicit its homonyms and thereby a host of associated meanings. The above comments are, of course, only speculations on characteristics of Chinese colour names that require verification.

Overview

To summarize this section, we do not expect that the actual perception or coding of colours is any different for the Chinese than for any other people, since there are common physiological bases for colour vision. But there is clear evidence for sub-universals and uniquenesses in feelings for colours indicated by the Chinese and others, side by side with universals reflecting the commonality of human experience of colours.

SOCIALIZATION, FIELD DEPENDENCE, AND COGNITIVE STYLE

In this section we will review cross-cultural studies of susceptibility to perceptual illusions, field dependence, and cognitive style. Two biosocial variables which are related to these cognitive processes will be discussed: the physical environment and the social climate in which people live. As mentioned above, geographical variation is vast in China, and we would expect the factor of physical environment to have different effects in diverse parts of China. But traditions such as the manner of child upbringing and socialization patterns probably vary less within the whole of China, and we would expect their effects to be more general. In any case, variation in these two factors will be contrasted in a comparison of the Hakka and Tanka communities of south China, whose environments and socialization patterns differ.

Visual Illusion and Field Dependence

According to the carpentered-world hypothesis (Segall, Campbell, and Herskovits, 1966) people who live in modern urban environments are expected to be more susceptible to some visual illusions, such as the Muller–Lyer figure and the Sander Parallelogram, because they have acquired visual inference habits which are more ecologically adaptive in a carpentered (that is, a right-angled, urban) environment. Configurations of lines in this environment, such as those forming the corners of rooms and buildings, have been useful cues for visual depth perception, and when similar inferences of depth are made in configurations of illusion figures, mistakes about length are made. For example, configurations forming the 'featherhead' of the Muller–Lyer figure (>—<) can be typically found in corners of rooms extending away from the observer. The test line in the figure tends to be interpreted as further away from us and therefore to be seen as longer. On the other hand, configurations forming the 'arrowhead' (←→) are found in corners of objects extending towards us, and therefore the test line is interpreted as shorter, even though the lengths of the test lines in the two figures are identical. Conversely, people living in open environments could be subject to illusions like the Horizontal/Vertical illusion, where again ecologically valid inference habits lead to misjudgements of length in an experimental situation. In this case, vertical lines are interpreted as greatly shortened lines extending into space in the environment such as the desert or sea. They are then interpreted as longer than horizontal lines. Dawson, Young, and Choi (1973) compared the illusion susceptibility of Hong Kong Chinese samples with Americans and Australian Aboriginal Arunta desert-dwellers. In the case of the Muller–Lyer illusion, the American subjects were most susceptible, and this would make sense if we consider their environment to be the most carpentered. The Chinese were intermediate, and the open-desert-dwellers least susceptible. A similar picture emerged with the Sander Parallelogram. With the Horizontal/Vertical illusion, the Arunta sample showed the greatest illusion, as expected. However, the Hong Kong Chinese sample showed less susceptibility than the American sample, and this is attributed to the more closed environment of the crowded city of Hong Kong. In such an environment, there is not much opportunity of seeing lines extended into very distant space.

Other factors are also related to illusions such as the Muller–Lyer. Berry (1972), for example, found a correlation between skin pigmentation and Muller–Lyer susceptibility, as well as a correlation between experience of a carpentered world and the illusion. Jahoda (1971) concluded that no single factor can adequately account for the observed variations in reaction to the Muller–Lyer illusion. Dawson, Young, and Choi (1973) reported negative correlations between the above measures of illusion susceptibility and measures of field independence for Hong Kong Chinese subjects. Field independence, as defined by Witkin, Dyk, Paterson, Goodenough, and Karp (1962), is the ability to separate a perceived item from its context. A field-dependent person, on the other hand, tends to orientate himself by reference to the environment, and his perceptions tend to be global. Measurement of field independence is usually done with such tests as the Embedded Figures test, Kohs Blocks, the Rod and Frame test, and the Three-Dimensional Pictorial Perception test (see Dawson, Young, and Choi 1973). In the Rod and Frame test, for example, a straight line (the 'rod') can be rotated independently of a square frame. Both can be tilted away from the horizontal/vertical orientation. Subjects look at the rod and frame through what amounts to a tunnel that cuts off cues from the background, such as corners of the room or furniture, which provide cues for the horizontal/vertical orientation. The ability of subjects to see the rod as horizontal or vertical, without being affected by the orientation of the surrounding frame, is measured.

Not only is field independence negatively correlated with illusion susceptibility, but it is also related to socialization and sex differences (Barry, Child, and Bacon, 1959; Witkin, Goodenough, and Oltman, 1979). Agricultural societies are conducive to the development of the obedient and compliant behaviour which is necessary for effective group effort in agriculture. Such behaviour patterns are usually associated with higher field dependence. In contrast, hunting and fishing societies have more permissive socialization, fostering the independence that is needed for survival in the harsh desert, sea, or snow environment. Generally, males are also expected to be more field independent and to have higher spatial ability than females, as a result of their traditional roles. In agricultural societies with strict socialization, there is a greater emphasis on conformity in the socialization of the female. But in hunting and fishing societies, a more equally permissive socialization is expected for males and females, and the result should be less marked sex differences in cognitive styles. Evidence for the above has been reported in the literature for peoples as diverse as Eskimos, Australian Aboriginals, Africans, and Chinese (Berry, 1966; MacArthur, 1967; Dawson, 1981a).

Socialization and Cognitive Style

In general, Chinese socialization patterns conform to the strict authoritarian variety. Thus it has been reported that Chinese parents exercise more severe discipline than Americans (Scofield and Sun, 1960). The Chinese also emphasize mutual dependence within the family more than Americans (Ando, 1965). Chinese children are taught to see things in terms of interrelations, are more tradition oriented, and live under their ancestors' shadows (Hsu, 1967). In a Hong Kong Chinese study, Dawson, Young, and Choi (1973) found positive correlations between the more modern attitudes held by subjects, as measured by the Dawson Tradition–Modern Scale, and susceptibility to perceptual illusions. This scale was constructed to measure the extent to which Chinese subjects hold more traditional Chinese attitudes and more modern attitudes. The correlation between modern attitudes and a higher susceptibility to illusions, indicating a carpentered-world experience, confirmed other studies in Sierra Leone (Dawson, 1967a; 1967b).

Perhaps a good way to illustrate the interaction of the physical environment and socialization, and their effects on cognitive style, is to compare two groups of Chinese, the Hakka agriculturalists and the Tanka boat-people of south China (Dawson, 1981b). This comparison also serves to remind us of the heterogeneity of the Chinese. The Hakka agricultural villagers studied are from a remote village in the New Territories of Hong Kong, and the Tanka fishermen are from a remote fishing village in the New Territories as well as from Aberdeen in Hong Kong. In socio-cultural matters, the Hakka have harsher socialization and firm social sanctions, a stratified society with lineages, and more conformity. The Tanka have more permissive socialization with no lineages, less conformity, and more individualistic values. Biologically, the Hakka have a more linear physique and a high-carbohydrate diet. The Tanka have a muscular physique with a high-protein diet. Amongst other measurements, these subjects were tested in (a) measures of field dependence like Kohs

Blocks, the Embedded Figures test, and the Rod and Frame test; (b) the Chinese Three-Dimensional Pictorial Perception test (3DPP), consisting of drawings and pictures designed to test depth perception; (c) illusion tests: the Muller–Lyer figure, the Sander Parallelogram, and the Horizontal/Vertical illusion; and (d) handedness.

The handedness data were consistent with a postulation of harshness of conformity. None of the Hakka subjects was left handed but 5 out of the 65 Tanka subjects were left handed. The Hakka subjects had a lower 3DPP performance, and a more field-dependent cognitive style performance. The sex differences for the Hakka showed that females had a more field-dependent cognitive style than males. But for the Tanka boat-people subjects, there was a less marked sex difference in this aspect of cognitive style, as expected in hunting and fishing communities. The geometrical illusion data, however, did not seem to support the carpentered-world hypothesis, since the Tanka subjects, who spend much time at sea were not significantly less susceptible. Nor did the Tanka subjects show greater Horizontal/Vertical illusion. These results were explained in terms of the geographical location of the fields of the Hakka farmers, which are situated at the Pearl River estuary. The Hakka agriculturalists have many opportunities for looking out to sea, and to that extent their visual environment resembles that of the Tanka fishermen. Data such as these support Dawson's biosocial model, where the biological environment and the social system evolved from the environment interact, to affect cognitive and other psychological patterns (see also Liu, Chapter 3 in this book).

Rigidity and Cognitive Complexity

Boey (1976) looked at the relationship between cognitive complexity and rigidity, and at parental attitudes amongst Chinese subjects in Hong Kong. The subjects were students of both sexes at a post-secondary college. Cognitive complexity refers to the number of differentiated dimensions a person has in perceiving or construing the stimuli in a given domain. A person with greater cognitive complexity is able to see more aspects and relations in any perceptual situation. Rigidity, on the other hand, refers to the persistence of a response or a response set when the demands of the situation have already been changed. Three domains of performance were included. In the interpersonal domain, cognitive complexity was assessed with the Role Construct Repertory test. Essentially, this test involves a list of roles like 'a person you dislike', 'your boss', and 'your friend', and subjects are asked to provide the names of people who fit each role. Subjects are then presented with triads of these people and are asked to indicate which two of them are alike in some important ways and at the same time different from the third. These 'ways' are the construct dimensions, and provide an indication of the various dimensions the subject uses to cope with the interpersonal world. In the physical domain, cognitive complexity was assessed with a Figure Comparison test. This resembles the Repertory Grid, in that sets of three geometrical figures are presented to subjects and they are asked to indicate important aspects in which two of the figures are alike and the third one different. From these answers, dimensions in the perception of physical forms are derived, such as shape, area, texture, height, volume, direction, position, structure, and colour. In the numerical domain, subjects were given a Digit Group test. They were shown 32 chips, each with a number, and were asked to group the chips in as many different ways as possible. They were asked for the underlying principles of their various groupings. Subjects were also asked to complete a Filial Piety Scale, and to request their parents to complete a Parental Attitude Scale, which measured authoritarian control.

In general, the results showed that, within each domain, rigidity was inversely correlated with cognitive complexity. There was, however, a certain amount of domain specificity, in that rigidity in one domain was not necessarily correlated with cognitive simplicity in another domain. With the Parental Attitude Scale, it was found that overprotection and overcontrol by the mother were related to cognitive simplicity in the interpersonal domain, but not related to the other two domains. Overcontrol and harshness by the father, and the extent to which the father emphasized hardship and repayment of the parents' kindness, were also related to cognitive simplicity in the interpersonal domain. The father's rigid orientation and discouragement of contradictory opinions were related to cognitive simplicity in the physical domain. The parents' attitudes towards filial piety, particularly that of the father, were all positively correlated with rigidity of the subjects as well as cognitive simplicity in the various domains. Not all of these correlations were statistically significant, but they were consistent in their direction. There was some tendency for the subjects' own attitude towards filial piety to be related to cognitive simplicity, but these relations were not significant. In sum, Boey's findings showed that the father's attitudes and authoritarian control have a marked influence on the development of rigidity in the subject's personality and the related lack of cognitive complexity. The general findings of Boey were collaborated by Chan (1979). He examined performance in four areas (verbal, non-verbal, numerical, and general intelligence), and found similar correlations with parental control as rated by the subjects (see also Ho, Chapter 1 in this book).

Social Orientation

Yang's (1981a) proposed distinction between self- or individual orientation and social orientation is related to some notions of biosocial psychology. Americans may be taken to represent self-orientation and the Chinese social orientation. The Chinese are brought up to remain an integral part of their families throughout their lives, instead of being trained to function independently of the family network. Authoritarianism, parental control, and norms of loyalty would be characteristics of the socially oriented society, with its related cognitive styles. Some other reports of Chinese cognitive style can be considered consistent with this view of the relation between socialization and cognition. Chiu (1972) compared American and Taiwanese Chinese subjects and found that the Chinese tended to have a relational-contextual style while the Americans had an inferential-categorical style. The former style is a response tendency to categorize stimuli on the basis of their functional and thematic relationships, and the latter is a tendency to classify stimuli on the basis of inferences made about the stimuli which are grouped together. In the experimental study, children were asked to select any two out of three objects in a set which were alike or went together and then tell the experimenter the reasons for their choice. An example of the relational-contextual style would be to classify human figures together 'because the mother takes care of the baby'. Examples of the inferential-categorical style would be reasons like 'because these are things to cut', 'because they are fruits', 'because they both have a motor', and 'because they both live on a farm'. Douglas and Wong (1977) compared Hong Kong Chinese and American high-school subjects and reported that the Chinese sample scored lower on tests of formal operation in the Piagetian model. In the case of probabilistic thinking, in which people estimate the likelihood of uncertain events, Wright, Phillips, Whalley, Choo, Ng,

Tan, and Wishuda (1978) reported that Hong Kong Chinese subjects, together with some other Asians, had a less differentiated view of uncertainty than British subjects. In this study, subjects were (a) asked questions about their views on uncertain events, such as 'Will you catch a head cold in the next three months?'; (b) asked questions on factual matters that most people are uncertain about, such as 'Is the Suez Canal over 100 miles long?'; (c) asked two-choice-alternative questions such as 'Which is longer: the Panama Canal or the Suez Canal?'; and (d) given a questionnaire to measure the fineness with which they could discriminate between probability words and phrases. The British subjects consistently showed a greater ability to adopt a probabilistic set, to discriminate uncertainty finely, and to express the uncertainty.

Bond (1980) suggested that this group of findings could be understood in terms of the socialization and upbringing of the Chinese, related to other aspects of cognitive style such as field dependence. Encouragement of obedience and parental authority are associated with the development of less differentiated functioning (Witkin and Berry, 1975). The use of the relational-contextual cognitive mode is probably associated with field dependence, which is in turn related to severe socialization. The same socialization and educational atmosphere would also discourage active searching modes of behaviour which are conducive to the testing of hypotheses and experimentation with formal thought. Independence of thought tends to be less developed in socially oriented cultures, and one therefore finds a relative slowness in the development of formal operations (Chiu, 1972). Similarly, the lower differentiation of uncertainty can be related to social orientation. In such cultures, there is less initiative to act independently and less perceived capacity to influence events (see Yang, Chapter 4 in this book) and therefore less opportunity to exercise the capacity to assess the outcome of such events.

Overview

The cognitive processes reviewed in this section are by and large what would be classified as top-down or conceptually driven processes, involving the interpretation of perceptual data. The exception is the possible relation between pigmentation and illusion perception (Berry, 1972) or similar physiological influences. The factors are directly connected either with the socialization process or with the physical environment which in turn affects socialization. The effects of these factors are felt on higher-order mental processes, rather than on the sensory process alone.

HANDEDNESS AND THE LATERALIZATION OF COGNITIVE FUNCTIONS

Handedness

Handedness, whether people prefer to use the right hand, the left hand, or are ambidextrous, is related to some cognitive functions. It is generally agreed that there is a genetic basis for handedness (Hardyck and Petrinovich, 1977), but genetic factors alone cannot adequately account for cross-cultural variations in handedness, and it has been suggested that socialization produces selective pressures to use the right hand in different cultures (Dawson, 1977b). Thus, while there is a universal preference for the right hand, the pressure to conform varies according to the permissiveness or harshness of socialization. Dawson (1977b) reported that the incidence of left-handedness amongst the more permissive Eskimo hunters, Australian Aboriginals, and the Chinese Tanka boat-people (male and female combined) was 11.3 per cent, 10.5 per cent and 9.4 per cent respectively. In contrast, the Temne of Sierra Leone, the Chinese Hakka villagers, and the Katanganese agriculturalists had incidences of 3.4 per cent, 1.5 per cent, and 0.6 per cent respectively. The corresponding percentages for the Scottish, English, and American samples were 7 per cent, 5.1 per cent, and 5.6 per cent, midway between the agriculturalists with severe socialization and high conformity, and the more independent and permissive hunters and fishermen. Furthermore, a sex difference in handedness also reflects the even greater pressure on females to conform in agricultural societies with authoritarian socialization. The Temne, Hakka, and Katanga males had 3.8 per cent, 2.5 per cent, and 0.8 per cent left-handedness respectively, and the corresponding female percentages were all zero. In the case of the Eskimo and the Australian Aboriginal hunters, there were no significant differences between males and females, and the Chinese Tanka boat-people actually showed a slightly higher incidence amongst females.

The above Chinese percentages were all obtained in Hong Kong. Guo (1984) reported results of a survey which included all areas of mainland China and a sample of over 10,000. The incidence of left-handedness for males and females combined was only 0.24 per cent (although over 8 per cent were classified as ambidextrous). This result would also be consistent with the predominantly agricultural environment and the probably harsher socialization patterns of the mainland Chinese sample than the Hong Kong sample. Bearing in mind the particularly low incidence of left-handedness among the Chinese, shown in this comprehensive mainland Chinese survey, we can review some evidence of the relation between handedness and cognitive style, although this evidence is not obtained directly from Chinese samples.

It has been reported that left-handed people are significantly more field dependent than right-handed people (Silverman, Adevai, and McGough, 1966). This is confirmed by Dawson (1977b) in a study of Eskimos. Fixed right-hand dominant subjects were more field independent than mixed-hand dominant subjects. Left-hand dominant subjects were more field dependent than both mixed-hand dominant subjects and fixed right-hand dominant subjects. Assuming that this pattern applies universally, it produces a somewhat paradoxical situation, to resolve which further work would be needed. We have already reviewed studies showing that severe socialization is related to more field-dependent cognitive styles. But severe socialization and pressure to conform is also related to higher incidences of right-handedness, and right-handed people tend to be more field independent. To make the picture more complicated, Kocel (1977) reported data showing that right-handed males had lower spatial abilities than left-handed males, but that right-handed females showed higher spatial abilities than left-handed females. On this topic, we can be sure only about two points: that handedness has a genetic and a cultural determinant, and that the incidence of left-handedness amongst Chinese is rather low. While there are suggestions about the cognitive implications of handedness, what these mean exactly for the Chinese is not entirely clear, mainly because there is a lack of research.

The Lateralization of Cognitive Functions

The lateralization of cognitive functions means that one half of the brain is more involved in some processing activity than the other. It should be noted that, just as handedness is not a clear-cut right or left matter, but is a dimension ranging from strong right-handedness, through weak right-handedness, ambidexterity, and weak left-handedness, to strong left-handedness, the lateralization of a particular function does not necessarily mean that one hemisphere is exclusively involved. It is more often a case of difference in the degree of involvement. Furthermore, inter-hemisphere communication is possible through the corpus callosum of the brain. The degree and type of handedness are assessed by detailed questionnaires and other means. Evidence for lateralization comes from studies of the impairment of cognitive functions in brain-damaged people, from experimental studies directing information to one or other hemisphere, and even from studies of patients with split brains as a result of medical necessity. Generally, the right hemisphere is more involved in handling holistic spatial perception, including the recognition of faces and emotions, and the left hemisphere is more capable in handling sequential and analytic information, including verbal material. But there are some individual variations. It has been estimated that over 90 per cent of right-handed people have their language functions lateralized in the left hemisphere, but that only 65 to 70 per cent of left-handed people have their language functions lateralized in the left hemisphere, and some of them are bilateral or have partial language functions in both hemispheres.

The lateralization of perception of Chinese characters is more complicated than the corresponding perception of alphabetical languages like English. In the latter, most right-handed subjects show a left hemisphere advantage. But in the case of the Chinese, lateralization depends on the nature of the material presented or the task required. In testing perceptual lateralization, a common procedure is the visual hemifield presentation. Verbal stimuli are shown to the subject by means of tachistoscopic projectors which permit precisely controlled and very short exposure times. Subjects are first asked to fixate at a point on the screen and the stimuli are then shown either to the right or to the left of the fixation point for less than a fifth of a second. This short time precludes the possibility of the subjects' moving their eyes to fixate at the item, either deliberately or not. In this manner, information presented in the left hemifield is conveyed to the right hemisphere and vice versa, as determined by the anatomy of our visual system. Performance, measured in terms of error rate or response time, allows a comparison of the facility with which either hemisphere is capable of handling the presented information (although, as noted above, the difference is not absolute but is only in terms of relative error rates or response times).

In the perception of Chinese materials, there is a difference between the perception of single characters and that of two-character combinations. Single Chinese characters, or the kanji characters used in Japan, are seen better in the left hemifield and therefore right hemisphere (Hatta, 1977), although Sasanuma, Itoh, Mori, and Kobayashi (1977) and Huang and Jones (1980) reported no significant difference. This difference in the perception of Chinese logographs and other types of language is demonstrated nicely when the two constituent scripts of the Japanese language, kanji and kana, are compared. Kanji were originally Chinese characters, which were borrowed by the Japanese and which retain their morphemic characteristic, while kana are syllabic symbols. Hatta (1977) and Sasanuma, Itoh, Mori, and Kobayashi (1977) found a left hemisphere advantage for kana.

The distinction between the lateralization of perception of Chinese characters and that of alphabetic symbols has been taken to indicate the significance of stimulus properties. Chinese characters are holistic symbols while alphabetical words are stimuli with sequences of letters. Tzeng, Hung, Cotton, and Wang (1979), however, found that the right hemisphere advantage for Chinese applied only to single characters. When two-character 'words' were shown to subjects, there was a left hemisphere advantage, just as with alphabetical languages. Ho and Hoosain (1984) also found a left hemisphere advantage when subjects were asked to decide if pairs of characters were opposites or not. Unlike individual characters, pairs of characters require sequential and analytical processing. Tzeng, Hung, Cotton, and Wang (1979) suggested that the lateralization of processing functions is not determined so much by stimulus properties as by the nature of task requirements. Holistic perception of single characters remains predominantly a right hemisphere function, but higher-order sequential analysis is still a left hemisphere activity. However, one question that remains to be answered by the task-specific view (as opposed to the stimulus-specific view) is why single English words, unlike single Chinese characters, are not processed in the right hemisphere when there is an indication that they too can function as perceptual wholes in the Gestalt sense (see, for example, Kolers, 1972; Osgood and Hoosain, 1974). On this consideration alone, they should be processed in the same way as holistic symbols. Furthermore, we need an explanation for the difference between the perception of characters and the perception of individual English letters, with the latter showing a left hemisphere advantage (Bryden, 1965), when no sequential processing is involved in either.

Overview

It has been suggested that the difference in the lateralization pattern for the perception of single Chinese characters probably matters less in the higher-order functioning of processing sentences (see Hung and Tzeng, 1981). The left hemisphere is eventually largely responsible for analytic language processing, no matter where the initial items were processed. This amounts to saying that language differences matter more in data-driven or bottom-up processes than in conceptually driven or top-down processes. The issue is complicated by the higher incidence of right-handedness amongst the Chinese, since handedness is related to the lateralization of cognitive functions. The Chinese process individual characters more in the right hemisphere. However, the higher incidence of right-handedness indicates that in more Chinese the left hemisphere should eventually be responsible for the analytic processing of larger units of language. This finding has implications for such matters as the impairment of language functions following strokes and other forms of brain damage (see Guo, 1984).

READING AND READING DISABILITY

The perception of Chinese language and its relation with other perceptual functioning could have applied implications. One main function of all written languages is to transcribe spoken words, but they could achieve this end differently. Chinese transcribes whole morphemes, the units of meaning. Each monosyllabic character almost always represents a unit of meaning which can itself be a word, although many words consist of two or more characters. But alphabets in languages like English transcribe phonemes, the units of sound. Investigations into the cognitive processes underlying the reading of different orthographies and their relations with reading difficulties have been based on this distinction. There is a general belief that the incidence of reading disability amongst the Chinese is low, possibly because of the nature of the orthography. There is even one report of success in teaching American children, who had reading difficulties, to learn English represented by Chinese characters, although the project was on a small scale (Rozin, Poritsky, and Sotsky, 1971).

Semantic Access and Reading

There are some indications that the meaning of Chinese characters is more manifest perceptually than the meaning of words in other languages. Biederman and Tsao (1979) found that the Stroop colour test effect was stronger for Chinese than for English. In this test, the time which subjects take to name the colour of patches of ink is compared with the time that they take for naming the colour of the ink of printed colour names. For example, the colour name 'red' could be printed in blue ink instead of red ink. Inconsistency between the colour name and the colour of ink of the printed name results in longer response times, even though subjects are asked just to name the ink colour and to try to ignore the meaning of the names. This means that some processing of the meaning of printed names is inevitable. The fact that the Stroop effect is stronger for Chinese suggests that the perception of the meaning of Chinese names is more unavoidable, that is, that the meanings of Chinese characters are more manifest than the meanings of words in English.

Similar effects are found with inconsistencies in the physical size of two numbers and their numerical values (for example, where the number 6 is printed in a larger size than the number 9), when subjects have to indicate which number is physically larger. Tzeng and Wang (1983) reported that the same effects were found with numbers written in Chinese characters, as when the subject had to indicate that the physical size of the character for 6 was actually bigger than that of the character for 9. However, native English speakers did not show any similar effect for the names of numbers in English — when the word SIX was printed larger than the word NINE. This again demonstrates that the meaning of Chinese words is more manifest than that of English words. Yet when Chinese subjects did the same test with English number names, they showed an interference effect, just as if the stimuli were Chinese characters. The explanation offered is that the Chinese/English bilingual subjects had transferred their reading habits from the Chinese characters, which are morphemic symbols of meaning, to the English alphabetical words. It might be recalled that earlier, when we looked at acuity for horizontal and vertical arrays, and at eye movements in reading Chinese and English texts, it was suggested that Chinese/English bilinguals could transfer their reading habits in their native language to their second language.

There are other indications of the distinction in accessibility of meaning between morphemic and alphabetical symbols. Hoosain and Osgood (1983) showed that perception of and response to the polarity of the affective meaning of words were faster for Chinese words than for English words. Subjects were presented with words like 'heaven' and 'hell' and were asked to indicate whether they meant something positive or negative (affective polarity). Chinese subjects could do this for Chinese words more quickly than American subjects for English translation equivalents, which were matched for mean number of syllables. Hoosain (1984a) also reported data contrasting the speed for getting at the sound of (phonological access to) Chinese and English words for numbers, with the speed for getting at the meaning of (semantic access to) these words. Hong Kong Chinese/English bilingual subjects could pronounce Arabic numerals more quickly in Cantonese than in English. Similarly, they could read numbers printed in Chinese characters more quickly than numbers printed in English — and by about the same amount of time. Comparing these two sets of results, we have an indication that, for these subjects, the phonological access for English words was not slower than that for Chinese words. In both sets, the cause of the difference is related to the motor response time discrepancy — the difference in the time taken to move the vocal apparatus to say the numbers in the two languages.

Contrasting simple pronunciation times for English and Chinese numbers with their translation times shows the time it takes to obtain access to the meanings of numbers in the two languages. Semantic access is not necessary for simple pronunciation. But it is a prerequisite for translating the numbers from one language to another. We have seen that access to the sounds of numbers printed in English did not require more time than the same process for Chinese. On the other hand, access to the meaning of English number names required more time than access to the meaning of Chinese numbers. Translating printed Chinese number names into English was much faster than translating printed English number names into Cantonese. This result might seem paradoxical at first glance, since translating into Cantonese meant pronouncing Cantonese numbers, which was itself a faster response than pronouncing numbers in English. The result makes sense only if we realize that translating from English meant having to obtain access to the meaning of the names in English, and vice versa for the Chinese number names. The translation results would suggest that the bilingual subjects required much more time for semantic access to English number names than to

Chinese number names. In fact, this difference overwhelmed the other difference in the opposite direction — that saying the response in Cantonese itself was significantly faster than saying numbers in English. It should also be noted that this difference in semantic access times for the two languages was obtained with subjects who reported that they actually had more experience with the number names in English than those in Chinese.

Reading research suggests that there are two possible routes by which to arrive at the meaning of written words, the visual route and the phonological route. In the former, the meaning of written symbols is arrived at through some internal visual representation. In the latter, the written symbol has to be converted to some code related to its pronunciation (phonological recoding) before its meaning can be arrived at (McCusker, Hillinger, and Bias, 1981). There have been some suggestions that access to the meaning of Chinese might require less phonological recoding than access to the meaning of English in comparable situations. For example, Hoosain and Osgood (1983) found that the pronunciation times for experimental English words were actually shorter than those for their Chinese translation equivalents. If the perception of the affective meaning of Chinese words requires the same kind of phonological recoding as that for English words, response times for Chinese should be slower, but this was not the case. Such findings do not mean, however, that phonological recoding is not needed in reading Chinese (see also Erickson, Mattingly, and Turvey, 1977; Tzeng, Hung, and Wang, 1977), but the possibility remains that the relation between visual and phonological processing might be different for Chinese, because of its unique orthography (Treiman, Baron, and Luk, 1981).

Eye Movements and Reading

Some interesting points about the perception and reading of Chinese arise if we compare evidence about the more manifest meaning of individual Chinese words and the eye-movement data for the reading of text which was reviewed earlier. On the one hand, we have indications that semantic access for individually presented words is faster for Chinese words than for English words. This would be due to bottom-up processes which are determined by the nature of the two orthographies. On the other hand, while Chinese print is more compact, Chinese requires more eye fixations per line for the reading of continuous text. More frequent eye fixations might seem unnecessary if the meaning of individual characters can be arrived at quickly, unless there are other considerations besides the meanings of individual characters. The syntactic 'density' of Chinese could be one possibility. Another could be the lack of information about variations in word length or shape for Chinese characters. For English, important information to aid reading speed comes from parafoveal vision, beyond the few letters we can see clearly in foveal vision. It has been reported that the reader can see clearly only about four letters to each side of the fixation point, but can discern the general shapes and lengths of words for another 10 or 12 letters (McConkie and Rayner, 1975). With some knowledge of the language, including the possible meanings of words of different shapes and lengths, the reader can preprocess words in parafoveal vision, before they come up for focal attention processing. In this case, of course, conceptually driven processes play an important role. Here we have a top-down interpretation of the blurred images as well as a hypothesis about their relations with what has been processed so far. In Chinese, all variations in strokes take place within the same generally square space in printed text (there are, for example, no letters such as *l* or *p* protruding from the line of print), and there are no specific spaces separating syntactic units like words from each other — whether what amount to words are single characters, or sets of two characters or more. Thus, there would be much less information from parafoveal vision in Chinese.

Liu, Yeh, Wang, and Chang (1974) tried to demonstrate any possible facilitation that might be provided to the reader if Chinese word boundaries were clearly indicated with extra space, in addition to the spaces separating individual characters. However, no facilitation was obtained in the experimental situation, possibly because of the subjects' lack of familiarity or long-term experience with the new format. Without the rich variations in word shape or length to facilitate parafoveal vision, the Chinese reader would need to pay focal attention to smaller chunks, that is, would need more fixations in reading.

Another possible explanation for the higher fixation frequency for Chinese is the habit of pronouncing individual characters when reading. This habit might have been handed down traditionally, and might be related to the lack of more obvious grapheme-phoneme rules to tell the Chinese reader how to pronounce individual characters. In any case, whether in the form of vocal or subvocal reading (McGuigan, 1984), this habit could unnecessarily slow down the Chinese reader, as it would require some attention to be paid to each single character. In the section on eye movements above, we noted some reports of smooth or pursuit-type movements in reading Chinese. It could be that these were produced by subjects who were not engaged in individual character pronunciation, and who therefore did not require frequent fixation stops. But more work in this area will be needed before we have a clearer picture of the relationship between eye movements and the phonological and semantic access of Chinese text.

Reading Disability

Orthography differences could be significant in the nature of reading disability in different language communities. We have mentioned that there is a general belief that reading disability is a Western phenomenon. However, Stevenson, Stigler, Lucker, Hsu, and Kitamura (1982) compared the incidence of reading problems amongst large samples of children in the United States, Japan, and Taiwan, and found comparable incidences of reading disability in all the children. But the pattern of difficulties found in the Chinese children was somewhat different from that of American children. Chinese children with reading disability were classified as such, because of their difficulty with the comprehension of meaning, rather than because of their performance in 'vocabulary' tests involving the sight-reading of isolated words (that is, in remembering pronunciations). American children had a relatively higher incidence of 'vocabulary' difficulty. In an earlier study of Chinese children, Ai (1949) estimated that the number of children who had difficulty identifying sounds of characters was only half the number of children who had difficulty identifying meaning. The findings of Stevenson *et al.* and of Ai could be related to the emphasis on pronunciation drill in Chinese lessons, as well as the unique relations between the visual form, pronunciation, and meaning of Chinese symbols. Ai (1949) showed that in experimental tests of memory, the association between word shape and sound deteriorated sooner than the association between word shape and meaning. Chinese also has a great number of homonyms, and this is one major consideration against the romanization of the Chinese language (as is contemplated from time to time). More recently, Tzeng and Wang (1983) reported that when subjects were asked to remember lists of words presented either orally or visually, the last couple of items were remembered better if they were auditory items than if they were visual items. And this applied to both English and Chinese lists. However, for the earlier items, it was only with Chinese that visual items were remembered better than auditory items. For English lists, there was no difference between the two modes of presentation. Visual presentation was better for the Chinese subjects, regardless of whether they were asked to recall the items orally or in written form. This study showed that visual memory might have distinctive functions for Chinese.

In view of the above distinctions regarding the Chinese language, it became relevant to ask if poor and good readers of Chinese might have different cognitive ability patterns. Woo and Hoosain (1984) compared the visual and auditory functioning of poor and normal readers. Two groups of Chinese children in Hong Kong were tested. In a Chinese-character recognition test, subjects were shown, in succession, two lists of characters and were asked to identify those items in the second list that were also in the first. The poor readers made more visual-distractor errors than normal readers. (Visual distractors were characters that looked somewhat like the original target characters and were used as distractors in the test list.) But the poor readers did not make more phonological-distractor errors than normal readers. (Phonological distractors were characters in the test list that had identical pronunciations to the original target characters, and served the same purpose as the visual distractors.) The two groups of subjects were also tested with the five subtests of the Frostig Developmental Test of Visual Perception (Frostig, Maslow, Lefever, and Whittlesey, 1963), including tests of eye-motor co-ordination, figure-ground perception, constancy of shape, position in space, and spatial relationships. In every test the performance of the poor readers was significantly poorer than that of the normal readers. The two groups of children were also tested with auditory tests, including a digit-span test measuring the ability to retain orally presented random numbers, and the Auditory Association Test of the Illinois Test of Psycholinguistic Abilities (Kirk, McCarthy, and Kirk, 1968) measuring their ability to provide the missing words in orally given questions like 'Cotton is soft. Stone is . . .'. There was less difference between the performances of poor and normal readers on these tests, although the latter still did somewhat better than the former. Thus the whole set of results showed that poor readers in Chinese were handicapped mainly because of their visual disability. This finding is consistent with the distinctive importance of visual characteristics in processing the Chinese language.

Related to the significance of visual processing for Chinese characters are findings suggesting that Chinese subjects tend to have better visual-form discrimination abilities. Lesser, Fifer, and Clark (1965) compared Chinese, Jewish, Puerto Rican, and Negro children in grade 1 of primary school. The Chinese showed the highest scores in space conceptualization and reasoning, the second highest scores in numerical ability, but were third in verbal ability. Carlson (1962) compared the acquisition of object concepts, form concepts, and number concepts. He reported that both Chinese subjects and American art students found form concepts easier than the other two types of concept, as distinct from American undergraduates and other adults. In this study, subjects had to learn nonsense names given to different instances of the same form, object, or number. Another study in this area was that of Chan (1976a), using the Raven's Progressive Matrices. Since this test is generally considered culture free and is widely used to assess general intelligence, differences in the level of performance of Chinese subjects should have particular implications for cross-cultural comparisons of intellectual ability. The Progressive Matrices require the subject to look at sets of visual patterns and their relations, choosing one pattern out of a few to complete the original set. Sets are presented in some ascending order of difficulty. Chan compared the performance of a group of Chinese students and a European group, and found that the Chinese did better in 47 out of the 60 items, five at the 5 per cent level of significance, 15 at the 1 per cent level of significance, and the rest not significantly. There were no differences in five other items, and the Europeans did better in the remaining eight items, but none significantly. Furthermore, it was on the most difficult items at the end of the test that the Chinese showed a significantly better performance. One possible reason for the better performance of the Chinese subjects in this and similar tests involving visual forms is their experience with learning the Chinese orthography (Chan, 1976a; Rohrl, 1979). We have already seen that it is mainly in their visual ability that normal Chinese readers differ from poor readers. The non-alphabetical Chinese script, with its more direct association between form and meaning, puts more emphasis on visual form discrimination. Chinese readers therefore have more experience in this mode of learning.

Overview

We might agree at the end of this section that there is considerable evidence of different perceptual or reading processes for the Chinese, which relate to their distinctive orthography. It would seem that, if we can accept the implications of the work of J. Chan and others, experience with the orthography produces effects in cognitive functioning beyond the language process itself. The Chinese, in fact, seem to conceive of and manipulate visual forms differently from others who have other kinds of script in their language. Returning to the notion of linguistic determinism, the language effects in the present case would be more pervasive than those originally conceived of by Sapir and Whorf — they go beyond the immediate effect of the conceptualizations depicted by the language items in question and extend to general information processing.

THE SOUNDS OF NUMBERS

In terms of possible implications, another distinctive feature of Chinese is the short pronunciation duration of numbers, at least those pronounced in the Cantonese dialect. Short sound durations are related to the number of items that can be retained in short-term memory. Baddeley, Thomson, and Buchanan (1975) asked subjects to remember words with short and long pronunciation durations. The words were matched for familiarity and number of syllables (for example, wicket and bishop as compared with coerce and harpoon). Words with short sounds were remembered better. It is generally agreed that when people hear or see words, the items in short-term memory are coded in a sound-related form (Loftus and Loftus, 1976). Assuming that the capacity for this sound code in short-term memory is limited, it makes sense that items with shorter sound duration would not overload this capacity as easily as those with long duration. Furthermore, in problem solving, information is not just passively stored in short-term memory, but is manipulated or processed towards a goal. It is agreed that our attention span is limited, and that a trade-off exists between simple storage and active processing functions (that is, the greater the amount of resources allocated to storage, the less the amount that is left for processing the stored information, and vice versa). Information with items of short sound duration can therefore be processed more easily than information with items of longer duration. We will now look at specific examples of these relations.

Ellis and Hennelly (1980) reported that the sound durations of numbers pronounced in Welsh were longer than those in English. Digit-span norms for Welsh-speaking children were also found to be lower than those for English-speaking children. Digit spans are measures of the short-term memory limits for the maximum sequence of random numbers pronounced by the tester, and are components of many tests of intellectual ability. Ellis and Hennelly also suggested that this language difference in pronunciation duration, as well as that for digit span, is related to the ability of Welsh children in arithmetic. Hoosain (1984b) found that the sound duration of numbers pronounced in Cantonese (all monosyllabic) is even shorter than that in English. For normal pronunciation, at the rate of about one number a second, as well as for the very rapid pronunciation of long sequences of random numbers, the durations of Cantonese are much shorter, although not every Cantonese number name is shorter than every corresponding English number name. Liu and Shen (1977) also reported that numbers were read more quickly in Mandarin than in German. Thus, it seems that sound durations of Chinese numbers are shorter than those of alphabetic languages. Digit spans tested in Hong Kong are also significantly higher than those of English-speaking subjects. For example, Hoosain (1979) found that the mean digit span for Hong Kong undergraduates was 9.9, about two digits higher than that reported for comparable samples in the West. Higher norms are also reported at other age levels, and this fact had to be taken into consideration in the Hong Kong Cantonese translation of the Wechsler Intelligence Scale for Children (Psychological Corporation, 1981), where digits are presented in pairs instead of individually to increase difficulty.

The suggestion that digit-span capacity is related to mathematical ability or the capacity to manipulate numbers in problem solving is more difficult to demonstrate directly. Hoosain (1984b) found that the correlation between English digit span and mathematics achievement grades (tested in English) for Hong Kong Chinese/English bilinguals was 0.38 for forward digit span, where subjects had to recall random numbers in the presented order, and 0.42 for backward digit span, where numbers were recalled in reverse order. Both correlations were statistically significant. Chan (1981a) reported a longitudinal study that reinforced the notion of a relationship between language and mathematics achievement. Two groups of Chinese children were compared in Hong Kong. They had comparable academic performance when they were 12 years old and all took the same Secondary School Entrance Examination in 1972. One group proceeded to Chinese secondary schools where Chinese was the medium of instruction, and the other group went to Anglo-Chinese schools where English was the medium. When both groups took the Certificate of Education Examination in 1977 in their respective languages of instruction, the Chinese group did better in the subjects of Chinese and mathematics, and less well in all other school subjects, than the Anglo-Chinese group. Their better performance in the Chinese language is understandable, since this was their medium of instruction. But their performance in mathematics, particularly in comparison with their inferior performance in other subjects, is singularly suggestive. Very often, when the superior performance of the Chinese in mathematics is noted, it is usually suggested that motivation or family interest in studies might be the crucial factor. From this study, however, it would seem that, at least at some level of manipulation of numbers, the characteristics of the language and the corresponding perceptual processes might have some relation to performance.

CONCLUSION

It is tempting to try to paint some composite picture of the perceptual outlook of the Chinese, and to contrast it with that of other people. On the other hand, it should be obvious that such a temptation ought to be resisted, at least for the moment, when all we have are individual studies of isolated aspects of Chinese perception. There is also the general question of the extent to which findings in the laboratory can be extended to real life. For example, one may question the relevance or significance to real life of the finding of a difference in acuity for vertical as opposed to horizontal arrays among English-speaking and Chinese subjects. Does this difference mean that the Chinese are actually able to see things in everyday life differently from other people? We have already seen that the acuity difference between Chinese and English was limited to linguistic items. Even so, there are no indications that this difference matters beyond finely controlled experimental tasks, or makes an impact in subjective experiences of cognition. This is not to say that none of the experimental findings reviewed could have such implications. In the following few paragraphs we will identify some of these implications.

Before doing so, we might make a distinction between those perceptual processes that are related to the Chinese language and those that are related to other aspects of the Chinese environment and to socialization processes. Interposed between these is the distinction between bottom-up processes and top-down processes. It has been suggested that language or orthography differences matter more in bottom-up processes than in top-down processes (Hung and Tzeng, 1981). This certainly seems valid in the case of reading. The strongest evidence comes from contrasting the perception of single and combined Chinese characters in visual hemifield studies — the lateralization of processing the more 'complex' two-character words becomes just like the perception of English words. Similarly, with reference to the question of the retrieval of meaning from individual words as well as from continuous text, we find that language differences matter more in the simpler processes. The Stroop effect, the speed of access to the meaning of individual words, and memory for individual words all indicate language differences. But when it comes to the reading of text, counteracting factors produce equalizing effects. For example, the evidence indicates that, in real life, reading speeds for texts of identical content are about the same for English as for Chinese — as can be verified by asking native speakers to read passages with identical content or comparing the reading of news items with the same content on radio or television (Peng, Orchard, and Stern, 1983). The need for phonological recoding to access meaning shows a similar effect. Findings of significant differences between Chinese and English tend to involve tasks that require the processing of only some aspects of single words. In cases where subjects have to process longer items, orthography differences tend to disappear (Tzeng, Hung, and Wang, 1977).

But there appear to be two respects in which such language differences can produce significant effects with practical implications beyond bottom-up processes. One is in the various instances we have seen where people seem to transfer behavioural patterns which are innate, or are appropriate for processing Chinese, to new situations when they come across a different language. We have reviewed studies of acuity, the Stroop effect for numbers, and eye-movement patterns. The latter, in particular, could have important educational implications. There is a suggestion that bilingual Chinese/English speakers transfer the eye-movement habits appropriate for Chinese text to English, and this results in a slower reading speed for the second language. This suggestion certainly calls for verification, and for the design of learning procedures to 'unlearn' the old habit in the new situation.

Another practical implication of the language difference relates to cognitive abilities that seem to develop or that are facilitated by learning or using Chinese. These include visual-pattern discrimination and the manipulation of numbers. Apart from the question of adjusting for cross-cultural or cross-linguistic differences in comparing intellectual abilities across cultures (as in the case of developing norms for cross-cultural comparisons), it should be pertinent to investigate any real cross-cultural performance differences in achievement outside the laboratory. We have all probably come across tales of super-achievement by some Chinese in mathematics (and visual-pattern discrimination and numbers are perhaps the two ingredients of cognitive manipulation in this field). However, in order to understand these cross-cultural differences in achievement, we need more than incidental observations or even survey data. What we really need are studies of the process *per se* of mathematical manipulations and the relation that these have with elements of the manipulations, such as numbers and spatial relations. In any case, the possibility of facilitating mathematical performance by means of the language used remains intriguing. If proved valid, this aspect of 'linguistic determinism' would be a new dimension of the original Sapir–Whorf hypothesis.

At times, some of the variables reviewed in this chapter might appear to contradict each other. While we have examined the possibility of distinctive cognitive abilities of the Chinese which are conducive to mathematics performance, we have also looked at socialization patterns that discourage independent thought. Surely these two sets of factors work in opposite directions in terms of cultivating achievement. One explanation that might help in understanding this conflict would be that people who experience a relatively less harsh socialization, and who have a more permissive upbringing, manage to exploit their advantage in cognitive abilities, resulting in superior achievement. In other words, one needs the right combination of factors.

The effects of biosocial factors on cognition are probably felt more on top-down than on bottom-up processes, although some of these, such as the judgement of lengths of lines in illusion tests, might at first appear rudimentary if not trivial. While it might be difficult for modern city-dwellers to do so, we should try to imagine the consequences of the misjudgement of distances in harsh environments such as the open sea, or expanses of sand or snow. In the context of the present chapter, the effects of the biosocial environment are mainly in terms of what is referred to as cognitive style. Quite obviously, this is a matter of conceptually driven processes, and typical studies would be those relating socialization to cognitive complexity, and the manner in which relations between things are perceived. Of all the factors affecting perceptual processes that are reviewed in this chapter, perhaps the pattern of socialization and orthography are the two that are most pervasive and probably apply more or less to most Chinese. We might also note that the distinctive Chinese language has itself served a purpose in the biosocial development of the Chinese people. The non-alphabetical orthography has allowed for the numerous variations of spoken dialect throughout China, while it has enabled the maintenance of a common written language which has served to unify this vast country throughout the centuries.

The effects of socialization are such that, while we do not expect the Chinese to see the world differently, they could differ in material ways from people in another culture in what they make of it, and therefore in how they act. Having said that, we should also note that this conceptual difference need not be unique to the Chinese. On the contrary, there are indications that it is likely to be shared by others with similar experiences of socialization. This is, of course, what we noted at the beginning of the chapter as a sub-universal. The perceptual processes of the Chinese, then, are characterized by a combination of processes that are uniquely Chinese, processes that are shared with some other people, and processes that are common to all humankind.

Note: This paper was completed while the author was Visiting Professor of Psychology at the Purdue University School of Science in Indianapolis. Facilities provided there are gratefully acknowledged.

3 Chinese Cognition

IN-MAO LIU

INTRODUCTION

Neisser (1967) defined cognitive psychology as including all processes by which the sensory input is transformed, reduced, elaborated, stored, recovered, and used. Thus cognition may simply be defined as human information processing. The concept of the Chinese does not refer simply to a race but to a people who have received a more or less unique set of internal and external experiences which distinguishes the Chinese from other peoples. External experience refers to the outcome of experiencing a different physical environment, while internal experience refers to the outcome of receiving information through conversation and written materials, and even through non-verbal communication.

The purpose of the present chapter is to describe the cognitive processes of those who have received a set of internal and external experiences that is unique to the Chinese. Before proceeding to describe the cognitive processes, some major theoretical assumptions are presented. One fundamental premise is that the cognitive processes of the Chinese people depend entirely on their unique set of internal and external experiences. Thus it is claimed that, if a non-Chinese person had received a set of similar experiences, this person's cognitive processes would not differ from those of the Chinese. According to this view, cross-cultural psychology has two main tasks: (a) to identify a set of internal and external experiences unique to some particular people, and (b) to find the relationships between these unique experiences and behaviour. Obviously the latter will be the more difficult task because it is frequently impossible to identify which unique experience is responsible for the observed behaviour.

GENERAL THEORETICAL SCHEME

It has long been known that behavioural differences can be attributed to either experiential or genetic factors. By emphasizing experiential factors in the present functional approach, the next natural question to ask is how different experience is retained within an individual to affect his or her behaviour. Past experience must be retained in memory as specifiable knowledge. In the following paragraphs, a simultaneous-processing model is proposed in order to explain how this type of specifiable knowledge comes to affect different people in different ways.

The Simultaneous-processing Model

Humans are capable of processing several stimulus conditions simultaneously. The notion of simultaneous processing is used here in a weak sense to mean that, in processing a particular stimulus condition, a person is capable of taking other stimulus conditions into account. If at the time of processing a particular stimulus condition, a person's behaviour is affected by the presence of other stimulus conditions, then this effect will be taken as presumptive evidence for simultaneous processing.

The main assumption of the simultaneous-processing model is that, at the time of processing a momentary stimulus condition, a person takes into account his or her past experience. It is therefore necessary to specify the exact nature of past experience so that it is possible to say that the acquisition of one type of experience by one people will affect the behaviour of this people in some specific way. For this purpose, let us consider the philosophers' claim that there are two types of knowledge (Ryle, 1949): procedural knowledge is knowledge about how to do something, while declarative knowledge is knowledge of facts about the world. Procedural knowledge will be considered first. Procedural knowledge in philosophy corresponds to the production systems of artificial intelligence as originally proposed by Post (1943). A production system consists of a set of rules, called productions, for rewriting strings of symbols and a specification of some initial strings. For simplicity, productions can be identified as rules for behaviour of the following type.

If C_i condition, then R_i behaviour. (1)

In other words, this rule of behaviour says that in the condition C_i, a person will behave in a way specified by R_j.

Therefore, when some people receive a set of experiences different from that received by other people, it is possible to express a partial set of experiences in terms of a set of acquired behavioural rules.

We say 'a partial set' of experiences because the remaining set of experiences cannot be directly translated into behaviour but represents declarative knowledge or knowledge about the world. Indeed, all individuals acquire an enormous set of behavioural rules from childhood. The following are two such common rules.

If you come to a street and see a green traffic light, then you cross the street. (2)
If you are driving to a crossroad and see a green traffic light, then you drive straight ahead. (3)

However, since there is a limit to human cognitive capacity, it is not expected that an individual takes into account all behavioural rules acquired in the past. He or she takes into account only those behavioural rules that are well learned and well practised.

Our next question is how a person's response to a momentary stimulus condition is affected by his or her stored behavioural rule, if this behavioural rule is taken into account at the time of the person's response. The notion of taking a behavioural rule into account will be explained first, and then the notion of compatibility will be defined. Taking a behavioural rule into account means taking into account the stimulus condition defined in a behavioural rule. A behavioural rule is defined as being incompatible with a stimulus condition that calls for an action, if the action defined in a behavioural rule is in conflict with the action called for by a stimulus condition. For example, let us consider the following behavioural rule.

If you pick up a purse, then you have to return it to the owner or send it to a police station. (4)

Suppose you pick up a purse full of money when nobody is watching. You may wish to keep it. However, this action is in conflict with the action of Rule 4. Therefore Rule 4 is incompatible with the stimulus condition of a purse which is left anywhere. Similarly, a behavioural rule is defined as being compatible with a stimulus condition that calls for an action, if the action defined in a behavioural rule is similar to the action called for by a stimulus condition.

On the basis of the main assumption of the simultaneous-processing model we obtain the following consequences. If a behavioural rule is incompatible with a momentary stimulus condition, a person's response will tend to be suppressed. On the other hand, if a behavioural rule is compatible with a momentary stimulus condition, a person's response will be facilitated. If a behavioural rule is neither incompatible nor compatible with a momentary stimulus condition, a person's response will not be affected.

There is only meagre experimental evidence in support of the above reasoning. In Liu's study (1985), a list of paired items was presented one pair at a time. The subject's task was to respond to each pair by pressing the left or right key according to condition-action rules such as 'If an English letter protruding upwards or downwards appears on the left (or right) side, then press the left (or right) key', or 'If two English capital letters in alphabetical order appear on the left (or right), then press the left (or right) key'. In such a procedure, the number of rules does not vary with the number of responses. It was found in Experiment 1 of this study that the number of highly compatible rules in a list had no effect on reaction time. But in Experiments 2 and 3 incompatible rules in a list adversely affected the reaction time.

In the above experiments, the notion of compatibility or incompatibility between two or more behavioural rules was defined. When this notion is applied to a well-learned behavioural rule and a momentary stimulus situation that calls for an action, it is expected that a more drastic effect will be shown.

Cognitive Development

Although a person is capable of processing a number of stimulus conditions simultaneously, this capability is not present from birth. The number of stimulus conditions which a person is able to process simultaneously increases gradually through the early stages of development and this increase can be used to characterize cognitive development. In the following discussion, let us use this notion to explain how a child develops from the preoperational stage to the concrete-operational stage as defined by Piaget (1952). According to Piaget, the range of the preoperational stage is from 2 to 7 years of age. This stage has as its primary development, the growth and utilization of the representational skills acquired in the sensori-motor stage. Children in this stage are described as being unable to solve conservation problems, transitivity problems, class-inclusion problems, and so on. Between the ages of 7 and 11 children enter the concrete-operational stage and master conservation, causality, transitivity, class inclusion, multiple classification, and seriation tasks.

The mastering of conservation problems after reaching the concrete-operational stage will be used as an example to demonstrate the fundamental characteristic of cognitive development — that children take into account an increasing number of other stimulus conditions at the time of processing a stimulus condition. Although preoperational children consistently answer correctly the simplest conservation problem of object permanence, they rarely solve conservation problems dealing with specific attributes of the material, such as quantity. In this type of task, children are first shown two or more identical objects, for example, two glasses of water. After the children agree that the two identical glasses of water are equal on the crucial dimension (the quantity of water), the experimenter transforms one glass of water in a way that changes its appearance but leaves the crucial dimension constant. For instance, the water is poured into a taller but thinner glass. Finally, the experimenter asks if the two glasses of water remain equal with respect to the quantity of water. Piaget believed that preoperational children fail to answer correctly because they base their judgements on appearances rather than on logical considerations. From the present standpoint, their failure to answer correctly is due to their being unable to take into account both the height and the cross-sectional dimension of the container. Taking these two aspects into account simultaneously appears to have created an informational overload for preoperational children.

Unique Experiences of the Chinese

Although the cognitive development of all peoples follows the same universal pattern of taking into account an increasing number of stimulus conditions, there are differences between peoples in which specific stimulus conditions are taken into account. The hypothesis was suggested earlier that these specific stimulus conditions are retained in individuals' memories in the form of condition-action rules to affect later behaviour.

If the majority of people acquire in their early life a set of behavioural rules and act according to these rules, a distinct pattern of behaviour should evolve in their later life. One of the major tasks of cross-cultural psychology is to identify distinct sets of behavioural rules acquired by different peoples. In the following discussion, we shall consider general and specific behavioural rules acquired by the Chinese in their childhood.

Some behavioural rules are quite general, in the sense that the conditions specified in the condition-action rules are very broad; the acquisition of such behavioural rules affects a wide variety of behaviour. From childhood, the Chinese are taught to respect and be obedient to their superiors under all circumstances.

If your superiors are present, or indirectly involved, in any situation, then you are to respect and obey them. (5)

The indirect involvement in the condition of this rule refers to the teachings and messages of superiors. The most important superiors are the ruler and parents. In ancient times, the ruler was the emperor, but is now called the leader.

Teachings about loyalty and filial piety are widespread. Some evidence may be obtained from the textbooks used in primary and secondary schools. However, a person acquires behavioural rules not only from school textbooks but also from daily newspapers and magazines. Liu, Chuang, and Wang (1975) sampled printed passages containing 1,000,000 words from newspapers, magazines, works of fiction and non-fiction, the textbooks of primary and secondary schools, as well as non-educational reading matter. All the sampled passages are likely to have been read by the typical educated Chinese adult. Although it is possible to pick out all passages related to Rule 5, for our purpose it suffices to consider the frequency counts of related words such as 'loyal' and 'filial'. Table 3.1 lists the Chinese and English usages of loyal- and filial-related words and their frequency counts. The frequency counts of the English words are based on the Thorndike and Lorge (1944) word book.

Following an examination of Table 3.1, it should be noted that, first, although characters are units of writing in Chinese and are morphemes by themselves, a character may or may not constitute a word. There are two-character and three-character words. Huang and Liu (1978) estimate that two-character words in all types of Chinese print comprise about 65 per cent of the total. Second, Table 3.1 includes only those Chinese words beginning with the character corresponding to the English words loyal and filial. There is a single character (morpheme) standing for the English words loyal or filial that constitutes a word, and there are also many Chinese words obtained by combining the character for English loyal or filial with another character to make the concepts more explicit and to differentiate them from one another. Thus there are more loyal- and filial-related Chinese words than those listed in Table 3.1, because the character

Table 3.1 Chinese and English Usages of Loyal- and Filial-related Words

	Frequency of Usage	
	Chinese	English
Loyal-related words		
Loyal	37	22
Loyal-person's-temple	1	–
Loyal-good	1	–
Loyal-advice	7	–
Loyal-honest-simple	6	–
Loyal-heart	13	–
Loyal-honest	3	–
Loyal-purity	4	–
Loyal-minister	2	–
Loyal-mind	8	–
Loyal-truth	8	–
Loyal-faithful	2	–
Loyal-word	1	–
Loyal-courageous	9	–
Loyalist	–	1
Loyally	–	1
Loyalty	–	19
Loyalty-filial	1	–
Total	103	43
Filial-related words		
Filial	20	4
Filial-dress (mourning dress)	2	–
Filial-piety	3	–
Filial-as-brother	2	–
Filial-respectful	2	–
Filial-heart	3	–
Filial-obedient	10	–
Filial-son	2	–
Filial-serving	1	–
Total	45	4

standing for loyal or filial may occupy the second position in two-character words. Although these words are excluded from consideration, Table 3.1 nevertheless shows that there are more loyal- and filial-related words in Chinese than in English and that the total frequencies of usage are also higher in Chinese than in English.

Persons regarded as superiors include not only the ruler and parents but also government officials who directly govern the citizens of a country. Table 3.2 presents official-related words in Chinese (those in which the first character corresponds to the English word official) and in English. The above observations again apply. Although there are many other two-character Chinese words in which the second character corresponds to the English word official, Table 3.2 shows that there are more official-related words of the type under consideration in Chinese than in English and that the total frequency count for the Chinese words is higher than that for the English words.

The influence of Rule 5 is always present, because a person behaves constantly in the presence of his or her superiors either at home or at work. Even when a person is not in the physical presence of his or her superiors, the teachings and messages of the latter cover so many types of situation that he or she is always affected by Rule 5.

Rule 5 is frequently incompatible or in conflict with an overtly assertive attitude. One of the best behavioural manifestations of an overtly assertive attitude is verbal and ideational fluency, for it is impossible for a person to assert himself or herself overtly without verbal and ideational fluency. It may therefore be predicted that because they take Rule 5 into account in many types of situation, the Chinese people will appear less fluent, verbally and ideationally, than Westerners.

As explained earlier, a behavioural rule is defined by both condition and behaviour, and specifies some type of behaviour as contingent on some condition. The generality or specificity of a behavioural rule is then dependent on the condition specified in the rule. If the condition is broad and includes a variety of situations, then a behavioural rule is general. Otherwise a behavioural rule is specific. One of the most conspicuous rules of the specific type acquired by the Chinese during their childhood is as follows.

If the purpose is to acquire the knowledge contained in an article, then the best strategy is to memorize the article. (6)

Let us consider the evidence for the widespread acquisition of this behavioural rule by Chinese from their childhood. Before the introduction of public schools in China, children attended so-called

Table 3.2 Chinese and English Usages of Official-related Words

	Frequency of Usage	
	Chinese	English
Official	102	more than 50
Official-bulletin	1	–
Official-troops (government troops)	20	–
Official-horse	1	–
Official-side	19	–
Official-dress	1	–
Official-of-high-rank	2	–
Official-road	2	–
Official-residence	2	–
Official-of-government	22	–
Official-bureaucrat	2	–
Official-king	3	–
Official-ranking	4	–
Official-army	3	–
Officer-academy	4	–
Officer-salary	1	–
Officer-post	2	–
Official-system	1	–
Official-in-charge	3	–
Officialdom	3	–
Officialdom-manner	1	–
Official-document	1	–
Office-of-government	3	–
Officer (for addressing)	34	–
Official-rank	1	–
Officer	84	more than 100
Official-porcelain-works	1	–
Officially	–	9
Officiate	–	1
Total	323	more than 160

'private schools' where young pupils recited moral and literary readings from ancient times. Even after the introduction of public schools, this practice has survived. A recent survey (Liu, 1984b) showed that most teachers in public schools (grades 1 to 6) in Taiwan still require their pupils to memorize every lesson in the Chinese language textbooks.

In junior high schools in Taiwan (grades 7 to 9), teachers also require their pupils to memorize every lesson written in the old literary style. Such lessons comprise about 30 per cent of texts in the first year (grade 7) and increase to about 60 per cent in the third year (grade 9). Another survey (Liu, 1984b) was made of two classes each of grades 7 to 9 from a typical junior high school in Taipei. The numbers of males and females were equal. The subjects completed a questionnaire which asked how well they memorized the lessons (of literary style) assigned by their teachers. The general findings were: (a) the percentage of children who memorized every assigned lesson decreased from 62.5 per cent (in grade 7) to 37.8 per cent (in grade 8) to 21.84 per cent (in grade 9); and (b) the percentage of children who memorized only some lessons increased from 6.25 per cent (in grade 7) to 23.17 per cent (in grade 8) to 55.17 per cent (in grade 9).

Another survey was made by S. Bond (personal communication, 10 November 1984) of an American school in Hong Kong in which the method of teaching is the same as that in the United States. The survey showed that primary-school children were not required to memorize English lessons, with the exception of spelling and some grammatical rules. Among secondary-school children, only those pupils who participated in dramatic performances were required to memorize anything. Thus Western children lack the opportunity which Chinese children have to practise memorizing skills in their early childhood. Although it is known that young children have difficulty in memorizing, because they are still ignorant of how to rehearse items, it is expected that Chinese children have developed more skills for memorizing (such as the use of rhythms) than Western children.

Another specific behavioural rule closely related to the 'memorize lesson' rule is the 'practise skill' rule.

If the purpose is to acquire any new cognitive skill, then the best strategy is to practise repeatedly. (7)

New cognitive skills include reading and writing, solving arithmetic problems, and so on. A simple survey made by the author in Taipei primary schools showed that a tremendous amount of homework is assigned to pupils every day. Whenever a new character appears in a lesson, pupils are required to write that character as many as 20 times, as part of their homework. Since each lesson contains several new characters, pupils are required to write several pages in their notebook for a one-day exercise in the language course. According to a recent cross-cultural survey by Stevenson and his associates (cited in Cunningham, 1984), American grade 1 pupils spent an average of 14 minutes each weekday on homework. Japanese grade 1 pupils spent 37 minutes and the Taiwanese students spent 77 minutes — more than five times longer than the Americans. Interestingly, American mothers rated ability as a stronger factor than effort in their children's success in school. The Japanese and Taiwanese mothers, on the other hand, rated effort as more important than ability. Of course, parents who believe that success depends more upon ability than effort are less likely to require their children to work hard in school and at home than parents who believe that effort is more important.

The consequences of acquiring specific behavioural rules such as the 'memorize lesson' and 'practise skill' rules may include the following. First, the 'memorize lesson' and 'practise skill' rules are generally compatible with what students are expected to learn in school. Therefore, by acquiring these two rules from their early childhood, Chinese students will perform better than Westerners at those school subjects that require memory and practice. Second, and more specifically, as a consequence of following the 'memorize lesson' rule, Chinese are expected to rehearse earlier in their childhood while memorizing and to develop more efficient memory strategies than Westerners. This conjecture has been alluded to in a preceding paragraph. Third, as a consequence of observing the 'practise skill' rule, Chinese children are expected to excel not only in language courses but also in sciences and mathematics. The reason for this conjecture is that achievement tests depend upon drill in solving science and mathematics problems. The following discussion reviews some pertinent empirical findings.

CHARACTERISTIC FEATURES OF CHINESE COGNITION

Although some biological changes are produced by physical environments (see, for example, Silver and Pollack, 1967), their effects on behaviour are generally restricted. Therefore, by emphasizing the experiential rather than the genetic determinants of behaviour, one naturally assumes that the cognitive capacities of different peoples are more or less the same. However, the cognitive capacity of an adult does not appear suddenly, but evolves through an orderly process of development. The fundamental characteristic of cognitive development is that a person comes to take into account an increasing number of stimulus conditions at the time of processing a particular stimulus. In the course of this cognitive development, a person also stores more and more behavioural rules. The main assumption of the simultaneous-processing model means that stored behavioural rules come to affect a person's behaviour.

The preceding section described how Chinese people have stored some unique behavioural rules. A person's behaviour will either be facilitated or will suffer, depending on whether the stored behavioural rules are compatible or incompatible with a situation that calls for action. The following paragraphs consider some important phenomena and findings bearing on this line of argument.

Verbal and Ideational Fluency

Chinese acquire the 'respect superiors' rule during their childhood. This rule should not be considered as a single behavioural rule, but as a large set of behavioural rules that include traditional ways of dealing with superiors in everyday life. Chinese have to take this rule into account in responding in almost any situation. Consequently, as the simultaneous-processing model predicts, a person's performance latency tends to be lengthened, and deviant responses tend to be suppressed. However, the characteristic that responses are deviant or rare is one precondition of originality and creativity. In other words, by taking into account the 'respect superiors' rule at the time of performing an act, Chinese tend to be less fluent, both verbally and ideationally.

The first area in which we shall examine verbal and ideational fluency is that of parent-child interaction. If Chinese children are to learn the 'respect superiors' rule from their early childhood, incompatible rules, such as assertiveness and eloquence, should simultaneously be suppressed or unlearned from the beginning. This means that Chinese children have to learn many rules at the expense of verbal skills. It is therefore expected that Chinese mothers have less verbal interaction with their children than American mothers. Although no study of this question has been done with Chinese, the result expected has been obtained with Japanese (Caudill, 1972). This expectation, however, is consistent with observations that Chinese children vocalize less and that they spend more time in close proximity to their mothers than American children (Kagan, Kearsley, and Zelazo, 1978). The latter finding points to the hypothesis that this closeness enables mothers to exercise physical control for the easy enforcement of behavioural rules. This hypothesis may be tested by analysing the verbal content of mothers' control. Even without making such an observation, however, it is the author's impression that Oriental mothers seem to teach their children what not to do more frequently than Western mothers. In order to enforce this type of teaching, mothers are expected to exercise some kind of direct physical control.

The second area in which verbal and ideational fluency may be measured is the performance of children. Lesser, Fifer, and Clark (1965) conducted one of the most comprehensive and careful studies designed to examine the patterns of various mental abilities in young American children from different cultural backgrounds. They used four tests from the Hunter College Aptitude Scales (Davis, Lesser, and French, 1960). The four tests measured verbal ability, reasoning, number facility, and space conceptualization in grade 1 children from four ethnic groups (Chinese, Jewish, Negro, and Puerto Rican), with each ethnic group divided into middle- and lower-class groups. They found that each ethnic group showed a distinctive pattern of abilities regardless of social class, with Chinese and Jews generally higher on reasoning, number facility, and space conceptualization than Negroes and Puerto Ricans. However, the Chinese group was much lower than Jews on verbal ability and even lower than the Negroes, although the Chinese were the highest on space conceptualization. In a follow-up study six years later, Lesser (1976) reported that these cultural patterns had remained quite stable.

The verbal ability test used by Lesser, Fifer, and Clark (1965) consisted of picture vocabulary and word vocabulary. The picture vocabulary test required the children to name the objects or the actions depicted in pictures. The word vocabulary test mainly required the children to define words by answering questions aloud. Since the Chinese children had acquired the 'respect superiors' rule by that time, it follows that their verbal performance tended to be inhibited.

It may be asked why Chinese children performed so well in the space conceptualization and reasoning tests. A close examination of these test items showed that they represented well-defined problems in which goals were explicitly stated. In solving this type of problem, children perform according to given problem rules. It may be assumed that Chinese children had learned more behavioural rules and had been required to practise explicit rules more frequently than Jews. As they would transfer this learned behaviour to the test situation, it follows that Chinese children would perform on this type of test at least as well as the Jewish group.

However, it is likely that Chinese subjects would suffer in solving ill-defined problems that require subjects to generate as many ideas as possible. There are two reasons for this conjecture. First, the 'respect superiors' rule is incompatible with a stimulus condition that calls for generating as many ideas as possible. Another plausible reason is consistent with the assumption of the preceding paragraph that Chinese have acquired, and have performed according to, more behavioural rules than Westerners. The main assumption of the simultaneous-processing model is that a person takes into account all relevant behavioural rules in responding to a momentary stimulus condition. If Chinese have to take into account more behavioural rules than Westerners in responding to a stimulus condition, then the resources of the former would be diverted more to behavioural rules than to their current action. On the other hand, the resources of Westerners would be focused more on their current action, resulting in a more efficient performance than that of Chinese. This reasoning is, of course, based on the assumptions that all human cognitive capacity is approximately equal and that the proportion of behavioural rules that are compatible with the action required is also about the same for all peoples.

Precisely this type of result was obtained in an extensive study by Liu and Hsu (1974), testing subjects from grade 2 to second-year university students with a Chinese version of the Torrance test of creative thinking (Torrance, 1966). This test measures (a) idea fluency, which is obtained by simply counting the number of ideas generated, (b) originality, which is scored by counting the number of completely unique ideas on the basis of statistical frequency, and (c) flexibility, which represents the number of different categories of idea produced. In all three measures, the Taiwan norms were below the American norms, as was expected. One interesting observation from the Taiwan norms is that the three scores levelled off after senior high school. The originality scores of university students were even lower than those of senior-high-school students. One interpretation would be that younger generations are becoming increasingly liberated from the 'respect superiors' rule than older generations, represented by university students.

In studies measuring cognitive development with Piagetian tests that require an active searching mode of behaviour, Chinese children who have to take the 'respect superiors' rule into account for their everyday actions should be at a disadvantage. Thus, Douglas and Wong (1977) showed that Chinese high-school students showed formal-level skills less frequently than American students of the same age. Similarly, Chen and Wu (1981) found that the ages of attainment for the Piagetian concepts such as quantity, levels, seriation, symbols, weight, sequence, inclusion, matrix, movement, probability, volume, angles, shadows, perspective, rotation, distance, classes, and so on, for elementary- and secondary-school children in Taiwan were later than those reported in the Piaget (1964) studies.

Finally, the verbal and ideational fluency of adults may be examined. It was reported above that, on the Torrance test of creative thinking, the norms of originality obtained from Taiwan university students were not only lower than the American norms but also lower than those from Taiwan senior-high-school students. However, this Torrance test was a verbal test. Paschal, Kuo, and Schurr (1980–1) used the non-verbal (figural), culture-free Torrance tests of creative thinking to test 120 randomly selected American and Chinese college students. They found again that American subjects scored significantly higher on the originality measure than Chinese subjects. Very interestingly, however, in this non-verbal test the Chinese scored higher on the fluency measure than the Americans. It is clear that the 'respect superiors' rule is not incompatible with non-verbal figural tests which invite subjects to express ideas by drawing. The originality measure is, of course, different from the fluency measure. Thus, the lower scores of the Chinese on the originality measure may be explained by (a) the incompatibility of the 'respect superiors' rule and (b) the assumption that Chinese have acquired more behavioural rules.

In connection with the 'respect superiors' rule, it may be asked whether children can become more creative as a result of teaching by their parents. In order for a specific behavioural rule to affect behaviour, it must be well learned and intensively practised. It must also be consistent with existing behavioural rules. If these two conditions are satisfied, then children may tend to behave creatively when instructed.

Memorization and Other Cognitive Skills

The 'memorize lesson' and 'practise skill' rules are more specific than the 'respect superiors' rule. Therefore, the effect on later performance of acquiring the first two rules is usually restricted to certain types of behaviour.

The first cognitive skill affected by these rules is memorization. Some cultures regard memory ability as the most important component of intelligence. Dube (1977) studied Botswanian categories related to Western conceptions of intelligent behaviour. He succeeded in showing that ratings of intelligence were related to the recall of stories: the higher the rated intelligence, the better the recall. My observation is that the ancient Chinese would have rated the possession of knowledge and the instant composition of poems and articles as most important.

Chen and Huang (1982) attempted to determine empirically the modern Chinese view of intelligence. Their subjects (Australian and Chinese students) rated items from two intelligence tests on the two aspects of relevance and difficulty. The two intelligence tests were the Stanford–Binet and the Wechsler Adult Intelligence Scale. On relevance ratings, the underlying three-factor structure (spatial-mechanical, verbal, and memory) of the Chinese sample accorded very well with that of the Australian sample, suggesting a basic common structure for the concept of intelligence across cultures. Both cultures considered spatial-mechanical items most important and memory items least important. However, the two samples differed in the mean difficulty scores on the three dimensions: the Australians regarded items requiring rote memory as much harder, and items requiring spatial-mechanical ability as much easier, than the Chinese group. The Chinese students tended to rate spatial-mechanical items as the most difficult and to consider memory items as no more difficult than verbal items. In line with the hypothesis that the Chinese have acquired a distinct behavioural rule (Rule 6), Chen and Huang attributed these rating differences to possible cultural differences in nurturing and in the provision of opportunities to practise the different skills.

Let us consider some observations bearing on the memorizing ability of the Chinese. With respect to digit span, Hoosain (1979) found that the mean digit span for Hong Kong undergraduates was 9.9, about two digits more than that reported for comparable samples in the West. However, this superior memory span may be an artifact, because Liu and Shen (1977) found that numbers were read more quickly in Mandarin than in German, and Hoosain (1984b) reported that the sound duration of numbers pronounced in Cantonese is shorter than in English. It was earlier found by Baddeley, Thomson, and Buchanan (1975) that words with shorter pronunciation durations are recalled from short-term memory better than words with longer pronunciation durations. Therefore, because of the inherent difference in the pronunciation durations, digit span cannot be used to compare the memorization abilities of Chinese and Westerners.

An unambiguous comparison of memory performance may be made if the items to be remembered are of the same type. As in the Peterson and Peterson study (1959) and the Murdock (1961) study, Liu and Ma (1970) used English consonant trigrams as items to be remembered, in order to obtain short-term forgetting curves from Chinese college students. With respect to the identical experimental condition of presenting consonant trigrams only once, Liu and Ma obtained more than 20 per cent recall from Chinese subjects at the retention interval of 27 seconds. Peterson and Peterson and Murdock, however, obtained less than 20 per cent recall from Western subjects at the retention interval of 18 seconds. The Western subjects, with the retention interval of 18 seconds, had an advantage over the Chinese subjects, with the retention interval of 27 seconds. Yet the former subjects recalled less than the latter subjects. Since the subjects of the Liu and Ma study memorized English consonant trigrams, they were at a further disadvantage. The Chinese subjects seemed to capitalize on their acquired rehearsal skill (Rule 6) to transfer more items to long-term memory during the exposure time of items, because the flat part of a short-term memory retention curve (including 18-second and 27-second intervals) signifies the number of items transferred to long-term memory.

The author has spent many years conducting verbal memory research with Chinese subjects. The memory ability of Chinese subjects is usually superior to that reported in the American literature. For example, a typical textbook of learning (Hulse, Deese, and Egeth, 1975, p. 320) states that from 8 to 20 pairs may constitute a paired-associate list. However, with a list consisting of 20 pairs or fewer, Chinese college students usually attain the criterion of perfect recall within two or three trials. In the Huang and Liu study (1978), a list consisting of 24 pairs of two-character words was used. It was found that second-year college students attained 95 per cent correct responses on the third study-recall trial. On the other hand, for instance, Paivio (1965) used a paired-associate list consisting of 16 pairs of English nouns. The nouns were those with frequencies of 50 or more occurrences per million, according to Thorndike and Lorge (1944). He found that the mean total numbers of correct responses on four trials were between 6 and 11 for various groups of subjects. These figures are comparatively low, because the mean total numbers of correct responses on the first trial alone were between 6 and 12 for various groups in the Huang and Liu study.

The second area in which the effect of the 'memorize lesson' and 'practise skill' rules may be observed is that of reading and writing skills. There is a widespread belief that alphabetic languages are more difficult to learn than Chinese logographs. In the first place, alphabetic systems were developed later than syllable-based writing systems or logographs. Secondly, explicit phoneme segmentation is supposed to be harder for the young child than syllable segmentation (Liberman, Shankweiler, Fischer, and Carter, 1974). Chinese characters are of course monosyllables. The general belief about logographs was strengthened by a finding that American children with reading problems could learn to read a handful of words represented in Chinese characters (Rozin, Poritsky, and Sotsky, 1971).

When we examine the process of how Taiwanese children learn logographs, however, a different picture emerges. In Taiwan, schoolchildren learn to use an alphabetic phonetic spelling system called *zhuyin fuhao* before studying Chinese characters. This system consists of a set of 37 symbols for which there is consistent grapheme-phoneme correspondence. The pronunciation of any Chinese character can be represented by no more than three of these symbols. Usually, the first symbol represents a consonant, and the remaining symbols a vowel or a diphthong, although many characters are pronounced without consonants. Teachers spend only modest amounts of time teaching the *zhuyin fuhao* system during grade 1, but the early lessons are written exclusively with *zhuyin fuhao*. After about two months of instruction, Chinese characters are introduced and thereafter, for the first few years of elementary school, *zhuyin fuhao* symbols are printed beside all characters in the reading text.

It is clear that schoolchildren in Taiwan learn phoneme segmentation earlier than they learn Chinese logographs. This fact has the following two implication. First, explicit phoneme segmentation is not necessarily harder than syllable segmentation for the young child.

Second, alphabetic systems can, ontogenetically, precede logographic systems. Therefore the general belief that alphabetic systems are more difficult to learn than logographs is not true. The finding regarding American children with reading problems who learned to read a few Chinese characters (Rozin, Poritsky, and Sotsky, 1971) cannot be generalized to the learning of the Chinese language (Taylor and Taylor, 1983). In other words, their finding refers only to the learning of some isolated Chinese characters.

Recently, in a large-scale cross-cultural study, Stevenson, Stigler, Lucker, Lee, Hsu, and Kitamura (1982) found that the reading achievements of elementary-school children are comparable in Taiwan, Japan, and the United States. Evidence was also obtained that reading disabilities exist among Chinese as well as among American children. From this evidence also, Chinese appears to be as hard to learn as English.

If we consider the writing of Chinese characters, the skills involved are much more complex than those required for writing English words. One way to measure the relative complexity of Chinese characters and English words is to compare the time required to write roughly equivalent material in English and in Chinese. Taylor (1981) found that it took three times as long to write a Chinese page as its English equivalent. Learning to write characters takes time and patience because of their variety and complexity. It is therefore expected that Chinese children spend a tremendous amount of time in practising the writing of characters. As was mentioned earlier, Taiwanese grade 1 students spend more than five times as long on homework as Americans. A large proportion of this time is probably spent in writing characters.

What is the effect of practising writing Chinese characters on language acquisition? Experiment 4 of Liu's study (1978) answers this question. New words were presented one at a time to grade 4 students. One group of subjects (the 'study' group) studied the pronunciation and meaning of each new word. Another group of subjects (the 'write' group), in addition to studying the pronunciation and meaning of each new word, attempted to write the characters for each new word during the same exposure interval. It was found that, by practising writing the new characters, the 'write' group achieved a greater improvement in acquiring the pronunciation and meaning of new words than the 'study' group.

Let us now consider the effects of extensive practising to write and read characters by Chinese children, remembering the influence of each activity on the other. The first possible effect is on scholastic achievement. According to a study by Stevenson *et al.* (cited in Cunningham, 1984), of students from Taiwan, Japan, and the United States, in which each nationality would be expected to have equal numbers of poor readers, in fact 47 of the 100 lowest scores on vocabulary tests were received by American grade 1 students. Similarly, Americans received 57 of the 100 lowest scores in reading comprehension. The figures were about the same for grade 5 students.

A second possible effect of extensive practice in reading and writing Chinese characters would be on the writing style of the Chinese. A distinguishing characteristic of Chinese writing is the frequent usage of idioms. Almost all Chinese idioms consist of four characters and originate from ancient passages of the literary style. Articles of the literary style are difficult to read and are not taught until secondary school. This is because the literary style is not used in conversation, nor in printing. In these ways, therefore, Chinese idioms are quite different from English idioms. Foreigners are not expected to use Chinese idioms appropriately, even after studying Chinese for many years. Only after considerable practice in reading ancient passages of the literary style can students become capable of using idioms appropriately in their writing. Casual inspection of the *Min Pao* newspaper on 18 October 1984 (Leung, 1984) showed that a dispatch of 2,000 characters in length contained 22 idioms.

A third possible effect of extensive practice in reading and writing Chinese characters would be reflected in superior performance in space perception. Bond (1980) also made this conjecture. Thus it is generally found that Chinese subjects consistently show higher functioning than their American counterparts when concepts or abilities involving space, form, or shape are being assessed (Carlson, 1962; Leifer, 1972; Lesser, Fifer, and Clark, 1965).

As a final comment on the effect of acquiring the 'practise skill' rule, Stevenson *et al.* (cited in Cunningham, 1984) found that the performances of American children on mathematics achievement tests were worse than those of Japanese and Taiwanese children. Thus, in a situation where each nationality would be expected to have equal numbers of students receiving low mathematics scores, 58 of the 100 lowest scores among grade 1 students were received by Americans. Among grade 5 students, 67 out of the 100 lowest were Americans. Only one American was among the top 100 grade 5 students in mathematics. It appears that the poor showing of American children in mathematics may be linked to their relative lack of practice at solving mathematics problems. Stevenson *et al.* also attributed their finding to the relatively small amount of classroom time spent on that subject by American children.

Representation and Categorization

So far we have been considering the effect on Chinese behaviour of acquiring procedural knowledge (that is, condition-action rules) in childhood. The effect on later behaviour of acquiring declarative knowledge (that is, knowledge about the world) in childhood is, at most, indirect. The latter effect is rather on the representation and categorization of world knowledge. The representation and categorization of such information can be studied through the associative method, which is based on the principle of frequency — that if two events are frequently experienced in a particular way, they will tend to be represented in that way. This principle can be traced to Thumb and Marbe (1901), who found that words of one type evoked a response of the same type and that more frequently preferred associations occurred more rapidly than less preferred ones. Another useful tool for studying representation and categorization is the semantic differential. Since this type of study is covered in Chapter 2 of this book, it will not be included here.

Cross-cultural comparisons of representational differences can be made. An extensive cross-cultural study of representational differences, using the associative method (Szalay and Deese, 1978), compared Koreans and Americans. In addition, category norms have been obtained from American subjects (Battig and Montague, 1969; Cohen, Bousfield, and Whitmarsh, 1957) and from Chinese subjects (Jeng, Lai, and Liu, 1973). The following account is largely from Liu (1973), who compared the American sample of Battig and Montague with the Chinese sample of Jeng *et al.* The purpose of both studies was to find out what items or objects people commonly give as belonging to various categories or classes. For each category name, the subjects in the American study were given 30 seconds and those in the Chinese study were given 60 seconds to write down as many items included in that category as they could. More time was allowed for the Chinese subjects because (as mentioned previously) it takes about three times as much time to write a Chinese page as its English equivalent (Taylor, 1981). In fact, however, the time allowed for the subjects to write down category instances is immaterial because the following comparison of the English and Chinese norms is based on the relative positions of equivalent items, arranged according to frequency.

The category names used in the two studies are of two types. One type of category name is related to the natural environment, such as the natural earth formation, weather phenomena, colours, flowers, insects, fruit, and so on. The other type of category name concerns social or cultural items, such as cloth, footwear, sport, relatives, human dwellings, occupations, ships, vehicles, weapons, crimes, and so on.

In the categories of the natural environment, marked differences in category norms were obtained from the American and the Chinese subjects. For instance, different plants grow and different animals live in the two countries, giving rise to differences in categorization. The most frequently mentioned bird in the United States norms is the *robin* which is not typical in Taiwan and occupies the twenty-first position in the Chinese norms. Similarly, the most typical American tree is the *oak* which is rather atypical in Taiwan and occupies the thirtieth position in the Chinese norms.

The cross-cultural difference in the categorization of the natural environment also extends to the categorization of social or cultural items. Thus, *hempen fabrics* (48.1 per cent of responses) are commonly used in subtropical Taiwan but rarely used in the United States (only one response in 442), reflecting the effect of different physical environments on the kind of cloth used by different peoples. However, in the category of sport, *football* appears in the first position (89.59 per cent) of the United States norms, but occupies the twenty-first position (10.27 per cent) in the Chinese norms. Similarly, in the category of substances for flavouring food, *soy* appears in the second position (65.94 per cent) for the Chinese, but fails to appear in the American norms at all. This is another indication of a difference in cultural traditions, but it does not reflect a difference in the physical environments, because soya beans are available in both countries.

If we consider the categories that are more heavily loaded with social convention, the effect of tradition and culture becomes even clearer. For instance, frequently used utensils such as *knife, spoon,* and *fork* (occupying the first three positions) in one culture occupy lower positions (fifth, eighth and thirteenth positions) in the other culture. For the categories of money, city, and state, the association patterns are also very culture-specific.

It may be concluded that the representation and the categorization of the human internal and external world are strongly affected by culture and cannot be understood simply from a universal viewpoint (see, for example, Heider, 1972). According to this viewpoint, categories are composed of a core meaning, which consists of the prototypes (best examples) of the category and is surrounded by other category members of decreasing similarity to the core meaning. The core meaning of categories is not arbitrary but is given by the human perceptual system. Heider concluded that the basic content and the structure of such categories are universal across languages, However, as is clear from Liu's (1973) comparison, some instances may be representative or typical of a category for one language, but other instances may be representative or typical of the same category for another language. It may be concluded that the degree to which an instance is representative or typical often depends on the unique set of internal and external experiences specific to a culture.

Invariant Features

We have seen that Chinese differ from Westerners in a variety of cognitive processes because the former have acquired in their childhood different sets of procedural and declarative knowledge. The acquisition of a different set of procedural knowledge by the Chinese tends to inhibit verbal and ideational flow and to enhance memorization and other cognitive skills in later life. The acquisition of a different set of declarative knowledge gives rise to a characteristic way of categorizing and representing the external world. In spite of these differences, there are many features that do not vary with the acquisition of different sets of procedural and declarative knowledge. Areas that have attracted vigorous research in the past few years are sentence comprehension and memory and counterfactual thinking.

The results of research into sentence comprehension and memory demonstrate the invariant nature of these skills. In the typical sentence-picture verification task first introduced by Wason (1959), a sentence and a picture are shown. The subject is timed while he or she reads the sentence, looks at the picture, and decides whether the picture is true or false with respect to the sentence. The sentence can be affirmative or negative, and the picture may or may not match the sentence, resulting in the following four sentence/picture combinations: true affirmative (TA), false affirmative (FA), true negative (TN), and false negative (FN). With English sentences, a pattern of verification times of TA, FA, FN, TN — in increasing length of time

— has generally been obtained (for example, Clark and Chase, 1972; Just and Carpenter, 1971). Using Chinese sentences, Cheng and Huang (1980) and Liu and Liang (1977) obtained exactly the same pattern of verification times, although in Experiment 2 of the latter study the word order of simple Chinese sentences differed from that of simple English sentences. Thus cognitive functioning at the level of sentence processing does not differ in English and Chinese despite grammatical variations.

Early investigators believed that the subject was unable to comprehend a sentence unless he or she was able to verify it against a picture; they also implicitly assumed that the converse was true, that is, that the subject was unable to verify a sentence against a picture unless he or she was able to comprehend the sentence. If both statements are correct, then the process of comprehension is equivalent to that of verification and the comprehension time should be equal to the verification time. On the basis of this assumption, early investigators attempted to measure sentence verification times. However the converse is not generally true. Recently Yu and Liu (1982) successfully separated comprehension time from verification time in conducting an experiment with Western subjects who were studying at National Taiwan University. The sentences in the experiment included: (a) left-embedded sentences (for example, 'Green car hit tree'), (b) right-embedded sentences (for example, 'Car hit green tree'), and (c) serial sentences (for example, 'Car is green, car hit tree' and 'Car hit tree, tree is green'). The same results were obtained with English, using Western subjects, as had previously been obtained with Chinese, using Chinese subjects. The comprehension time for right-embedded sentences was shorter than that for left-embedded sentences, and the two types of embedded sentence were comprehended faster than serial sentences. The results are as predicted by a model of sentence comprehension proposed by Liu (1984a) and establish the generality of the model.

With respect to sentence memory, Tsao (1973) used Chinese/English bilingual subjects to replicate Bransford and Frank's (1971) study. He investigated the integration of ideas across sentences when sentences were presented entirely in Chinese or in English (single-language condition), or half in Chinese and half in English (mixed-language condition). The term 'integration of ideas' refers to the finding that subjects tend to recognize complex sentences as having been presented before even though they were presented previously in small idea units rather than as complex sentences. Tsao found that linguistic integration occurs across different languages as well as in the same language. In Experiment 2, he used Kintsch and Monk's (1972) method to examine the storage of sentence information presented in different languages. After his Chinese/English bilingual subjects comprehended mixed-language or single-language paragraphs, he found that the reaction time for answering inferential questions about the contents of the paragraphs was the same for both mixed-language and single-language conditions. Tsao concluded that the underlying representation of information from connected discourses is propositional; the process of reasoning is not affected by verbatim details.

The second area of cognitive processes which is invariant is counterfactual thinking. The Whorfian hypothesis (1956) of linguistic relativity is now frequently interpreted in either the strong or the weak version. The strong version which is espoused by Whorf himself holds that language *determines* thought and behaviour patterns. The weak form merely asserts that certain aspects of language can *predispose* people to think or act in one way rather than another. Recently Bloom (1981) noticed that Chinese grammar does not have any simple device corresponding to the English subjunctive. While the English subjunctive unambiguously distinguishes a counterfactual sentence from an implicated one, Chinese offers only the 'if . . . then' construction for both types of sentence. In support of the weak version of the Whorfian hypothesis, Bloom collected both anecdotal and experimental evidence that Chinese speakers are less likely than English speakers to think counterfactually.

Bloom (1981) offered anecdotal evidence of a Chinese speaker's inability to answer counterfactual questions. The evidence is, however, open to different interpretations, and should not be regarded as conclusive, especially as English speakers frequently refuse to answer counterfactual questions, for reasons unrelated to whether or not they understand the questions.

Let us therefore consider Bloom's (1981) experimental evidence in support of the Whorfian hypothesis. He prepared a counterfactual story in English and Chinese. The Chinese version was given to Chinese speakers in Hong Kong and Taiwan, the English version to English speakers in the United States. Following each story, subjects were asked whether or not the counterfactual conclusions (for example, 'would have made a contribution') had actually happened. He found that only 7 per cent of the Chinese-speaking subjects gave counterfactual interpretations to the story, whereas 98 per cent of the English-speaking subjects did. In another study, he asked Taiwanese bilingual students and non-students to respond to a similar version of the story written in English. Among the non-students, only 6 per cent of whom had given counterfactual responses to the previous version in Chinese three months earlier, 86 per cent gave counterfactual responses to the new version written in English. Therefore Bloom concluded that the bilinguals' inclination to think counterfactually seemed to depend significantly on whether or not the language they were using had a linguistic construction for the counterfactual.

Recently, Au (1983) noted that in Bloom's (1981) study, every counterfactual conclusion in the English versions was marked with a counterfactual cue ('would have'), but that there was no corresponding cue in the Chinese versions. He also noted that Bloom's findings in the second study were confounded by the non-student bilinguals' previous exposure to the story. He then conducted a series of better controlled experiments and found that bilingual Chinese showed little difficulty in understanding Bloom's original story or his new story in either Chinese or English.

Finally, let us consider the concept of linguistic relativity in some depth. With respect to the cognitive processes at the level of sentence comprehension and beyond, we have seen that language does not determine how to process nor does it predispose people to process in one way rather than another. After reviewing the available literature, Hung and Tzeng (1981) reached essentially the same conclusion.

From the standpoint of empirical data, the strong and weak forms of the Whorfian hypothesis are hardly distinguishable. However, most people would agree that different people think differently and represent at least some aspects of the external world differently. This idea is, in fact, the main theme of the present chapter; it was earlier demonstrated that the acquisition of unique sets of procedural and declarative knowledge affects people's behaviour quite profoundly.

It is proposed that semantic relativity rather than linguistic relativity holds. Semantic relativity is the concept that the thought conveyed by a language affects the thinking of the people who use that language. When the Chinese read classical stories and novels bequeathed from earlier generations, they learn how to think and behave like the characters in these stories and novels. It is not the linguistic structure but the semantic content that affects the people's thought and behaviour. There is a precedent for this idea, in a study by Furth (1964), in which he studied deaf and hearing adults and found no significant differences in basic cognitive abilities, though most of his deaf subjects could barely read, write, or speak English. He then concluded that (a) language does not affect intellectual development in any direct, general, or decisive way, and (b) the influence of language may be indirect or specific and may accelerate intellectual development by providing the opportunity for additional experience through the giving of information and the exchange of ideas.

RELATED CONCEPTUALIZATIONS

One of the most extensive cross-cultural theories is Witkin's differentiation theory (Witkin, Lewis, Hertzman, Machover, Meissner, and Wapner, 1954; Witkin, Dyk, Paterson, Goodenough, and Karp, 1962). This theory is said to be a theory of cognitive functioning. Dawson (1963; 1967a; 1967b) pioneered the extension of the concept of psychological differentiation into the cross-cultural sphere. Berry (1966; 1967; and 1971) further developed a sophisticated model based on this work, relating ecology, type of subsistence, and social behaviour. Another conceptualization that is related to the present approach is that of primary and secondary control (Rothbaum, Weisz, and Snyder, 1982), although this conceptualization was developed in the context of personality and social psychology. Piaget's theory of cognitive development has inspired a considerable amount of cross-cultural research. However, his theory will not be treated further here because it has been discussed from time to time throughout this chapter.

Psychological Differentiation

Witkin and his associates (Witkin et al., 1954; Witkin et al., 1962) have put forward a theory of differentiation underlying the so-called field-dependent and field-independent or global and analytic cognitive styles. According to this theory, psychological development involves a progression from undifferentiated functioning with little specialization towards the emergence of articulated subsystems. On the empirical side, the determination of one's location on the field-dependence/field-independence dimension is usually achieved by one of a number of tests. In the Rod and Frame test, the subject is seated in a completely darkened room and is presented with a luminous rod, contained within a tilted luminous square frame. The subject is required to adjust the rod to a position he or she perceives as upright, while the frame remains at its initial tilted position. Depending on the extent to which the rod is adjusted close to the axes of the tilted frame and away from the vertical, the performance is scored as field dependent. The other two tests, called the Embedded Figures test and the Body Adjustment test, are similar to the Rod and Frame test in the sense that subjects are required to abstract a stimulus from its context.

After examining the empirical basis of the differentiation theory, it seems misleading to use such terms as 'cognitive style' to describe the result of isolating figure elements by subjects. Thus Serpell (1976) proposed that what Witkin (1967) and Berry (1976) labelled as cognitive style is best viewed as increased skill in dealing with pictorial stimuli. Similarly, the differentiation theory predicts superior performance on spatial-abilities tests by people from low-food-accumulating societies, on the grounds that such people typically engage in hunting and fishing for their food, activities which obviously require a high degree of spatial skill. It was found (Berry, 1966), for instance, that the Eskimo samples exceeded all others tested on all three tests, and that the Temne, an agricultural and high-food-accumulating people, earned scores nearest to the 'undifferentiated' end of the psychological differentiation continuum. However, agricultural people also have to develop a high degree of spatial skill in order to distinguish among a variety of grains and to separate wheat from weed, and so on.

Cole and Scribner (1974) also questioned the relation between ecology and psychological processes which was claimed by Berry. For example, it might well be that it is not hunting but some other aspect of these peoples' lives that accounts for the pattern of test performance. If hunting experience is of critical importance, one should see a difference in spatial skill between hunters and non-hunters within a society that emphasizes hunting. One way to test this notion is to compare men's and women's performances among Berry's two hunting samples — the Eskimos and the Australian Aboriginals. Although the women in these societies are not hunters, no significant sex differences in test performance occur in these societies.

In brief, at the beginning of this chapter the process of cognitive development was conceived of as children's coming to take into account an increasing number of stimulus conditions at the time of processing a particular stimulus condition. This characterization of ontogenetic development is essentially the same as that of differentiation theory, because the latter draws its evidence from observations of the performance of tasks that test a person's ability to isolate some stimulus by taking into account some external contextual stimuli. It is not, however, correct to generalize these ontogenetic differences as cross-cultural differences. It has repeatedly been emphasized that cross-cultural behavioural differences are obtained because different peoples come to take different stimulus conditions into account at the time of processing a particular stimulus condition. In other words, cognitive differentiation takes place along different dimensions for different peoples. Thus, on a task that requires subjects to identify a component letter from passages written in English, Americans would perform better than Chinese. On the other hand, on a task that requires subjects to identify component characters from passages written in Chinese, Chinese would be superior to Americans. In conclusion, the performance of a particular people on the Rod and Frame test, the Embedded Figure test, and the Body Adjustment test depends on how closely the performance demanded by these tests simulates a set of experiences that is unique to that people.

Another difference between differentiation theory and the proposed simultaneous-processing model is that the former emphasizes the 'condition' side of condition-action rules while neglecting the 'action' side, so that it is not easy to make specific predictions of cross-cultural behavioural differences. The following discussion therefore considers another theoretical approach of cross-cultural psychology that emphasizes the 'action' side of condition-action rules without paying great attention to the 'condition' side.

Primary and Secondary Control

Morris and his colleagues (see, for example, Morris, 1956; Morris and Jones, 1955) studied values in the United States, China, and elsewhere, asking subjects to rate 'Thirteen Ways to Live'. The Americans preferred a way which emphasized the autonomous pursuit of self-actualization and did not emphasize alignment with others. By contrast, the Chinese and the Japanese tended to stress close alignment with others. Morris (1956) concluded that 'the value pattern of the Chinese young people is actively and socially oriented to an extreme degree and hence is antithetic to those modes of life directed primarily towards the self or towards nature' (p. 60).

Recently Rothbaum, Weisz, and Snyder (1982) described the concept of social or self-orientation in terms of the concept of control (Rotter and Mulry, 1965). Rothbaum *et al.* labelled the process 'primary control', whereby people attempt to gain control by influencing existing realities, often by means of acts involving personal agency, dominance, or even aggression. When control is sought by means of alternative paths, which is labelled 'secondary control', individuals attempt to align themselves with existing realities, leaving them unchanged but exerting control over the psychological impact that those realities induce. In other words, a person often attempts to associate or closely align himself with other individuals, groups, or institutions in order to participate psychologically in the influence they exert.

Although it is possible to describe the value systems of various cultures, as Morris (1956) does, these systems are very remote from observable behaviour. There should be some mediating construct that can bridge the gap between the value systems and observable behaviour. Many unique condition-action rules acquired by the Chinese (as proposed earlier in this chapter) can be used to fill just such a gap.

Rothbaum, Weisz, and Snyder (1982) claim that, in primary control, individuals adopt a general strategy of attempting to influence existing realities and that, in secondary control, people adopt a general strategy of attempting to accommodate to existing realities. It is obvious, however, that a person does not indiscriminately attempt to influence existing realities nor to accommodate to existing realities. An individual's behaviour must depend in part on the situation. It is therefore important to specify under what condition an individual will attempt to influence, or to accommodate to, realities. In this respect, the notion of condition-action rules which is proposed in the present chapter provides a more precise account of specific behaviour as being guided by some general behavioural rules.

SUMMARY AND SPECULATION

In accounting for cross-cultural differences in behaviour, the present approach emphasizes experiential rather than genetic factors. If experiential factors are responsible for differences in behaviour, a set of internal and external experiences that is unique to a people must be stored as acquired knowledge in memory to affect later behaviour. Knowledge stored in memory can be classified into two forms: (a) knowledge of behavioural rules that specify certain actions to take place under certain conditions, and (b) knowledge of facts that are about the external world without any reference to an individual's behaviour tendency. According to the proposed simultaneous-processing model, at the time of responding to a particular stimulus condition, an individual takes into account those behavioural rules that are relevant to the particular stimulus condition. When the behavioural rules are in conflict, or are incompatible, with the behaviour called for by the particular stimulus condition, an individual's behaviour suffers. When the behavioural rules are compatible with the particular stimulus situation, his or her behaviour is facilitated. In this way, cross-cultural differences in behaviour can be attributed to unique sets of behavioural rules acquired by different peoples.

The explanation of cross-cultural differences in behaviour, in terms of different peoples' taking into account different sets of behavioural rules at the time of processing a particular stimulus condition, can also clearly be seen in the process of cognitive development. This is because, in responding to a particular stimulus condition, children can take only a small number of stimulus conditions into account. Thus the process of cognitive development can be conceived of as children's coming to take into account an increasing number of stimulus conditions. Because of their unique set of internal and external experiences, the Chinese come to take into account certain behavioural rules at the time of responding to particular stimulus conditions. Such behavioural rules may be identified as the 'respect superiors', the 'memorize lesson', and the 'practise skill' rules.

As a consequence of their having acquired the 'respect superiors' rule from their childhood, the verbal and ideational flow of the Chinese is less smooth than that of Westerners. On the other hand, because of their acquisition of the 'memorize lesson' and the 'practise skill' rules, the Chinese excel in the performance of tasks requiring memorization, and Chinese schoolchildren score highly not only on language but also on mathematics achievement tests. In addition to a unique set of behavioural rules, the Chinese also acquire a unique set of world knowledge, which is reflected in their unique way of representing and categorizing the external world. At the level of higher cognitive functioning, however, such as sentence comprehension and memory or counterfactual thinking, the Chinese think and behave in much the same way as Westerners. If the Chinese think differently from Westerners, the difference is superficial and can be explained by the semantic relativity hypothesis that the contents conveyed by a language, rather than its syntactical structure, affect the thinking of those people who use that language. Similarly, the available evidence does not warrant the common belief that the Chinese are affected at the level of higher cognitive functioning by the script they use.

Finally, the two related conceptualizations of psychological differentiation and primary and secondary control were contrasted with the simultaneous-processing approach. It was pointed out that differentiation theory emphasizes the 'condition' side of condition-action rules without reference to the 'action' side, while the notion of primary and secondary control stresses the 'action' side of condition-action rules without paying proper attention to the 'condition' side. For this reason, neither of these conceptualizations is a satisfactory theory of cross-cultural psychology.

To conclude the present chapter, it may be worthwhile to examine the optimal behavioural rules in China today. Although the 'respect superiors' rule hinders verbal and ideational flow, it may have the positive consequence of contributing to the emotional stability of an individual and the stability of family life and society. Perhaps it may be better to follow the 'respect superiors' rule moderately, rather than to its extreme — as in ancient China, because in this way creativity will not be stifled and at the same time social stability will be secured. (In this connection, it is interesting to speculate whether the reason for the early burst of technological inventions followed by a long period of silence in the history of China may be attributed to a strict observance of the 'respect superiors' rule after the teachings of loyalty and filial piety became widely accepted during the Han Dynasty about 2,000 years ago.)

Chinese people in Hong Kong and Taiwan are more liberal today than in ancient times and no longer subscribe to extreme forms of the 'respect superiors' rule. This is also true of the 'memorize lesson' rule. However, it may be a surprise to note that the 'practise skill' rule is more strictly observed by present-day Chinese than it was in ancient times. In a recent study, Stevenson *et al.* (cited in Cunningham, 1984) found that Taiwanese and Japanese children are far superior to American children on achievement tests of mathematics. Essentially, he attributed this difference to American children's lack of practice. Perhaps lenient 'respect superiors' and 'memorize lesson' rules, plus a strict 'practise skill' rule may be optimal. If this is true, then Asian countries, including Hong Kong, Japan, Korea, Singapore, and Taiwan, will continue to advance. Whether this conjecture turns out to be true awaits the outcome of one of the great natural 'experiments' of this century which is currently taking place. Finally, it should be noted that only a few studies conducted on Chinese cognition were reviewed in the present chapter. In the areas of social psychology, personality, and clinical psychology, the same or translated tests and questionnaires are frequently used across different cultures. Therefore, almost any study done in these areas has some cross-cultural significance, because it can be compared with similar studies done in different cultures. This is not the case in the area of experimental or cognitive psychology. Almost any researcher working in the area of cognitive psychology believes that the fundamental cognitive processes are the same across different cultures. He or she then devises a new experiment to explore the nature of cognitive processes. Therefore, very few cognitive psychologists pay close attention to the cross-cultural perspective in cognitive psychology. However, as is clear from the present chapter, cross-cultural research on cognitive processes may open new frontiers for cognitive psychology in the future.

4 Chinese Personality and its Change

Kuo-shu Yang

INTRODUCTION

International interest in the study of Chinese character dates back at least to the last decade of the last century (Smith, 1894). Early writings on this subject were usually based on impressionistic observations or conceptual analyses of quotations from Chinese classics. Serious relevant attempts by more rigorous empirical methods have been reported in the literature mainly within the last three decades, by scholars trained in psychology, anthropology, sociology, and political science. These reports are scattered in various professional journals of the different academic disciplines. Many of these studies were conducted by native Chinese scholars, whose publications (mostly in Chinese) have rarely been accessible to the Western reader because of their relatively inconspicuous locations in the literature or because of the language barrier. This unsatisfactory state of 'affairs obviously necessitates a systematic review of the empirical research on Chinese personality, including both English and Chinese studies. This chapter endeavours to accomplish such a literature review.

The studies to be reviewed may be properly considered investigations of what is called national character, which has been defined by Inkeles and Levinson (1954; 1969) as relatively enduring characteristics and patterns that are modal among the adult members of a society. As pointed out by Inkeles, Hanfmann, and Beier (1958), two main steps are encompassed by the study of national character: determining the modal personality patterns of a particular national group or a major subgroup and studying the interrelations between the personality modes and various aspects of the social system. The present chapter will cover empirical findings belonging to both of these two steps in the study of Chinese national character. Among studies of the second kind, however, only those which can throw light on the understanding of the transformation of Chinese personality under the influence of social change will be included. More specifically, this chapter will first review the major empirical studies of the enduring personality characteristics of Chinese and then examine investigations unravelling the change in those characteristics under the impact of modernization. Finally, a section will be devoted to the discussion of several methodological issues in the study of Chinese character.

Before reviewing the relevant literature, one point should be clarified. Chinese social and behavioural scientists in China have been slowly recovering from the traumatic shock of the Cultural Revolution. For ideological and political reasons they have done almost no empirical research on Chinese personality in the last 20 years or so. Because of numerous restrictions on the flow of information from mainland China, even the very few studies which have presumably been completed have been unable to reach the outside world. For this reason, most of the work to be reviewed in this chapter was conducted after 1948, when the Chinese Communists took power, and uses Chinese people drawn from Taiwan and Hong Kong as respondents or subjects. While this limitation is inevitable at present, it is reasonable to make inferences or generalizations about the typical Chinese character from what has been observed in the Chinese of Taiwan and Hong Kong. One reason for this is the fact that people in these two Chinese societies are not local natives in the usual sense. On the contrary, they have come, not long ago, from almost every major province of mainland China. (This is especially true of people in Hong Kong.) In other words, Chinese in Taiwan and Hong Kong are diversified enough to provide a fairly representative sample of the overall Chinese population. Another reason is the fact that the Communist ideology and social reform have been unable to change significantly the basic values and personality of Chinese in mainland China. As Lew (1979) pointed out, in spite of superficial discontinuities, there are basic continuities in the latent cultural and psychological traits of mainland Chinese and Overseas Chinese. When a Chinese person from mainland China meets a Chinese person from Taiwan or Hong Kong, it is unlikely that they would think that they were people from different national cultures. More probably, they would feel that they were 'birds of the same flock'.

CHINESE PERSONALITY CHARACTERISTICS

Numerous empirical studies have provided information about the stable personality traits of Chinese. In this section, we will deal mainly with those studies which were better designed and yielded results with some cross-cultural meaning. While many of them used an assessment procedure originally designed for cross-cultural purposes, others applied to the Chinese sample a measuring instrument specifically developed within the cultural context of some other country (usually the United States). Research of the latter type has been labelled by Triandis (1972) as 'pseudoetic', rather than 'etic' (using truly universal concepts or categories), in the sense that it imposes the 'emic' (culture-specific) categories of one culture (usually a Western culture) on another (in this case the Chinese culture) as quasi-universal categories. Any cross-cultural differences found in this type of study should be interpreted with special caution.

One of the most inclusive definitions of personality traits is that of Guilford (1959). He defined a trait as any distinguishable and relatively enduring way in which one individual differs from others. This rather broad definition is adopted hereafter to accommodate the various conceptions of personality disposition in the studies to be reviewed. In his well-known model, Guilford was able to distinguish seven kinds of trait (physiology, morphology, aptitudes, temperaments, needs, attitudes, and interests) to represent different aspects of personality. The review which follows is organized according to a modification of Guilford's classification. The scheme to be used is based upon a purely psychological conception of personality, and includes four classes of personality trait: aptitudinal traits, motivational traits, evaluative-attitudinal traits (corresponding to attitudes and interests in Guilford's model), and temperamental traits. Our review, however, will focus on the last three categories since no cross-culturally valid data provided by well-designed research on general and specific aptitudes are available.

Motivational Characteristics

Motivational dispositions have much to do with what a person does, with providing reasons for choosing different courses of action, and with performing with different degrees of effort. While Guilford (1959) distinguished needs, interests, and attitudes as three basic kinds of motivational trait, only those psychogenic needs which are broadly generalized desires will be featured in this section. Most of the perennial needs, in terms of which the Chinese motivational pattern will be described, are socialized motives with self-evident cross-cultural relevance.

Previous studies of Chinese motives have used both self-report inventories and projective techniques as assessing instruments. The most frequently utilized inventory is the Edwards Personal Preference Schedule (EPPS) (Edwards, 1959), a multidimensional standardized test measuring 15 psychological needs. At least three Chinese versions of EPPS have been used by different investigators in their studies of the need patterns of Chinese students at different universities in Taiwan. Among more than 10 such studies, the following are relatively representative: (a) Peng (1963), the first user of the EPPS in Taiwan, tested 296 students from National Taiwan University and National Normal University in 1963; (b) Hwang (1967) collected data for 660 students from National Normal University in 1964; (c) Lu (1970) administered the EPPS to 1,076 students from National Taiwan University in 1968; and (d) Chang (1975) reported data for 844 students assessed at Tunghai University in 1970. In order to obtain a more stable estimation of the central tendency on each of the 15 need variables, the data from these four studies were pooled by computing grand means (from their respective means and sample sizes on the same variable) across the total sample of 2,876 Chinese students. These grand means are given in Table 4.1. Also included in the table are K.S. Yang's (1967b) EPPS results for 367 overseas students of Chinese ancestry who had returned to Taiwan from Indonesia, Malaya, Singapore, Vietnam, Burma, and Hong Kong for college education. To enable a cross-cultural comparison, Edwards' (1959) norms for American students and Fuster's (1962) data for a sample of 288 Indian students from St. Xavier's College in Bombay are shown in the same table.

An inspection of the average scores in the first two columns in Table 4.1 reveals that the patterns of the means on the 15 needs of the two Chinese samples are quite similar, although the two groups of Chinese students had been brought up in very different societal environments. Both groups scored relatively high on Achievement, Order, Affiliation, Intraception, Abasement, Nurturance, Change, and Endurance and relatively low on Exhibition, Heterosexuality, and Aggression, with Deference, Autonomy, Succorance, and Dominance falling in between. The Overseas Chinese students had grown up with their families in foreign lands with a different culture, before they came to Taiwan for advanced education. If we can agree with contemporary researchers of the *Hua-Chiao* (Overseas Chinese) that migration to different foreign countries with diverse cultures has provided a ready-made 'experimental laboratory' for the study

Table 4.1 Mean Scores on the Edwards Personal Preference Schedule for Chinese, American, and Indian Students

Scales	Chinese Students		American Students	Indian Students
	Pooled Sample (n = 2,876)	Yang (1967) (n = 367)*	Edwards (1959) (n = 1,504)	Fuster (1962) (n = 288)
1. Achievement	15.46	15.29	14.38	15.22
2. Deference	12.57	12.67	11.80	12.84
3. Order	14.38	16.08	10.24	12.34
4. Exhibition	9.64	10.10	14.34	12.55
5. Autonomy	13.06	13.21	13.31	12.70
6. Affiliation	15.44	15.23	16.19	14.02
7. Intraception	15.53	14.15	16.72	15.92
8. Succorance	13.83	13.16	11.63	11.86
9. Dominance	13.99	13.46	15.83	14.29
10. Abasement	15.02	16.56	13.66	16.73
11. Nurturance	15.97	17.34	15.22	16.64
12. Change	14.43	15.33	16.35	16.15
13. Endurance	15.28	16.80	12.65	14.90
14. Heterosexuality	8.53	9.45	16.01	9.89
15. Aggression	9.29	10.62	11.70	13.72

Note: *Composed of male and female students of Chinese origin who had returned from Indonesia, Malaya, Singapore, Vietnam, Burma, and Hong Kong for college education in Taiwan.

of cultural acculturation and change (Fried, 1958), we must say that this 'experiment' over many generations has been unable to change the overall need pattern of the Chinese 'subjects'. Furthermore, if a need pattern has such robustness or resistance to change under long-standing foreign cultural pressure, it must be very basic and crucial to the everyday social life of a Chinese person.

Table 4.1 also reveals some interesting cross-cultural differences. First, Chinese students tended to express a higher need than their American counterparts on Achievement, Deference, Order, Succorance, Abasement, Nurturance, and Endurance, a lower need on Exhibition, Intraception, Dominance, Change, Heterosexuality, and Aggression, and an approximately equal need for Autonomy and Affiliation. This general pattern of differences has been repeatedly confirmed in comparisons of the EPPS needs of Chinese and Americans, on the basis of the more limited samples reported in Fenz and Arkoff (1962), Hwang (1967), Lu (1970), Peng (1963), Singh, Huang, and Thompson (1962), and Yang (1965). These studies have all compared university students, who are the most modernized group in the Chinese population in Taiwan and in other Chinese societies. Had the general populations of China and America been compared, larger differences in needs would have been found.

When compared with the Indian students, Chinese students were inclined to be higher on Order, Affiliation, and Succorance, lower on Exhibition, Abasement, Heterosexuality, and Aggression, and about equal on Achievement, Deference, Autonomy, Intraception, Dominance, Nurturance, and Endurance. Hwang (1967) and Singh, Huang, and Thompson (1962) have reported data supporting this general pattern of difference. It should be pointed out here that Chinese students are similar to Hindu students on more needs than they are to their American counterparts. China and India are, of course, both Eastern, Asian countries which have important societal and cultural similarities (Hsu, 1963).

Among the 15 needs so far discussed, three (achievement, affiliation, and dominance or power) have also been investigated in other studies using Chinese people as subjects. One of these studies was Abbott's (1970) analysis of psychosocial functioning in Chinese society, in which he used a carefully translated Chinese version of Gough's (1960) California Psychological Inventory (CPI) as the major tool for the assessment of Chinese personality. Abbott compared the CPI profiles of his Chinese (40 in Taipei) and Chinese American (52 in San Francisco) adolescents to those of a sample of Japanese adolescents and those of Gough's (1960) normative sample of American adolescents. His results showed, among other things, that the Chinese and the Chinese American samples were strikingly similar to each other on Achievement via Conformance (Ac) and Achievement via Independence (Ai), and their mean scores were both higher than those of the Japanese and American samples on these two measures of need for achievement.

Other studies on needs for achievement (nAch), affiliation (nAff), and dominance or power (nPow) have used projective techniques or materials as the means for data collection. One was carried out by McClelland (1963), in which a number of stories were randomly selected from public-school reading books used in three South-east Asian countries (China, India, and Pakistan) in the years 1950–9. The stories were carefully scored with respect to the needs for achievement, affiliation, and power. He found that all three countries were relatively high (above the world average) in nAch and nPow and relatively low (below the world average) in nAff. He was also able to find two distinctive patterns of the three needs in Chinese reading books collected from mainland China and Taiwan. His results revealed a pattern of high nAch and nPow and low nAff for mainland Chinese, and a pattern of low nAch and nAff and high nPow for Taiwan Chinese. McClelland's findings must be interpreted with great care, however, because the writing, editing, and publishing of public-school reading books are usually under the strict control of the government in most South-east Asian countries. Therefore the stories in these books cannot be regarded as spontaneous expressions of the inner desires of the populations of these countries. This is especially true of the Chinese Communist stories. The validity of data on nAch is particularly vulnerable to political influence, and the contents of the stories tend to reflect the ideological emphasis on collective achievement of the Chinese Communist regime. Subsequent observations from mainland China indicate that the level of nAch of the mainland Chinese should have been much lower than that reported by McClelland. It is very likely that, in the 1950s, Chinese in China and Taiwan were relatively low in their nAch, and that this low need might not be naturally projected on material like stories selected from public-school reading books.

Evidence for the rather low nAch of the Chinese, as compared with Americans, can also be found in another study using a projective procedure. The research was completed by Watrous and Hsu (1963), who collected a large number of Thematic Apperception Test

(TAT) stories from several samples of college students in Hong Kong, Taiwan, India, and the United States. It was found that the Chinese groups showed lower percentages of achievement imagery than the American students and the most Westernized Indian groups and higher percentages than the least Westernized Indian groups. The Chinese fantasies also conveyed less gregariousness and less concern with peer acceptance than did the American TAT responses, suggesting a relatively weak nAff on the part of Chinese. In addition, the Chinese students appeared to have a lower need for Aggression (nAgg) and a higher need for Dependence (nDep) or Succorance (nSuc).

So far we have reviewed most major studies on the Chinese motivational pattern and have found certain inconsistencies in the findings on some of the needs. One of these inconsistencies becomes clearer when we compare the personality-inventory data on nAch and the projective-test data on the same need. It will be recalled that Chinese were found to be higher than Americans on the Achievement scale of the EPPS and lower on nAch, as revealed in children's readers (McClelland, 1963) and TAT stories (Watrous and Hsu, 1963). This inconsistency seems to suggest that the self-report and projective measures of what appears to be the 'same' need may not measure the same thing. There have already been studies reporting zero or very low correlations between self-report and projective measures of achievement motivation (for example, McClelland, 1958; Weinstein, 1969).

The need for achievement is a highly complex motive saturated with strong social significance. In order to understand better the meaning of the above-mentioned inconsistency, it is necessary for us to go deeper into the content of this need construct. McClelland and his associates (1953; 1961) originally defined achievement motivation as a propensity to strive for success in any or all situations in which a personal standard of excellence is thought to apply. However, as K.S. Yang (1982a), Yang and Liang (1973), and Aeroff (1977) have already pointed out, there may well be several varieties of achievement motivation. McClelland's conceptualization of the achievement motive as a well-internalized predisposition in the self-reliant individual as a result of independence training is probably only one variety. Dissatisfaction with this highly individualistic conception of achievement motivation as a cross-cultural research variable has been voiced among investigators (for example, De Vos, 1973; Kubany, Gallimore, and Buell, 1970; K.S. Yang, 1982a; Yang and Liang, 1973) studying people in collectivistic societies like Japan, Taiwan, and the Philippines. A strong and pervasive preoccupation with achievement and accomplishment is commonly observed among people in the family and related social settings in Chinese and Japanese societies. In order to do justice to this preoccupation, K.S. Yang (1982a) and Yang and Liang (1973) proposed to distinguish between two basic varieties or types of achievement motivation: individual oriented and social oriented. They defined individual-oriented achievement motivation as a kind of functionally auto-nomized desire, in which the course of achievement-related be-haviour, the standards of excellence, and the evaluation of the per-formance or outcome are defined or determined by the actor himself or herself. They define the social-oriented achievement motivation as a kind of functionally unautonomized (hence still extrinsic and instrumental) desire in which the course of the achievement-related behaviour, the standards of excellence, and the evaluation of the per-formance are defined or determined by the significant others, the family, the group, or the society as a whole. The former type is con-ceived of as resulting mainly from independence-emphasizing socialization in an individualistic society and the latter type from dependence-emphasizing socialization in a collectivistic society. Yang and Liang (1973) have been able to demonstrate empirically that these two varieties of need for achievement are related in different ways to other variables (for example, socio-economic status).

With these two types of achievement motive in mind, it will be much easier for us to realize the complexities and pitfalls involved in the measurement of this motivational variable. My contention is that the individual-oriented type of achievement motivation, because of the unconscious nature of its thorough internalization and func-tional autonomy, will be most effectively assessed by a projective procedure; the social-oriented type of achievement motivation, however, because of its conscious sensitivity to the influences of others, the family, group, and society, will be most effectively measured by a self-report inventory. Partially supportive evidence is available in the literature. In a study replicating McClelland's pro-cedure for arousing and measuring achievement motivation, Yu (1974) found that Chinese familism and filial piety correlated positively with verbal reports (a conscious measure) of achievement and had no relationship with TAT projections (an unconscious measure) of nAch. Furthermore, he found that the conscious achievement statements and the unconscious achievement imagery did not correlate with each other to any significant extent.

Up to this point, it should be clear that self-report and projective measures of achievement motivation plausibly represent two different varieties of the same need, namely, the individual oriented and the social oriented. Since the Chinese are inclined to have a much stronger social-oriented need for achievement and a much weaker individual-oriented need for achievement than Americans, they would of course have higher scores on conscious measures of this need on such self-report tests as the EPPS and the CPI and lower scores on unconscious measures of this need on such projective procedures as TAT and reader stories. The inconsistency between the self-report and projective findings concerning achievement motivation can thus be resolved.

In concluding this section, the Chinese motivational pattern may be tentatively summarized as follows: relatively strong on Abasement, Achievement (social oriented), Change, Endurance, Intraception, Nurturance, and Order, moderate on Autonomy, Deference, Dominance, and Succorance, and low on Achievement (individual oriented), Affiliation, Aggression, Exhibition, Heterosexuality, and Power. While this contemporary Chinese need pattern is essentially a continuation of the traditional Chinese motivational proclivities with a collectivistic orientation, it encompasses new elements which convey a flavour of the modern individualistic outlook. One of these new elements, for instance, is the relatively high need for change, especially among Chinese students in Taiwan.

Evaluative-attitudinal Characteristics

We shall consider three evaluative-attitudinal characteristics. The first concerns values and value orientations. Values, which are usually considered to be more general than attitudes and interests, are mainly motivational. A value may be defined as the core component of a class of generalized attitudes concerning what is desirable or undesirable, which directs behaviour on a long-term basis towards some goals in preference to others. A person's value system is usually composed of values at different levels, for which different assessment instruments have been designed.

The modal value system of Chinese has been empirically investigated by psychologists and anthropologists using various methods suitable to the measurement of values at different levels. At the highest level of one's value system are what may be called value orientations, which were defined by Kluckhohn and Strodtbeck (1961) as complex but definitely patterned (rank-ordered) principles, resulting from the transactional interplay of three analytically distinguishable elements of the evaluative process — the cognitive, the affective, and the directive elements. Value orientations can serve as guides to behaviour and have directional functions in the solution of problems that may be categorized by four modalities of human experience: activity, relation, time, and the relationship between man and nature.

There have been at least four studies of the value orientations of Chinese (Chang, 1959; Y.N. Lin, 1978; Liu, 1966; Yang and Chang, 1975), which made use of either Kluckhohn and Strodtbeck's original questionnaire or a newly derived questionnaire. While all these studies used Chinese students in Taiwan and Hong Kong as subjects, their findings are consistent on some orientation modalities but inconsistent on the others. All of these studies found that Chinese students' dominant orientation on the relational modality was individualism rather than collaterality (peer orientation) or lineality (collectivism); and that on the time modality their orientation was to future rather than past or present perspectives. These orientation patterns are at variance with the common image of traditional Chinese as people who typically had a collectivistic and hierarchical (linear) emphasis in human relationships and a past emphasis in time perspective (Cheng, 1946; Hsu, 1948; 1971a; King and Bond, 1985; Kluckhohn and Strodtbeck, 1961; Lin, 1939; Tseng and Hsu, 1969–70). These findings thus reveal a drastic movement away from the traditional Chinese pattern in these respects by Chinese young people in Taiwan and Hong Kong. On the time and relational modalities, Chinese students now tend to have value orientation patterns fairly similar to those of American students as reported in studies by Green (1979) and Nordlie (1968).

On the other hand, in the spheres of activity and the relationship between man and nature, the findings are inconsistent. On the activity modality, Yang and Chang (1975) reported a dominant preference for inner development (being-in-becoming) rather than expression (being) and achievement (doing) among a group of 108 Chinese university students in Taiwan, whereas Y.N. Lin (1978) found a dominant preference for achievement rather than inner development and expression among a group of 705 junior-high-school students in Taiwan. The factors that are responsible for this difference are by no means clear. Since inner development has been one of the major goals for the self-improvement or cultivation of the typical Chinese intellectual in traditional Chinese society, the difference may be interpreted as an important aspect of Chinese university students' developmental reidentification with the traditional Chinese culture (Dawson, Law, Leung, and Whitney, 1971). As for the man-nature modality, Y.N. Lin (1978) and Yang and Chang (1975) found that Chinese students were predominantly inclined toward a mastery-over-nature orientation, while Liu (1966) reported that most Chinese students in Hong Kong valued a submission-to-nature orientation. It seems that Liu's 1962 Hong Kong students were distinctly traditional in this regard, whereas, more than 10 years later, Y.N. Lin's and Yang and Chang's Taiwan students tended to be moving away from this traditional characteristic to such an extent that their dominant man-nature orientation was rather similar to that of American students (Nordlie, 1968). It is not clear, however, whether this disparity should be attributed to differences in the type of Chinese society or to social changes over a period of more than 10 years.

Another study dealing with values at a rather high level is Morris's (1956) 'Ways to Live' survey. Research on Chinese values by means of his questionnaire has produced copious data, some of which will be reviewed here and in a later section of this chapter. In 1948, Morris administered a Chinese version of his questionnaire to 743 Chinese college and high-school students in mainland China, and obtained the first set of preference ratings for a Chinese sample on the 13 Ways to Live. According to his data, these Chinese students gave the highest ratings to Ways 13, 5, 6, and 3:

Way 13. Obey the cosmic purposes.
Way 5. Act and enjoy life through group participation.
Way 6. Constantly master changing conditions.
Way 3. Show sympathetic concern for others.

At the same time, they gave the lowest ratings to Ways 2, 4, 9, and 11:

Way 2. Cultivate independence of persons and things.
Way 4. Experience festivity and solitude in alternation.
Way 9. Wait in quiet receptivity.
Way 11. Meditate on the inner life.

It must be pointed out that this preference pattern cannot represent the value judgements that the Chinese students of 1948 would have made if China had been at peace. When Morris administered his questionnaire to his Chinese respondents, China had been in a state of political turmoil and social unrest for a long time and the nation-wide civil war had reached such a stage that only a year later the Communists took over mainland China. Facing an unknown but challenging future full of uncertainties and opportunities, these Chinese students should have become highly action oriented and should have experienced a sense of strong social concern. It is not surprising that they placed a high value on Way 5 (act and enjoy life through group participation and collective resolute activity) and Way 6 (constantly master changing social and physical conditions), and a low value on Way 9 (wait in quiet receptivity) and Way 11 (meditate on the inner life).

In his cross-cultural comparison of mean preference ratings for the 13 Ways to Live, Morris found that Chinese students were the only group most favouring Way 13 (obey cosmic purposes) and that all the other cultural groups (from India, Japan, Norway, and the United States) uniformly rated it as one of the least acceptable ways. The fact that the Chinese gave the highest rating to Way 13 was partly due to a serious fault in the Chinese translation of one of the statements in the description of Way 13 (Morris, 1956, p. 36). The first sentence, 'A person should let himself be used', became, in the Chinese translation, 'A person should make himself useful'. This highest rating cannot, however, be completely attributed to an error in translating one sentence out of eight in the description of Way 13. There must have been some other factors. For example, these Chinese students had a fairly good reason to like Way 13, for it represents a mixed stress on subjugation to, and harmony with, an irresistible nature or environment, which is usually supposed to be one of the main components of the traditional Chinese value system (Li, 1975). Since Morris's 1948 value ratings for Chinese students were heavily influenced by the then overwhelming national factors in China and admittedly were plagued by translation errors, it does not make much sense to compare these ratings cross-culturally with those collected in other countries as Morris himself (1956) and his followers (Jones and Bock, 1960) did.

About 10 years later, Singh, Huang, and Thompson (1962) administered the English version of Morris's questionnaire, among other instruments, to 37 American, 37 Chinese, and 37 Indian students at Ohio State University. They found that the Chinese students most preferred Way 5 (act and enjoy life through group participation), Way 1 (preserve the best that man has attained), Way

3 (show sympathetic concern for others), and Way 6 (constantly master changing conditions); and they least favoured Way 4 (experience festivity and solitude in alternation), Way 9 (wait in quiet receptivity), Way 11 (meditate on the inner life), and Way 2 (cultivate independence of persons and things). It is interesting to note that the above list of the most and least preferred Ways to Live is almost the same as that obtained by Morris for mainland Chinese students, except that Way 1 replaced Way 13 as one of the most favoured. While the subjects in Singh, Huang, and Thompson's study were all graduate students, the authors failed to tell the reader how old these subjects were and where they came from (Taiwan, mainland China, or Hong Kong). It is very likely that a considerable number of these older students had received their college or high-school education in mainland China before they left or escaped from that land. In other words, Singh, Huang, and Thompson's subjects might have had similar experiences to Morris's 1948 sample of Chinese students and the value pattern of the two groups should have partly reflected the influence of the same political and social factors.

Given the small size and the unknown composition of Singh, Huang, and Thompson's sample with respect to age and background, its representativeness is questionable. In order to obtain a better picture of such preferences in Chinese students, more representative samples should be tested in typical Chinese societies. While no such research has been possible in mainland China since 1948, several studies have been completed in Taiwan.

One of these studies was conducted by Yang (1972) during the period 1964–5, only a few years after Singh, Huang, and Thompson's (1962) study. Yang collected preference-rating data from 787 Chinese university students in Taiwan, using a new Chinese version of Morris's questionnaire. These Taiwan students were found to prefer the following Ways most:

Way 1. Preserve the best that man has attained.
Way 3. Show sympathetic concern for others.
Way 7. Integrate action, enjoyment, and contemplation.
Way 10. Control the self stoically.

The Ways that they favoured least were the following:

Way 4. Experience festivity and solitude in alternation.
Way 13. Obey the cosmic purposes.
Way 11. Meditate on the inner life.
Way 2. Cultivate independence of persons and things.

Comparing this Chinese value pattern with those found by Morris and by Singh *et al.*, several similarities and differences may be pointed out: (a) Way 3 is among the most favoured ways in all three studies, thus representing one of the most stable aspects of the Chinese value system; (b) Ways 7 and 10, while most preferred by Taiwan students, are not among the most favoured ways for mainland and overseas students; (c) Ways 4, 11, and 2 are among the least preferred in all three studies, thus reflecting a stable tendency among the Chinese to despise certain aspects of the Ways to Live; (d) Way 13, while least preferred by Taiwan students, is not among the least favoured ways for mainland and overseas students.

Yang's results indicate that the best way of life for Chinese students in Taiwan may be summarized as follows. One should build a moderate and balanced life with action, contemplation, and enjoyment combined in proper proportions. In leading such a life, sympathetic concern for other persons should be greatly emphasized, social restraints should be willingly accepted, and good human achievements and traditions should be carefully preserved. In order to function properly and effectively, one must be vigilant and strict in the control of oneself, and warm and benevolent in the treatment of others. Sensuous enjoyment, sheer meditation, excessive independence from persons or things, and silent submission to nature and forces should be avoided or abandoned.

When Yang's data are compared with those obtained by Morris (1956) and Singh, Huang, and Thompson (1962) for American and Indian students, it is found that Chinese and Indian respondents tended to place greater emphasis upon self-control, to be concerned for other people, and to derive more satisfaction from social life. In contrast, American students preferred an enjoyable life with much self-indulgence and little passivity. In spite of these differences, the three groups all rated Way 1 (preserve the best that man has attained) and Way 7 (integrate action, enjoyment, and contemplation) among the most favoured, and Way 2 (cultivate independence of persons and things) among the least.

So far we have reviewed the major relevant studies which use value-orientation and Ways to Live questionnaires as measuring instruments. Both of these instruments assess values at a fairly general level. Previous research on Chinese values has also employed tools which examine values at a relatively more specific level. These include Allport, Vernon, and Lindzey's (1951) *Study of Values*, Gordon's (1960) *Survey of Interpersonal Values*, and Rokeach's (1967) *Value Survey*.

Rodd (1959) was the first researcher to administer a Chinese version of the Study of Values questionnaire to Chinese respondents in Taiwan. He collected data for 1,290 Chinese (525 mainlanders and 765 Taiwanese) and then compared these data with those from Japanese and Americans. It was found that the two Chinese groups, while closely alike, differed from the other two cultural groups in their value patterns. In general, Chinese tended to show a high interest in the Theoretical, Political, and Religious values and a low interest in the Social, Economic, and Aesthetic values. In contrast, the dominant values for Japanese were the Economic, Aesthetic, and Political, and the subordinate values were the Theoretical, Social, and Religious; the stronger values for Americans were the Economic, Political, and Religious, and the weaker values were the Aesthetic, Social, and Theoretical.

During the same general period, Singh, Huang, and Thompson (1962), in their comparative study of selected personality variables, reported data collected on the English version of the Allport, Vernon, and Lindzey scale for relatively small samples of American students and Chinese and Indian students studying in the United States. Their results indicated that the three highest values for the Chinese group were Theoretical, Aesthetic, and Social, and the three lowest were Political, Religious, and Economic; the three highest values for the Indian group were Economic, Theoretical, and Political, and the three lowest were Social, Aesthetic, and Religious; and the three highest values for the American group were Theoretical, Religious, and Aesthetic, and the three lowest were Economic, Political, and Social. The value profiles here obtained for Chinese and Americans were thus quite different from those obtained in Rodd's study for the corresponding cultural groups.

Two years later, in 1964, Li and Yang (1972), using a Chinese version of the Allport, Vernon, and Lindzey scale, collected relevant data for 306 university students in Taiwan. This time the young Chinese were found to place a higher value on Theoretical, Aesthetic, and Social, and a lower value on Political, Economic, and Religious. In 1966, Chiu (1967) administered the same Chinese version to 1,075 students at the National Normal University in Taipei and found that they were relatively high on Theoretical, Aesthetic, and Political, and low on Social, Economic, and Religious. Recently, Lei and Yang (1984), in their study on the change of values as a result of societal modernization, reported relevant data for 905 university students, indicating higher mean scores on Theoretical, Aesthetic, and

Political, and lower mean scores on Social, Economic, and Religious. An almost identical pattern was obtained by Wu (1984) from a large sample of 2,250 college students.

All the studies using the Allport, Vernon, and Lindzey scale, except that by Rodd, reported a highly similar Chinese value profile: Theoretical and Aesthetic were the two highest values and Economic and Religious the two lowest, with Political and Social being in between. It may also be noted that the Theoretical value is among the highest two and the Economic among the lowest two even in Rodd's study. It appears that the empirically identified modal value profile described above is fairly close to the stereotypic value pattern of a typical traditional Chinese intellectual. This is by no means surprising, since almost all the subjects in the studies using the Allport, Vernon, and Lindzey scale were college and university students, who were contemporary counterparts of the traditional Chinese intellectuals.

Only one study has administered Gordon's Survey of Interpersonal Values to a Chinese sample in Taiwan. This is the study by Tarwater (1966), which used a Chinese adaptation of Gordon's scale, carefully translated to preserve the original psychological meanings of the constructs measured. This investigator obtained results for 801 Chinese students from several universities and colleges in Taiwan and Hong Kong and compared these data with those for Gordon's original American sample. His cross-cultural comparisons showed that Chinese students were higher in their valuing of Conformity and Benevolence and lower on the scales of (interpersonal) Support, (social) Recognition, and Leadership than were American students. Benevolence is the closest Western equivalent to *jen* (仁), which is one of the most central traditional Chinese virtues (King and Bond, 1985). Tarwater's finding about this particular interpersonal value means that even among contemporary Chinese young intellectuals, who are supposed to be the most modernized group in the population, *jen* is still a predominant cultural value. Furthermore, as Benevolence has a mutually supportive and nurturant quality, Tarwater's finding is in accordance with the finding that Chinese students have a strong need for Nurturance on the EPPS (as discussed in the last section).

Appleton (1970; 1979) is probably the only political scientist who surveyed the values of Chinese respondents in Taiwan before 1970. Utilizing a Chinese version of Rokeach's (1967) Value Survey, he collected rank-order data for 754 college and university students and

395 vocational-high-school students. Among the terminal values (of personally or socially preferable end states), the most important were found to be National Security, Freedom, a World at Peace, and a Meaningful Life, and the least important were Salvation, Maturity, a Comfortable Life, and Respect from Others. Among the instrumental values (of personally or socially preferable modes of conduct), the most important were Responsible, Honourable, Trustful, and Clean, and the least important were Intellectual, Tender, Self-disciplined, and Courageous.

In 1970, Grichting (1971) conducted a large-scale survey throughout Taiwan, by administering an adapted short version of Rokeach's inventory of terminal values to a stratified sample of households (rather than individuals). His data for 1,874 respondents showed that the average rank of the nine terminal values included placed them in the following order of decreasing importance: Family Security, a World at Peace, Inner Harmony, a Comfortable Life, True Friendship, Social Recognition, Faith, Religion, and a Happy Afterlife.

At least three Chinese value studies using the Rokeach Value Survey as a major instrument have been published recently. Ng *et al.* (1982) collected data from university students (100 in each cultural group) in Taiwan, Hong Kong, and seven other Asian and Pacific countries with a modified version of the Rokeach survey. Since their research purpose was to identify major value dimensions in terms of which the different cultural groups could be located, their results are not very informative in describing the specific value profiles of the Chinese groups. More detailed and representative relevant data obtained by the Rokeach procedure come from two large-scale studies conducted by Wang (1981) and the Committee for Education Planning (CEP) (1983) in Taiwan.

Using a modified version of the Rokeach Value Survey (Form E), Wang (1981) collected data for 5,971 junior-high-school students and found that for these students the most important terminal values were National Security, the World as a Commonwealth, a World at Peace, Freedom, and Equality, and the least important were Spiritual Salvation, Happiness, a Comfortable Life, an Exciting Life, and a World of Beauty; the most important instrumental values were Filially Dutiful, Patriotic, Benevolent, Honest, and Responsible, and the least important were Cheerful, Imaginative, Capable, Intellectual, and Clean.

Similar results (with certain exceptions) were reported in another study (CEP, 1983), in which 5,466 adolescents of senior-high-school age and 478 teachers were tested for their value preferences by Rokeach's method (Form D). The data obtained disclosed that among the terminal values the adolescents ranked as the most important: National Security, a World at Peace, Family Security, Freedom, and Equality/Brotherly Love, and as the least important: a Comfortable Life, Social Recognition, and Spiritual Salvation; among the instrumental values they considered the most important to be Ambitious, Broad-minded, Honest, Responsible, Capable, and Intellectual, and the least important to be Clean, Obedient, Loving, Imaginative, and Observing Etiquette. It was also found that the degree of consistency in the rank ordering of the values between the students and their teachers was high, even higher than that between the students and their parents.

It is noteworthy that the ranked patterns of terminal values obtained in the four major studies are quite similar, all expressing a proclivity to emphasize collective welfare and social concern and to de-emphasize sensuous enjoyment and personal feeling in one's life. On the other hand, the pattern of instrumental values obtained in the last study is somewhat different from those in the others. While social and moral values unequivocally preceded personal and competence values in the studies by Appleton, Grichting, and Wang, a pattern with thoroughly mixed social and personal values was observed in the CEP study. The latter finding seems to imply the leaking in of an individualistic, self-oriented spirit.

In addition to the above studies employing a standardized Western scale, there have been quite a number of relevant studies utilizing a questionnaire specifically designed for use with Chinese respondents. Findings in these studies, however, are too voluminous and unsystematic to be thoroughly reviewed here. For the sake of brevity, only some studies which deal with values at a similar level to those reviewed thus far will be mentioned here as examples. One of these studies was completed by the Chinese Psychological Association (1979), in which a comprehensive questionnaire was given to 17,000 Chinese college and university students in Taiwan. One of the items asked the respondent to rate the importance of 22 personal characteristics. Ratings for this item showed that the young Chinese tended to rate the following as the most important: Filial Duty and Respect for Parents, Loving and Protecting Own Nation, Cultivating Good Character, Regard for Public Welfare, and Observance of Law and Order; and the following as the least important: Recollecting the Past, Being Good-looking, Enjoying the Present, Being Independent, and Letting Things Proceed Naturally.

Another item requested each respondent to indicate how much he liked or disliked each of 16 goals of life. It was found that the highest in the list of liked goals were Successful Marriage and Happy Family, Beating One's Brain in Pursuit of Knowledge, Understanding and Facing Oneself, Handsome Income and Good Life, and Stability and Security in Life; and the lowest were Religious Belief and Spiritual Pursuit, as a Leader to Dominate Others, Living in Tranquillity and Idleness with a Pure Heart and Few Desires, Labouring and Exercising Intensively to Develop Physical Capabilities, and Being Successful in Social Life.

Still another item asked what the respondent thought was the most valuable achievement in one's life. Responses to this item revealed that the students were inclined to choose Health, Learning, Morality, and Friendship as the most valuable, and Pretty Face, Longevity, Power, and Status as the least, with Love and Wealth being in between. This value pattern is confirmed later by another large-scale study (Bureau of Social Welfare, 1980), in which 4,000 Chinese youths aged 12–20 years were surveyed.

We have so far reviewed more than 20 studies on Chinese values and value orientations. Briefly speaking, contemporary Chinese students in Taiwan tend to have a dominant profile of value orientations consisting of inner development, individualism, future perspective, and mastery over nature. This profile obviously represents a drastic change from the traditional Chinese pattern of inner development, collectivism (lineality), past perspective, and submission to nature. These young Chinese are also found to prefer a moderate and balanced life with action, contemplation, and enjoyment combined in proper proportions. It is quite important for them to accept social restraints, to express sympathetic concern for others, and to preserve good human achievements and traditions. They consider that sensuous enjoyment, sheer meditation, and silent submission to external forces should be avoided. Moreover, they are relatively high in theoretical and aesthetic interests and low in economic and religious ones. Their valuing of conformity and benevolence is high, and of interpersonal support and social recognition is relatively low, when compared with American students. Their perception of the relative importance of terminal values indicates a tendency to stress collective welfare and social concern and to de-emphasize personal enjoyment and feeling in one's life. As to the instrumental values, they place greater significance upon social and moral values than upon personal and competence ones, although the latter values are moving to a higher level of importance, suggesting a gradual change in the direction of being more individualistic and self-oriented.

The second type of evaluative-attitudinal characteristic to be considered is attitudinal syndromes. Attitudes are closely related to values, but have a more specific content and are more peripheral in the individual's personality structure than values. An attitude is a relatively enduring organization of beliefs and feelings around a person, object, or situation, predisposing one to respond in some specific manner. Each person usually has an extremely large number of attitudes towards various specific things or categories of things. Numerous investigations have been carried out into Chinese people's political, religious, economic, cultural, and fertility attitudes. Findings of some of these studies are reviewed in Chapter 6 of this volume. In this chapter, we will discuss only those studies that are concerned with three broad attitudinal syndromes, namely, authoritarianism (Adorno, Frenkel-Brunswik, Levinson, and Sanford, 1950), Machiavellianism (Christie and Geis, 1970), and locus of control of reinforcement (Rotter, 1966).

Authoritarianism is a complex pattern of dispositions, attitudinal in nature, marked by a high degree of conventionality, superstitiousness, aggressiveness, rigidity in thinking, submissiveness to authority, and several other characteristics. The first set of Chinese data on this broad attitudinal dimension was collected by Singh, Huang, and Thompson (1962) in their comparative study of Chinese, American, and Indian students. The Chinese scored slightly lower than Indians, but much higher than their American counterparts, on authoritarianism as measured by Sanford and Older's (1950) Authoritarian/Equalitarian Scale. In another study, Meade and Whittaker (1967) gave the English version of the California Fascism (F) Scale (Adorno *et al.*, 1950) to 62 Chinese university students from Hong Kong and five other groups of students of comparable sample size from India, Brazil, Arabia, Rhodesia, and the United States. Indians and Rhodesians showed the highest level of authoritarianism. The scores of Chinese and Arabians exhibited no difference and together they constituted the next level. Brazilians came next, followed (much further down) by the Americans. Relevant data were also reported in a study by Earle (1969), who administered Rokeach's (1960) Dogmatism Scale in both English and Chinese to 101 Chinese students at the University of Hong Kong and an English version of the same scale to 82 British university students. The results revealed that the Hong Kong mean scores on both language versions were higher than the British mean score. Since dogmatism is conceptually and empirically related to authoritarianism (Rokeach, 1960; Kerlinger and Rokeach, 1966), Earle's finding may be interpreted as indicating that the Chinese group was higher on authoritarianism than the British. From the data obtained in the above three studies, Chinese may be said to be higher in their authoritarian attitudes than Americans, British, and Brazilians, and lower than Indians and Rhodesians.

The high Chinese authoritarianism may also be inferred from a study by Ho and Lee (1974) with 135 Taiwan teachers as subjects. These researchers gave adult Chinese not only a Chinese version of the F Scale but also a scale of attitudes towards filial piety, and obtained a moderately positive correlation between authoritarianism and filial piety. Since Chinese people have long been known for their extremely strong sense of filial piety, it may be inferred from this substantial correlation that they are also high in their authoritarian attitudes. Furthermore, since both authoritarianism and filial piety presumably involve traditionalism, Ho and Lee's finding seems to suggest that socialization factors responsible for the formation of attitudes of filial piety might also be responsible for the formation of authoritarian attitudes. Exactly what these factors are is an important empirical question awaiting systematic future research.

One of the main components of authoritarianism is unconditional submissiveness to authority. Research findings in several studies have shown that Chinese are quite conspicuous by their deferential attitudes towards whomever or whatever they consider an authority. Thus, in an interesting study, Chu (1967) ran persuasion experiments in order to reveal various differences in the ease or reluctance with which Chinese subjects, from different sectors of Taiwan society, would change their opinions. His experimental results on persuasibility, as compared with non-Chinese data, were consistent with the conventional assumption of Chinese submission to the authority of age, status, and tradition. In the same vein, Hiniker (1969) conducted an ingenious experiment adopting a forced-compliance paradigm for attitude change. The Hong Kong Chinese subjects, all of whom were adult refugees who had left Communist China after 1959, were easily induced to comply overtly with authority, although this compliance by no means implied private acceptance.

Supportive data were also provided in Yang's (1970) study, in which a newly constructed authoritarianism scale with a forced-choice format and an adaptation of the Triandis Role Differential (Triandis, Vassiliou, and Nassiakou, 1968), both in Chinese, were administered to 227 university students in Taiwan. For the subordinate/superordinate role-pairs (for example, son/father, student/teacher, employee/employer) and for those of equal power (for example, friend/friend, classmate/classmate, colleague/colleague), authoritarianism was found to correlate positively with the appropriateness of such role-behaviour factors as nurturance, acquiescence, subordination, and dependency. For the superordinate/subordinate role-pairs, authoritarianism was found to correlate positively only with the appropriateness of the role-behaviour factor of superordination. Of particular interest and significance is his finding of a positive correlation between authoritarianism and the appropriateness of such role behaviour as acquiescence, subordination, and dependency in an equal-power relationship. The importance of this correlation is that the more authoritarian students were likely to consider it appropriate for the actor to assume the subordinate part in an equal-power role-pair. This suggests that, for a typical traditional Chinese (however authoritarian he is), the best policy is always to behave like a subordinate and to treat the other as an authority, unless he clearly knows that he himself is the authority in a role relationship.

In another relevant study (Bloom, 1977a; 1977b), 336 Hong Kong residents (including businessmen, professionals, workers, and students) were compared with 74 French university students and 52 American college students, in terms of their relative positions on the dimension of social principledness concerning socio-political thinking processes. It was found that the Chinese group scored markedly lower than the two Western groups, whose mean scores were almost identical. According to Bloom (1977a, p. 69), a low level on social principledness

would be marked by a capacity for understanding the abstract notion of socio-political responsibility at the societal level, but be limited to the view that socio-political responsibility consists in unanalytic adherence to the demands of existing political authority, i.e., in placing obedience to that authority above any individual intuition as to what might constitute proper action.

The low social principledness of the Chinese thus represents a strong authoritarian orientation to defer without question to conventional authority and to accept unconditionally conventional norms and values. The second major attitudinal syndrome to be discussed here is Machiavellianism, which has been defined by Christie and Geis (1970) as the generalized belief that people are manipulable and capable of being deceived for personal gain. Oksenberg (1970) is the first of the few investigators who have ever put Chinese attitudes towards manoeuvring behaviour to empirical test. He began with a bidirectional hypothesis about the relative level of Chinese Machiavellianism: on the one hand, the popular Western stereotype of Chinese character predicts that the Chinese would be more Machiavellian than Westerners; on the other hand, the greater importance of social expectations, role requirements, and behaviour standards in interpersonal transactions in traditional Chinese society implies that the Chinese would be less Machiavellian. To shed light on this controversial problem, he administered a Chinese version of Christie and Geis's Mach IV Scale to 67 Hong Kong secondary-school students who had received a relatively traditional Chinese education and 146 comparable students who had received a relatively Western education. Comparison of the mean scores of the two groups revealed that the traditional subjects tended to be less Machiavellian than their Westernized counterparts. It appears that Westernization, in the Chinese context, will strengthen Machiavellian attitudes. From this finding, it may be inferred that the Chinese are less Machiavellian than Westerners. Another study with a somewhat different purpose was completed by Hwang and Marsella (1977), comparing 64 Taiwan Chinese and 64 Caucasian American students at the University of Hawaii on the Mach IV Scale. While there was no significant difference in mean scores, the factorial structures of the Mach IV Scale were found to be different for the two groups. For the Chinese, the scale appears to be measuring such monopolar attitudinal factors as suspicion, distrust, duplicity, traditional morality, and negative view of human nature, which may not be components of Machiavellianism as Christie and Geis defined it for Western people. On the other hand, with Americans the scale mainly covers a set of variables that load highly on such bipolar factors as integrity versus vulnerability, authenticity versus duplicity, and a positive versus a negative view of human nature. The results thus suggest that the Mach IV Scale does not assess equivalent attitudinal components for Chinese and Americans.

The third major attitudinal syndrome on which Chinese data have been reported is locus of control, which was defined by Rotter (1966) as a set of generalized beliefs or expectancies about how positive and negative reinforcements are obtained. At one extreme is internality, the belief that one can obtain rewards and avoid punishments by one's own skill, effort, foresight, and acceptance of responsibility. At the opposite extreme is externality, the belief that reinforcements depend upon such uncontrollable outside factors as chance, luck, the behaviour of those more powerful, and complex events in one's surroundings.

The earliest cross-cultural study on locus of control involving Chinese subjects is that by Hsieh, Shybut, and Lotsof (1969). These investigators administered Rotter's Internal-External (I-E) Control of Reinforcement Scale to 239 Anglo-Americans, 343 Hong Kong Chinese, and 80 American-born Chinese, and found that Americans exhibited a stronger belief in internal control of reinforcement and the Hong Kong Chinese a stronger belief in external control of reinforcement, with the American-born Chinese in between. This higher externality of the Chinese was later confirmed by M.S. Tseng's (1972) study using the Rotter Scale with 67 Asian and 61 American students at an American university.

Another relevant study was conducted by Lao (1977), using a multidimensional I-E Scale developed by Levinson (1974) to measure three major factors of locus of control: the belief in internal control, the belief in powerful others, and the belief in chance. This study compared 517 Chinese (243 males and 274 females) with 423 American college students (180 males and 243 females), in terms of their scores on the three I-E factors. The Chinese were reported to be stronger in their belief in powerful others than Americans of either sex. While Chinese females had a weaker tendency to believe in internal events than American females, the two male groups were not significantly different from each other on this factor. Finally, no significant cross-cultural difference was found on the chance factor in either sex.

Lao, Chuang, and Yang (1977) also reported data on sex differences in the three I-E factors. For Chinese students, males scored higher on internality and lower on chance and powerful others than females. For American students, there was no significant sex difference on any I-E factor. These findings revealed that Chinese male students were consistently more internal-oriented than their female counterparts on all three factors, whereas no such sex difference existed among American students.

The relevant literature on Chinese authoritarianism, Machiavellianism, and locus of control shows that Chinese people have relatively high authoritarian attitudes and low Machiavellian and internal-control attitudes. With regard to Machiavellianism, however, this conclusion should be considered with great care, because it is difficult to make a valid cross-cultural comparison with the Mach IV Scale, which has been found to have questionable conceptual equivalence when applied to Chinese subjects (Hwang and Marsella, 1977).

Finally, in addition to the studies on Chinese values and attitudinal syndromes reviewed so far, empirical research has also been carried out to provide data for the Chinese on some other evaluative-attitudinal aspects. One important aspect concerns organized judgements and orientations that are predominantly moral in nature. Two major lines of cross-cultural research on Chinese moral dimensions have been performed, one adopting a Kohlbergian and the other a Wilsonian paradigm.

According to Kohlberg (1969; 1976), there are six universal stages in the development of moral judgements: punishment orientation (Stage 1), reward orientation (Stage 2), good-boy/good-girl orientation (Stage 3), authority orientation (Stage 4), social-contract orientation (Stage 5), and ethical-principle orientation (Stage 6). This stage theory of moral reasoning has instigated a number of empirical studies in Taiwan. Most of these studies have attempted to relate moral judgement to such variables as age, intelligence, cognitive development, role-taking skill, cheating behaviour, delinquency, parental education, parental socio-economic status, family constellation, and urban or rural residence. For the sake of brevity, again, only those studies which have sufficient cross-cultural relevance will be reviewed here.

The first set of cross-cultural data on Chinese moral development was collected in 1962 by Kohlberg (1969) himself. He individually presented a series of stories, each portraying a moral dilemma, to a group of Chinese boys in Taiwan, scored their answers to the stories according to a standardized scheme, and compared the age trend of their moral development with that of American boys as reported in his doctoral dissertation research (Kohlberg, 1958).

His results showed that, at the age of 10 in each group, the observed rate of moral judgements monotonically fell off from Stage 1 to Stage 6. In other words, among subjects of 10 years of age in each group, the order of the six stages in terms of the rates of moral reasoning involved was the same as their order in terms of developmental difficulty or maturity. In the American sample, the order was generally reversed by the age of 16, although moral reasoning of the Stage 6 type was still little used. In contrast, their Chinese counterparts of the same age were found to make more moral statements at Stage 3 (good-boy orientation) and fewer statements at Stage 5 (contractual-legalistic orientation) and Stage 6 (principle or conscience orientation). The difference in moral orientation between the American and Chinese samples emerged at the age of 13 and increased gradually as their age progressed to 16 years.

Fifteen years after Kohlberg's pioneer Taiwan study, Chern (1978) presented 390 Chinese children, aged 8 to 16, with three stories involving a dilemma, and interviewed them with the standard questions. His results generally supported Kohlberg's finding that Stage 5 moral thinking is more salient among Americans than among Chinese in Taiwan.

Cheng and Lei (1981) carried out a similar investigation by applying a Chinese version of the 1978 standard moral interview format (Colby, Gibbs, and Kohlberg, 1978) to 213 Chinese children and adolescents with an age range from 7 to 23. By analysing the collected judgements about the moral issues, these investigators found that the authority orientation of Stage 4 (emphasizing the maintenance of social order) was the predominant type of reasoning for Chinese subjects older than 17 years. This finding confirmed Kohlberg's (1969) claim that Stage 4 is the most dominant stage among adults in most societies. In comparing their results with those of Weinreich's (1970) British study and Kohlberg's (1958) Chicago study, Cheng and Lei came to the conclusion that the major cross-cultural differences appeared in the rate of development of moral reasoning of Stage 2 (reward orientation), Stage 4 (authority orientation), and Stage 5 (social-contract orientation). To be specific, the Stage 2 type of reasoning decreased slightly more slowly and the Stage 4 type of reasoning appeared earlier in the American sample than in the British and Chinese samples. The rate of development of Stage

5 reasoning was slower among Chinese subjects than among American and British subjects. As to the developmental level of moral reasoning, older Chinese subjects exceeded their Western counterparts in the percentage of moral judgements or concerns at Stage 3 (good-boy/good-girl orientation) and Stage 4, and fell behind in those of Stage 5.

Two important cross-cultural differences become clear from the findings of the above studies with a Kohlbergian paradigm. First, Chinese children and adolescents not only develop Stage 5 moral reasoning (social-contract orientation) more slowly than their Western counterparts, but also end up with a lower level of that type of reasoning when they become adults. The Chinese lag in these aspects of moral development may be accounted for by the fact that the concept of the social contract, the balance of individual rights, and legalistic thinking are emphasized constantly in daily life and socialization in Western industrialized societies, but are usually neglected in Chinese societies.

Second, Chinese people at and beyond adolescence tend to display a higher level of Stage 4 moral reasoning (authority orientation) than Western people. As a moral man of the Stage 4 type, the average Chinese usually identifies himself with the goals and expectations of his society or the group to which he belongs, and judges things from a perspective which he believes is shared by other 'typical' members of the society or group. He upholds social norms and rules to avoid censure by the authorities, to avoid feelings of shame, guilt, and anxiety, and to maintain the social order for its own sake. This heteronomous orientation was termed 'Moral Type A' by Kohlberg and Tappan (1983), but it is conceptually distinct from 'Moral Type B', which is characterized by an inclination to make autonomous moral decisions without being influenced by external sources of power or authority. Thus, given the autonomous nature of the American normative values, one would expect that 'Moral Type A' will prevail among Chinese and 'Moral Type B' among Americans. Partial support has been provided by Lei and Cheng's (1984) reanalysis of the data from their 1981 study in accordance with the Piagetian criteria which are listed in the Moral Type Scoring Manual (Kohlberg and Tappan, 1983). They found that the percentage of 'Moral Type B' usage was consistently smaller in the Chinese sample than in the American sample.

Conceptually similar to the twin orientations of heteronomy and autonomy, as first defined by Piaget (1932), are Wilson's (1974)

dimensions of heterocentrism and autocentrism. He defined heterocentrism as the social reasoning orientation, in which particular
others are cited as the authority for behaviour, and autocentrism
as the social reasoning orientation, in which rules and principles are
cited as the basis for action. He constructed a tool of the forced-
choice type, the Autocentric/Heterocentric Questionnaire, for their
measurement. He administered this to children in grades 3, 5, and
7 in Taiwan (335), Hong Kong (362), Chinatown, New York City
(90), and New Jersey (293), to make a comparative study of the
political socialization of Chinese and American youngsters. His data
indicated that, among all the groups, children from Taiwan generally
had the most autocentric attitudinal orientation. They were more
apt to legitimize their behaviour by reference to universal rules or
principles than children from Hong Kong, Chinatown, or New
Jersey. American children were relatively lower in autocentrism and
more likely to cite particular others as the reference for their
behaviour.

Given the conceptual correspondence of heterocentrism and
autocentrism to heteronomy and autonomy, Wilson's finding of
higher autocentrism on the part of Chinese children seems to be in
conflict with Cheng and Lei's (1981) finding of more Stage 4 moral
reasoning (a kind of heteronomous orientation) and Lei and Cheng's
(1984) finding of less 'Moral Type B' (autonomous orientation) usage
on the part of Chinese adolescents. A closer look at the differences
between Chinese and Americans in all age groups in these studies
indicates that the contradictory findings may be at least partially
reconciled with each other by the factor of age difference and the
phenomenon of Chinese adolescent regression. In the cross-cultural
comparison made by Cheng and Lei (1981), although Chinese adolescents older than 16 years showed a higher percentage of Stage 4
moral judgements than their American counterparts, Chinese
children younger than 14 years tended to show a lower level of moral
reasoning of the same type than American children. In Wilson's
study, all subjects were children under the age of 13 and the higher
autocentric orientation of the Chinese group was consistent with the
lower heteronomous orientation of the Chinese children in Cheng
and Lei's cross-cultural comparison. Furthermore, Wilson identified
a trend of childhood precocity and adolescent regression, which
meant that Chinese children (especially those from Taiwan) were
ahead of American children in the development of social reasoning,
but that the advent of adolescence was apparently accompanied for

many of them by a shift from their earlier, heavily stressed autocentric attitudes and by a renewed increase in their heterocentric orientation. Eventually, this change would result in a higher level of Stage 4 thinking on the part of Chinese adolescents, as found in Cheng and Lei's study. Wilson suggested that this developmental phenomenon of childhood precocity and adolescent regression was due to the well-known emphasis in Chinese societies on moral training. He pointed out that such training was more intensively and systematically carried out in Taiwan and its influence was reflected in a rapid increase in autocentrism until grade 5. Beyond this point there was generally a regressive tendency of decreasing autocentrism and increasing heterocentrism. For Chinese youngsters in Taiwan and Hong Kong, this reversal phenomenon appears to be related to the increasing demands for adherence to well-defined social expectations and behaviour patterns and to the vivid threat of group ostracism and shaming sanctions against deviants in these Chinese societies.

From the above results and discussion, it may be inferred that the difference between Chinese and Americans in the autonomous versus heteronomous orientation or the autocentric versus heterocentric orientation is a complex function of age: the Chinese tend to be higher in autonomy or autocentrism during childhood and higher in heteronomy or heterocentrism during adolescence (and probably adulthood as well).

Temperamental Characteristics

After reviewing the major studies on the hormetic and attitudinal aspects of Chinese personality, we come to a discussion of Chinese temperamental dispositions as revealed through empirical research. In the literature of personality psychology, the concept of temperament has been poorly defined, and has sometimes included personality traits left over when the other categories have been accounted for. As delineated by Buss and Plomin (1975), Guilford (1959), and Thomas and Chess (1977), temperament differs from aptitude, which reflects the *what* and *how well* of behaving, and from motivation, which deals with *why* a person does what he is doing. It has much to do with the *way* or *manner* in which an individual behaves. More specifically, temperament is concerned with style rather than content, with expressive behaviour rather than instrumental or coping behaviour, and with what a person brings to a role or situation rather than what either of these demands of him. Although temperament usually includes a hereditary component (Buss and Plomin, 1975), it can be more or less influenced by cultural and environmental factors in its development and expression (Thomas and Chess, 1977). Chinese people, as a hereditarily and culturally unique group, must have certain temperamental traits that are different from other ethnic and cultural groups. In fact, previous research has indeed provided us with data bearing upon the characteristic styles of Chinese cognition, emotionality, and behaviour. Since the temperamental domain is too broad and uncertain for us to review all the potentially pertinent literature, only those empirical studies that deal with general Chinese stylistic dispositions will be briefly discussed here. The following are among these cognitive, emotional, and behavioural temperaments, some of which are more and some less culturally bound: emotionality and anxiety, self-restraint and cautiousness, sociability and extroversion, realistic-mindedness, and holistic proclivity.

The first temperamental characteristic to be considered is emotionality. This is one of the basic temperaments suggested in Buss and Plomin's (1975) temperamental theory. Closely related to emotionality are anxiety and neuroticism. There have been numerous empirical studies of this temperamental dimension using mainland Chinese as subjects. Early comparative studies were done by Chou and Mi (1937), Hsiao (1941), Lei, Kuo, and Chen (1945), Pai, Sung, and Hsu (1937), Shen (1936), Shen and Liu (1935), Smith (1938), and Westbrook and Yao (1937) with questionnaires and scales such as the Bernreuter Personality Inventory (BPI), Gordon's Personality Data Sheet, Thurstone's Neurotic Inventory and Personality Schedule, and the Woodworth, Cady, and Mathews Questionnaire. The results reported from these studies in general indicate that the Chinese mean scores on emotionality or neuroticism were higher than those in the American norms.

While early research on Chinese emotionality and related variables exclusively used mainland Chinese as subjects, recent studies have mainly selected Chinese people in Taiwan and Hong Kong as respondents. Within the last 20 years or so, more than 15 such studies have been conducted, of which most made use of self-report measures. Among these studies, several (Chiu, 1963; Scofield and Sun, 1960; Sun, 1968) gave the Cattell 16 Personality Factor Questionnaire (16 PF) to different samples of Chinese students in Taiwan, Hong Kong, and the United States. Of these, only that by Chiu tested a sample (453) large enough to provide statistically stable results.

According to this study, Chinese students were lower in Ego Strength (calm, emotionally stable) and higher in Premsia (sensitive, sentimental), Guilt Proneness (timid, worrisome), Protension (suspicious, jealous), and Identity Significance (frustrated, tense).

In her attempt to revise the Thurstone Temperament Schedule (TTS), Kao (1962) obtained results for 2,398 college students in Taiwan and compared them with Thurstone's norms for American students. It was found that the Chinese group's average emotionality score was similar to that of the American group in both sexes. In the standardization of a Chinese version of the Guilford–Zimmerman Temperament Survey (GZTS) with 2,265 college and high-school students, Chang and Lu (1969) reported that the Chinese norm for Emotional Stability was lower than that for Americans. Several years later, Sue and Kirk (1972) reported data collected for 236 Chinese American students by the application of the Omnibus Personality Inventory (OPI). In comparison with their non-Chinese American counterparts, Chinese Americans were found to be lower on Personal Integration (less at ease with themselves and others) and higher on Anxiety Level (more apt to be uncomfortable and anxious). At about the same time, Abbott (1970) published relevant results for 40 Chinese adolescents in Taipei, obtained by the CPI. Comparison of these data with the American norms revealed that the Chinese were lower in Self-acceptance and Well-being, among other personality variables.

Other studies of Chinese emotionality and anxiety adopted simple anxiety or neuroticism scales rather than multidimensional tests. Thus Chiu (1971) compared Chinese and American children in grades 4 and 5 — 613 Taiwanese and 381 American — on the Children's Manifest Anxiety Scale. The Chinese showed a small but significantly greater degree of anxiety than Americans. Paschal and Kuo (1973) compared 60 Chinese and 60 American university students, matched with respect to several demographic and scholastic variables, in terms of Cattell's (1963) IPAT Anxiety Scale. Their statistical analysis indicated that Chinese subjects scored higher on manifest anxiety than their American counterparts. Another study of this sort was done by Chan and Eysenck (1981), in which a Chinese version of the Eysenck Personality Questionnaire (EPQ) was administered to 732 adults in Hong Kong. Chinese males were found to score slightly higher than British males, but Chinese females to score significantly lower than British females, on the Neuroticism Scale. In a more recent relevant study, Gong (1984) gave the EPQ to 2,517 adults in

13 provinces in mainland China and compared the results with those obtained for English and Greek adult samples in Dimitriou and Eysenck's (1978) study. One of the conclusions from the comparisons is that the Chinese scored slightly higher than the English on Neuroticism and both were more neurotic and emotionally labile than the Greeks.

The early and recent studies so far reviewed generally indicate that the Chinese mean scores on emotionality, anxiety, and neuroticism tended to be higher than those of American samples. Some of the previous investigators (for example, Chou and Mi, 1937; Smith, 1938; Paschal and Kuo, 1973) have literally interpreted this difference in score as meaning that the Chinese were actually more emotional, anxious, or neurotic than Americans. They have even advanced many possible but not very plausible reasons to explain this Chinese 'temperamental' characteristic, including such factors as racial difference, social change, excessive competition for jobs, strict up-bringing at home, parental pressure for young people to go abroad, and political, economic, and social uncertainty in mainland China and Taiwan. The first of these explanations, racial difference, needs a little special discussion or clarification. When Smith (1938) first offered racial difference as an important responsible factor, he failed to provide any evidence to support his contention. However, empirical results obtained since, in the studies by Freedman and Freedman (1969) and Kagan, Kearsley, and Zelazo (1978) strongly suggest that the contrary is true. By directly observing the behaviour of children in nursery schools, ranging in age from one day old to two-and-a-half-years old, these rigorous investigations found that Chinese children were more calm and passive and less excitable than American children. Nobody can infer from this reliable evidence any genetic or constitutional disposition for the Chinese to be more emotional, anxious, or neurotic than American Caucasians.

Our contention is that the observed difference between Chinese and Westerners in the test scores of emotionality, anxiety, or neuroticism should not be glibly interpreted as reflecting some real difference in emotional temperament between the two cultural and ethnic groups, unless we can demonstrate that no seriously confounding factors were involved in the comparison. In this regard, Hsu (1951) has pointed out that the difference in the emotionality or anxiety score may be explained in terms of material differences in culture. Many items of the temperament tests or scales standardized with American and British subjects mention material elements (such as subway systems, 10-cent stores) which may not be found in mainland China, Taiwan, or even Hong Kong (where an underground railway system was constructed only recently). This lack of certain elements of material culture makes the Chinese application of many of the items impossible.

Hsu (1951) went even further, doing an interesting empirical study to demonstrate that an anxiety or neuroticism score *per se* could be meaningful only when it is referred to a given culture and judged according to the norms of that particular culture. A behavioural trait may be called 'emotional', 'anxious', or even 'neurotic' in one culture because it hinders the happiness and efficiency of living. But the same trait is not necessarily 'emotional', 'anxious', or 'neurotic' in another — just the other way around. Hsu's penetrating analysis shows that the positive attitudes of the Chinese towards, for instance, sex taboos, depreciation of self, interpersonal prudence or suspicion, and meditative absent-mindedness must not be interpreted as emotional, anxious, or neurotic responses. It is such temperamental traits, in fact, that make it possible for a typical Chinese to live efficiently and happily in the traditional agrarian Chinese society. It may thus be argued that most, if not all, of the differences in emotionality scores of Chinese and Westerners can be convincingly accounted for by cultural differences in the specific and special meanings of some common behaviour patterns in the two contrasted traditions.

Because of these and other seriously confounding factors, no definite conclusion can be reached about cross-cultural comparisons of Chinese emotionality and anxiety. At the present stage of our empirical knowledge, we are simply unable to say that the Chinese are in general more emotional, anxious, or neurotic than their American counterparts. Nor can we definitely portray Chinese people as having little anxiety or low neuroticism, as have some interdisciplinary observers (for example, Cheng, 1946; Hsu, 1953; La Barre, 1946), although previous research using projective instead of self-report methods has suggested that this may be true (Hsu, Watrous, and Lord, 1961; Richards, 1954; Watrous and Hsu, 1963). In short, the question of Chinese emotionality is still open to further research, but requires much better conceived studies that are free from the invalidating factors discussed above.

The second temperamental characteristic to be considered concerns self-restraint and cautiousness. Impulsivity is another basic temperament in Buss and Plomin's (1975) theory, involving the tendency to respond quickly rather than to inhibit the response. They assumed two main components for this temperamental dimension: (a) yielding to as opposed to resisting urges, impulses, or motivational states; and (b) responding immediately and impetuously to a stimulus as opposed to waiting and planning before making a move. The opposites of impulsivity are such temperamental traits as inhibition, suppression, cautiousness, and reflection (Kagan, 1966).

Many commentators (for example, Cheng, 1946; Hsu, 1949; Tseng, 1973a) have frequently characterized Chinese as being cautious, repressed, patient, humble, modest, and non-aggressive. These psychological and behavioural characteristics constitute a temperamental syndrome that may be summarized as self-restraint, in contrast to impulsivity. Relevant empirical research has confirmed that the Chinese indeed tend to display such a temperamental pattern.

More than 20 studies have obtained data useful in locating Chinese on the impulsivity versus self-restraint dimension. Of these studies, some used self-report inventories or questionnaires, and others relied on projective techniques, as measuring tools. Scofield and Sun (1960) and Chiu (1963), in their self-report studies with the Cattell 16PF, found that the Chinese students were higher on Controlled Will (careful, playing safe) and lower on Parmia (adventurous, bold). In standardizing a Chinese version of the TTS in Taiwan, Kao (1962) reported a higher score on Reflectivity and a lower score on Impulsivity for Chinese students, as compared with their American counterparts. In another standardization study (Chang and Lu, 1969) using a Chinese version of the GZTS, Taiwan students were found to have higher scores on Thoughtfulness (reflective, introceptive) than the American norms and to be equal to them on Restraint. The data collected by Sue and Kirk (1972) with the OPI revealed a marked tendency on the part of Chinese Americans to be lower on Impulse Expression (more inhibited and conventional and less ready to express their impulses). In Abbott's (1970) study employing the CPI, Chinese adolescents from Taipei were found to be higher on Self-control and Good Impression than the American norms. There are similar findings from Chan and Eysenck's (1981) and Gong's (1984) studies using the EPQ, in which Chinese adults in Hong Kong and mainland China scored higher on Social Desirability than British subjects.

Relevant data also come from Hwang's (1974a; 1974b) and Lu's (1978) studies, both of which were conducted in Taiwan. In Hwang's study, 502 Chinese (Taipei) and 487 Scottish junior-high-school students were compared in terms of their semantic differential ratings on a number of bipolar adjectives. In comparison with Scottish adolescents, the Chinese group was reported to give lower scores on such adjective pairs as Bad-Good, Ugly-Beautiful, and Calm-Lively for the target concept of Myself. Hwang interpreted these differences as expressing a striking tendency to be humble and modest on the part of the Chinese adolescents. In Lu's study, 2,613 college and high-school students in Taiwan were given a Chinese version of the Gordon Personal Inventory. Data analysis, and comparison with the corresponding American norms, revealed a stronger proclivity for the Chinese to be cautious, and this cross-cultural difference did not vary with the sex of the subjects.

In addition to these self-report studies, there have also been relevant investigations that used a projective method as the main procedure. One of the earliest such investigations was completed by Abel and Hsu (1949), who gave the Rorschach Ink-blot Test (10 ambiguous, vague, and therefore meaningless ink-blot pictures as stimuli for free association) to 56 adult Chinese Americans. Analysis of the subjects' projective associations revealed that the Chinese were good at controlling their impulses and refraining from expressive spontaneity. The Rorschach results, however, also indicate that males and females born in China appeared to experience freedom for enjoyment and satisfaction, and for expressing emotions in a spontaneous manner, in the area of nature and especially in that of food. The finding concerning the food or oral sphere as an allowed area of emotional freedom and enjoyment seems to confirm La Barre's (1946) hypothesis on Chinese orality, a hypothesis which was later extensively discussed by such psychoanalytically inclined scholars as Muensterberger (1951) and Weakland (1950; 1956). The finding about the sphere of nature or physical environment as a permitted area for spontaneous responsivity was later corroborated by Watrous and Hsu (1963) in their TAT study.

In another related investigation, one of Hsu's associates (Richards, 1954) made a 'blind' evaluation of each of 35 Rorschach records drawn from a larger sample of Chinese adults tested in Hawaii. The results indicated that the male Chinese were preoccupied with role-playing as well as with the subjugation of basic feelings to demonstrations of *politesse* and manners; to them, spontaneity was fearsome and there was security in making the right impression.

Other relevant research using the Rorschach Test was done by Yang and his associates, who administered the test to a carefully selected sample of 347 normal Chinese adults from northern Taiwan. A series of articles has been published to report various findings concerning normal Chinese personality. In one article, Yang, Tsai, and Hwang (1963) reported that Chinese adults tended to produce a smaller number of total responses (associations), and a larger number of total refusals (pictures with no reported associations), than the American norms found in the Rorschach literature. In another article, Yang, Chen, and Hsu (1965) presented data indicating that Chinese adults had a much longer average first-reaction time (time needed to voice the first response to a picture) as well as a much longer average time (time needed to produce a response) than the American norms. These striking differences in the volume and speed of Rorschach responses were interpreted by Yang and his associates as indicating more inhibited, cautious, and patient, and less spontaneous, natural, and impulsive behaviour on the part of normal Chinese adults.

There has also been relevant research involving the application of the TAT. One of these studies was carried out by Watrous and Hsu (1963), in which 40 Taiwan and 50 Hong Kong Chinese students were found to appear more cautious, restrained, and thoughtful, and less spontaneous, egocentric, and aggressive than American students. In a study by Han (1974), 80 Chinese undergraduate students in Taipei were given the first 20 cards of the TAT in two sessions, and were reported to have a much longer first-reaction time and total time than the American norms. Han inferred that these differences expressed a tendency for Chinese people to be more inhibited and cautious. In his original and follow-up studies comparing social attitudes of Chinese and Scottish adolescents, Hwang (1974a; 1975) gave a selected set of TAT cards to groups of university and high-school students in Taipei and comparable groups of students in Scotland. Thematic analysis of the protocols obtained in the two studies consistently demonstrated that Chinese adolescents displayed a greater amount of inhibition, which restrained them from being active and spontaneous.

Also relevant is Hwang's (1968) investigation with the Rosenzweig Picture Frustration Study (Rosenzweig, Fleming, and Clarke, 1947), a projective test of 24 cartoon-like drawings, each representing a two-person incident of everyday life. Hwang asked 320 Chinese university students to write down, for each picture, the verbal responses that one person would make while the other was saying something of frustrating significance to him. The reactions of Chinese subjects were strikingly different from Rosenzweig's American norms: they were far more intropunitive (aggressively attributing the frustration to oneself, presumably as a consequence of the inhibition of its outward expression) and less extrapunitive (aggressively attributing the frustration to someone or something in the external world) when confronted with frustrating situations. This finding may be conceived of as a manifestation of the traditional Chinese emphasis on self-examination and self-restraint in order to maintain a harmonious interpersonal relationship.

All the studies reviewed, using either a self-report or a projective technique, have unanimously shown that Chinese people in general are inclined to be more restrained, cautious, patient, and self-contained, and less impulsive, excitable, spontaneous, and natural than Americans. Previous research has demonstrated that these temperamental differences seem to have a genetic basis. Freedman and Freedman (1969), for example, applied neurological, sensory, and motor tests to Chinese American and Caucasian American newborn infants at a mean age of 33 hours — an age at which any differences in maternal handling could not have any appreciable effect. Chinese infants were reported to be more calm and impassive, even when a cloth was placed over the face, and to habituate more readily to a blinking-light stimulus. While there was no difference in the amount of crying, the Chinese stopped more quickly and were easily consoled. In another study, Freedman (1974) tested Chinese American and Caucasian American infants and new-born babies of other ethnic groups with the Brazelton–Freedman Neonate Scale, which covers a variety of behavioural items and neurological signs. Besides the temperamental difference in excitability, the Chinese showed less rapid changes of mood from content to upset, although their Central Nervous System (CNS) maturity and their sensory and motor development were very similar to those of their Caucasian counterparts. Judging from findings in these and other related studies, it may be justifiably concluded that the imperturbability of Chinese babies and the excitability of Caucasians as distinctive temperamental patterns seem to have their respective genetic bases. Moreover, in the case of the Chinese, the innate imperturbability will be further enhanced by traditional Chinese cultural norms and socialization practices that place great stress on obedience, conformity, humility, self-abasement, and harmonious relationship (see, for example, Ho, 1981a; Hsu, 1949; Hummel, 1960).

The third basic temperamental characteristic in Buss and Plomin's

(1975) system is sociability, which consists mainly of affiliativeness — a strong inclination to be with others and to be responsive to others. A closely related, but somewhat different, temperamental variable is extroversion. There is a general agreement among researchers (for example, Howarth and Browne, 1972; Morris, 1979; Vagg and Hammond, 1976) about the centrality of the trait of extroversion as defined specifically as sociability. The sociability dimension, as the most salient component of extroversion, may even be seen in what Guilford (1934) called social extroversion. In fact, Guilford and Zimmerman (1949) used the term 'Sociability' to replace 'Social Extroversion' as a label for one of the 10 personality factors measured by their temperament test.

Where do the Chinese generally tend to be located on the sociability and extroversion dimensions? Pertinent scattered data can mainly be found in the studies cited in the above discussion of Chinese emotionality and self-restraint. In one of the earliest relevant investigations, conducted in mainland China, Shen (1936) reported that Chinese high-school students were higher in introversion (hence lower in extroversion) on the BPI. In the 1960s, Kao (1962) collected data in Taiwan by the TTS and found that Chinese college students scored lower on Sociability than the American norms. Through the use of the Cattell 16PF, Chiu (1963) obtained a lower average score on Cyclothymia (easy going, warm hearted) and Surgency (talkative, cheerful) for Chinese university students in Taiwan, than that of their American counterparts. In Chang and Lu's (1969) study, Chinese university students, also in Taiwan, scored much lower on the Sociability scale of the GZTS than Americans.

Sue and Kirk (1972), in their assessment of temperamental traits by the OPI, found that Chinese American students exhibited attitudes and behaviour characteristics of less socially extroverted people (lower Social Extroversion). Abbott (1970), however, failed to identify any significant difference on the Sociability dimension of the CPI between Taiwan adolescents and the American norms. In Chan and Eysenck's (1981) and Gong's (1984) EPQ studies, Hong Kong and mainland Chinese adults received a lower score on Extroversion than British subjects.

Evidence supportive of low sociability by Chinese has also been provided in Zimbardo's (1980) cross-cultural research on shyness and loneliness. According to the self-report data he collected by questionnaire for 87 Taiwan respondents and other cultural groups of various sample sizes, the Chinese, along with the Japanese, showed the highest prevalence rate of shyness among the 10 cultural groups compared, including Americans. If shyness is inversely related to sociability, Zimbardo's finding supports the general conclusion of the above studies. Little research by projective techniques has been done on this temperamental dimension. Piecemeal relevant data may be found in Watrous and Hsu's (1963) TAT study, in which Chinese fantasies were found to convey less gregariousness and less concern with peer acceptance than American responses. It was also reported that, although Chinese are far less concerned with personal enjoyment than Americans, they can enjoy themselves alone as well as with others, whereas Americans showed a much stronger urge to seek the company of others for the purpose of enjoyment.

Taken together, these studies generally reveal a weaker tendency for the Chinese to be sociable and extroverted and a stronger tendency to be self-contained and introverted. This temperamental pattern, together with the high self-restraint and low impulsivity previously described, suits the traditional Chinese social life in which people were required to maintain a pliant but distanced role in interpersonal relationships so as to achieve a balance between the self and others.

In addition to the three major temperamental dimensions we have already discussed, there are other major temperamental dimensions on which empirical data have been collected for Chinese subjects. These data will enable us to have a broader view of the Chinese temperamental pattern. Two additional temperamental variables will be briefly considered in concluding this section of the chapter. The first is the well-known Chinese practicality or realism. As repeatedly pointed out by some Oriental and Western observers (for example, La Barre, 1946; Nakamura, 1964; Pedersen, 1983), the Chinese have been characterized as valuing common sense and utilitarian ways of thinking highly; and even their philosophical teachings have been based on practical subjects, including everyday examples of ethics, politics, and social relations. Empirical research on this Chinese way of thinking has been meagre and only two relevant studies may be mentioned here. One was conducted by Hellersberg (1953), using a projective test known as the Horn–Hellersberg Test. The test consists of squares which contain a few lines, and one square which contains no lines. The subject is asked to draw in each square whatever picture he likes, utilizing the given lines, if any. An interview then follows in which the subject gives information on each picture, including an explanation of why he has drawn these items and what the details of the drawings mean to him. Hellersberg administered this test to 70 adult and child subjects of Chinese birth or background. Among other things, she found that the objects the Chinese drew appeared to be concrete and practical, and numerous references were made to their immediate surroundings and places where they had lived in the past. She described this tendency as Chinese realism. The other study that provides relevant data on Chinese practicality is Sue and Kirk's (1972) research by the OPI. Their comparative study of Chinese American and non-Chinese American students indicated that the former scored higher on Practical Outlook (a stronger tendency to evaluate ideas on the basis of their immediate practical application). Thus, results from both studies seem to support the common international image of the Chinese as a practical-minded people.

Another temperamental characteristic is holistic proclivity, a tendency for the Chinese to perceive stimuli in wholes rather than in parts. One of the earliest sets of relevant data was reported in Abel and Hsu's (1949) Rorschach study on the personality of Chinese Americans. In their study, the Chinese Americans born in China were found to make more whole responses than detail responses to the ink-blots, while those born in America made more detail than whole responses (rather in the pattern found for Caucasian American samples). This change from taking a whole view of the blots to a more detailed one may be interpreted as a change of perceptual style due to American acculturation on the part of the Chinese. It should also be mentioned here that both groups of Chinese Americans in Abel and Hsu's study took in the blots as a whole much more frequently than did the Caucasian American sample in De Vos' study (1966).

Relevant Rorschach data can also be found in a study by Nih, Cheng, and Chang (1954), in which 600 junior-high-school students and 70 adults from Taipei were individually tested. These researchers reported a smaller number of whole-blot responses for Chinese adolescents and a greater number for Chinese adults than the American norms. They also found that the number of detail responses tended to correlate positively with scholastic achievement. This and other evidence seem to suggest that the smaller number of part-blot responses among high-school students might have resulted from the influence of the overwhelming and special educational environment in which they found themselves. Very briefly, these adolescents had been taught ever since their primary-school years to emphasize, memorize, and cram fragmentary details and facts in order to be successful in the keenly competitive joint examination for entrance into schools of a higher level.

In their report of the 10 popular (P) Rorschach responses for a sample of 347 Chinese adults from Taiwan, Yang, Tsai, and Hwang (1963) provided data clearly showing that whole blots dominated in forming the P responses and detail responses seemed to be highly associated with colour in the blots concerned. The same is true in Hwang's (1955) smaller study of popular Chinese Rorschach responses.

In his comparative study of the social attitudes of Chinese and Scottish adolescents by the use of the Sentence Completion Test and the TAT, Hwang (1974b) came to the conclusion that Chinese adolescents had a tendency to perceive things in wholes rather than in parts. This conclusion was also partially supported by his follow-up study on the social attitudes of these subjects.

Another study bearing on this subject was done by Chiu (1972), who administered the Siegel–Kagan Categorizing Test (which includes 28 items, each showing three pictures) to groups of primary-school children — 221 Taiwanese and 316 American children of comparable age and socio-economic status. Each child was asked to select two pictures that were alike and to state why the two were similar. Chinese used the relational-contextual style as their dominant type of categorization and the descriptive-analytic as the least frequent. In contrast, American children were high in the inferential-categorical and descriptive-analytic styles but low in the relational-contextual style. These findings generally reveal that the Chinese preferred to categorize on the basis of interdependence and relationship, whereas Americans liked to analyse the components of stimuli and to infer common features. Since interdependence and relationship are conditions conducive to the formation of an organized whole, Chiu's results may be interpreted as indicating a dominant style among Chinese of being synthetic rather than analytic, on the basis of their performance in categorizing stimuli or objects.

Put together, all these studies seem to support the hypothesis that Chinese people, especially adults, tend to display a cognitive style of seeing things or phenomena in wholes rather than in parts while Westerners tend to do the reverse. This proclivity for global or holistic perception, so emphasized by some scholars (for example, Abbott, 1976; Hang, 1966; Hwang, 1982) as a major Chinese psychological characteristic, is consistent with the widely discussed synthetic (rather than analytic) orientation of the Chinese. This generalized propensity may be a result of the intuitive approach as a dominant Chinese way of thinking, which was alluded to by the renowned philosopher Northrop (1946). However, as rightly pointed out by Moore (1967), the same orientation may also be regarded as an application of the Chinese spirit or principle of harmony in the realm of the intellect. In this spirit, the Chinese will try to synthesize the constituent parts into a whole so that all parts blend into a harmonious relationship at this higher level of perceptual organization. In fact, Chinese people tend to be highly sensitive to outside conflicts and inconsistencies, and they usually manifest a strong tendency to find some way to reconcile the incongruent parts in a higher integrated framework. This powerful holistic approach is widely found not only in the realm of Chinese intellectual activities, but also in the realm of Chinese practical and ethical life. From this perspective, the famous Chinese collectivism may be seen as a special application or case of the Chinese holistic orientation operating in the domain of social life.

Finally, it should be pointed out that practical realism and holistic proclivity, as temperamental characteristics, are rather different from the more basic ones (that is, emotionality, self-restraint, and social introversion). For one thing, while these last two traits are predominantly perceptual and cognitive, the first three are mainly social and emotional in nature. Although each of these temperamental characteristics is able to affect the style or manner of the behaviour of Chinese in most major areas of life, the first three should have a greater influence in the social and emotional facets, and the last two a stronger effect in the perceptual and cognitive facets, of daily functioning.

CHINESE PERSONALITY CHANGE

So far, we have reviewed the major empirical studies, published either in Chinese or in English, on the characteristics of Chinese personality. This systematic literature review should have enabled us to achieve a better understanding of the motivational, evaluative, and temperamental traits of Chinese as a separate cultural group. Research findings from the study of psychological traits in different modalities all converge on the same common pattern of Chinese character, generally reflecting such interrelated features as social harmoniousness, group-mindedness, mutual dependency, interpersonal equilibrium, relationship-centredness, authoritarian syndrome, external-control belief, heterocentric orientation, self-suppression, social introversion, practical realism, and holistic eclecticism. These characteristics portray the Chinese as a highly social, practical, and eclectic people with a strong collectivistic orientation. This Chinese personality pattern has been conceptualized by Hsu (1953; 1963) as situation centred, by Wilson (1974) as relationship oriented, and by K.S. Yang (1981a; 1981b; 1982a) as social oriented.

The historical genesis of Chinese national character has received little serious attention from scientific scholars. Sporadic attempts have been made by social scientists and sinologists to identify those economic, social, and cultural factors that are in one way or another responsible for the formation of Chinese personality in a historical context. Representative scholars who have made such an attempt include Chien (1979), Fried (1976), Hsu (1948; 1961; 1963; 1965; and 1971a), King and Bond (1985), La Barre (1946), Tseng (1973a), Wei (1972), Wen (1972a; 1972b), Wilson (1970), and Yang (1981b). Among them, some have emphasized the influence of Confucian and other social-philosophical thoughts on Chinese character, some have singled out certain aspects of traditional social structure (including kinship structure) as powerful determinants, and others have stressed the importance of the economic system as a basis for the historical development of Chinese personality. It was La Barre (1946) and Wen (1972a) who, among others, have rightly pointed out the paramount significance of an agricultural economy as an essential factor for understanding Chinese history, society, and character. La Barre went even further to state that an economic system of the agricultural type had fostered in China a unique familial organization of society, which in turn shaped the theory and practice of statecraft, the structure of social control, the nature of religions, and the distinctive national personality and 'ethos'.

Along the same lines, Yang (1981b) proposed an interactionistic cultural-ecological analysis of the development and change of the character and behaviour patterns of Chinese people. This point of view emphasizes the pivotal role of environmental factors in explaining cross-cultural regularities. It also supposes that the ecological characteristics of the human habitat in which a particular group of people develops its distinctive life-style interact with the physical and behavioural traits of the group's members in determining the cultural form of the group and the mode of its cultural adaptation. From such a perspective, the modal personality of a cultural group may be seen as a function of the group's cultural pattern (mainly comprising the economic system, social structure, and socialization practices), which in turn results from its members' adaptation to their ecological environment. More specifically, in order to adjust to the characteristics or properties of their ecological environment, members of successive generations of an ethnic group with certain morphological, physiological, and psychological traits will create a special type of economy, which in turn necessitates an appropriate social structure. A unique pattern of socialization then evolves to train members of subsequent generations to form a set of personality and behaviour traits that will make them compatible with the particular social structure and function.

Using such a simplified cultural-ecological model as a guide, Yang (1981b) reviewed some historical and archaeological findings to describe the characteristics of the ecological environment in which the Chinese civilization began to develop. He also discussed why a self-sufficient and self-sustaining agricultural system as a subsistence economy could be formed and could have persisted since the New Stone Age (5000 BC). He then proceeded to identify five crucial attributes of Chinese social structure and functioning that resulted from this agricultural economy: (a) hierarchical organization (society mainly organized in terms of, and social power allocated solely according to, vertical relationships defined with respect to seniority, position, and sex); (b) collectivistic functioning (individual required to submit himself to his family, group, or other collectives in social functioning); (c) generalized familization (family as a general model for the organization and functioning of all outside-family groups); (d) structural tightness (social roles and their relationships highly rigid in their prescriptions and enactment); and (e) social homogeneity (social norms stressing local uniformity rather than diversity).

These and other social structural factors, interacting with certain dominant moral and religious thoughts and doctrines (notably vulgar Confucianism, Taoism, and Buddhism), would lead to a special mode of socialization through which a traditional Chinese learned how to live effectively in the social web of this agricultural society. Yang listed the following as the central practices of Chinese socialization: (a) dependency training, (b) conformity training, (c) modesty training, (d) self-suppression training, (e) self-contentment training, (f) punishment preference, (g) shaming strategy, (h) parent-centredness, and (i) multiple parenting (every adult member in a family acting as a parent or parent-surrogate to a child). He considered these to be the major antecedent factors that had acculturated the Chinese into social, practical, and eclectic human beings with a strong collectivistic inclination, or more simply, social-oriented persons. This Chinese personality, as a product of the specific cultural aspects of Chinese agricultural society, enabled the Chinese person to adjust himself or herself smoothly to such a society.

China has been an agricultural society for several thousand years. However, during approximately the last 100 years, Chinese society and its people have undergone a significant change under the impact of modernization. The social change has been particularly rapid and drastic in Taiwan in the last 30 years or so. The entire society has been transformed from a traditional agricultural society to a modern industrial state. One obvious indication of this transformation is the fact that 75 per cent of all employees are in non-agricultural employment. As the first industrial society created on Chinese soil by Chinese people, the Taiwan experience has contained very many economic and social aspects that are qualitatively different from those of traditional Chinese society. According to the cultural-ecological perspective, the drastic qualitative change from an agricultural to an industrial economy during such a relatively short period should have resulted in a rapid corresponding change in Chinese social structure, which would in turn induce substantial change in Chinese socialization practices and, finally, national character. From this point of view, Taiwan may be considered a unique social laboratory in which the change of Chinese society and personality can be readily observed.

Indeed, a number of empirical studies, using both quasi-longitudinal (diachronic) and cross-sectional (synchronic) approaches, have dealt with changes, of one sort or another, in Chinese character. No true longitudinal research using a panel design (assessing the same sample of persons on two or more occasions) has been done, apparently because this design confounds the effect of social change with that of ontogenetic development and because it generally yields too small a sample size. Instead, in studies using a diachronic approach (for example, Hwang, 1976; Yang and Hwang, 1984), the same measuring instrument was administered to two or more samples which were comparable with respect to sex, age, and other demographic variables. The time interval between the tests was long enough to allow social change to occur.

Quasi-longitudinal data, however, are difficult to obtain. More studies on Chinese personality change have been conducted through the use of the cross-sectional method. In order to 'manipulate' the effect of social change due to societal modernization, different cross-sectional variables have been used by different investigators, including observing respondents in communities of varying degrees of modernization (for example, Wen, 1979) and testing subjects of successive generations, usually parents and their adolescent or adult offspring (see Abbott, 1970; 1976).

Another type of cross-sectional research that has been more frequently found in the literature on Chinese personality change is the individual-difference approach, involving the use of a tool that assesses the degree of modernization at the individual level. Using this approach, Yang and his associates (Hchu, 1971; Hchu and Yang, 1972; Yang, 1981b; Yang and Hchu, 1974) developed the Chinese Individual Traditionality/Modernity Scale (CITMS) to provide a measure of degree of individual modernization. A current revised version of this test is composed of 50 items, each with a six-step rating scale of agreement or disagreement, concerning such attitudinal topics as family, culture, education, politics, law enforcement, economic affairs, sexual behaviour, and so on. They have treated Chinese individual modernity, as measured by the CITMS, as the central intervening variable and studied its antecedent determinants, personality correlates, and behavioural consequences in a systematic way. What they have found in these studies concerning the relationship of individual modernity to personality and behaviour characteristics may serve as a basis for inferring the relationship of societal modernity to the same psychological characteristics as a result of social change. In other words, if individual modernization is a direct effect of societal modernization, we can infer the effects on personality and behaviour of the latter from the psychological correlates and consequences of the former. Recent empirical research (Lei and Yang, 1984; Yang and Hwang, 1984) has demonstrated that this kind of relational inference has considerable validity.

There have been more than 20 quasi-longitudinal and cross-sectional studies on the change of Chinese character in Taiwan. The majority of them will be briefly reviewed in terms of the three main modalities of personality so that the general trends of Chinese personality change under the impact of modernization may be readily understood.

Changes in Motivational Characteristics

A review of the literature discloses that there have been several studies on changes in Chinese needs. Some have adopted a cross-sectional and others a quasi-longitudinal approach. The cross-sectional studies were mostly carried out by Yang and his associates, using an individual-difference approach. In one of their studies, Hchu and Yang (1972) gave the CITMS and a Chinese version of the EPPS to 150 college students and found that individual modernity positively correlated with needs for Autonomy and Heterosexuality and negatively with needs for Deference and Abasement. In another study, Hwang and Yang (1972) reported data for a sample of 247 university students, indicating a low but statistically significant negative correlation between individual modernity and need for social approval, as measured by a Chinese version of Marlowe and Crowne's (1964) social desirability scale. In a third study, using a projective technique of the TAT type, Yang and Liang (1973) obtained a positive relationship of individual modernity to nAch among 69 high-school boys. More interesting is their finding that individual modernity was negatively related to the social-oriented type of achievement motive and positively to the individual-oriented type of achievement motive. One implication of this finding is that, under the impact of modernization, the Chinese in Taiwan tend to change from social orientation to individual orientation in their need for achievement. This trend is consistent with my earlier assertion that typical Chinese are characterized by a strong social-oriented need for achievement (see the previous discussion of motivational characteristics). The change also means that the process of modernization makes the Chinese become gradually more like people in a modern industrialized society such as the United States, where the individual-oriented type of achievement motivation prevails.

Yang (1976) also investigated the relationship of individual modernity to some needs of a more specific type, using Chinese adults as respondents. He interviewed 161 husbands and 161 wives with a 23-page questionnaire which included 20 items for the measurement of individual modernity. One of the findings was that individual modernity had a negative correlation with the following need variables: (a) need to maintain and raise status in the family through having a son; (b) need to maintain and raise status in the family through having a daughter; (c) husband's tendency to withdraw affection from wife due to sonlessness; and (d) wife's fear of loss of her husband's affection due to sonlessness. Individual modernity was also reported to correlate negatively with actual and ideal family size and son preference, and positively with contraceptive behaviour. More direct evidence for change in the Chinese motivational pattern has been provided by Hwang's (1976) quasi-longitudinal study. He tested 660 National Normal University students with a Chinese version of the EPPS in 1963 and administered the same instrument to 269 students in the same institution in 1975. He compared the two sets of data and found that the two groups differed from each other on eight EPPS scales: an increasing trend was observed on Exhibition, Autonomy, Intraception, and Heterosexuality, and a decreasing trend on Deference, Order, Nurturance, and Endurance. The findings of increased Autonomy and Heterosexuality and decreased Deference are consistent with those in Hchu and Yang's (1972) cross-sectional research.

To summarize the relevant results obtained in previous studies, we may tentatively say that, as social change continues, the Chinese in Taiwan tend to have a higher need for exhibition, autonomy, intraception, heterosexuality, and individual-oriented achievement and a lower need for deference, order, abasement, nurturance, endurance, social approval, social-oriented achievement, and the attainment of social status and affection through traditional means. In other words, they have been developing a greater concern with self-expression, self-assertion, independence, and personal achievement, as well as becoming freer of their self-imposed inhibition about associating with people of the opposite sex. On the other hand, they have become less concerned with conforming to customs, achieving organization and orderliness, blaming and belittling self, helping and giving sympathy to others, persevering in a task or activity until finished, seeking approval or admiration from others or society, and striving to achieve goals set by others or society.

Changes in Evaluative-attitudinal Characteristics

At least nine studies have provided data relevant to the change in Chinese evaluative characteristics. In their study of Chinese value orientations, Yang and Chang (1975) gave the revised version of the CITMS, along with a value orientation questionnaire of 44 forced-choice items derived from Kluckhohn and Strodtbeck's (1961) instrument, to 104 university students. The data obtained showed that more modernized students manifested a stronger tendency to prefer achievement (doing) and a weaker tendency to prefer inner development (being-in-becoming) in the activity sphere, and a stronger tendency to prefer individualism and a weaker tendency to prefer lineality (collectivism) in the relational sphere. Data which support the Chinese students' decreasing preference for lineality also come from a study by Liu, Chen, Chen, and Yang (1973), in which higher scorers on modernity reported a lower tendency to consult their parents and a higher tendency to consult their friends when they were in trouble or had a problem.

Yang and Hwang (1984) studied the influence of social change on preferences for ways of life, with a joint application of quasi-longitudinal and cross-sectional approaches. They administered Morris's (1956) Ways to Live Questionnaire and the revised version of the CITMS to 969 university students in 1984, a sample comparable in sex, age, and other demographic variables to the 787 students similarly tested by Yang (1972) in 1964. They compared the two groups in terms of their preferences for the 13 Ways to Live and found that the 1984 group had a lower mean preference score on Way 1 (preserve the best that man has attained), Way 3 (show sympathetic concern for others), Way 5 (act and enjoy life through group participation), Way 6 (constantly master changing conditions), Way 10 (control the self stoically), and Way 11 (meditate on the inner life), and Way 12 (chance adventuresome deeds); a higher score on Way 4 (experience festivity and solitude in alternation), Way 7 (integrate action, enjoyment, and contemplation), Way 8 (live with wholesome, carefree enjoyment), and Way 9 (wait in quiet receptivity). They also correlated individual modernity with preferences for various ways of life and found that the former was negatively related to preference ratings on Ways 1, 3, 5, 10, 11, 12, and 13 and positively to those on Ways 4 and 7. It is interesting to note that, with the exception of Way 13, whenever individual modernity correlated in a certain direction with preference for a specific way to live, the 1984 group would differ from the 1964 group in the corresponding direction on that particular way of life. It is in this sense that the quasi-longitudinal data validated the cross-sectional data for individual modernity as a 'predictor' of psychological and behavioural change due to societal modernization. Taken together, these two sets of findings may be summarized as indicating a decreasing trend in Morris's Factor A (social restraint and self-control) and Factor B (enjoyment and progress in action) and an increasing trend in Factor E (self-indulgence and sensuous enjoyment) during the process of social change.

Also using quasi-longitudinal and cross-sectional designs in the same study, Lei and Yang (1984) applied a Chinese version of the Allport, Vernon, and Lindzey Study of Values and the revised version of the CITMS to 905 university students in 1984. They compared the 1984 data to those of the 195 university students tested by Li and Yang (1972) in 1964, finding that the 1984 group scored higher on the Aesthetic and Political values and lower on the Theoretical, Economic, and Religious values. Individual modernity was found to correlate positively with the Aesthetic value and negatively with the Economic and Religious values. As in Yang and Huang's study described above, most of the cross-sectional results were validated by the quasi-longitudinal ones. Although individual modernity was not significantly related to the Social value in Lei and Yang's study, these two variables were found to correlate negatively with each other in an earlier study by Hchu (1971), in which 222 university students were used as subjects.

In Hchu's study (1971), individual modernity was also found to correlate with authoritarianism as an attitudinal variable. A negative correlation between these two variables was also reported in Yang's (1976) study on psychological correlates of fertility attitudes and behaviour, with Chinese adults as respondents. Recently, Chen (1977) and Hu (1977; 1982) have repeatedly found a negative correlation between authoritarianism and individual modernity in a series of studies on Chinese political behaviour, using students and adults as respondents or interviewees.

Hu and his associates (for example, Hu, 1982; Liang, 1984) reported data indicating a positive correlation of individual modernity with various measures of democratic attitudes. In Liang's (1984) study of the organizational identification of 508 civil servants in Taipei, a positive correlation was obtained between individual modernity and sense of alienation. In Yang's (1976) study concerning fertility psychology, individual modernity was observed to be negatively related to Rotter's (1966) Internal-External Control Scale, with the more modernized having a greater tendency to believe in their own skill, effort, foresight, and acceptance of responsibility as major determinants of reinforcements and punishments. Corroborative data can also be found in K.S. Yang's (1982b) study of *yuan* (緣), a unique Chinese conception of predetermined interpersonal affinity. *Yuan* attribution represents a set of fatalistic attitudes in which the traditional Chinese believe that almost every interpersonal relationship or transaction is predetermined by fate, some unknown force, or what one did in one's last life. Yang reported that, among the 543 Chinese students he surveyed, those scoring high on individual modernity tended to display a weaker tendency to believe in *yuan* than those who scored low. Since *yuan* represents a kind of belief in external control, this finding may be interpreted as revealing a weaker tendency among the more modernized students to have such beliefs.

On the basis of the studies reviewed so far, several statements about changes in the evaluative-attitudinal modality may be made. During the process of modernization, Chinese students' value orientations have changed from a preference for inner development and lineality (collectivism) to a preference for achievement and individualism. Their liking for ways of life stressing social restraint and self-control and those emphasizing action and progress in action has been decreasing, and their liking for ways accenting self-indulgence and sensuous enjoyment has been increasing. As a concomitant of social change, they have become more interested in aesthetic experience and power and influence, and less interested in theoretical thinking, practical utility, social commitment, and religious experience. Moreover, they have been changing in the direction of becoming more democratic, alienated, and internal controlled and less authoritarian in attitudes.

Changes in Temperamental Characteristics

The CITMS and its revised version have been used in a number of studies on Chinese temperamental traits. In one study, Hchu (1971) applied Eysenck's Maudsley Personality Inventory to 209 university students and reported that individual modernity was negatively related to Neuroticism but had no statistically significant relationship with Introversion-Extroversion. In a recent study by Yeh (1981), individual modernity was found to have a positive correlation with tolerance of life stress and stimulation among 437 college students. A particularly interesting finding from this study is that individual modernity could effectively function as a moderating variable, so that life stress had a positive correlation with the number of personal bad habits, used as a measure of mental health, in the low and moderate modernity groups but a zero correlation in the high modernity group.

While Hchu's and Yeh's research is mainly concerned with change in the temperamental dimension of emotionality and anxiety, there have been studies that have dealt particularly with change in the temperamental dimension of self-restraint and cautiousness. In one of these studies (Hwang and Yang, 1972), a *male* experimenter asked each *female* university student to do a word-recognition task in front of a tachistoscope under a procedure of progressive prolongation of exposure time. It was found that high scorers on individual modernity tended to need a shorter exposure time for the correct recognition of taboo (that is, sex-related) words displayed one at a time. This finding suggests a weaker tendency to suppress the responses that they thought might be socially inappropriate. No such difference was found for the neutral words. In another experiment, the subject first performed a simple, tedious, and boring task (picking up chess pieces from one box and putting them into another) for 20 minutes and was then requested to rate his evaluation and feeling about the experiment as a whole. The results showed that the more modernized students gave lower ratings to the usefulness of the experimental procedure as a method of measuring motor skill and to the scientific significance of a report which would be based upon the results obtained in the experiment; they also expressed less willingness to return to take part in another experiment of a similar nature. In a third study, higher scorers on modernity were found to show a weaker tendency to consider others' opinions before they made decisions about such important personal matters as election of courses of study, extracurricular activities, selection of a marriage partner, and expression of opinions in public. These three experiments reported in Hwang and Yang's (1972) article seem to indicate that more modernized students consistently tended to express a lower degree of self-restraint and social cautiousness in their social relations.

Yang (1974) completed another relevant study in which more than 100 university students were administered the Rosenzweig Picture Frustration Study, along with the CITMS. His data revealed that individual modernity positively correlated with extrapunitive reactions and negatively with intropunitive reactions to frustration. These findings may be interpreted as indicating that the more modernized students had a higher tendency to attribute the frustration aggressively to someone or something in the external world, and a lower tendency to attribute the frustration aggressively to themselves (after having inhibited its outward expression).

Still another study of this sort was also done by Yang (1981a). He selected 46 high and 46 low scorers on individual modernity from a larger sample of university students and then tested them with the Rorschach Test. More modernized students were found to have a larger total number of responses and a smaller number of popular responses. They were also found to take a shorter time to produce the first and subsequent responses. It was considered that these findings showed a weaker tendency among the more modernized Chinese to be socially inhibited and cautious.

The most comprehensive study of the relationship of individual modernity to temperament was conducted by Lee (1973), providing data relevant to several temperamental dimensions. She gave Cattell's 16PF, Guilford and Zimmerman's GZTS, Gough's CPI, and the CITMS to various groups of college students ranging in sample size from 165 to 297. On the 16PF, individual modernity was found to correlate positively with Ego Strength (calm, emotionally stable), Dominance (assertive, competitive), Surgency (talkative, cheerful), Parmia (adventurous, bold), and Radicalism (liberal, free-thinking); and to correlate negatively with Super-ego Strength (conscientious, persevering), Guilt Proneness (timid, worrisome), and Controlled Will (careful, playing safe). On the GZTS, individual modernity tended to be positively related to Ascendance and Masculinity and negatively related to Restraint, Friendliness, and Personal Relations. On the CPI, individual modernity was reported to have a positive correlation with four of the 18 variables: Social Presence, Sense of Well-being, Tolerance, and Flexibility. Also using the CPI as a measuring tool, Abbott (1970) found that Chinese adolescents in Taipei and San Francisco had been moving away from their parents' modal temperamental pattern in that they scored higher on Flexibility and Tolerance and lower on Good Impression, Self-control, and Femininity.

To summarize the above findings of studies on the change of Chinese temperaments, it may be tentatively concluded that, under the influence of social change, Chinese people have been becoming higher in their sociability (extroversion), dominance (ascendance), flexibility, tolerance, and masculinity; and lower in their emotionality (anxiety), self-restraint (cautiousness), friendliness (harmonious relationship), conscientiousness, perseverance, and femininity.

So far in this section, we have reviewed most of the empirical studies of Chinese personality change under the impact of societal modernization. For the sake of simplicity and clarity, these changes, empirically confirmed to a greater or lesser degree through quasi-longitudinal and cross-sectional data, may be listed as shown in Table 4.2.

This pattern of change in the Chinese character is neither complete nor definite. Its configuration and contents will certainly be revised and extended upon the production of new findings by future research. However, given the apparently uncertain nature of this pattern of change, we can still identify, from the whole set of *decreasing* characteristics, such interrelated basic traditional Chinese proclivities as collectivistic orientation, other-orientation, relationship orientation, authoritarian orientation, submissive disposition, inhibited disposition, and effeminate disposition; and, from the whole set of the *increasing* characteristics, such interrelated basic new proclivities as individualistic orientation, self-orientation, competitive orientation, equalitarian orientation, autonomous disposition, and expressive disposition. The former set of proclivities may be simply subsumed under K.S. Yang's (1981a; 1981b; and 1982a) concept of social orientation, and the latter under the concept of individual orientation. The decrease of the former characteristics means that the Chinese in Taiwan have been moving away from the traditional syndrome of social-oriented traits, which were needed for adjustment to everyday life in the Chinese agricultural society. And the increase of the latter characteristics reveals that these Chinese have been gradually acquiring some of the individual-oriented traits that will make their life easier in Taiwan's industrializing society. Thus the central trend of Chinese psychological transformation due to modernization has been from social orientation to individual orientation.

In this section, we have briefly expounded a cultural-ecological view of the formation of the Chinese character and systematically described the changes in this character as a result of societal modernization. The major classes of factors and variables involved in these processes may be summarized simply in Figure 4.1.

SOME CONCLUDING REMARKS

Most of this chapter has been devoted to a description and discussion of Chinese personality and its change under the impact of societal modernization. Numerous relevant studies published in Chinese have been reviewed, all of which are rarely accessible to the

Table 4.2 The Impact of Societal Modernization on Chinese Personality

Decreasing	Increasing
Motivational Characteristics	
n Deference	*n* Exhibition
n Order	*n* Autonomy
n Abasement	*n* Intraception
n Nurturance	*n* Heterosexuality
n Endurance	*n* Achievement
n Achievement (social-oriented)	(individual-oriented)
n Social approval	
Evaluative-attitudinal Characteristics	
Preference for inner development	Preference for achievement (activity)
Preference for collectivistic (lineal) relationship	Preference for individualistic relationship
Preference for social restraint and self-control	Preference for self-indulgence and sensuous enjoyment
Theoretical value	Aesthetic value
Social value	Internal-control beliefs
Religious value	Democratic attitudes
External-control beliefs	
Authoritarian attitudes	
Temperamental Characteristics	
Self-restraint and cautiousness	Sociability and extroversion
Friendliness and harmoniousness	Ascendance and dominance
Conscientiousness	Flexibility
Perseverance	Tolerance
Femininity	Masculinity

Western reader and have therefore not been covered in reviews on Chinese behaviour and personality by such Western scholars as Abbott (1970), Fried (1976), Grichting (1971), and Vernon (1982). Through the present systematic review, readers should have obtained a clearer idea about what psychological characteristics the Chinese possess and how these characteristics have been transformed as a result of social change. In addition, readers should have become

Fig. 4.1 A Simplified Interactionistic Cultural-ecological View of the Genesis and Change of Chinese Character

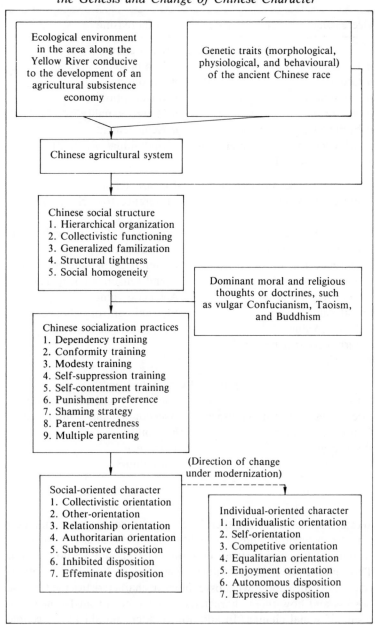

familiar with the methods that investigators in this field have adopted in their research and the concepts they have used in interpreting their results.

Although we have been primarily concerned in this chapter with the pattern of Chinese personality and its change as revealed in research findings, it is also useful to dwell briefly on some of the main shortcomings of the research methods utilized in previous studies. Such a methodological discussion will enable the reader to make a better evaluation of the internal and external validities associated with the conclusions and generalizations from these studies. It is hoped that, as a result, future investigators will be able to conduct better conceptualized and designed research in this area.

Methodological defects can easily be identified in studies of Chinese personality. First, there have been obvious inadequacies in the formation of research problems. Typically researchers have failed to make a clear statement of what specific questions, not to mention well-developed working hypotheses, they were proposing to answer by their investigations. While lack of theoretical orientation is a common disadvantage in this area, many studies have fallen prey to the additional characteristic of method- or tool-centredness. In many cases, the investigator seems to have been so interested in a certain test or scale of personality that it was mechanically applied to the Chinese whether it was culturally appropriate or not. Some of the researchers, notably local Chinese ones, have not made a sufficiently extensive review of the existing literature before formulating their research problems and have thus failed to realize that studies similar to their own had already been completed by others years ago. This unknowing repetition of similar studies, while providing potentially useful cross-validation data, is not likely to advance the depth of our knowledge about Chinese personality. In order to improve research in this field in the future, it is essential for the investigator to conceptualize and formulate his or her research problem or hypothesis on the basis of related literature. The best way to do this is to develop the research question from a relevant theoretical or conceptual paradigm. Only in this way can Chinese personality and its change be adequately explored in depth.

More seriously, the soundness of the basic strategy and design of most previous studies on Chinese character may be questioned. True cross-cultural research, simultaneously collecting data for two or more cultural groups, has been reasonably infrequent in the psychological literature on Chinese character. Among the very few such studies, most, if not all, have made their cross-cultural comparisons in an uncontrolled way. Usually the effects of cultural difference have been appraised without any empirically confirmed comparability between the construct concerned and its measuring instrument. In fact, the uncertainty of conceptual as well as methodological equivalence has been a common problem of almost all recent studies of Chinese personality, cross-cultural or not, which have adopted a non-projective method. In most such studies, the investigator has administered an instrument developed and standardized in a Western culture to a sample of Chinese. A research practice like this has been labelled by Berry (1969) as 'imposed etic' and by Triandis (1972) as 'pseudoetic', in the sense that it imposes categories, variables, concepts, or constructs derived from past research in one culture on to the behaviour of members of another culture. Using such a strategy, the researcher is employing not only an 'imposed etic' theoretical framework but also an 'imposed etic' methodology. Thus it is a 'double imposed etic' approach and this, according to Berry (1969), is one of the worst types of cross-cultural research. With a 'design' like this, it would be impossible for the investigator to be sure either that cross-culturally equivalent concepts or constructs are being examined or that methods or tools with sufficient cross-cultural equivalence in the assessment of these concepts or constructs are being brought to bear.

In order to avoid these conceptual and methodological uncertainties, future researchers on Chinese behaviour should adopt some cross-cultural form or extension of Campbell and Fiske's (1959) multi-trait, multi-method paradigm for establishing construct validity, as recommended by Irvine and Carroll (1980). The investigator should at least ensure that he or she is measuring constructs that are cross-culturally equivalent or valid before accepting the test scores as measures of these constructs. It is essential to collect data to indicate whether or not an assessment instrument or procedure standardized in an alien culture still retains its original construct validity when its translated version is applied to the study of Chinese behaviour. There are many ways to achieve this end. One way is to intercorrelate and carry out a factor analysis of the items of the test in question, using data collected from a heterogeneous sample drawn from a target Chinese population. If the factorial structure obtained is highly similar to that reported for the foreign standardization sample, the tool may be said to have retained its original construct validity when applied to Chinese subjects. Another way is to collect data from a heterogeneous Chinese sample by the test in question and by several other carefully chosen instruments which measure variables that have been reported to have specific relationships with scores on that test in its culture of standardization. If the pattern of relationships between scores on the major test and on the other variables is highly similar in the two cultural groups, this particular test can be considered to have cross-cultural construct validity when used with Chinese subjects. The latter approach has been exemplified in a study by Yang and Yang (1974), in which the cross-cultural validity of a Chinese version of Byrne's (1961) Repression-Sensitization (R-S) Scale was empirically evaluated. Yang and Yang found that, in the Chinese sample, scores on the R-S Scale positively correlated with actual- versus ideal-self concept discrepancy, value versus feeling incongruency, and neuroticism; negatively related to actual-self concept and extroversion; and had no linear relationship with ideal-self concept. Exactly the same results were found in an American sample as reported by American psychologists (for example, Altrocchi, Parsons, and Dickoff, 1960; Byrne, Barry, and Nelson, 1963; Golin, Herron, Lakota, and Reineck, 1967).

Closely related to the cross-cultural validity of a measuring instrument is the problem of its translation. It is apparent that investigators of Chinese personality have not paid enough attention to this problem. With very few exceptions, most past studies, in translating a written test into Chinese, have not used a back-translation check, or a more complicated and sophisticated translation procedure as described by Brislin and his associates (Brislin, 1976; 1980; Brislin, Lonner, and Thorndike, 1973), Prince and Mombour (1967), and Werner and Campbell (1970). As a result, the linguistic equivalence of the original and Chinese versions of the test cannot be guaranteed. To be exempt from this shortcoming, future research should take back translation or some analogous procedure as a minimum requirement for adapting a foreign instrument for use with Chinese subjects.

Other obvious methodological defects concern the appropriateness and comparability of the samples used. Previous relevant studies purporting to be cross cultural have made comparisons without ensuring that the Chinese and foreign samples are demographically comparable. In many cases, the description of the samples has been simply too brief to enable any assessment of the composition and comparability of the samples. An additional problem is the narrow range of Chinese people who have been used as subjects in the study of Chinese personality. Most of the studies in this field have employed captive students in schools as samples for data collection. Since these student samples are not representative of the general Chinese population, conclusions drawn from data on these subjects are likely to lose their external validity when generalized to other groups of Chinese people. Fortunately, relevant empirical studies using non-student samples have been gradually increasing in number and their findings enable checks on the feasibility of generalization from student results. It is, however, still imperative for future investigators in this field to conduct more studies using large enough samples drawn from non-student Chinese of different ages, at different educational levels, and in different walks of life.

Before concluding this chapter, several points about the direction and orientation of future research in this field must be stated. First, more and better studies should be done on the structure of Chinese personality. Under this rubric, at least four directions of empirical inquiry can be seriously pursued.

1. Research gaps can easily be identified by a careful reading of the preceding section on Chinese personality characteristics. There is no formal, systematic, empirical test of the hypothesis that Chinese have a stronger social-oriented achievement motivation, as revealed in self-report measures, and a weaker individual-oriented achievement motivation, as revealed in projective measures, than Caucasians. Another gap is the need for a well-designed study to enable a comparison between Chinese and Caucasians in emotionality, anxiety, or neuroticism, by means of a cross-culturally valid measuring procedure.

2. An 'etic' approach using universal categories or constructs, no matter how carefully executed, will be unable to unravel those psychological characteristics that are unique to, and most representative of, Chinese people as a cultural group. In order to understand Chinese personality better, an 'emic' approach using specific Chinese categories or constructs should be given more weight in future research. K.S. Yang (1982a) has advocated the Sinicization of psychological research in Chinese society, and some Chinese psychologists (for example, Cheng, 1982; Chu, 1983; Yang, 1982b) in Taiwan have already completed a number of empirical studies on such indigenous psychological concepts as face and *yuan*. Research projects are being carried out by Yang and his associates for the systematic study of Chinese familism and Chinese filial

piety, beginning with the construction of standardized scales for their measurement. More and better studies along these lines will uncover the unique psychological and attitudinal make-up that underlies the behavioural functioning of the Chinese as a social-oriented people.

3. While previous studies of Chinese character have been predominantly psychometric in nature, future research in this area should take a more dynamic and interactionistic approach. This should give us a better knowledge of the modal behavioural processes of the Chinese as a result of their unique interaction with social and other situations. The most defensible methodology is an approach based upon the notion of dynamic interactionism. As defined by Magnusson and Endler (1977), dynamic interaction refers to a pattern of behavioural functioning, in which person variables and situation variables are integrated to describe and explain the process whereby individual behaviour develops and maintains itself. Such a person-situation (environment) interaction model will be able to incorporate the psychometric approach by treating personality variables as person variables. This interactionistic research paradigm may be utilized to find out not only how Chinese personality interacts with situations in affecting Chinese behaviour but also how these dynamic interactions differ as a function of culture.

4. Relatively little research has been conducted on the ethnogenetic and ontogenetic (individual) development of Chinese personality. There is a need for studies based upon historical documents and materials (especially those concerning social life, folk customs, ethical rules, domestic disciplines, and parental precepts) as these will shed light on the genesis of Chinese character in a historical context. Also important are studies of the socialization process, through which the psychological characteristics and behavioural patterns of the Chinese are transmitted, as cultural elements, to individuals of a new generation in significant social settings such as the family, the school, and society at large. In view of the dearth of knowledge about the historical formation and ontogenetic development of Chinese character, any well-documented or designed investigation in this area will be extremely welcome. Findings from such research are, *de facto*, an essential part of the basis for the construction of a full theory of Chinese personality and behaviour.

Second, more and better studies should be carried out into the change of Chinese character under the impact of modernization. In this area, there are at least three major lines of research.

1. Systematic cross-sectional research on the antecedents, correlates, and consequences of Chinese individual modernity should be continued with a conceptual scheme such as the one adopted by Yang (1974). But better assessing instruments or procedures should be used, which reflect recent theoretical progress in the conceptualization of individual modernity as a syndrome of attitudes and actions. Previous research has demonstrated, for example, that individual modernity and traditionalism do not correlate highly enough to justify the assumption that they are the two poles of the same continuum; and that the same individual is not necessarily uniformly modernized or traditional across attitudes, values, and behaviour in different domains of life; that modernity and traditionalism are each composed of a number of psychological and behavioural components or dimensions that can be separately measured. Future investigation in this area should use a new measuring tool that has taken such points into consideration. A multi-dimensional test of this type is being constructed by a team of Chinese social psychologists headed by the present author. The new instrument will consist of separate scales for Chinese modernity and traditionalism, each providing separate scores for different domains of life (for example, family, economic, political, religious, and educational areas) as well as for different psychological components.

2. The study of Chinese personality change cannot rely solely on the cross-sectional approach. More and better quasi-longitudinal research should be carried out in order to trace accurately the transformation of Chinese character during social change. An easier way to do this is to replicate a Chinese personality study completed a number of years ago (for example, 10, 15, 20 years, or more), as Lei and Yang (1984) and Yang and Hwang (1984) have done in their comparative studies. Such studies require the establishment of a data bank in which researchers into Chinese personality and behaviour from all over the world can deposit their raw data for permanent storage. Any interested scholar who wishes to replicate an earlier study may request a usable copy of the original data in whatever form is necessary for comparative analysis. In this way, quasi-longitudinal replications can be more easily performed by someone other than the original investigator

(who may not be interested in carrying out such a study or may not live long enough to do so).

A potentially more fruitful way to undertake quasi-longitudinal study of Chinese personality and behaviour is to design a systematic multi-stage study from the very beginning, so that one or more standardized tests or questionnaires are carefully chosen or constructed and then administered to a large comparable sample of people from the same Chinese population every four, five, or more years. Data to be collected by this periodic procedure are stored and analysed for quasi-longitudinal and other comparisons. Such a large-scale long-term endeavour is possible only when the resources of a government research institution are actively and resolutely involved. As a first attempt in this direction, a group of behavioural scientists (mainly psychologists, sociologists, and anthropologists) in the Institute of Ethnology of the Academia Sinica in Taiwan have designed and initiated such a periodic study. Two long questionnaires concerning social attitudes, values, and behaviour have been constructed and administered to two large heterogeneous samples of Chinese adults in Taiwan. The same two questionnaires will be administered to two comparable samples every three years and the quasi-longitudinal data from this long-term study will be analysed to explore the psychological and behavioural effects of societal change in Taiwan.

3. While there have been a number of studies of the change of Chinese personality, virtually no systematic research has been done to attempt to understand why and how specific Chinese personality characteristics have been changing in certain directions under modernization. We know very little about the dynamic processes by which these changes take place as a result of societal change, although we do know that these processes must be so complicated that they are not easily subject to empirical investigation. However, no matter how difficult research in this area is, it should be given a high priority in the future.

Third, as a field for scientific research and discourse, the study of Chinese personality and its change has been theoretically underdeveloped, in the sense that previous attempts at theory building have been few and fragmented. With the possible exception of Francis Hsu's (1961; 1963; 1965; 1971a; and 1971b) theoretical formulations, the conceptual schemes or models advanced by other researchers, such as those of Dawson, Law, Leung, and Whitney (1971) and K.S. Yang (1981b; 1982a; 1982b), are either limited in scope or preliminary in nature. None of these theoretical positions has successfully functioned as a conceptual device for generating working hypotheses and thus there has been no close interplay between theory and empirical research activities. This may be one reason why past studies of Chinese personality and its change were in most cases not theoretically oriented and their findings were usually simplistically interpreted. To remedy this unsatisfactory condition, better theories should be constructed anew or developed from the old, so that they can be used as tools for integrating previous findings, generating testable hypotheses, and explaining new phenomena in the formation and change of Chinese personality. Such theories must be able to explain adequately how modal Chinese personality patterns have been formed in a historical context, have developed as a result of socialization, and have changed under the impact of modernization.

5 Psychopathology Among Chinese People

FANNY M.C. CHEUNG

PSYCHOPATHOLOGY among Chinese people has been studied mainly from the medical perspective. With the growth of interest in cultural psychiatry, the focus has centred on cultural aspects of psychiatric epidemiology, symptomatology, and aetiology. In this chapter, these reports will be briefly summarized. Attention will be directed to psychological and social factors in the manifestation of abnormal behaviours, and psychological forms of treatment among Chinese.

HISTORICAL PERSPECTIVE

Historical reviews of Chinese psychopathology have referred to traditional medical beliefs in both the classical and folk traditions. The traditional Chinese medical system has been described in detail in a number of books and reports (Chin and Chin, 1969; Koran, 1972; Lin, 1981; Liu, 1981; Topley, 1970). In the classical tradition, illnesses are discussed in terms of the balance of the *Yin* and *Yang* forces, the five fundamental elements (metal, wood, water, fire, and earth), the *ching-lo* (meridian) system, and the circulation of *chi* (vital energy). The aetiology of illnesses is attributed to three groups of factors: six seasonal influences (wind, heat, fire, cold, moisture, and dryness), seven internal emotions (joy, grief, fear, anger, love, hatred, and desire), and situational conditions, such as trauma, fatigue, deregulation of diet, and insects.

The first references to mental illness in Chinese classical medicine appeared in the *Huang-ti Nei-ching* (Yellow Emperor's Classic of Internal Medicine, third to fifth century BC), when the term *tien-k'uang* (craziness) was used to describe symptoms of disturbed affect and behaviour, with *tien* referring to the passive symptoms and *k'uang* referring to the more agitated symptoms of certain psychoses. Some authors have traced the root of the character *k'uang* to dog, and suggested that the aetiology might have been attributed to rabies at that time (Zhang, 1980). Later, *hsien* (seizure) was added as a third category of mental illness.

The aetiology of mental illness in the system of classical medicine follows the same principles as other forms of illness. A holistic system involving external and internal conditions, and physical and psychological factors was postulated (Lin, 1981). Traditional Chinese medicine integrated psychological and physiological functions as the major sources of imbalance and disease. Behavioural and somatic observations were equally important for diagnosis and treatment.

In the folk tradition of Chinese medicine, supernatural as well as Taoist beliefs including divination, sorcery, spirits, and ghosts were held to be responsible for illnesses. These beliefs persist in present-day Chinese societies. The practices of fortune-telling, astrology, physiognomy, geomancy, and shamanism are still used by some as indigenous forms of healing (Lee, 1975; 1980; Lin, 1981). Mental illness is a common reason for consultation with shamans and fortune-tellers. Nevertheless, the medical model remains the dominant paradigm in the study of psychopathology in Chinese culture.

There is little direct reference to the psychodynamics of mental health and illness in classical Chinese writings. The apparent lack of emphasis on psychological factors had led to the allegation often made against the Chinese that they tend to somatize their emotional problems (Kleinman, 1977; Tseng, 1975a). More recent reviews of classical writings and Chinese philosophy have tried to identify mental health concepts in these early writings. Mok (1984) studied Confucius's works with reference to mental health. From a study of *The Great Learning*, three types of mental attitudes were identified as relevant: humility, jealousy, and abnormality. The factors which affected mental ill-health were internal imbalance and bias against others. From a study of the *Doctrine of the Mean*, Mok discussed the Confucian principles for maintaining mental health which included 'being careful about one's motive' (愼獨), 'attaining equilibrium and harmony' (致中和), 'behaving according to one's place' (素位而行), 'bearing loyalty and forgiveness' (存忠恕), and 'achieving the three virtues — wisdom, "*jen*", and courage' (行三達德— 智、仁、勇). The essence of mental health may be summarized in the three axioms: 'the wise will not be confused' (智者不惑); 'the human-hearted (*jen*) will not be worried' (仁者不憂); and 'the courageous will not fear' (勇者不懼). An overview of the Confucian paradigm of human nature may be found in King and Bond (1985), while an assessment of selfhood in the neo-Confucian tradition may be found in Metzger (1981a).

Contemporary psychiatry and psychology were imported into China in the 1920s when departments of neurology and psychology were established in Beijing University. In Taiwan and Hong Kong, Western psychiatry was developed after the Second World War, by Professors T.Y. Lin and P.M. Yap respectively. University departments of psychology were not established until the late 1940s in Taiwan and the mid-1960s in Hong Kong. Little work has been done to integrate traditional Chinese beliefs with Western models of psychopathology. The history of Chinese psychiatry has been summarized briefly by Cerny (1965) and Koran (1972). Research on medical psychology in China between 1949 and 1966 may be found in the book by Chin and Chin (1969).

STUDIES OF PSYCHIATRIC MORBIDITY

Early studies of psychopathology in Chinese societies have focused primarily on epidemiological surveys and clinical case-studies based on Western diagnostic categories. These studies have been reviewed by Lin, Kleinman, and Lin (1981), and updated by Lin and Kleinman (1981) for the People's Republic of China and by Yeh (1985) for Taiwan.

The major epidemiological studies of mental disorders among Chinese were conducted on a sample of 20,000 in three Taiwan communities representing village, small town, and city during the years 1946–8 (Lin, 1953), and again 15 years later on a sample of 30,000 during the years 1961–3 (Lin, Rin, Yeh, Hsu, and Chu, 1969). The prevalence rates for schizophrenia and manic-depressive psychosis were 2.1 and 0.7 per thousand respectively and were basically unchanged between the two surveys. However, the prevalence of neurosis rose from 1.2 to 7.8 per thousand. Four tribes of 11,442 Aborigines in Taiwan were also surveyed in the period 1949–53 (Rin and Lin, 1962). Reports on psychiatric epidemiology in mainland China have been published recently in Chinese journals, involving populations ranging from 200,000 to 2,000,000 in regions close to major medical centres such as Shanghai, Beijing, and Nanjing (Lin and Kleinman, 1981). The prevalence rate for schizophrenia ranged from 0.77 to 4.8 per thousand, and for manic-depressive psychosis from 0.03 to 0.09 per thousand. Unfortunately, vast differences in criteria and methodology in these studies make it difficult to compare the prevalence rates within as well as outside China. The prevalence of specific disorders, including schizophrenia (World Health Organization, 1973) and affective disorders (Yap, 1965b), has also been studied among Chinese.

Although reviews of these epidemiological studies have indicated that the overall prevalence rates for psychoses among Chinese are roughly similar to the rates reported in other cultures, T.Y. Lin (1983) cautioned that differences in the methodology of these studies may limit the value of comparisons of the overall rates. He also pointed out the existence of discrepancies between prevalence rates and hospital admission rates, which should be taken into consideration before cross-cultural comparisons are made.

In the case of minor mental disorders among Chinese, lower prevalence rates of depressive illness (especially neurotic depression), obsessive-compulsive neurosis, and alcoholism have consistently been observed (T.Y. Lin, 1983; Lin, Kleinman, and Lin, 1981). On the other hand, neurasthenia is one of the most common diagnoses or self-diagnoses among psychiatric out-patients in China (Chin and Chin, 1969; Kleinman, 1982; T.Y. Lin, 1983). The bases for these cultural differences in rates may be explored in terms of symptom manifestation and pathogenetic conditions, as well as in definitions of psychopathology. Changes in rates for neurosis, suicide, and psychophysiological reactions have been observed in the follow-up epidemiological study in Taiwan, suggesting the role of migration and urbanization on adaptation and mental health (Lin, Kleinman, and Lin, 1981; Yeh, 1985).

In Hong Kong, the first community-wide epidemiological study of the rates for mental disorders has just been launched by the Psychiatric Epidemiological Unit of The Chinese University of Hong Kong (Chen, 1984; Wong, Lai, Wong, Hong, and Chen, 1984). Using the General Health Questionnaire (Goldberg, 1978) and the Diagnostic Interview Schedule (Robins, Helzer, Croughan, Williams, and Spitzer, 1979), the study will use a two-stage design for case identification on a target of 20,000 subjects. Until these results are available, the only community survey of mental stress symptoms comes from data arising from a sociological survey in 1974 (Lee, 1976; 1981). Using the 22-item Langner Scale (Langner, 1966), Lee found that almost one-third of the stratified sample of 3,983 urban household heads between the ages of 20 and 59 were suffering from four or more symptoms indicative of psychological disturbance. Other statistics on psychiatric disorders are obtained mainly from patient attendances at and admissions to the Government Mental Health Service centres, which are the major sources of psychiatric services in Hong Kong. On the basis of in-patient admission rates, the majority (63.5 per cent) of psychiatric patients are schizophrenics. The pattern of diagnoses is quite different among out-patients, of whom about 45 per cent are neurotic cases and only about 20 per cent of whom are schizophrenics. Cases of affective disorder and depression are comparatively rare (Lo, 1981). Morbidity studies based on attendances at psychiatric service centres are, however, inadequate indicators of prevalence rates. In Chinese societies, attendance and hospitalization are affected by the availability of services as well as conceptualization of illness and the pattern of seeking help among the afflicted and their families (Cheung, 1985b).

Rates of mental disorders among Overseas Chinese have been based mainly on treated cases in mental health or health facilities. Tsai, Teng, and Sue (1981) reviewed the studies of the utilization of mental health facilities by Chinese in the United States and concluded that their psychiatric admission rates were low. While Chinese Americans underutilized treatment facilities, those who became patients were more disturbed. Tsai et al. (1981) suggested that the low utilization rates reflected inhibition about approaching professional mental health facilities as a result of factors such as the fear of stigma, the inaccessibility of mental health services to Chinese, and the Chinese systems of beliefs about mental health. Similar findings have been reported by Chiu and Tan (1985) in Melbourne, Australia, where they identified cases of Chinese origin who had used psychiatric services in private practices, general hospitals, and psychiatric hospitals. The most common diagnosis found among the hospitalized cases was schizophrenia while that found in private practice was neurotic disorder. In Singapore, where Chinese comprise 76 per cent of the population, the majority (61.8 per cent) of the patients admitted into the main psychiatric hospital were diagnosed as schizophrenics (Tsoi and Chen, 1979). Among these patients, 78.8 per cent were ethnic Chinese. Neurotics constituted about 46 per cent of the new patients at psychiatric out-patient clinics (Tsoi, 1985). However, in a mental health survey conducted by the Ministry of Health in Singapore in 1978 using the Langner Scale, only 7.9 per cent of the Chinese scored four or more symptoms (Tsoi, 1985), far fewer than the percentage found in the Hong Kong study (Lee, 1976). Unfortunately, insufficient information is provided by the Singapore report to enable a comparison of the results of the two studies.

Psychiatric epidemiological studies of Chinese children and young people have been conducted in Taiwan and, more recently, in China. In Taiwan, a four-year longitudinal study of university students was carried out in a Taipei university during the years 1963–7 (Yeh, Chu, Ko, Lin, and Lee, 1972). The results showed that university students had a lower rate of psychosis than the same age-group in the general population. While there was no difference among the females in terms of the rates for psychophysiological disorders and neurosis, the male students were found to suffer from a higher rate of neurosis but a lower rate of psychophysiological disorders than males in the general population. Hsu (1966; 1973) studied the prevalence rates of behaviour problems among primary-school and junior-high-school students using teacher ratings, and found the rates to be around 10–13 per cent, with higher rates among boys.

Recent epidemiological studies of child mental health in China have included pre-school children and adolescents. Large-scale studies have been conducted in Beijing, Nanjing, Shanghai, and Sichuan. Behaviour problems at home and in schools were identified using standardized rating forms. In one study in Nanjing (Yu, 1985), high rates were found for problems including partiality for food, overdependence on parents and adults, emotional instability, sluggishness in daily life, finger sucking and nail biting, but low rates for truancy, school failure, and rudeness. Different patterns of problems were found in the city and the countryside.

Since the implementation in China of the policy of one child per couple, greater attention has been directed at the mental health of the single child. The first Child Mental Health Research Centre was set up in Nanjing in 1984. Epidemiological studies undertaken in Nanjing included an investigation of the mental health conditions of 1,246 pre-school and primary-school children, and the prevalence of mental retardation in the Nanjing area (Nanjing Child Mental Health Research Centre, 1984). Comparisons between single children and non-single children, and the prevalence of minimal brain dysfunction are the central themes covered in a number of community studies (Shanghai Mental Hospital, 1981; Yang, 1985; Yu, 1981). These studies have generally concluded that the mental health of single children was as sound as, if not better than, that of non-single children. However, the prevalence of minimal brain dysfunction was found to be high (about 8.6 per cent) compared to Western standards. Unfortunately, differences in case identification and methodologies render comparison of the studies difficult.

On the basis of existing epidemiological studies and international collaborative studies, T.Y. Lin (1983, p.862) pointed out that psychopathology among Chinese has basic similarities to that in Western culture. The two major similarities are that 'the entire range of psychopathology observed in the West and in other cultures in terms of symptoms and syndromes [has] been observed in the Chinese' and 'all types of mental disorder . . . as described in Western literature, have been identified among the Chinese when standard Western diagnostic criteria are applied'.

Many of the clinical case-studies of psychiatric disorders among Chinese have concurred about the overall similarities in the symptomatology and the course of illness to cases reported in Western psychiatry. In Hong Kong, follow-up studies of schizophrenics (Lo and Lo, 1977) and of obsessional neurotics (Lo, 1967) have found comparable courses and prognoses to those reported in Western literature. Singer, Chang, and Hsu (1972) and Singer, Lieh-Mak, and Ng (1976) found that the correlations among biological variables, physique, personality, and mental illness resembled those reported for Caucasians. Singer, Ney, and Lieh-Mak (1978) went on to examine child psychiatric disorders and concluded that, despite the influence of culture, the forms of psychopathological manifestations were similar to Caucasian cases.

More direct comparisons of diagnostic criteria for schizophrenia with Western standards were made in Taiwan in conjunction with the WHO International Pilot Study in Schizophrenia in the period 1966–72 (World Health Organization, 1973). Using the Present State Examination Schedule (Wing, Cooper, and Sartorius, 1974), the study found that schizophrenics identified in Taiwan were basically similar to those in other cultures. Among the schizophrenic patients, however, more were diagnosed as paranoid type and hebephrenic type. Higher rates of paranoid symptoms were also reported by Yeh, Fan, and Tien (1979), and by Rin, Schooler, and Caudill (1973).

The diagnosis of schizophrenia in Singapore has adopted a different set of criteria (Tsoi and Chen, 1979). Although the psychiatrists concerned were Western trained, they did not base their diagnosis on Western criteria such as disorders of thinking, emotions, conation, and motor behaviour, nor did they use Schneider's First Rank symptoms. Instead, their diagnosis was based mainly on a cluster of 'commonly known abnormalities' with the patients' relatives as the chief informants. The most common abnormalities were paranoid ideas, hearing voices, talking to oneself, insomnia, and aggressive behaviour. However, paranoid ideas of harm and influence were found in less than one-third of the Chinese schizophrenic patients (Tsoi, 1985).

Greater interest has been shown in the discussion of cultural differences between Chinese and Western psychopathology. One source of interest has been differences in the manifestations of affective disorders. Yap (1965b) found a lack of reference to sin and a low frequency of feelings of guilt and unworthiness among Chinese depressives. He acknowledged, however, that these differences might be more of degree than of kind. Later, Yap (1971) reversed his position on these cultural differences, stating that feelings of guilt were not particularly rare among Chinese depressives. Tseng (1975a) and Kleinman (1977) noted that Chinese depressives tend not to report their affective symptoms and, instead, manifest their psychological problems through somatic complaints. Singer (1977) reviewed the literature on depressive disorders and concluded that, given the methodological problems of many of the reported studies, there was insufficient evidence to suggest that depressive disorders among Chinese have outstanding features deviant from their Western counterparts. The topic of somatization as a Chinese cultural characteristic has been a subject of much controversy and will be discussed in a later section of this chapter.

In the 1950s and 1960s, much discussion took place on culture-bound syndromes among Chinese, the best known being *koro* (Gwee, 1963; 1968; Ngui, 1969; Tan, 1981; Yap, 1965a; 1971). *Koro* consists of an acute panic state relating to concern about the shrinking of one's penis. The disorder was believed to be based upon the practice of castration as a penultimate form of punishment in the tenth century AD in imperial China (Gwee, 1963). Gwee regarded *koro* as a 'hysterical dissociative state' while Yap (1965a) considered it a 'culture-bound depersonalization syndrome'. Wen and Wang (1981) subsumed *koro* under the core *shen k'uei* syndrome, a sexual neurosis associated with kidney deficiency. Wen and Wang made a distinction between disease and illness and suggested that the *shen-k'uei* syndrome may be regarded as a universally occurring disease of sexual neurosis, although its manifestations and conceptualizations, that is, the illness, may be culture specific. Tan (1981) concurred with this distinction between disease and illness. He pointed out the basic emotional conflicts underlying *koro* as a type of neurotic disorder and equated *koro* with an acute anxiety state. He concluded that

Westernization may modify the manifestations of culture-bound syndromes as may the massive and radical changes in modern Communist China.

What has not changed in the various modern Chinese societies is the continued emphasis on the culture-specific syndrome of neurasthenia. In Chin and Chin's (1969) review of research in medical psychology in Communist China between 1949 and 1966, a common topic for research was found to be neurasthenia — its incidence, aetiology, and treatment. It is a popular form of diagnosis or self-diagnosis in China, Taiwan, and Hong Kong (Cheung, in press; Kleinman, 1982; T.Y. Lin, 1983), despite its declining usage in Western psychiatry. Neurasthenia as a diagnosis has been loosely applied by patients, their families, or professionals to refer to a variety of symptoms of both a somatic and a psychological nature. Kleinman's (1982) study found that many of the neurasthenic patients who presented themselves at the Hunan psychiatric out-patient clinic were given the diagnosis of depression or anxiety neurosis. Cheung (in press) discussed the two separate clusters of symptoms used in various descriptions of neurasthenia in advertisements for popular folk medicines in Hong Kong. One cluster included more psychological symptoms including moods and cognitive problems. The other cluster of symptoms referred to mostly somatic concerns such as lack of vital energy (*chi*), lack of blood, fatigue, or *shen k'uei*, which could be alleviated through tonic care. Yap (1965a) has also discussed *shen k'uei* as a neurasthenic state associated with sexual excess. This ambiguity in the definition of neurasthenia and its association with somatic weakness by intellectuals and mental health workers may provide a more socially acceptable context for one to seek help for psychiatric and sexual problems (Cheung, in press).

DEFINITIONS AND MANIFESTATIONS OF PSYCHOPATHOLOGY AMONG CHINESE

Traditional medical beliefs about mental illness emphasized psychosomatic integration. Consequently, behavioural and physiological indicators were used for diagnosis and treatment. Since the main categories of mental illness, *tien* and *k'uang*, referred to psychotic disorders, only the more disturbed forms of behaviours were considered pathological. In line with the Confucian doctrine of the mean, excesses in any form would be inappropriate. Lin (1981) discussed traditional psychiatric beliefs which regarded excess and incongruence of emotions as psychopathogenic. Later differentiation of the terms *feng-tien* (瘋癲) and *feng-k'uang* (瘋狂) suggested that these two psychotic disorders had the same rapid onset as wind in the radical of the word *feng* (風). The inclusion of wind in the character of craziness was probably derived from the unpredictability of the behaviour of the afflicted.

Behavioural disturbances were particularly recognized when they jeopardized harmonious interpersonal relationships and disrupted the personal roles assumed by the afflicted. In the Confucian view, a person is a relational being interacting in a prescribed role system (King and Bond, 1985). It would therefore be expected that in Chinese society the agitated and disturbed symptoms of psychoses would be less tolerated, whereas lethargic and intrapsychic symptoms would be more acceptable.

For non-psychotic disorders, the medical emphasis has been placed on the manifestation of somatic symptoms even though their aetiology in psychological factors may be acknowledged. Minor mental illnesses were traditionally combined with other physiological problems. In such diagnoses, either the organic or the psychological symptoms may have been included as the primary symptoms (Lin, 1981). These traditional medical approaches are often reflected in the manifestations of minor psychiatric disorders among Chinese even today. Many neurotic patients seek help from general practitioners. This focus on somatic symptoms by the patients as well as by the physicians has led to the impression that the emotional symptoms are masked (Cheung, Lau, and Waldmann, 1980–1; Kleinman, 1977; Tseng, 1975a). However, given the distinction made between psychotic disturbances, which were labelled as mental illness in traditional and folk beliefs, and minor psychiatric disorders, which would not have been considered mental illness, the focus on somatic treatment in the case of the latter can be understood. Cheung and her associates (Cheung and Lau, 1982; Cheung, Lau, and Wong, 1984) found that in Hong Kong many neurotic patients at psychiatric clinics have previously consulted general practitioners, to whom they have tended to report a combination of both somatic and psychological symptoms.

Cheung (1982; 1985b) further pointed out that studies of non-patients have indicated that, among the normal population, admission of psychological symptoms was as frequent as that of somatic symptoms, if not more so. Chinese have been found to score generally higher than other groups on psychological inventories such as the MMPI (Cheung, 1985a; Song, 1981; Sue and Sue, 1974). In these studies, both the normal population and psychiatric patients had particularly high scores on two clinical scales of the MMPI, 2 and 8. Cheung (1985a) suggested that these high levels may reflect cultural differences in the endorsement frequencies and social desirability of items depicting interpersonal responses, general activity level, and values, rather than reflecting higher rates of psychopathology among Chinese. In general, Chinese prefer less active involvement and are more reserved in casual interpersonal relationships. In addition, they tend to be less optimistic in their outlook. If the Chinese results are interpreted according to American norms, Chinese would appear more lethargic and 'depressed' than Americans. Given this baseline, it may be understandable that the affective features of depression are less readily recognized by the afflicted and their significant others than the more disturbed symptoms in psychotic disorders.

The emphasis on moderation and restraint in social behaviour and in the display of emotions may be reflected in the lower tolerance of disturbance among children. This may partly explain the higher rates of minimal brain dysfunction (MBD) reported among Chinese children in China. When teachers' observations were used as the basis of case identification (as is the case with many of the studies reported in China), it would be expected that deviance in activity level and the drifting of attention in a structured classroom among other well-behaved students would be more readily diagnosed as cases of MBD.

In view of the sudden increase in reported rates of MBD in China since 1978, T.Y. Lin (1984) has raised the question of 'category fallacy', that is, the possibility that the introduction of the concept of MBD after China resumed international scientific exchanges might have led to an indiscriminate application of the diagnostic criteria among interested psychiatrists. The presence or absence of a concept for a certain psychological disorder will probably have a direct impact on the recognition of that problem even among professionals. Given the lack of familiarity with Western psychiatric concepts among the Chinese, the initial recognition of psychiatric disorders by the afflicted, the family, or significant others would be low. The symptoms would be labelled as minor disturbances and explained by reference to various situational factors. The labelling of psychiatric disorder by physicians is mostly done after long delays (Cheung, Lau, and Wong, 1984; Lin, Tardiff, Donetz, and Goresky, 1978).

On the other hand, the effect of public mental health education might have been to arouse the sensitivity of concerned parents, as in the case of MBD in China. During the author's visit to Jiangsu province in 1984, she discussed the problem with a psychiatric social worker who indicated that, after the showing of a television programme on hyperkinesis, the psychiatric hospital had an enormous increase in consultation by concerned parents. The smaller size of the modern Chinese family has allowed parents to pay more attention to their children's well-being, and has increased their concern for any given child.

Even when patients become aware of their problems, the decision on whether and where to seek treatment may determine how the problems will be presented. Cheung and her associates (Cheung, Lee, and Chan, 1983; Cheung, 1984) found that students generally do not seek professional help for mild emotional problems and that, when they do, they tend to approach a medical practitioner. Cheung and Lau (1982) further found that the complaints presented in various medical settings differed. When patients attended a psychiatric out-patient clinic, they reported many symptoms as the reason for their consultation. On the other hand, patients at a prison's psychiatric observation unit reported on the events which had led to their imprisonment. These patients differed from patients attending a psychiatric out-patient clinic or a general out-patient clinic in terms of their stated intention for consultation, the type of symptoms expressed and presented, and the process of help-seeking behaviour. Situational variations then, apparently play an important role in eliciting expectations and behaviour from Chinese patients.

Cheung, Lau, and Waldmann (1980–1) made a distinction between the expression mode and the recognition mode of symptom presentation. Although depressed patients presented initial complaints of somatic symptoms to the medical doctor, they recognized and admitted psychological features of depression when the doctor directly asked about them. In their studies, Cheung and her associates (Cheung and Lau, 1982; Cheung et al., 1984) also found differences in the complaints cited by the patients and the presenting symptoms observed by the psychiatrists. In the 1982 study, 29.3 per cent of the 75 psychiatric out-patients cited psychological factors among their complaints while 45.3 per cent cited somatic factors (Cheung and Lau, 1982, Tables 1 and 2). The manifest somatic, affective, cognitive, and behavioural symptoms noted by the psychiatrist were, however, all greater in number. In the 1984 study, 38.3 per cent of the psychiatric patients from public and private psychiatric out-patient clinics cited psychological problems as one of their reasons for the psychiatric consultation, while 29.2 per cent cited somatic problems (Cheung *et al.*, 1984, Table 7). In terms of manifest symptoms noted by the psychiatrists, 89.7 per cent of the patients presented affective symptoms, 54.4 per cent cognitive-perceptual symptoms, 30.7 per cent behavioural symptoms, and 68.6 per cent somatic symptoms (Cheung *et al.*, 1984, Table 8). In these two studies, the distribution of symptoms of the patients differed partly because of the mixed diagnostic groups of patients. In both studies, however, the psychiatrists noted many more manifest symptoms than those cited by the patients.

To further illustrate the discrepancy between symptom reporting and symptom manifestation, the patterns of presenting complaints among Chinese depressives at a medical clinic in Hong Kong (Cheung *et al.*, 1980–1) will be examined in greater detail. None of the depressed patients reported any subjective feeling of sadness to the general practitioner. Instead, the most common complaints were sleep disturbances, tiredness and malaise, headaches, menopausal symptoms, loss of appetite, abdominal pains, palpitations, bodily weakness, fearfulness, and epigastric pains. When directly asked, most of the patients admitted sadness or the lowering of spirits, tiredness and proneness to fatigue, aches and pains, gastro-intestinal and cardio-vascular symptoms, feelings of tension and nervousness, and experience of agitation and restlessness (Cheung *et al.*, 1980–1, Tables 1 and 4). Many of these psychological symptoms would have been missed if the patients had not been directly asked about them.

Kleinman (1982) studied 100 neurasthenia patients who attended a psychiatric out-patient clinic in Hunan, and found that 93 could be diagnosed as having some forms of depression, 69 had some forms of anxiety state, and 44 had a chronic pain syndrome according to DSM-III criteria (Kleinman, 1982, Table 4). Among the 93 depressive cases, 90 per cent presented headaches as one of their chief complaints, followed by insomnia (78 per cent) and dizziness (73 per cent). The common psychological complaints were poor memory (43 per cent), anxiety (39 per cent), irritability (23 per cent), and disturbing dreams (22 per cent) (Kleinman, 1982, Table 13). The percentage of psychological symptoms elicited from the depressive patients was much higher. All of the 93 cases admitted having some forms of dysphoria including feelings of depression, sadness, displeasure, unhappiness, and irritability. Difficulty in thinking or concentrating was admitted by 84 per cent, with 'mind slowing down' (62 per cent), anhedonia (61 per cent), and worthlessness (60 per cent) among the commonly elicited symptoms (Kleinman, 1982, Table 15). Although the patients were aware of their psychological symptoms, 30 per cent of the patients diagnosed as having a major depressive disorder presented entirely somatic complaints, 70 per cent presented somatopsychic complaints with the somatic ones viewed as the most important, whereas none presented entirely psychological complaints (Kleinman, 1982, Table 12). Kleinman concluded that depression as a disease entity was socially and culturally shaped. Among Chinese depressives, the illness experience was somatized and presented in the form of neurasthenia.

Symptomatology of depression among Chinese has been studied in cross-cultural comparisons. Marsella, Kinzie, and Gordon (1973) showed that the cluster of symptoms characterizing ethnic Chinese depressives differed qualitatively from that characterizing Caucasian depressives. Somatic complaints were more common among Chinese depressives. Marsella (1980) suggested, along the same lines as Kleinman (1977; 1982), that the construct of depression was conceptualized and communicated differently across cultures.

The patterns of depressive symptomatology among Caucasians, Blacks, and Overseas Chinese college students in the United States were compared by Chang (1984), using the Zung Self-rating Depression Scale. She found cultural differences in the configurations and underlying dimensions of the symptoms of depression. The pattern among the Overseas Chinese group was characterized by somatic complaints. For the Black students, the pattern was characterized by a mixture of affective and somatic complaints, whereas that for the White students was characterized by cognitive and existential concerns.

Somatic complaints constitute an important clinical feature not only of depression, but also of other psychiatric illnesses among Chinese (Wong and Chan, 1984). Using a health questionnaire originally designed for psychiatric case identification, Wong and Chan derived a somatic scale which could differentiate between psychiatric patients and control subjects. This scale included questions relating to appetite, physical strength, sleep, headache, pallor, palpitation, and neurasthenia. The item on neurasthenia was originally intended to measure psychological symptoms, but was found to correlate negatively with other psychological symptoms and positively with the somatic symptoms. The sensitivities of the somatic scale were highest for affective psychoses and neurotic disorders but lower for schizophrenic cases. Wong and Chan concluded that somatic symptoms form an important part of the phenomenology of affective psychosis and neurotic disorders for Chinese patients in Hong Kong. These descriptive studies on the manifestations of psychopathology showed that patterns of symptoms among Chinese psychiatric patients differed from those of Western patients. Whether these cultural differences were due to different practices in seeking psychiatric help or basic differences in the nature and aetiology of disorders could not readily be answered from these descriptive studies. However, several groups of aetiological factors have been studied in relation to Chinese psychopathology. In the following sections, three main groups of factors — physical and physiological correlates, social factors, and cognitive factors — will be reviewed.

PHYSICAL AND PHYSIOLOGICAL CORRELATES

Chin and Chin (1969) summarized the research in medical psychology in mainland China between 1949 and 1966. Influenced by the Pavlovian experimental tradition and the support for a more 'scientific' approach to psychology, research on mental illness has adopted a physiological as well as an experimental approach. One of the major foci of research within medical psychology has been the investigation of the physical correlates of mental illness, especially schizophrenia, neurasthenia, mental retardation, and more recently, hyperkinesis.

Neurasthenia is a common diagnosis in China and has been studied in relation to various physiological processes. Kung (1963) found unusually quick electroencephalogram (EEG) reactions to external stimuli and delayed after-effect reactions among neurasthenia patients. He attributed these reactions to a weakening in the tensile strength of the nervous system, which led to direct responses to external stimuli and delay in returning to the normal state.

Chen (1964) used the psychogalvanic reflex (PGR) as a measure of the physiological indications of 'self-sensitivity' among neurasthenic patients. He found that neurasthenic patients who were oversensitive and those who were excessively tired differed from the normal population in their resting scores as well as in their greater reactivity. Chen explained the similarity between the two groups of neurasthenic patients in terms of the lessened selectivity of the brain as a result of the weakening of the tensile strength of brain tissues. Chen, Zhang, Shih, Xu, Chen, and Hu (1980) later utilized electrodermal activity as an index of arousal level to examine psychophysiological deficits of schizophrenia. They found that schizophrenic patients were more overaroused than the normal population. Comparisons of paranoid and non-paranoid schizophrenics showed that the latter group had higher basal levels, more spontaneous electrodermal fluctuations, and slower habituation of response amplitude during repeated stimulation.

Studies of psychopathology among Chinese outside mainland China have placed less emphasis on physical and physiological factors. Instead, greater interest has focused on social and cultural factors. In Hong Kong, two studies have tried to relate biological variables, physique, personality, and mental illness among Chinese men and women (Singer, Chang, and Hsu, 1972; Singer, Lieh-Mak, and Ng, 1976). Compared with the normal population, schizophrenic and neurotic patients had smaller body size and higher linearity whereas, among affective patients, males had larger body size but females had smaller body size. The authors concluded that the correlations they obtained for these variables were similar to those reported for Caucasians.

A more recent investigation has been made by an anatomist who integrated the Chinese meridian system with an anatomic system for measuring posture in studying the relationship between posture types, personality, and mental illness. Plummer (1982) studied the relationship between acupuncture, *tai-chi*, and Rolfing, fields which relate to posture, muscle balance, gait, and the psyche. She suggested that postural homeostasis would be related to physiological as well as psychological homeostasis, and has begun to study these variables among psychiatric patients in Hong Kong.

Studies of physical and physiological correlates of mental disorders among Chinese are few in number. One area of investigation which has suggested possible ethnic differences in physiological factors is alcohol reactivity. Wolff (1972) compared Asian and Caucasian adults and infants in terms of their autonomic responsivity to alcohol. He found more face-flushing among the Asians after alcohol consumption, even after cultural differences in diet and environmental influences were controlled. Wolff suggested that these ethnic differences were due to genetic factors. A similar genetic hypothesis was postulated by Ewing, Rouse, and Pellizzari (1974) who found more face-flushing and higher heart rates among Asian students in the United States. They attempted to explain the lower rates of alcohol abuse among Asians on the basis of the aversive physiological reactions to alcohol. Sue and Nakamura (1984) summarized the evidence on alcohol metabolism and cardio-vascular sensitivity of Chinese and Japanese. They concluded that the physiological responses of these two ethnic groups differed from those of Caucasians although the mechanisms underlying these differences were not yet clear. However, Sue and Nakamura pointed out that the genetic-physiological factors could not explain the different rates of drinking among groups of Chinese and Japanese who differed in terms of socio-cultural factors such as cultural assimilation. They proposed, instead, an integrative model in which physiological factors, socio-cultural factors, and alcohol consumption reciprocally affect one another. Some of these socio-cultural factors will be examined in the next section.

SOCIAL FACTORS

The role of social factors has been emphasized in the theory of behaviour, behaviour deviations, and corrective measures in modern Communist China. Chin and Chin (1969) summarized the theoretical position of medical psychology in China in 1965, a position based on dialectical materialism, according to which psychological activities are regarded as the reflection of social conditions. External influences such as conditions of 'work, *hsueh-hsi* (learning), and living' constitute the conditions of change for the individual. Given different conditions of social life, individuals vary in their 'internal causes' (which include the nervous system, recognition processes, attitudes, and emotions). This theory of behaviour deviation is, however, politicized in its conclusion that, under socialism, a society takes care of its people and thus mental disorders are lessened and more easily remedied. The existence of mental disorders is explained as a remnant of capitalistic society. This polemical social causation theory was prevalent among party officials and mental health professionals up to the fall of the Gang of Four and the Cultural Revolution (Cheung, 1981a).

Since social science was not given important emphasis in China until the 1980s, there have been few empirical studies which specify what social conditions are related to mental disorders and how. These factors have been given more attention in studies from Taiwan and Hong Kong.

Socio-demographic Factors

Socio-demographic data have been included in the large-scale epidemiological studies conducted in Taiwan and Hong Kong. In T.Y. Lin's (1953) original survey of mental disorders in Taiwan, he found a relatively high concentration of total mental disorder in the lower class. The upper class, however, had higher rates for paranoid schizophrenia, manic-depressive psychosis, and psychoneurosis. Hebephrenic schizophrenia, senile psychosis, mental deficiency, psychopathic personality, and alcoholism were more prevalent in the lower class. Lin also found diagnostic differences on the basis of educational status and occupation. While mental deficiency, epilepsy, psychopathic personality, senile psychosis, and alcoholism were more highly concentrated among illiterates and the less educated, schizophrenic reaction, manic-depressive psychosis, and psycho-neurosis were found to be fairly evenly distributed. Among occupational groups, professionals and the unemployed had higher rates of total mental disorders. Results on sex differences indicated higher rates for females on schizophrenic reaction, manic-depressive psychosis, and hysteria. Males had higher rates of mental deficiency and psychopathic personality. In terms of age, the rate of mental disorders for every 1,000 people showed a higher concentration in the middle age-groups than in the younger and older age-groups. Lin concluded that these findings were generally in accord with other cross-cultural surveys.

In their 15-year follow-up survey of the same three communities in Taiwan, Lin, Rin, Yeh, Hsu, and Chu (1969) found similar patterns of distribution across the key socio-demographic variables. Although the prevalence of schizophrenia was still higher among the lower class, there was a significant decrease in its rate among this group. A considerable increase in the prevalence of mental deficiency and psychoneurosis among the uneducated group had occurred.

One of the three communities in these epidemiological studies in Taiwan was further surveyed on the prevalence of psychophysio-logical reactions and their relations to socio-environmental factors (Rin, Chu, and Lin, 1966). Differential rates of psychophysiological reactions were found across the variables of age, sex, marital status, social class, period of migration, and religion. Higher rates were obtained among middle-aged people, the lower-class mainland Chinese, older females, married younger persons, and the older age-group which had converted to Christianity. In conclusion, the authors suggested that these socio-demographic factors shaped the milieu of the individual. The relationships between socio-environmental stresses and psychophysiological reactions varied according to the individual's milieu.

In Hong Kong, Lee (1976; 1981) studied the relationship of sex roles and social class to the prevalence of psychiatric symptoms using the Langner Scale (Langner, 1966). Higher rates of symptoms were found among females, the lower socio-economic group, the less educated, and the older age-groups. Even controlling for education and age, the relationships of stress symptoms to sex and socio-economic status continued to hold. Lee explained the social class differences in terms of general satisfaction with daily life. However, life satisfaction could not account for the sex differences in the symptom rates. Instead, Lee postulated that females were more expressive and willing to admit their personal difficulties, whereas Chinese males, especially those in the lower social class, were less expressive. The greater sex differences in the rate of symptoms among the lower socio-economic group supported his hypothesis.

While these socio-demographic variables provide descriptive information on rates of psychiatric disorders among Chinese, they do not explain the dynamics of psychopathology. More specific social factors have been included in recent studies to explain psychiatric and psychological disorders. In the following discussion these factors will be subsumed under social change, stressors and buffers, and socialization and family dynamics.

Social Change

Chinese societies have undergone rapid and dramatic changes. Some of the patterns of psychopathology observed in one society at a certain period may change in another. Tan (1981) suggested that social and cultural changes in different Chinese societies may modify traditional cultural beliefs and the mode of manifestation of culture-bound syndromes. The sources of social changes that have been studied are migration, modernization, and urbanization.

Migration was offered as a major explanation for the increase of neurotic disorders in the 15-year follow-up study undertaken by Lin,

Rin, Yeh, Hsu, and Chu (1969) in Taiwan. The increase was especially significant among people who had moved to the surveyed communities within the previous 15 years. The rates of psychoneuroses were higher among migrants from within Taiwan and migrants from mainland China than among the original inhabitants of the communities.

The type and the period of migration were studied more closely in the survey by Rin, Chu, and Lin (1966) of psychophysiological reactions in Taiwan. They found that Taiwanese females who had migrated to the community under investigation after the Second World War were particularly at risk. Among the migrants from mainland China, the younger age-group of both sexes and particularly those of the lower class reported more psychophysiological reactions during and after the migration following the Second World War, an exodus which took place under drastic circumstances.

Chinese migration to the United States, as a source of social stress in relation to mental health, has been discussed by Tsai, Teng, and Sue (1981). Abrupt life changes requiring substantial social readjustment, coupled with the social and material deprivation in the new environment, strain the adaptive capacity of the immigrants. Hinkle (1974) found that Chinese immigrants in the United States experienced more medical problems than a comparable age-group of White Americans. The immigrants and their children may experience cultural conflicts, as opposing demands are made on their allegiance to traditional and Western cultures (Sue and Sue, 1971). A high level of distress was also found among Chinese students from Taiwan studying in the United States (Klein, Miller, and Alexander, 1981). Problems of transcultural adaptation for these sojourners were discussed.

Within Chinese societies, social changes have been discussed mainly in terms of modernization and urbanization. The former has been associated with adaptation to Western values and style of life. In the study by Rin, Chu, and Lin (1966) in Taiwan, the prevalence rate of stress reactions was related to identification with traditional or modern values. The traditional value index included items on religion, language used at home, family structure, type of social and recreational activities, and concept of illness. A modern-life contact index was also used, consisting of education, style of dwelling and equipment, household arrangement, frequency of modern social and recreational activities, and contact with modern knowledge through other people. The results showed that those who had high modern-life contact and who at the same time upheld their own traditional value systems were capable of dealing with stress. On the other hand, people with the least modern-life contact and who also lacked a firm identification with their traditional values showed heightened rates of stress reaction.

With increasing urbanization in modern Chinese societies, high-density living has become a topic of concern to mental health professionals. The direct impact of high-density living on mental health is not, however, immediately apparent. In Lin's (1953) epidemiological study in Taiwan, he found a striking difference in the concentration of schizophrenic reaction and neurosis in the central area of each community (which consisted of the market district and business offices). In the years 1961–3, the concentration of schizophrenia in the more densely populated central area was no longer evident (Lin, Rin, Yeh, Hsu, and Chu, 1969). However, a higher rate of neurosis was still observed in the central residential areas.

The population density in Hong Kong is particularly high, and most of the population live in high-rise buildings. These dwellings are also small in size. The relationship between population density and psychiatric stress was a major concern in a biosocial survey conducted by Millar (1976; 1979), the same survey which Lee (1976) used to study the prevalence of stress symptoms. Millar used both neighbourhood density and household density to derive a composite index of population density. She found a small but significant difference in the amount of stress felt by residents in high-, medium-, and low-density situations. In explaining the mild effect on stress despite the extremely high population density, Millar (1979) suggested that Chinese in Hong Kong held a more tolerant attitude towards overcrowding. Over two-thirds of the urban sample reported moderately tolerant or very tolerant attitudes toward high-density living. This tolerance was especially prevalent among the older, the less educated, and the poorer people, and among immigrants from mainland China. Millar concluded that intolerance of high density rather than the actual density itself constituted a source of stress in Hong Kong. Lee (1985) described many coping mechanisms within Hong Kong households which might reduce the need for space. He cautioned, however, that with the fading of the 'immigrant culture', the younger generation born and brought up in Hong Kong may expect the comfort of a spacious living environment and thus may be less tolerant of overcrowding than their parents' generation.

Hwang (1979) in Taiwan proposed a similar explanation for adjustment to high-density living among Chinese. He differentiated two indicators of population density which elicited different types of coping response. The indicator of average size of space utilized by each resident was closely related to other life stresses associated with low socio-economic status. A second indicator — sharing a dwelling with many people — was related to stress, which implied that it might be the interpersonal conflict rather than the lack of space itself which was the source of stress. Residents of dwellings shared by many others adopted various coping strategies to alleviate the stress of living in overcrowded conditions. For individuals who valued the traditional cultural norm of interpersonal co-operation and getting along with others on friendly terms, little conflict and few psychopathological disturbances were experienced. On the other hand, residents in overcrowded dwellings who adopted the individualistic values of self-assertion and personal striving for achievement suffered from more interpersonal hostility and suspicion. They were also more likely to report psychosomatic symptoms and agitated depression.

Like adjustment to urbanization and high-density living, the impact of social change on psychopathology has been explained in terms of the breakdown of traditional Chinese values and social organization. This hypothesis has been used to account for the increasing trend of alcoholism among Chinese. The previous rarity of alcoholism among Chinese has often been noted (Harrell, 1981; Lin, 1953; Lin and Lin, 1982; Singer, 1972; 1974). Harrell (1981) suggested that in the Chinese community, drinking fitted into the system of folk biomedical beliefs and into the pattern of social relations. Lin and Lin (1982) further elaborated this socio-cultural hypothesis, characterizing the traditional pattern of Chinese drinking in terms of drinking with others and drinking with eating. These social prescriptions provided the control mechanism for preventing alcohol abuse. With the adoption of a Western lifestyle and the breakdown of traditional social organization, however, the original control mechanism has lost its importance. Although the prevalence of alcoholism is still relatively low, a rising trend of alcoholism and alcoholic psychoses has been reported in Hong Kong (Singer, 1972; 1974). Similar increases in these trends have been observed in Singapore (Khoo and Fernandez, 1971) and Taiwan (Yeh, 1985).

In the above studies, the socio-cultural hypothesis about Chinese psychopathology has been discussed in general terms. Other studies have focused on the role of stressors and social support in the Chinese culture for explaining and predicting psychopathology.

Stressors and Buffers

Most studies of Chinese psychopathology have been atheoretical. One of the few exceptions is Ko's (1980) Model of Mental Health. Ko proposed an interactionistic model to predict mental health on the basis of pressure and ego-strength. Pressure is a source of stress while ego-strength is the buffer against stress. When internal and external pressure exceeds ego-strength, mental health problems will arise. According to Ko's definition, ego-strength consists of one's tolerance of stress, problem-solving ability, and social support. Huang, Hwang, and Ko in Taiwan (1983) found that objective and subjective life stresses among university students were positively correlated with depressive symptoms. These stressful life events included economic difficulties, interpersonal problems, and academic failure. On the other hand, social support from the family and friends was negatively correlated with depressive scores.

Stressful life events have been studied in greater detail by Hwang (1981). On the basis of the responses by male university students to an adapted version of the Social Readjustment Rating Scale of Holmes and Rahe (1967), Hwang obtained three dimensions for the perception of life events: magnitude, uncontrollability, and stability. High stress events included death of spouse or close relatives, serious illness or accident, divorce, marriage, imprisonment, and bankruptcy. Uncontrollable events usually posed greater stress to the individuals, although some controllable events such as marriage and divorce were equally stressful. Events which were related to one's family and one's career were rated as more stressful than those related to one's life habits such as social activities, diet, and living conditions.

Hwang (1978) further examined interpersonal stress in terms of the nature of the conflicts and the distance in interpersonal relationships. In one's conflicts with others, most emotional uneasiness was found when family members or friends were involved; less conflict and emotional uneasiness were involved with strangers. Hwang explained these differences in terms of the social norms which regulate interpersonal behaviour between people who are related to each other in different ways. These norms are internalized to become interpersonal expectations: one would expect more from family members and friends than from strangers.

Perception of stressful life events was studied by Chan and his associates in Hong Kong (Chan and Chan-Ho, 1983; Chan, Chan-Ho, and Chan, 1984). Using a 69-item event list derived from Paykel,

Prusoff, and Uhlenhuth (1971), they found a similar pattern of upsetting events among university staff and students as were found in the American sample studied by Paykel *et al*. The most upsetting events were death of spouse, death of child, jail sentence, death of close family member, and divorce. The greatest difference in rank between the Hong Kong and the American sample was for divorce, which was considered more upsetting by the Hong Kong sample. The least upsetting events were vacation, a move in the same city, child married with respondent's approval, and wanted pregnancy. Six varimax rotated factors were extracted from the list of events: loss and failure, gain and achievement, environmental and role change, personal catastrophe, minor interpersonal problems, and legal and court-related problems. Chan and his associates suggested that the relationship between stress and illness may be mediated for Chinese people by their social support systems and by their help-seeking behaviour. They recommended that this hypothesis be tested in a multivariate study.

The role of life events as stressors for the individual has been widely accepted. On the other hand, the function of social support is less clear. Social support may act as a 'preceding factor' which prevents the onset of disorders directly, or as an intermediate buffer against the drastic consequences of life changes (Lin, Simeone, Ensel, and Kuo, 1979; Lin, Dean, and Ensel, 1981). In a study of a representative sample of Chinese Americans in Washington, DC, Lin *et al.* (1979) found that although stressors were positively related to the incidence of psychiatric symptoms, the negative correlation between social support and psychiatric symptoms was larger. The social support scale which was used in this study focused on non-kin support, and included items measuring involvement in Chinese activities and associations. Although involvement in the Chinese subculture was an important source of social support for some Chinese, items measuring involvement with neighbours and friends nearby, as well as with friends from their home country, were found to be more important in the assessment of overall social support. The results of this study did not, however, show any relationship between stressors and social support. There was no strong evidence supporting either the 'preceding factor' explanation or the 'buffering' explanation.

Ko (1980) included social support as one of the components of ego-strength in his interactionistic model of mental health. He proposed that psychopathology had a positive relationship with pressure and a negative relationship with ego-strength. The role of social support in the manifestation of depression was studied by Huang, Hwang, and Ko (1983) as a test of Ko's model. Support from the family and friends was measured in terms of 'adaptation', 'partnership', 'growth', 'affection', and 'resolve'. The overall scores on social support from family and friends were negatively correlated with depression scores. Again, social support on its own may be insufficient in moderating the relationship between stress and depression. Huang *et al.* (1983) suggested that the other components of ego-strength — tolerance and problem-solving ability — should be included in the prediction of depression. This suggestion awaits empirical testing.

The role of social support has been further studied in terms of resources in the help-seeking process. Lin, Tardiff, Donetz, and Goresky (1978) found that Chinese mental patients in Vancouver tended to resort to their family for support before seeking help from medical professionals, and were finally referred to mental health professionals after a period of delay. Similar patterns of reliance on the family and close friends were found among students and psychiatric patients in Hong Kong (Cheung, Lau, and Wong, 1984; Cheung, 1984). Most psychiatric patients consulted their families or friends about their problems prior to seeking professional help. When they did seek help, most approached a medical physician first (Cheung *et al.*, 1984). As a consequence, professional consultation with psychiatrists was usually much delayed.

Chinese who believed their problems to be primarily psychological tended to turn to their families and friends for support and not to seek any professional help at all. Cheung (1984) found that, among Hong Kong university students, friends were the major source of support for psychological symptoms listed on the Langner Scale (Langner 1966). Few of these students would seek help from professionals or, indeed, seek any help at all for these problems. However, for physiological and psychophysiological problems, the medical physician would be the major source of professional consultation. Similar reliance on the medical physician has been found in another study with university students in Hong Kong (Cheung, Lee, and Chan, 1983). Given five common health or mental health problems faced by students, including weakness and fatigue, tension and anxiety, difficulty in sleeping, 'hollow-emptiness', and headache, most Chinese students would attempt a variety of self-help measures initially. If the problems persisted or became serious, the students would first approach a medical doctor for most of the problems except 'hollow-emptiness'. In the latter case, the students would turn more to their own primary social network, namely, friends and family.

The nature of support from family members has been studied in relation to the mental health of secondary-school students in a lower socio-economic community in Hong Kong by Chan (1983). Social support was measured in terms of tangible aid, concern and encouragement, information and advice, and feedback. For the 498 male and female students, most support came from their mothers. Support from fathers, siblings, or peers was generally rarer. Support from the family was negatively related to mental health, as indicated by the smaller number of problems reported on the Mooney Problem Check List (Mooney and Gordon, 1950). Support from friends or peers was much less related to mental health. Among family members, support from the father was even more strongly related to mental health than that from the mother, especially in connection with school and personality problems. While Chan (1983) found a direct relationship between mental health and family support, there was also evidence that the latter provided a moderating influence when severe stress from life events such as examination failure was experienced. Chan pointed out the important role of fathers as a source of support to adolescents, and the need for fathers in Hong Kong to become more concerned with their children's problems.

Socialization and Family Dynamics

The influence of the Chinese family on mental health extends beyond its role as a source of social support. Given the central importance of the family as a unit over the individual in Chinese society, mental health professionals have focused on the functions and interpersonal relationships within the family system to explain mental health issues (Li, 1985; Lin and Lin, 1981; Singer, 1976a). Li's simple summary, for example, tried to point out how the mental health of Chinese in mainland China was affected by the family, in contrast to the manifestation of mental disorders in the West. In particular, he pointed to the care of the young and the elderly, and the stability of the marriage institution. His conclusions were based primarily on personal experience as a psychologist and were illustrated by case material.

Singer (1976a) wrote from his experience in psychiatric practice in Hong Kong and discussed major sources of problems in the Chinese family, especially in view of cultural changes in Hong Kong. He observed that a number of influences are causing present-day Hong Kong families to become smaller. These influences include 'urbanization, housing shortage, immigration, notions of romantic love, of value of the conjugal family and of individualism, and the greater independence of women' (p. 47). He found the main sources of family conflict to be the mother- and daughter-in-law relationship, the challenge to parental authority, and the rising position of women in society and in the family. This change in the role of women also threatens the traditional stability of Chinese marriage.

Among studies of the relationship between the family and mental health, the most important function of the family which has been studied is that of socialization. Chinese patterns of socialization are reviewed in detail by Ho in Chapter 1 of this book. He discusses the literature on child-rearing practices in conjunction with impulse control and achievement. Self-control, emotional self-reliance, and frustration habituation are emphasized in traditional Chinese culture (Ward, 1970) and have been cited as possible sources of resistance to stress and mental illness (Lee, 1982; Tseng and Hsu, 1969–70).

The push for achievement, on the other hand, has been suggested as a source of pressure for Chinese children (Law, 1978; Singer, 1976a; Yeh, 1985), especially for the eldest son (T.Y. Lin, 1984). The high value that Chinese parents have placed on education, coupled with the intense competition for the limited number of places in higher education, have been cited as reasons for school phobia, psychosomatic disorders, and neurotic disorders (Law, 1978; 1979). The level of anxiety among secondary-school students in Hong Kong, for example, was found to be higher than that in the United States (Cheung and Lee, 1984). Similar concerns have been raised in Taiwan. T.Y. Lin (1984) described the ill effects among schoolchildren as a result of the pressure to do well in examinations in order to enter prestigious schools. He labelled this social phenomenon the 'Narrow Gate Syndrome'. Given the push from parents and teachers, schoolchildren strive for scholastic success so as to gain approval from their parents and praise from their teachers. The parents' values on educational success are incorporated into the children's own aspirations. Consequently, the children's fear of failure at examinations often leads to anxiety, depression, and psychosomatic symptoms. In his description of the 'Narrow Gate Syndrome', Lin has tried to delineate the process of socialization in the Chinese family. Support for this socialization process may be found in Ho's discussion on achievement in Chapter 1.

Singer (1976a) cautioned that observations on Chinese socialization practices should take into account social-class differences as well as social changes in different Chinese societies. The extent to which these socialization practices may be conducive or detrimental to mental health is further complicated by the differential rates of recognition of disorders in the Chinese family. Previously, childhood psychiatric disorders were often ignored or dismissed by parents. This shortfall in identification must then qualify earlier suggestions that such occurrences were rare among Chinese children (Lin, 1985). Recent concern with children's mental health may be strengthened by a general increase in the educational level of parents, greater access to mental health facilities, and smaller family size. With fewer children in a family, more attention is paid to the individual child. This situation is epitomized by the surge of interest in mainland China in the mental health of the single child, since the implementation of the one-child policy — as discussed in an earlier section of this chapter.

The change in social context may in turn change the meaning of certain socialization practices. Take the case of harsh punishment, which was the traditional means of maintaining parental authority and children's obedience. Wu (1981) suggested that harsh discipline was one of the two mechanisms for training filial piety, the other being the inducement of physical and emotional closeness to ensure a lifelong bond. Wu hypothesized that parents who have not undertaken a period of socialization of a child, which creates a bond of attachment with the child, would be more likely to inflict abuse on the child. He cited as examples the acknowledged custom of cruel treatment of stepchildren by Chinese stepmothers, and the institutionalized practice of child abuse against adopted daughters. Child abuse as a mental health problem in Taiwan and Hong Kong has been recognized only in recent years, whereas previously harsh punishment would not have been considered as abuse or identified as a mental health problem. The assumption that a hierarchical parent-child relationship prevails in the Chinese family needs to be re-examined in modern Chinese societies.

COGNITIVE FACTORS

Explanatory Models

In line with the attention given to cognitive social learning approaches in the study of personality, psychopathology, and psychotherapy, cognitive schema have been used to explain psychological problems among Chinese. Mechanic (1972; 1977) and Kleinman (1980) have discussed the concept of explanatory models in relation to illness behaviour as it varies across cultures. Kleinman referred to explanatory models as 'the notions about an episode of sickness and its treatment that are employed by all those engaged in the clinical process', including the patients and the practitioners (p. 105). Explanatory models are used to conceptualize particular illness episodes of the individual and include questions regarding aetiology, the onset of symptoms, pathophysiology, the course of sickness, and treatment. Kleinman used the example of the illness experience and the behaviour of Chinese patients to illustrate the importance of understanding the cognitive constructions of patients in the healing process.

On the basis of his observations that Chinese patients rarely complained of anxiety, depression, and psychological problems, Kleinman (1977; 1980) suggested a model of somatization to explain how Chinese managed dysphoric affect and affective disorders. When the dysphoric affective states were initially recognized, Chinese patients and their families used non-specific terms to refer to these feelings without differentiation. These feelings may further be suppressed through minimization or denial, dissociated and expressed in isolation, or substituted for by somatic preoccupation. Kleinman proposed that these 'cognitive coping processes' may be unique to the Chinese culture.

Kleinman and Lin (1981) acknowledged that somatized affects were not the only externalizing cognitive coping process for the Chinese. However, they admitted knowing little about the other coping responses such as experiencing and expressing distress in moral, cosmological, or social terms. Further, the assumption that affective factors are suppressed in the somatic presentation of symptoms among Chinese has been questioned (Cheung, 1982; 1985b; Cheung and Lau, 1982; Cheung, Lee, and Chan, 1983; White, 1982). These authors found that Chinese used multiple causes and solutions in their conceptualization of problems. Somatic conditions were not considered to be the predominant or the only causes.

Cheung, Lee, and Chan (1983) studied the cognitive schema used by university students in Hong Kong to explain five commonly experienced health and mental health problems. Each problem was attributed to multiple causes including somatic, psychological, social, situational, and existential factors. No single category of causal factors was identified by the students as the prevailing causal factor for the five problems. The pattern of multiple causal attributions differed significantly across the problems. The problems of headache and weakness were seen as predominantly caused by physical illness and a dysfunctional somatic lifestyle. Sleeping difficulties were commonly attributed to psychological factors. Situational factors, especially those related to school problems, were cited as the major causes for the problem of anxiety. The problem of emptiness was attributed mostly to interpersonal and existential causes, with little reference being made to somatic or situational factors. The nature of the attributed cause of a problem was related to the intended solution only when a problem was mild. Most Chinese students indicated that, when their problems were severe, they would seek the professional help of medical doctors, except in the case of emptiness.

Psychiatric patients in Hong Kong were also found to describe their problems using multiple categories which included psychological as well as somatic factors (Cheung and Lau, 1982; Cheung, Lau, and Wong, 1984). Cheung and Lau further found that patients at three medical settings differed in the expression of their reasons for consultation. In contrast to patients attending a psychiatric clinic, psychiatric patients at a prison clinic mostly cited the process leading up to their arraignment and the court's referral as their reasons for consultation. This study illustrates the important role played by situational factors in eliciting expectations and responses from Chinese patients. The psychiatric patients' previous experience in medical settings where they expected to have their physical symptoms treated may have led them to present somatic symptoms in these settings. These presentations might have biased the earlier suggestions of a somatization tendency among Chinese. Cheung (1982) suggested that 'Chinese seeking help at different medical and non-medical settings may constitute different subgroups who, through diverse paths of help-seeking, would present their problems in different ways' (p. 1343). The simple somatization hypothesis derived only from observations on patients needs to be refined.

The Locus of Control

Chinese culture has been described as situation-centred in that the behaviour of the individual is often determined by interpersonal transactions within specific situations (Hsieh, Shybut, and Lotsof, 1969; Hsu, 1971b; Kuo, Gray, and Lin, 1979; Kleinman, 1980; Kleinman and Lin, 1981). In Chapter 4 of this book, Yang discusses the literature on the internal-external locus of control which shows that Chinese subjects scored higher on externality than Anglo-Americans. Kuo *et al.* (1979) further found that the locus of control was an important determinant of symptoms of psychological distress among Chinese Americans. Chinese Americans who believed that one's rewards in life were contingent upon social forces which were beyond one's personal control tended to score higher on an index of psychiatric impairment and on a depression scale, and manifested more symptoms such as low self-esteem, apprehension, insomnia, headaches, and other psychophysiological symptoms. The authors asserted that internally oriented Chinese Americans would be better prepared to deal with adjustment problems as they would feel that they had better control over the adversities of their lives.

In models of helping and coping, the locus of control has been incorporated into theories of attribution and helplessness (Brickman, Rabinowitz, Karuza, Coates, Cohn, and Kidder, 1982; Seligman, 1975; 1978; Seligman, Abramson, Semmel, and Von Baeyer, 1979). Brickman *et al.* distinguished between the attribution of responsibility for a problem and the attribution of responsibility for its solution. This distinction was expounded in a cross-cultural context by Sue (1978). Emphasis on the internal or the external locus of control in the conceptualization of the problem and on the internal or the external locus of responsibility in the conceptualization of the solution distinguished the mental health approaches among different ethnic minority groups in the United States.

The attribution of psychological problems to external factors has been considered a protective mechanism by Yang (1982b) and Lee (1982; 1985). An important external attribution for success or failure in interpersonal and person-object relationships among Chinese may be embodied in the concept of *yuan* (緣). Originating in Buddhism, the concept of *yuan* is used as a *post hoc* explanation for a personal outcome by alluding to fate, predetermination, and external control (Lee, 1982). In the modern application of the concept, Yang found that *yuan* may be used as a force of destiny to foster interpersonal relationships, as a psychological state which promotes the development of such relationships, or as a description of the harmonious relationship itself. As a stable external factor, *yuan* serves the function of maintaining interpersonal harmony by attributing the success or failure of relationships to forces beyond one's personal control, thereby ridding oneself or others of the responsibility for the outcome. Thus, *yuan* not only protects the individual by enabling him or her to save face, but also saves the face of others. It helps the individual to rationalize failure, by reducing his or her self-blame and blame of others. Both Yang (1982b) and Lee (1985) argued that the belief in *yuan* is a defence mechanism which may be conducive to mental health, although excessive dependence on these concepts may impede active attempts to cope. Yang, however, suggested that, in the modern application of the concept, *yuan* may be seen as an unstable factor which may be changed by individual or social efforts, whereupon internal control may be exercised.

The contribution to mental health of the belief in *yuan* was studied by Huang, Hwang, and Ko (1983). They found that attribution to *yuan* was used with events relating to the affiliative orientation, especially in positive instances. Students who scored low on depression tended to attribute negative interpersonal relationships to lack of *yuan* more frequently than the students who scored high on depression. It is consistent with Yang's (1982b) suggestion that university students did not view *yuan* as an entirely deterministic and stable force. In the same study, it was also found that depression scores were highest among those students who attributed negative life events to internal, stable, and global factors. Depressive students tended to attribute both positive and negative events to uncontrollable factors.

Chung and Hwang (1981) studied the attributed causes of school performance from the perspective of learned helplessness among high-school students in Taiwan. Six attributional factors were extracted, representing internal versus external locus of control, and stable versus unstable dimensions. Learned helplessness was related to the pattern that attributed academic failure to causal factors which are internal and stable in locus of control, such as lack of ability. At the same time, these students tended not to attribute their academic success to stable internal factors, including ability and effort. Learned helplessness was manifested in their expectation of low performance, their lack of persistence in studying, and in their poor self-esteem. These students were found to have a lower sense of well-being and poorer academic achievement.

The perception of controllability and stability was related to the magnitude of stress resulting from life events in Hwang's (1981) study using university students in Taiwan. A negative linear relationship was found between controllability and magnitude of stress. Uncontrollable life events were perceived to be more stressful. Stability was not directly related to the magnitude of stress, with both stable and unstable life events rated among the more stressful. Hwang suggested that these perceptual dimensions were important psychological considerations in coping.

Coping Strategies

The pattern of coping strategies among Chinese has been studied by Hwang in Taiwan (1977; 1978; 1979). From interviews with 180 married men of different age-groups and socio-economic status, patterns of responses were identified for the coping strategies used to deal with daily problems. Four major types of strategy were classified. The strategy of relying on oneself included facing the problem and devising a solution, enduring and persevering, striving, and having confidence. The second major category involved asking for help from one's social resources, and especially the use of private interpersonal relationships, such as those with friends and relatives. The third coping strategy was through appeals to supernatural power or prayers for blessings. The fourth category was related to the more passive Taoist philosophy of doing nothing and letting nature take its course. Hwang found that these coping strategies were not contradictory or mutually exclusive. Subjects often mentioned the use of more than one strategy for dealing with their problems. From these interview responses, it may be seen that the common coping strategies adopted by Taiwanese men were related to cognitive processes, either by the more passive means of learning to live with their problems, or facing the problems and persevering. The more active, self-reliant, and problem-solving approaches were adopted more often by subjects from the higher social class and from the younger age-group.

Hwang (1978) further developed six factor scores for coping strategies, based on the responses of the same group of married men to a structured questionnaire on coping dispositions. He identified three patterns of coping which were relevant to the process of dealing with different types of interpersonal conflict. The first group of men were described as 'men of action'. When involved in interpersonal conflicts with persons outside the family, they preferred to face reality, analyse the situation cognitively, and take some immediate action. They would attribute blame for the conflict either to themselves or to others. The symptom patterns associated with this pattern included agitated depression, psychosomatic disorders, and sleep disturbance. Active coping mechanisms were also employed by the second group of men who were characterized by their task orientation. They differed from the first group in terms of their self-assertion and competitiveness. When involved in interpersonal conflicts, they tended to attribute the fault to others; they relied on themselves to solve their own problems. Like the first group, they also had symptom patterns which were psychosomatic in nature, especially in the oral or gastro-intestinal system. The third pattern of coping was more passive in nature and was used by men who were inclined to strive for excellence in order to gain recognition. These men would persevere and ignore the problems instead of analysing them objectively. Their typical symptom pattern was disturbance in cognitive functioning, social withdrawal, and existential complaints.

In the study by Cheung, Lee, and Chan (1983) in Hong Kong of university students' intended solution to five common problems, psychological endurance and active coping were also found to be adopted frequently when the problems were mild. Psychological endurance included telling oneself to be calm, to accept or forget the problem, and to control one's thoughts. Active coping methods included analysing the problem, resetting goals, and working harder. These self-reliant solutions were used when the students were faced with mild problems of anxiety, feelings of emptiness, and sleep disturbances. But these cognitive coping methods gave way to consultation with medical professionals when the problems became severe.

Similar reliance on self-directed psychological approaches in the initial attempts to cope with psychiatric problems was found among psychiatric patients in Hong Kong (Cheung, Lau, and Wong, 1984). Patients at a public clinic, who were mostly from a lower socioeconomic background, differed from patients attending a private psychiatric clinic. About half of the public patients sought professional assistance for their initial problems, although one-third of them also resorted to self-directed methods of coping, especially by ignoring the problem, controlling oneself, or avoiding the situation.

In contrast, the private patients were not inclined to seek any professional assistance at all for their initial problems. Instead, more of them would consider that nothing could be done except to accept the reality through self-control or passive endurance. The apparent difference in the passive versus active coping styles among the subjects of higher social class in this study and in Hwang's (1977) study in Taiwan has to be viewed in the context of the different types of subject employed. In the former study, the subjects were self-selected psychiatric patients who were already seeking treatment. In the latter case, the subjects were male heads of household sampled on the basis of an age and socio-economic status matrix.

The tendency to resort to self-directed coping strategies may be understood in terms of the Confucian tradition of self-discipline. Wu (1982) suggested that stress avoidance was associated with the person's ability to 'correct the mind and train the temperament' (p. 297). Self-discipline implies that a person has an even temperament and is not easily disturbed, and that therefore his or her social conflicts and psychological stress are diluted. The cultural ideal expects self-discipline of persons with high education and high social standing. If this expectation is valid, educational level should be related to the use of self-related cognitive coping strategies. This hypothesis awaits further empirical testing.

Shame and Guilt

A popular distinction between Oriental and Western cultures has been in terms of shame and guilt. Influenced by Freud's notion of the role of guilt in the development of Western civilization, anthropologists and sociologists have attempted to investigate the differences between shame cultures and guilt cultures (Benedict, 1947; Mead, 1937; Leighton and Kluckhohn, 1947). Chinese societies have been described as shame oriented (Eberhard, 1967; Hsu, 1949).

C.L. Chu (1973) suggested two major influences on the Chinese shame culture: Confucianism and humanism. He defined shame in terms of an interpersonal orientation in which behaviour would be compared to social norms, and guilt in terms of an intrapsychic orientation in which behaviour would be compared to one's personal standards. Confucianism was oriented towards shame through its emphasis on social norms and reference to ideal types as models of behaviour. At the same time, humanistic concerns in Chinese culture placed great importance on harmonious interpersonal relationships, especially among the extended family. Socialization and control were exercised through social sanctions. The roots of guilt-orientation in Chinese culture were traced to Buddhism and Christianity. Comments on Chu's paper at the 1973 Symposium on the Character of the Chinese have raised issues such as the lack of a clear-cut distinction between shame and guilt, and the lack of sufficient evidence from folk culture, apart from the ideals expounded in classical literature. The roles of shame and guilt in Oriental societies have also been discussed in depth by Wilson (1974) from the perspectives of socialization and moral development.

Yap (1965b; 1971) criticized the dichotomy between shame and guilt and considered it to be unhelpful in understanding affective disorders. He found no grounds for distinguishing between 'depression with guilt' and 'depression without guilt'. He argued that the earlier attempts at distinguishing between shame cultures and guilt cultures were futile and concluded that 'it is increasingly clear that the opposition of "shame" to "guilt" is intellectualistic, arbitrary, and without empirical justification' (Yap, 1965b, p. 100). He suggested that it would be more useful to conceptualize shame and guilt in a linear order, from unconscious guilt feelings, to conscious guilt feelings, to conscious moral shame feelings. Conscious shame feelings would be generated by the anticipation of discovery of wrong conduct by others, whereas the two guilt feelings would not be witnessed by others. While all these feelings would assume the acceptance of a moral standard and a sense of moral obligation to conform, the degree of internalization would be strongest with unconscious guilt feelings. According to Yap, this unconscious guilt feeling would be less pathogenic than the other conscious feelings. Using this model of linear ordering, Yap (1965b) found lower incidences of guilt and feelings of unworthiness among Chinese depressives than among Western depressives. In a later study (Yap, 1971), this cultural difference was not replicated. Unfortunately, however, Yap's attempts at cross-cultural comparisons of shame and guilt suffered from problems of definition, the same defects in earlier studies which Yap himself had criticized.

In addition to having a role as aetiological concepts, shame and guilt have been cited as important constructs in the understanding of social dynamics among Chinese in response to mental disorders. Lin and Lin (1981) described the dynamics of shame and guilt as a complicated mix in the family of the afflicted. Shame would be felt by the family, especially the head of the family, and not by the afflicted, towards the outside world. Lin and Lin suggested that the stigma attached to mental illness might originate in the family's fear of exposure to criticism and disgrace. Guilt over mental illness might be felt by the afflicted towards their family or by the family towards the afflicted as well as towards ancestors. However, no recent attempt has been made to provide any empirical support for the delineation of these processes. It would be interesting to test Lin and Lin's hypothesis that shame may be related to different views on the aetiology of mental illness, including moral, psychological, and religious causes.

TREATMENT

Given the lack of a distinct psychological theory of mental disorders in traditional Chinese medicine, forms of treatment have not distinguished between psychological and physical approaches. In traditional medical treatment, the state of mind and the state of health are considered simultaneously. The relevance of psychological factors to the cause and treatment of physical and mental health problems has been acknowledged. However, although psychological approaches have been used in traditional medicine, there have been few descriptions of or research reports on the detailed process of the treatment. Traditional forms of mental health care in Chinese societies have been summarized by Lin (1981), Tseng (1973b; 1975b), and Wu (1982).

Traditional Chinese medical treatment of so-called 'insanity' has tended to use herbs (Tseng, 1973b), coupled with diet, acupuncture, moxibustion, and other measures intended to restore internal balance. It has been suggested that Chinese mental patients distrust talk therapies (Kleinman, 1977; 1981; Kleinman and Lin, 1981). Wu (1982), however, pointed out that these findings were contradictory to the fundamental principle of traditional Chinese medicine which emphasized the psychological aetiology of disease. He found that in Chinese medical texts, the psychological approach, though not treated independently, was an important aspect of the health care system. Human emotions were included as prominent explanations of pathology and were noted in diagnosis. The emphasis on emotion may be missed because it is often expounded in the form of preventive measures such as the promotion of a balanced or disciplined life, the regulation of emotions and desire, and adjustment to physical changes.

Emotions have been manipulated by therapeutic procedures in the traditional treatment of illnesses which were believed to have been caused by emotions. Wu (1982) located 15 illness episodes in historical documents, popular literature, and personal notes which supported the psychotherapeutic approach. Counter-emotions were used to treat emotional illnesses including those due to an 'imbalance of emotions', 'sickness with longing' (being 'lovesick'), and 'delusion-induced illness'. In all of these historical episodes, the Chinese physician attempted to achieve the cure 'directly' by intervening in the patient's daily life or social relations. These social realities were believed to be the 'true' causes of sickness; solutions to these immediate problems would provide the cure. In this direct approach, the Chinese physician side-stepped the talking procedures, intended to provide insight, which are used in most Western psychotherapies. Wu concluded that traditional medical models of aetiology and treatment included psychotherapeutic procedures, although Chinese practitioners did not label their treatment as such. In traditional medical treatment, discussions about psychosocial problems would have been incorporated in the four means of diagnosis — inspection (*wang* 望), interrogation (*wén* 問), auditory and olfactory perception (*wen* 聞), and palpation of the pulses (*ch'ieh* 切). There was thus no need for a separate form of psychotherapy.

The relevance of Western talk therapies, especially those oriented towards gaining insight, has been raised by many mental health professionals working with Chinese clients (Cheung, 1981b; Kleinman, 1977; Kleinman and Lin, 1981; Lin, 1982; Lin and Lin, 1978; Sue, Ino, and Sue, 1983; Sue and Kirk, 1975; Sue and Sue, 1973; Sue and Sue, 1972). Some psychiatrists (Kleinman, 1977; Tseng, 1975a) have suggested that Chinese have difficulty expressing their emotions in clinical situations. Wu (1982), however, pointed out that Chinese have rich although subtle ways to display their emotions. While direct and full expression of feelings may be considered inappropriate under certain circumstances, there are culturally based 'display rules' for communicating emotions without resorting to open verbal discussion. Wu suggested that the Chinese patient may expect an 'authoritative' doctor to have the competence to detect physical or psychological disorders from these clues and 'non-verbal leakages', so that the patient does not need to make elaborate verbal complaints.

Expectations about treatment among Chinese clients often differ from the assumptions stemming from Western psychotherapies. Findings on Chinese expectations about counselling have mostly been obtained in studies of international students in the United States, among whom Chinese students formed a subgroup (Alexander, Workneh, Klein, and Miller, 1976; Tan, 1967; Yuen and Tinsley, 1981). Tan found that Asian students expected their counsellors to be more directive and authoritative. However, the small sample of Asian students in Tan's study limited the degree of generalization possible from his results. Using a more comprehensive questionnaire on expectancies and a sample of international students balanced in terms of acculturation, Yuen and Tinsley differentiated between the pattern of expectancies of Chinese students and those of American, Iranian, and African students. The Chinese students scored low on responsibility, motivation, openness, confrontation, and concreteness. They expressed more concern about their counsellor's being courteous, respecting their privacy, and keeping a distant and smooth relationship. Yuen and Tinsley concluded that, because of these expectancies and their unfamiliarity with counselling as a helping resource, Chinese students may be less inclined to approach professional counselling services for solutions to their psychological problems.

Lack of access to psychotherapeutic services has been given as one of the reasons that Chinese do not seek professional help or only approach medical physicians for their emotional problems (Cheung, 1984; Sue and Sue, 1977). Cheung pointed out that there are few trained psychotherapists and counsellors in Chinese societies. Only a small number of clients can therefore be served. In mental health settings, medication is the major form of treatment. The heavy caseload of psychiatrists discourages involvement in psychotherapy. Even in American society where psychological services are more common, there are other cultural and social barriers to counselling. Sue and Sue identified these barriers as language difficulties, value conflicts, and differences in expectations from counselling: there are few bilingual and bicultural counsellors to whom Chinese Americans would readily relate; Western insight-oriented talk therapies are considered to be culture bound and class bound.

What forms of psychotherapy, then, would be more appropriate for Chinese clients? Little empirical research has been addressed to this issue. Counselling process and outcome studies in Chinese societies are limited by the number of trained counsellors who could participate in the studies. Most of the reports in the literature are based on case-studies using Western treatment methods on an individual patient or in a hospital ward. Cheng and his associates in Taiwan (Cheng and Fan, 1976; Cheng and Lui, 1976; Cheng and Wu, 1977) studied the effectiveness of non-directive and directive counselling on high-school and university students. In short-term counselling which involved only one or two sessions, the directive approach was found to be more effective in relieving tension and worries initially. On the other hand, Cheng and Wu found that the non-directive approach was superior in long-term counselling, and refuted the belief that, given the 'authoritarian personality' of the Chinese (see Yang, Chapter 4 in this volume), the directive approach to counselling would be preferred. Generalization from these results, which were based on circumscribed problems among students in an experimental situation, may, however, be limited.

Psychological counselling constitutes only a small part of the various psychiatric services available to Chinese. Tseng (1975b) outlined the utilization of different services for various psychiatric problems by high, middle, and low social classes in Taiwan. The choice of services used depended on the nature of the problems and the social background of the clients. For major psychiatric disorders, the most common form of treatment for patients from all social classes was modern psychiatry. For the lower social class, shamanism was still part of familiar daily activities and served a wide range of psychiatric and medical problems. For minor psychiatric disorders with predominantly somatic symptoms, the upper social class utilized Western medicine, while more of the lower social class used traditional medicine. The middle class used both types of medical service. For general psychological problems, it was mainly clients from the upper social class who utilized psychological counselling. For such problems, the middle and the lower social classes were more likely to resort to fortune-telling, physiognomy, and divination. Tseng noted that throughout all these forms of psychiatric care, there was an orientation towards the Taoist value of harmony and regulation in the natural world as the means for obtaining a condition of normality. The clients' choice of the available services was based on their beliefs about the services and the nature of their problems. Often they utilized several kinds of service simultaneously. Tseng concluded that psychiatric care in Chinese societies may be provided in various ways and that folk and traditional forms of care should be accepted. The role played by folk-healers in Chinese societies has likewise been emphasized by researchers and scholars who have studied Chinese health care systems (Kleinman, 1980; Kleinman and Gale, 1982; Kleinman, Kunstadter, Alexander, and Gale, 1975; Lee, 1975; 1980). Indigenous resources have been utilized more systematically under schemes providing community mental health care in the People's Republic of China. The community mental health system there has been described by visitors like Ho (1974b), Kleinman and Mechanic (1979), Y.C. Lu (1978), the Sidels (Sidel, 1973; Sidel and Sidel, 1972; Sidel and Sidel, 1973), and by local professionals like Shen (1985) and Xia and his associates (Xia, 1985; Xia, Yan, and Wang, 1980). In large cities such as Shanghai and Beijing, resources at different levels of the community are co-ordinated to provide continuing services for psychiatric patients. For example, in Shanghai, a three-tier network at the municipal, district, and community levels is set up to mobilize co-operation among medical personnel, employers, family members, and neighbourhood committees in providing a comprehensive plan of treatment for the patients (Xia *et al.*, 1980). Neighbours, retired workers, and family members help to observe the patients' condition, to guide and educate them, to solve social or psychological problems, and to administer prescribed medication. The mobilization of these community resources not only helps to alleviate the burden on mental health professionals, but in fact provides better after-care in a supportive and familiar community. This Chinese model of community mental health holds much promise for psychiatric care in Chinese societies where a shortage of professionals will continue for a long time to come, and where modern psychiatric and psychological forms of treatment are still foreign to many patients. The literature at present available on these systems is still confined to descriptive reports. Despite the enthusiasm expressed by international visitors, the effectiveness of these programmes still needs to be demonstrated in empirical studies.

SUMMARY AND CONCLUSIONS

This chapter has examined the Chinese concepts of, and approaches to, mental health and psychopathology. Studies of epidemiology, aetiology, and treatment have been reviewed. Some of the key issues in the study of Chinese psychopathology have been discussed within the context of the available studies. Comparisons of studies are, however, difficult, since different definitions and methodologies are often used. In addition, many of the studies are only descriptive or are weak in research design. The findings are thus more suggestive than definitive.

Lin, Kleinman, and Lin (1981) criticized the quantitative epidemiological surveys of Chinese populations as 'superficial and culturally naive'. They suggested that epidemiological studies of culture-bound syndromes and somatization would help to explain how Chinese culture influenced psychopathology. However, epidemiological studies alone will remain descriptive in nature. Studies need to be based on theories, in order to advance the understanding of Chinese psychopathology. Despite numerous studies on various topics derived from Western theories, there is no core theory of Chinese psychopathology to integrate the range of themes being investigated.

The present review of the Chinese concepts of mental health and the traditional systems of mental health care suggests that modern Western psychiatric models do not provide an adequate paradigm for the study of these indigenous concepts. Some of the early studies, such as those on shame and guilt or on somatization, which were based on a Western conceptual framework, have forged dichotomies of the underlying mental processes. Empirical studies of patients and normal subjects have found that Chinese adopt multiple causal attributions and coping strategies in dealing with their problems. These cultural characteristics suggest the importance of an interactionistic paradigm, in which psychological processes, somatic factors, and the situational and social contexts all contribute to an understanding of Chinese psychopathology. A systems model is needed to examine the role of these multiple factors in the precipitation, manifestation, and recognition of psychological disturbances, and in seeking help and treatment for them. Interestingly, the interactionistic and organismic approaches found in Oriental systems of medicine have been advocated in recent calls for Western medicine to move towards a biopsychosocial model of medicine (for example, by Schwartz, 1980). Such a theoretical paradigm would provide a more relevant and useful research framework for the study of psychopathology among the Chinese.

6 The Social Psychology of Chinese People

MICHAEL HARRIS BOND AND KWANG-KUO HWANG

Balance is the great schema of the cosmos;
Harmony is the universal path of life as a whole.

(Adapted from Chuang Tzu)

INTRODUCTION

The legends and folk stories of a culture often reveal the central preoccupations which inform day-to-day behaviour. Solomon (1971, Chapter 2) discusses one such traditional tale taken from the Chinese theatre. The protagonist, Jen-kuei Hsueh, is an accomplished soldier who left his pregnant wife 18 years before to fight a distant campaign for the emperor. Returning home, he notices a young man shooting wild geese with great skill. Provoked, he challenges the youth to a test of marksmanship. The rival readily accepts whereupon Hsueh immediately puts an arrow through his heart, saying 'a soldier like me could not let another live if he was a superior in marksmanship with the weapons in which I excel'.

Of course, it turns out that the youth is Hsueh's son whom he has never seen. The remorse of the father is tempered by the fact that the son has violated two cultural imperatives. First, he did not recognize his father: so strong are the bonds of family and the imperatives of filial piety that a son should know his father regardless of any factors which may disguise his identity. Secondly, the son has committed the cardinal sin in the Chinese tradition: he has challenged his father and thereby affronted social order. As a Chinese proverb tersely puts the matter, 'In a family of a thousand, only one is the master'. A threat to the family is a threat to the body politic and a violation of heaven's mandate. It must therefore be ruthlessly put down.

This disturbing story underscores the Chinese preoccupation with social order in the same way as the Oedipal drama underscores the Western preoccupation with individual freedom. One purpose of this chapter is to show how this cultural concern for harmony-within-hierarchy can be used to explain Chinese social behaviour. We begin with a discussion of Confucian social philosophy. This philosophy lies at the heart of the theories that have been advanced by Chinese and American scholars to help explain and predict Chinese social interaction. Analysis of these theories leads to a consideration of the empirical data collected to date within the traditional areas of social psychology. We conclude with suggestions about areas and approaches for future research.

This chapter will summarize the hypotheses and discoveries that have been made about Chinese social behaviour, thereby showing that Chinese culture can be compared with other cultures and fitted into a wider cross-cultural framework. It is hoped that this framework will be used to generate predictions in other as yet unexplored areas of Chinese interaction.

THE CONFUCIAN HERITAGE

The centre stage in almost all approaches to Chinese social behaviour is commanded by Chung-ni K'ung or Confucius, as he is known in the West. Confucius was born in the town of Chou, a part of the kingdom of Lu, in 551 BC. This was a time of political instability in the Eastern Chou Dynasty with the various kingdoms contending against one another for pre-eminence. These unsettling events impinged directly on the life of Confucius, as he moved in and out of political appointments with the ebb and flow of political fortune. Personal experience of such vicissitudes imparted to his work a fundamental concern with the problem of achieving social harmony.

The predominance of Confucianism in China can be traced to its origin in the Han Dynasty about 2,000 years ago. Wu Ti, an Emperor of the Han, set up at court five 'colleges' for the five Confucian classics and assigned official students to these five colleges, thus creating a sort of state university. From this time, China began to develop a system of educating and selecting potential officials, a system which was primarily based upon the mastery of Confucian ethics. Confucianism gradually became recognized as the official philosophy of the state (Fairbank and Reischauer, 1973).

Confucianism was espoused by most rulers throughout the history of China not only because it emphasized the duty of officers to serve with dispassionate loyalty, but also because its ideology was congruent with the cultural system of traditional China, basically an agrarian state (Stover, 1974). This agricultural economy tied the vast majority of the population to the land and its constraints, supporting the peasants at only a subsistence level. Their livelihood became even more precarious in years of famine when a great portion of China's huge population faced starvation. This kind of ecological backdrop predisposed the Chinese peasantry to accept Confucian philosophy, which encourages restraint over one's desires and equal distribution of the limited resources among members of a group (the family in most cases). The educated élite became members of the ruling class by passing examinations based on the Confucian classics. They then exercised power according to Confucian prescriptions. As cultural transmitters, they advocated Confucian philosophy as a way of rationalizing the political and social order by writing legends, drama, folk stories, and folk songs for the peasantry. Thus all Chinese people were enmeshed in the Confucian tradition.

Numerous publications are available for those wishing to pursue the philosophy of Confucius in detail (for example, Fung, 1948). Our concern is to extract themes from this body of work which have immediate implications for the daily functioning of Chinese people. In this respect, the discussion must begin with the fundamental Confucian assumption that man exists in relationship to others (King and Bond, 1985). The Western starting point of the anomic individual is alien to Chinese considerations of man's social behaviour, which see man as a relational being, socially situated and defined within an interactive context.

In the Confucian tradition, certain relationships were accorded a position of paramount importance. These were the so-called Five Cardinal Relations (*wu lun*), namely, those between sovereign and subject, father and son, elder brother and younger brother, husband and wife, and friend and friend. As with the order of nature itself, these relationships, even those between friends, were constructed in hierarchical patterns (Fairbank, 1966). In each case, the senior member was accorded a wide range of prerogatives and authority with respect to the junior.

Both parties to the relationship, however, were circumscribed by rules of correct behaviour (*li*), which entailed both rights and responsibilities for each. Harmony would be realized if each member of the unit was conscientious in following the requirements of his or her role. So, for example, the state would prosper if the sovereign ruled justly and the subjects served loyally. Failure to follow the dictates of proper role behaviour would imperil the relationship and disrupt the harmony of society (Wright, 1962).

This potential for disharmony was particularly troubling since the cardinal relationships involved considerable inequalities of power. Abuse of one's superior position put the opposite party in serious jeopardy. The antidote for this frightening possibility was to inculcate and enjoin a morality of compassion and righteousness upon those in positions of authority. Indeed, violations of these moral prescriptions by superiors constituted justification for rebellion (Hsiao, 1954); the prized virtue of sincerity entailed a steadfast adherence to what was right even if the consequence was disobedience to one's superior (King, 1981).

It should be noted in passing that a given individual could be enmeshed in a variety of relationships at a particular moment in the life cycle. So, a man could be subject to his sovereign, father to his son, son to his father, husband to his wife, and young friend to his elder friend. From an individual perspective, this tapestry of dualities may seem unmanageable, as it may call forth seemingly incompatible patterns of behaviour of superordination and subordination from the same person. This apparent contradiction is, however, not an important issue when seen from a relational perspective on the nature of social life; one is human in one's relationships and develops the skills necessary to fulfil all one's responsibilities. Adaptability, not consistency, becomes a focal issue in considering character.

In summary, the essential aspects of Confucianism in constructing a Chinese social psychology are the following: (a) man exists through, and is defined by, his relationships to others; (b) these relationships are structured hierarchically; (c) social order is ensured through each party's honouring the requirements in the role relationship. As we will subsequently attempt to show, many aspects of Chinese social behaviour can be linked to this distillate of Confucianism.

MODELS OF CHINESE SOCIAL BEHAVIOUR

There is, of course, a wealth of acute observations about the social behaviour of Chinese people, both from Westerners (for example, La Barre, 1945; Smith, 1894) and from Chinese (Hsu, 1953; Lin, 1935). Most of what has been written, however, is episodic and unsystematic, lacking the synthesis and the power to predict that are the hallmarks of scientific theorizing. What follows is an attempt to summarize the theories that approach these criteria. The theories represent tentative first steps and vary in their range of applicability and potential for testability, as will be seen. Given their historical precedence, however, they cannot be overlooked.

Readers will notice that all these models of Chinese social behaviour are implicitly cross-cultural, that is, they contrast the Chinese dynamics with those of another cultural group, Americans or Westerners. This feature of their authors' theorizing is hardly surprising, given that each has lived in, and studied, both cultural groups. Furthermore, the vast bulk of social science data has been gathered from the United States, which therefore constitutes an unavoidable point of departure in developing alternative conceptions. American authors, however, rarely show any cross-cultural concern in developing their theories of social behaviour, behaving in print as if their conceptualizations were innocent of historical and cultural overlay (Gergen, 1973; Sampson, 1977). It is hoped that these theories of Chinese social behaviour, especially the indigenous ones, will catalyse a responsiveness to cultural issues in future Western theorizing about social behaviour.

A contrast is drawn between American and indigenous theories. By 'American' we refer to the ethnic origin of the authors and to the tradition out of which their theorizing arises. By 'indigenous' we refer to the fact that the authors of the theory are Chinese and the intent of their theorizing is to develop concepts responsive to Chinese social 'reality'. There has been a self-conscious and deliberate movement among Chinese social scientists to avoid being intellectually colonized, so that they can more sensitively portray the nature of Chinese social life. We respect this healthy development by grouping the theories below into American and indigenous categories.

American Theorizing

Two American theories will be discussed: Solomon's dependency orientation and Wilson's theory of autocentrism versus heterocentrism. Solomon (1971) attempted to develop a theory of child socialization which would help to account for subsequent adult, and especially political, behaviour. He approached this problem by examining the logic of Confucianism, the essence of which he considered to be the hierarchical interdependencies discussed above. The first of the *wu lun* encountered in the individual life cycle was that between parent and child, and it was to interactions of this type that Solomon turned his attention.

At the time of Solomon's study, there was a scanty data base on comparative socialization practices for him to use in developing his argument (see Ho's chapter, this volume). To supplement this base, Solomon interviewed recent Chinese refugees from China who had fled to Hong Kong. From these interviews, he was impressed by the reports of early indulgence of all children followed by the imposition of strict (often physical) discipline once the child came 'of age' and began school. He hypothesized that this abrupt reversal developed a strong dependency orientation in the children — a desire to be cared for by the authoritarian providers, their parents, coupled with fear and anxiety about contravening their demands. He asserted that this pattern of child-rearing inhibited the development of internal controls, so that principled moral action and modulated emotional expression were not possible. He considered that it did, however, provide the character structure necessary to the smooth functioning of the subordinates in the remaining *wu lun*.

This argument was useful for the development of Solomon's thesis, but it is suspect on a number of grounds: (a) the evidence about the relative indulgence or punitiveness of Chinese socialization practices at any stage in the life cycle is either conflicting or lacking (Bond and Wang, 1983, p. 63); (b) it has a strongly ethnocentric flavour, presuming that independence is the normal end-state of healthy human development (Hogan, 1975). This concern is amplified by Solomon's characterization of the Chinese as weak willed in their conformity and deference to leadership. As Wong (1982, p. 11) has pointed out, 'What is involved in Chinese conformity and acquiescence may only be a prudent and expedient motive to avoid disrupting the present relations. It has nothing to do with a lack of autonomy or self-assertion.' And (c) it ignores an extensive area of activities outside those prescribed by the *wu lun*, where Chinese engage most purposefully and energetically in voluntaristic undertakings (King and Bond, 1985). Even if the Solomon thesis were true, recent evidence on the situational specificity of behaviour (Bandura, 1969; Mischel, 1968) would surely permit different patterns of behaviour outside specified relationships. Finally, (d) the Solomon thesis fails to suggest how Chinese develop the leadership skills necessary for the superior person in a *wu lun* relationship.

The second American theory under consideration is Wilson's

autocentrism versus heterocentrism theory. Like Solomon, Wilson (1970; 1974) is a political scientist interested in illuminating Chinese political behaviour. He, too, begins with the socialization process and relies on interview data — in this research project, from mothers in Hong Kong, Taiwan, and the United States. Wilson's argument, however, is that Chinese child-rearing is characterized by the withdrawal of maternal love and the use of group shaming as punishments for misbehaviour. The consequences for the Chinese child are a high degree of anxiety and fear about losing love and being abandoned.

Wilson argues that these socialization practices function to facilitate the internalization of values which guide behaviour independently of others, that is, autocentrism. This orientation contrasts with heterocentrism where particular others are cited as authorities for behaviour. Wilson (1974, p. 255) and Bloom (1977a) then provide data supporting the argument that Chinese children are more autocentric than American.

What is the consequence of this argument? To quote Wong (1982, p. 11) again:

Solomon may still have a point in arguing that there is a general lack of self-assertation in Chinese children ... However, such a lack of self-assertion should not be construed as entailing a lack of moral autonomy or of independent, internalized and principled control of one's emotions.

In a sense, Wilson's work has served to counterbalance Solomon's ethnocentric interpretation of Chinese character structure. The former affirms that the moral self (chi) lies at the core of Chinese personality; the negative reading to their accommodative response tendency is thereby undercut. Also affirmed is what Metzger (1981b) called the transformative mode in Chinese responding, that is, 'an ethic of ultimate ends ... bearing on interpersonal relationships [and] stressing personal integrity and righteousness' (Wong, 1982, p. 15). This aspect of the Chinese harkens back to the traditional Confucian justifications for rebellion against tyrannical authorities — independent assertion in the service of propriety in human relations.

The implications of Wilson's arguments for a psychology of Chinese social behaviour are less clear than those of Solomon (1971). Under what circumstances will the autocentric orientation of the Chinese lead to different social behaviour from that predicted by a dependency orientation? One may be principled or craven in one's conformity to group demands or one's avoidance of conflict, but the result is the same. More thought is needed in order to distinguish between the predictions for actual social functioning made by these two theories.

Indigenous Theorizing

Three theories by Chinese social scientists will be considered: Hsu's *ren*, Yang's social orientation, and Hwang's model of resource distribution. Francis L.K. Hsu has spent considerable energy in print assailing the limited perspective of theorizing by American social scientists. His earlier work used concepts derived from Western theory to contrast Chinese with American behaviour. So, for example, in a 1949 article, he used the Freudian concept of a defence mechanism to classify Chinese as 'repressors' and Westerners as 'suppressors' in order to explain differences in their sexual behaviour. Similarly, in a 1965 article, he used the concept of a dominant kinship relation to classify the Chinese as 'father-son' and Westerners as 'husband-wife' in order to explain a variety of differences, from mate selection to authority patterns.

In his 1971 paper, however, Hsu (1971b) turned to an indigenous Chinese concept, *ren*, which he used to encourage a shift of theoretical perspectives in approaching human social behaviour. Hsu maintained that the Westerner's emphasis on individual personality and its development has side-tracked fruitful inquiry. 'Since personality is seen as a distinct entity, there is an inevitable failure to come to terms with the reality of man' (p. 23). This reality for Hsu is that human needs are three in number, namely, sociability, security, and status. These needs are satisified through interpersonal transactions. Consequently, the fundamental irreducible, the 'human constant', is what Hsu calls *ren*, and designates as 'personage'. He chooses the Chinese term for man 'because the Chinese conception of man . . . is based on the *individual's transactions with his fellow human beings*' (p. 29, emphasis in original).

This alteration of focus means that scientific attention is rerouted from the individual's 'deep core of complexes and anxieties' to the relationship between the individual's social behaviour and 'the interpersonal standards of the society and culture'. Satisfaction of human needs arises out of the match between a person's behaviour and these social norms. This spider's-web view of human reality then leads to a set of hypotheses which Hsu uses to explain a variety of contrasts between Chinese and Westerners and Chinese and Japanese.

Hsu does not offer a theory of behaviour, but rather an approach to theorizing about behaviour. The emphasis is shifted from the individual to the individual's relationships. We accord such attention to Hsu's paper because his clarion call for a realignment of approach is so quintessentially Chinese. From this emphasis on relationship have emerged two indigenous theories of Chinese social behaviour, Yang's social orientation and Hwang's model of resource distribution.

In a number of publications, Kuo-shu Yang (see Yang and Hchu, 1974, and Yang, this volume, for a review) has explored the behavioural implications of the contrast between a traditional Chinese and a modern Western position on values, attitudes, and beliefs. He tried to integrate these differences in a 1981 article where he described the traditional Chinese pattern as the 'social orientation'. At the other end of the pole was what he labelled the 'individual orientation' (see also Hsu, 1953).

Recalling the Confucian emphasis on interrelatedness, Yang (1981a, p. 161) maintains that Chinese, in deciding upon their behaviour, attach a great weight to the anticipated reactions of others to that behaviour.

Basically, it represents a tendency for a person to act in accordance with external expectations or social norms, rather than with internal wishes or personal integrity, so that he would be able to protect his social self and function as an integral part of the social network.

Westerners and more modern Chinese give greater weight to their own personal standards in making the same behavioural decisions. Yang (1981a, p. 161) considers that some consequences of the traditional Chinese concern for the reactions of others are their

submission to social expectations, social conformity, worry about external opinions, and non-offensive strategy in an attempt to achieve one or more of the purposes of reward attainment, harmony maintenance, impression management, face protection, social acceptance, and avoidance of punishment, embarrassment, conflict, rejection, ridicule, and retaliation in a social situation.

A number of important issues are worth noting in considering Yang's social orientation. First, it bears a close conceptual resemblance to Snyder's (1979) analysis of self-monitoring. Both psychologists are concerned with the internal or external orientation of an actor in directing his or her behaviour.

According to the self-monitoring formulation, an individual in social settings attempts to construct a pattern of social behaviour appropriate to that particular context. Diverse sources of information are available to guide this choice, including (a) cues to situational or interpersonal specifications of appropriateness and (b) information about inner states, personal dispositions and social attitudes.

Furthermore ... individuals differ in the extent to which they rely on either source of information. (Snyder, 1982, p. 93.)

Snyder's fertile conceptualization has spawned an awesome body of research, as his 1979 summary suggests. Its close resemblance to the social orientation of Yang, however, may provide an important bridge linking Chinese and Western social behaviour. If Chinese are high in self-monitoring and Westerners low, then a treasure trove of already unearthed behavioural differences immediately suggest themselves to the consideration of social scientists.

A second noteworthy issue concerns morality. The internal standards used by Yang's moderns to control their behaviour may be characterized by narrowness and self-seeking or by magnanimity and self-sacrifice (see Waterman's 1981 comparison of Hobbesian and ethical individualism). Conversely, a social orientation may reflect either fear of sanctions or consideration for others. Far too frequently, Chinese analyses of Western behaviour and Western analyses of Chinese behaviour have fallen prey to the ethnocentric temptation of seeing the typical behaviour of out-group members as psychopathic or craven. This temptation is reinforced by the vernacular. The terms 'individualistic' in Chinese and 'collective' in English have negative connotations, which are sustained by their respective political implications in each cultural group. Clearly, both social and individual orientations are capable of accommodating the whole gamut of moral considerations.

A third point constitutes an agenda for future research. From a social orientation, the critical question becomes, 'Who are the relevant others?'. In a laboratory study this problem is less marked, as the subjects' social field is artificially restricted by the experimenter. In less constrained settings, with a wider range of participants, the question is critical. Family members, work groups, close friends, one's ethnic group, classmates, leaders, and so forth can become relevant references for behavioural guidelines in various situations.

But which groups, and when? These are the same questions with which Triandis (in press) is trying to grapple in his consideration of collectivism, and they are fundamental for a theory of Chinese social behaviour.

The third Chinese theory we shall consider is Hwang's model of resource distribution. *Guanxi*, which is a term used to denote particularistic ties in China, is a key concept for understanding Chinese behaviour in social (Fried, 1969), political (Jacobs, 1979), and organizational (Walder, 1983) contexts. Having evolved from an agricultural society where the major social resources were controlled by a few powerful figures, traditional Chinese developed a complicated cultural system focused on *li* (courteous ritual), which encourages an individual to maintain hierarchical order and harmonious interpersonal relationships in a relatively stable and permanent social fabric. The Chinese cultural norm of *li* demands that an individual interact with people across different *guanxi* in accordance with various standards of social exchange. Thus the manipulation of interpersonal relationships has long been a strategy for attaining desirable social resources in Chinese society (Chiao, 1981).

In order to explain how Chinese interact with one another, K.K. Hwang (1983a) developed a conceptual framework for Chinese power games to integrate such indigenous Chinese concepts as *guanxi* (relationship), *renqing* (favour), *mianzi* (face), and *bao* (reciprocation). His model conceptualizes the two parties to a dyadic interaction as petitioner and resource allocator. Since either party in a dyadic interaction may control some kinds of social resource that are desired by the other, either party in the dyad may play the role of petitioner in one instance, and resource allocator in another.

Owing to the relation-oriented character of Chinese people, when a petitioner asks a resource allocator to distribute a certain kind of social resource under his control, the resource allocator will first consider the relationship (*guanxi*) between them and adopt appropriate rules of social exchange to interact with the petitioner. According to Hwang's model, interpersonal relationships in Chinese society can be classified into three main categories on the basis of their expressive and instrumental components.

1. Expressive ties. The most important expressive ties in Chinese society are the relationships between members in a family. The rule governing social exchange and resource distribution in a Chinese family is the *need rule*: the members with working abilities

(usually the parents or adults) have the responsibility to strive for resources to satisfy the legitimate needs of each member. When the parents become too old to work, their children have to assume an equivalent responsibility to support them.

2. Instrumental ties. An individual may establish temporary and anonymous relationships with other people solely as a means to attain his or her personal goals. Some examples of instrumental ties are the relationships between customer and salesgirl in a large department store, passenger and taxi driver, and so on. The expressive ingredient involved in instrumental ties is very slight; and the rule for social exchange with a person in this type of relationship is the *equity rule* whereby a constant ratio is maintained between the inputs and gains of each party. The use of this rule enables both parties to bargain with each other for their self-interest on the basis of universal and impersonal standards.

3. Mixed ties. The mixed tie is a kind of interpersonal relationship in which an individual is most likely to play the power games surrounding *guanxi*. In Chinese culture, persons who are said to have *guanxi* usually share one or more important characteristics. Such characteristics may be ascriptive, for example, common birthplace, lineage, or surname, or may involve shared experience, such as attending the same school, working together, or belonging to the same organization (Jacobs, 1979). The *guanxi* outside an individual's immediate family are conceptualized as mixed ties in Hwang's framework. Generally speaking, both sides to a mixed tie know each other and maintain a certain expressive component in their relationship, but it is not as strong as that in the expressive tie. Furthermore, persons having *guanxi* may be acquainted with one or more persons in common. All the acquaintances thus constitute an interpersonal network or reticulum, they may expect to meet one another in the future, and they may anticipate that other people in their network will evaluate the exchanges between them in accordance with Chinese norms, such as the necessity to reciprocate (Yang, 1957).

Basing his ideas on Foa's (1971) analysis, Hwang (1983a) proposed that the resources for social exchange may include money, goods, information, status, service, and affection. When a resource allocator is asked to distribute the resource under his or her control in such a way as to benefit any other in the social network, he or she has to take the rule of *renqing* (favour) into account and consider the following factors: (a) the cost of paying out the resources; (b) the affective component (*ganqing*) between them; (c) the probability of reciprocation from the petitioner; and (d) social evaluations from other people in the same social network. On the whole, the stronger the affective relationship between the two parties, the higher the status of the petitioner, the more resources there are under his or her control, the larger the probable future reciprocation, and the better social relations with important people that he or she keeps, the more likely it is that the resource allocator will accept the petition.

In order to strive for social resources controlled by a particular allocator, an individual may adopt several strategies to enhance his or her influence over the allocator. The most popular strategy for strengthening *ganqing* and *guanxi* in China is to increase the social interaction between two parties deliberately, by visiting, the giving of gifts (C.F. Yang, 1982), and inviting the other person to banquets on such occasions as weddings, funerals, or birthday parties in one's family, and festivals in one's home village (Fried, 1969; Jacobs, 1979). Even if an individual is barely acquainted with a resource allocator, he or she may 'pull' or 'work' the connections (*la guanxi* or *gao guanxi*) by asking an intermediary of high social status to introduce the petitioner to the allocator and to solicit a favour from the allocator on his or her behalf. Once the strategy of utilizing *guanxi* has been successful, people generally say that a 'back door' has been opened (Jacobs, 1979; Walder, 1983).

Another strategy which is frequently used for enhancing one's influence over others in Chinese society is face-work. Since an individual's power and status as perceived by others can guarantee an allocator's help, it is important for a Chinese to maintain his or her face and to do face-work in front of others in the mixed tie. He or she may deliberately arrange the setting for social interaction, take particular care with his or her appearance, and behave in a specific manner, in order to shape a powerful and attractive image when dealing with others. The more skilled this impression management is, the more likely the allocator will be to accept his or her request. If the allocator dares to reject his or her plea, the petitioner will lose face and both sides may feel disaffected in the long run. Thus, the allocator is generally well advised to 'do a favour' (*renqing*) and grant the request. When the allocator is neither willing to grant the petitioner's request, nor to hurt his or her face, the allocator may adopt the strategy of deferment and give no definite answer to the petitioner. The latter may then 'forget' the request and both parties proceed as if it had never been made, but with a clearer understanding of the limits to their relationship. Should, however, the request be pressed further, the potential for disruption to the two parties and their social network escalates seriously.

Hwang's theory is more domain-specific and testable than the theories discussed so far. Like Yang's (1981a) theory, however, it is an indigenous theory and uses common-sense constructs, much in the tradition of Heider (1958). As such, it is not explicitly cross-cultural or comparative. One is left to speculate about how universally applicable it may be and where cultural variability could be introduced into the model. Certainly the conceptual distinctions he draws make sense and connect directly with a large body of Western research, for example, that on distributive behaviour (covered later in this chapter). Cultural variations will, however, probably be found in a variety of areas (such as the following), and could profitably be explored in future research:

    (a) the breadth of social roles included in each of the three ties;
    (b) the distribution rules used within each category of tie;
    (c) the extent to which elements such as allocator status, likelihood of future interaction, expectation of repayment, strength of petitioner's social network, and so forth influence the decision to grant the request.

LOCATING THE CHINESE CROSS-CULTURALLY

Important psychological functions are served by the belief that one's group is unique and distinct from other groups (Tajfel, 1974; 1978). In the Chinese case, such a belief is an aspect of what Yang (1968) labelled 'Sinocentrism'. Such a perspective is anathema, however, in a cross-cultural approach to the understanding of a group, since it denies its comparability to other groups. If we are to see the Chinese case in the context of other world cultures, we must move beyond idiographic descriptions and locate the Chinese in some broad nomological network.

This agenda is doubly important, as people who describe themselves as 'Chinese' can be found in a host of cultures outside China. The political, social, and economic forces acting on these Chinese vary considerably. In what ways can behaviour patterns found in one of these groups be generalized to any of the others? Such extensions can only be undertaken if the various cultures can be demonstrated to occupy similar locations on some map of cultural dimensions.

Persons of Chinese ethnicity constitute over one-quarter of the world's population. Empirical data about these enormous numbers, however, are minuscule by comparison. This disparity is particularly marked when we consider the People's Republic of China, where psychology was not practised during the Cultural Revolution and is only now beginning to reappear (Brown, 1981). Social psychology in particular was always politically suspect (Kuo, 1971), received little support, and has only recently been revived with the formation of the Chinese Association of Social Psychology in the early 1980s. How could one position the Chinese in some set of scientific dimensions with such an inadequate data base?

The Hofstede Study

While working for a large multinational organization, Hofstede (1980; 1983) distributed a work-related value survey to comparable populations of company employees in 53 cultural units. Three were Chinese: Hong Kong, Singapore, and Taiwan. Hofstede simplified the mass of data using factor analysis, extracting four dimensions of cultural variation along which his cultural units could be located.

Two of these dimensions are of critical importance for our consideration. The first is collectivism–individualism. As described by Hofstede (1983, p. 83):

Individualism stands for a preference for a loosely knit social framework in society wherein individuals are supposed to take care of themselves and their immediate families only. Its opposite, Collectivism, stands for a preference for a tightly knit social framework in which individuals can expect their relatives, clan, or other in-group to look after them in exchange for unquestioning loyalty (it will be clear that the word 'Collectivism' is not used here to describe any particular political system). The fundamental issue addressed by this dimension is the degree of interdependence a society maintains among individuals. It relates to people's self-concept: 'I' or 'we'.

This cultural construct is a fundamental aspect of cultural variation and has been receiving increased attention from psychologists. Triandis (in press), for example, has reviewed and integrated literature related to the concept of collectivism, proposing an approach to its measurement across various cultural contexts. He makes considerable use of Hsu's (1953; 1971b) ideas of 'situation centredness' and *ren*;

indeed, the close relationship of these ideas and Yang's (1981a) model of social orientation to the construct of collectivism is obvious.

The second dimension of cultural variability is large versus small power distance. Again, as described by Hofstede (1983, p. 83):

Power distance is the extent to which the members of a society accept that power in institutions and organizations is distributed unequally. This affects the behaviour of the less powerful as well as of the more powerful members of society. People in large power distance societies accept a hierarchical order in which everybody has a place which needs no further justification. People in small power distance societies strive for power equalization and demand justification for power inequalities. The fundamental issue addressed by this dimension is how a society handles inequalities among people when they occur. This has obvious consequences for the way people build their institutions and organizations.

As with collectivism, the dimension of power distance has received increasing attention from cross-cultural psychologists, particularly from Berry (1979) who accords it a central position in his biosocial model. An emphasis on filial piety leads inevitably to a culture of larger power distance, and the relationship of this cultural dimension to Solomon's (1971) dependency orientation and to K.K. Hwang's (1983a) emphasis on the role of favour and face is clear.

These two dimensions are important for our purposes because all three Chinese samples occupied similar positions on these scales in the Hofstede results (highly collective and moderately high in power distance). The similarity of positions strengthens our confidence in generalizing results relevant to these dimensions across Chinese cultures in different places.

This confidence is enhanced by the results of recent research by Chong, Cragin, and Scherling (1983) in the People's Republic of China (PRC). They administered the Hofstede survey to a wide variety of managerial groups. Comparing their results with those of Hofstede, one can see a close correspondence among all four Chinese samples on the critical dimensions of individualism and power distance. This finding gives us greater assurance when applying data from Chinese samples outside the PRC to predict and explain the behaviour of Chinese inside the PRC.

Another point of critical importance is the fact that Hong Kong, Singapore, and Taiwan are all developing countries, industrialized and prosperous in comparison with the rest of South-east Asia and China. That certain fundamental Chinese values have remained intact throughout this modernization process suggests that they will likewise prove resistant to change as the People's Republic of China develops. Thus, when trying to understand and anticipate mainland Chinese behaviour, present results should enjoy future currency.

CHARACTERISTICS OF THE AVAILABLE DATA

Social psychology is primarily American in its origin and practitioners. Early cross-cultural research using Chinese subjects followed the inevitable pattern of 'safari' research, with visiting American psychologists carrying their models and procedures with their luggage while on sabbatical leave to Chinese societies (Brislin, Lonner, and Thorndike, 1973, p. 14). The consequent yield of these early data thus reflects Western preoccupations and biases (Hogan and Emler, 1978; Pepitone, 1976; Sampson, 1977).

A fascination with things Western eventually led to the advanced training of some Chinese social psychologists in the United States and Britain. In addition, a number of Western social psychologists established permanent residence in various Asian countries, plying their profession at local universities. These two factors slowly worked to 'decentre' the research undertaken (Brislin et al., 1973, pp. 37–9), so that recent data reflect more indigenous Chinese concerns and theoretical approaches. With a number of Chinese universities offering graduate programmes, this movement towards an indigenization of Chinese social psychology is bound to continue.

The bulk of research in the social sciences originates from the United States. Consequently, most empirical comparisons across cultures contrast the target culture with the American. This state of affairs is fortunate for our purposes, however, since American culture differs from Chinese cultures most strongly on precisely those dimensions where the Chinese cultures cluster, namely, individualism and power distance. A difference between American (indeed most Western) samples and a given Chinese sample is thus likely to generalize to the other Chinese cultures, provided the difference reflects the dynamics of individualism and/or power distance.

RESEARCH IN SOCIAL PSYCHOLOGY — PERSON PERCEPTION

This well-established area of research in social psychology (Schneider, Hastorf, and Ellsworth, 1979) covers a wide variety of topics. Our discussion will touch only those which are most frequently explored using Chinese subjects — emotions and their recognition, attribution processes, trait salience, implicit personality theory, the self, and stereotypes.

Emotions and their Recognition

This is a time-honoured area of interest in social psychology, dating back to the early studies of Landis (1929) on the judgement of facial expressions. The correct identification of the emotion felt by another is a critical input in the modulation of one's behaviour during interaction, and misjudgements in this respect become an obvious spawning ground for difficulties in cross-cultural relations.

There is a fundamental distinction in the field between the emotions experienced and the emotions expressed by a person during a social exchange. For tactical reasons, one is not always free to display what one feels. Norms governing the public manifestation of emotions are termed 'display rules' (Ekman, 1971), and may function to transmute felt anger into surprise, felt boredom into joy, felt delight into indifference, and so forth. It is these display rules which are likely to result in the wide range of variation in emotional expressions from culture to culture. Klineberg (1938) was the first to comment on Chinese patterns of emotional expression, distilled from a reading of some Chinese classics. As he pointed out, the displays of anger appear especially strange to Westerners, because Chinese expression of this emotion is so strongly censured.

Numerous studies have explored whether different cultural groups can identify *unmasked* expressions of emotions with equal levels of agreement (see Ekman and Oster, 1979, for a review). Those involving Chinese subjects (Chan, in press; Vinacke, 1949; Vinacke and Fong, 1955) agree with the pattern of results found elsewhere: that with minor exceptions for specific cultures, there are high levels of agreement in recognizing the facial expressions ōf happiness, anger, disgust, sadness, and fear or surprise. This universality in recognizing facial expressions of emotion also extends to vocal expressions of emotion (Bezooijen, Otto, and Heenan, 1983), in this case contrasting Taiwanese with Dutch and Japanese.

This research paradigm does not address the questions of whether emotions are felt and expressed more frequently in some cultures than in others. Consistent with Wilson's (1974) discussion of Chinese socialization, there is evidence that Taiwanese respondents report a higher frequency of shyness than Western populations (Pilkonis and Zimbardo, 1979, p. 155). Likewise, consistent with Ho's (1981) analysis of the timing and relational focus of Chinese socialization, it appears that Taiwanese kindergarten children are more willing to express the emotion of anger than their American counterparts (Borke and Su, 1972; Niem and Collard, 1972), but less willing to express sadness. This comparative pattern of results will probably be reversed however, after the Chinese have been socialized into the 'adult' world.

In their four-culture study of relationship rules, Argyle, Henderson, Bond, Iizuka, and Contarello (1984) identified a number of interpersonal areas governed by norms whose strength varies crossculturally. 'As expected in the East, there are more rules about obedience, avoiding loss of face, maintaining harmonious relations in groups, and *restraining emotional expression*. However, these differences were more marked for Japan than for Hong Kong' (p. 21, emphasis added). The heightened concern for controlling affect display is consistent with the higher collectivism of Japanese and Hong Kong Chinese cultures. The Chinese counsel against showing joy or sadness functions to maintain harmony by avoiding the imposition of one's feelings on others.

This concern about emotional restraint is reflected in Chan's (in press) study on the recognition of facial displays of emotion. He asked his subjects to examine a large number of photographs and to make similarity judgements on all possible pairs of photographs, so that he could discover the structure of the ratings through multidimensional scaling. A two-factor solution emerged as the best explanation of the data. The first factor tapped the dimensions of evaluation, activity, and relaxation found in studies elsewhere (for example, Schlosberg, 1954). The second factor was unique to this study, ordering the emotions in terms of the degree of emotional control each involved, from fear and anger to distress and contempt. From this experimental approach, also, one can discern a convergence on the basic Chinese issue of controlling emotional expression.

Attribution Processes

Briefly, the study of attribution addresses the question of how people make judgements about the causes of behaviour. More specifically, there is considerable interest in discovering the conditions under which people assume that the characteristics of the actor are responsible for producing his or her observed behaviour.

An avalanche of American work in this area has been directed towards testing the theories advanced by Heider (1958), Jones and Davis (1965), and Kelley (1967). Far too little energy has been expended to test the ecological validity of attributional activity itself (see, for example, Harvey, Yarkin, Lightner, and Town, 1980). Such questions as how much attributional activity people undertake (and when), what categories they use when trying to understand interpersonal events, and so forth (Bond, 1983a), are relatively neglected.

These concerns are of critical importance when examining attribution processes in non-Western cultures. There is suggestive evidence from philosophical, anthropological, and psychological perspectives to indicate that the frequency and type of attributions made in other cultures are likely to differ (Bond, 1983a; Shweder and Bourne, 1982). As attribution theory is so closely linked to conceptions of human nature and causality, it is essential to approach such studies in other cultures with openness and sensitivity towards one's informants (Jahoda, 1979; Selby, 1977) and to avoid imposing theoretical constructs imported from other cultures.

In a number of class projects at The Chinese University of Hong Kong, students from social psychology classes have undertaken such unstructured approaches to explanations about interpersonal behaviour. It certainly appears that the categories of Heider (1958), such as effort, ability, task difficulty, and luck, and those of Kelley (1967), such as person, stimulus, and circumstance, are used in Chinese explanations of behaviour. As reported in Bond (1983a, p. 152), however, certain more finely drawn categories appear in such explanations and may reflect cultural variables. So, for example, when using the stimulus category, Hong Kong Chinese students mention relationship considerations more frequently than American students, and vice versa for need considerations. Given the greater demands of binding relationships in collective cultures, this finding is not surprising. Further analyses of unstructured attributions are needed at this finer level to substantiate and extend these suggestive findings.

Given this backdrop of support for Western approaches, greater confidence can be placed in the work on attributions already done. It has been established that Hong Kong Chinese make both self-serving (Wan and Bond, 1982) and group-serving attributions (Bond,

Hewstone, Wan, and Chiu, 1984; Hewstone, Bond, and Wan, 1983). Under certain political restraints, Chinese will make group-effacing attributions (in Malaysia) or avoid group bias altogether (in Singapore) — see Hewstone and Ward (in press). When the social impact of verbal attributions has been examined, Chinese in Hong Kong have been found to prefer those who make self-effacing attributions for their own performance (Bond, Leung, and Wan, 1982a), but group-serving attributions for their group's performance (Bond, Chiu, and Wan, 1984).

Stimulated by Weiner's attribution theory of achievement-related behaviour (Weiner, Heckhausen, Meyer, and Cook, 1972), some psychologists in Taiwan have conducted research to investigate the relationship between the causal attributions for one's own success or failure, achievement-related behaviour, including expectancy of future success or failure, and academic achievement (Cheng and Yang, 1977; Chung and Hwang, 1981; Kuo, 1984). The results generally supported Weiner's theory, in that achievement motivation was positively correlated with internal attributions to effort and ability, and negatively correlated with external attributions to luck and task difficulty, while academic achievement had no significant relationship with causal attribution.

The research on causal attribution for others' behaviour formulated within the theoretical framework of Western psychology (for example, Taylor and Fiske, 1975) also provided support for Western theories and showed no cultural variation. For instance, Yee and Yang (1977) conducted two experiments to investigate the differences in attributions by actors and observers under different cheating situations. The results were consistent with what was found in the Western world — that actors tend to attribute their cheating behaviour to external causes, whereas observers tend to attribute that of others to internal causes; the more unjustifiable the cheating behaviour, the larger the difference in attribution between actor and observer.

So the bulk of research to date has been generally supportive of hypotheses derived from Western models. As researchers move beyond replications and incorporate more social variables into the context of data collection, distinctive cultural processes are certain to be unearthed. In the Bond, Hewstone, Wan, and Chiu (1984) study, for example, Chinese were found to moderate their group-serving bias before an audience whereas Americans did not. This

Chinese concern for avoidance of public conflict has been seen in other social behaviour and will undoubtedly affect attributional processes in ways that are as yet unexplored.

Trait Salience

As McArthur and Baron (1983) recently argued, the how and what of social perception can be closely tied to objective considerations that guide and discipline our daily functioning. This 'ecological' approach allows researchers to integrate cultural considerations into their research on social perception, since it suggests that basic cultural concerns will influence the way we understand the interpersonal world. So, for example, one would anticipate that information about a person's status would be of greater moment in guiding the perceptual-based responses of persons from cultures high in power distance.

Bond and Forgas (1984) argued that one such 'cultural agenda' in collectivist cultures was maintaining the integrity of groups against the divisive forces of self-interest. A person's degree of conscientiousness and good-naturedness is closely tied to his or her responsibility towards others and co-operativeness during interaction. As these characteristics are of critical importance in group functioning over a period of time, it was argued that collectivist Chinese in Hong Kong would be more responsive to these personality characteristics than would more individualistic Australians. These predictions were confirmed using behaviour intentions as dependent variables.

Implicit Personality Theory

This area of study concerns the ways in which a given group of people organize the constructs they use to perceive other people. The trait lexicons of any language contain a whole host of possible terms to describe personality. These overlap considerably and can be simplified into underlying dimensions that people employ in perceiving others.

Norman (1963) addressed this issue in the English language using American subjects and found that five dimensions were sufficient to exhaust the perceptual ratings of both self and others, namely, extroversion–introversion, good-naturedness–ill temper, conscientiousness–unreliability, emotional stability–neuroticism, culturedness–boorishness (see also Goldberg, 1980). These results

have been replicated in Hong Kong using university students responding to Norman's polar descriptions written in English (Bond, 1979).
The obvious question arises, however, about what dimensions of
personality perception are involved when Chinese raters use the
discriminations about another's personality which are provided by
the Chinese language. Yang and Bond (1983) attempted such an examination by first culling trait descriptors from Yang and Lee's
(1971) list of 557 common adjectives for personality traits. All the
adjectives in the list were first broadly categorized with respect to
several dimensions. About 150 frequently appearing descriptors were
then sampled from these categories and used as the end-points on
trait-rating scales of various target persons, such as father, mother,
self, most familiar friend, most familiar teacher, and so forth. Factor analyses of these ratings yielded from three to six factors depending on the target (see also Hanno and Jones, 1973). Regardless of
target, however, there was always a large first factor, labelled 'social
morality'. This factor involved items such as kind, modest, reliable,
and so forth, which seem important in maintaining the strength and
harmony of interpersonal relationships against the fragmentation
of individual abrasiveness and self-seeking. As mentioned in the
section on trait salience above, these integrative characteristics of
people are of signal importance in highly collectivist cultures and
account for a relatively high percentage of the trait variance (see also
Lew, 1983).

Confirmation of this reading of the data comes from similar
analyses run on ratings made by the same subjects of the same targets
but using the Norman (1963) *descriptions*, written this time in
Chinese. Regardless of target, there was again a disproportionately
large first factor, typically consisting of a blend between Norman's
second factor of good-naturedness and his third factor of conscientiousness. The prepotency of this dimension labelled as social morality thus appears to be robust across both indigenous and imported
scales, as long as they are presented in the Chinese language. This
prepotency appears to reflect important aspects of the collective
experience.

The Self

There has been a resurgence of Western research interest surrounding the topic of the self (see, for example, Wegner and Vallacher,

1980). Such interest has traditionally been lacking in Chinese research, perhaps because of the unhealthy alliance between self and individualism in the minds of the Chinese. The topic of the self becomes doubly fascinating in a collectivist culture, however, precisely because concern with the self is often derided and played down in favour of group considerations.

As with attribution studies, it seems judicious in the early stages of research to approach such a topic with a more open-ended approach. Bond and Cheung (1983) used the unstructured Twenty Statements Test (Kuhn and McPartland, 1954) to examine the categories used by Hong Kong Chinese to describe themselves. Were they more or less likely than comparable Americans and Japanese to represent themselves by social roles (for example, student, daughter), by psychological attributes (such as friendly, unstable), by concrete behaviour (for example, 'I walk my dog every day'), and so forth? Contrary to expectation, the Chinese students were similar to the Americans in the ways they talked about themselves; together, both groups differed sharply from the Japanese whose responses were much more concrete. Given that Hong Kong students generally study curriculum materials written in English by British authors, it is important to replicate this result in Chinese societies less influenced by a Western intellectual input.

The content of self-descriptions is also consistent with what one might predict from a knowledge of Chinese collectivism. So, Gabrenya and Wang (1983) found that Chinese from Taiwan and Hong Kong were more likely to endorse group-orientated self-concepts than were Americans. Similar results would be expected for aspects of the self-concept related to power distance.

The only other area where there has been some previous research on the self is that of self-esteem (Huang, 1971; Paschal and Kuo, 1973; Shen, 1936). These studies were comparative, and showed Chinese levels of self-esteem to be lower than American. Bond and Cheung (1983) confirmed this result using a different instrument and population of subjects, so that some confidence should be placed in the finding. As they pointed out, however, such a difference is consistent with the pressure for self-effacement in collective cultures (Bond, Leung, and Wan, 1982a). In the absence of further research, one cannot assume that low self-esteem in the Chinese has the same implications for social functioning as the same low level in respondents from some other cultures. Within Chinese culture, however, it does appear that a more positive self-concept is associated with more satisfactory interpersonal relationships (Chang, 1982) and more favourable life events (Huang, Hwang, and Ko, 1983).

Stereotypes

There have been several studies on the stereotypes Chinese hold of people from other countries over the last 20 years. For instance, Yang and Yang (1970; 1972) adopted Katz and Braly's (1933) method to measure the stereotypes of undergraduate students at National Taiwan University about people of various countries in 1962 and 1971 respectively. It was found in 1962 that their subjects held very favourable impressions of Germans, Americans, French, and Chinese. Their stereotypes of Indians, Russians, and Arabs tended to be negative; while their stereotypes of Japanese, English, and Black people consisted of both desirable and undesirable traits in equal proportions. Yang and Yang replicated their research in 1971 and found that, compared with their 1962 counterparts, students of the National Taiwan University had become less extreme in their stereotyping overall, and their stereotypes about Japanese and Americans had become more negative. Yang and Yang believed that these changes were caused by a series of setbacks to Taiwan in international affairs during the autumn of 1971, including disputes with Japan about sovereignty over nearby fishing islands, President Nixon's declaration of his intended visit to China, and Taiwan's expulsion from the United Nations.

Hsiung (1965) took students of Cheng-chi University in Taiwan as subjects and studied their ranking of people from 14 races or countries. The results showed that their order of preference was Chinese, Germans, Americans, French, Koreans, English, Japanese, Italians, Filipinos, Jews, Blacks, Russians, Indians, and Indonesians. The traits they chose for Americans were mostly desirable characteristics such as cheerful, active, exuberant, innocent, clean, materialistic, frank, and innovative, while the traits chosen for Blacks were undesirable characteristics such as stupid, dirty, foolish, unhygienic, lazy, unambitious, and rude. Maykovich (1980) provided further data revealing Chinese stereotypes about American Whites and Blacks. She applied a modified version of the Bogardus Social Distance Scale to college students and farmers in Taiwan, asking about their willingness to engage in various types of social interaction (such as marrying, becoming an intimate friend, sharing a taxi) with White, Black, and Chinese Americans. She found that Chinese students felt closest to the Chinese Americans, next closest to the Whites, and most distant from the Blacks. Farmers were either uncertain of their sentiments towards Americans or did not wish to have any transactions with them (see also F.S. Lin, 1978, on the influence of the mass media).

Situational factors as well as psychodynamic processes have been shown to affect Chinese stereotypes of a particular group. President Carter declared on 16 December 1978 that the United States would normalize its diplomatic relationship with the People's Republic of China on 1 January 1979, sever its diplomatic ties with the government of the Republic of China, and discontinue the Sino-American Mutual Defense Treaty one year later. The announcement astonished the Chinese in Taiwan, firing widespread patriotic zeal, which was accompanied by a strong dissatisfaction and bitter criticism directed towards the Carter Administration. Many social scientists noted the psychological impact of these political events on Chinese living in Taiwan. Maykovich (1980) suggested that the perception of Sino-American social distance was probably affected by such events, especially the United States' decognition of the Republic of China. Considerable research examined the change in stereotypes held by Chinese students about Americans as a result of these events (Huang and Hwang, 1979; Huang and Lin, 1979; Hwang, 1980). For example, Huang and Hwang administered Chinese versions of the F-scale, D-scale, and semantic differential scales for evaluating American people and the American Government to subjects aged from 16 to 40 years. At the time the mass media emphasized that the severance was caused by a few 'short-sighted' politicians in the American Government and that actually the majority of American people were friendly and wanted to support Taiwan. Not surprisingly, the results of the research showed that the subjects as a whole continued to hold a positive attitude towards the American people; their attitudes towards the American Government, however, tended to be negative. Further canonical correlation analyses indicated that a set of personality traits, consisting of Dogmatism, Traditionalism, and non-Cynicism, were associated with the most typical attitudes towards the American people and the American Government which the mass media advocated at that time.

All the previous research has examined stereotypes in Chinese people who have had little or no opportunity for face-to-face contact with foreigners. As suggested by earned reputation theory (Brigham, 1971; Triandis and Vassiliou, 1967), ethnic stereotypes can reveal a 'kernel of truth' when they are elicited from people who have had the experience of interacting with the group being stereotyped. Bond (1984a) examined the mutual stereotypes of two interacting groups at The Chinese University of Hong Kong. He asked 30 American exchange students and 130 local Chinese undergraduates to rate a typical in-group member (auto-stereotype) and a typical out-group member (hetero-stereotype) on 30 bipolar trait scales. Analysing the results on four dimensions obtained from factor groupings of the Chinese data, he found that both groups agreed that the typical Chinese student is more emotionally controlled but less open and less extroverted than the typical American exchange student. These stereotype differences are compatible with those found in previous studies (Yeh and Chu, 1974; Young, 1980). The transtemporal and trans-target stability of these findings suggests that the differences arise from real behavioural differences which characterize the two groups. In addition, the perceptual agreement may function to structure expectations about how interactions across group lines will proceed. The research also showed that both groups rated the other group higher on the fundamental dimension of prosocial orientation. Mutual out-group enhancement on this dimension probably undercuts the tendency to confine interactions to in-group members, and suggests that both groups are eager to seek contact with the out-group.

In the same vein, findings of research on sex-role stereotypes can be explained in terms of earned reputation theory. Sex-role stereotypes are formed as a result of an individual's experience of interaction with people of both sexes. They reveal not only biological sex differences, but also the relative social status of both sexes in a given culture. For instance, Huang (1971) adapted a questionnaire from Rosenkrantz, Vogel, Bee, Broverman, and Broverman (1968) to compare the sex-role stereotypes of American college students with those of their Chinese counterparts in Taiwan. Li and Wong (1980) did similar cross-cultural research using a revised version of the same instrument (Broverman, Broverman, Clarkson, Rosenkrantz, and Vogel, 1970). Both studies indicated that Chinese and American students showed similar features in their stereotypes of both sexes. Men and women in both cultures generally agreed on which sex was the more adventurous, dominant, independent, and so on. Nevertheless, the Chinese sample showed greater sex-role differentiation than did the Americans: they rated the male stereotype, for example, as more 'manly' than did the American subjects (for example, as more independent, more self-confident, makes decisions more easily, acts as a leader more, and so on). This difference could be interpreted in terms of the fact that the social structure of the Chinese family has traditionally shown a greater degree of sexual differentiation and has been more male centred (see also Braun and Chao, 1978).

Sex-role stereotypes can also be reflected in activities and school subjects which are supposed to be appropriate for people of different sexes. Keyes (1979) took Hong Kong Chinese adolescents as subjects and found that 'outdoor activities', such as ball games and hiking, were rated as appropriate for males, while 'activities inside the family', such as minding children, singing, housework, cooking, needlework, and dressmaking, were appropriate for females. These results are consistent with several surveys of role attitudes and status of Taiwanese women in the family. For instance, Lu (1980; 1982) pointed out that, even though women's participation in the workforce was common in Taiwan, women's familial role was still regarded as more important by most people. In fact, the major consideration by most women in choosing their occupation was their familial role, and the ideal employment pattern stated by most women was to have work compatible with their familial role. Gallin's (1982) research suggested that the assumption of new roles in the work-force by married women during the 1970s was not accompanied by appreciable changes in their status relative to men. Chiang's (1982) large-scale survey showed that the typical pattern of power in the Taiwanese family was of the husband-dominant type. In nearly all families, however, the wife undertook responsibility for the family tasks. Assignment of subordinate status to women did not vary with such factors as the respondent's employment status, occupational category, educational attainment, level of income, age, or area of residence, which are often taken to be indicators of modernization. She thus concluded that the traditional role of women remains as an unchanging core value in Taiwanese society. This role and the strength of male and female stereotypes appear to work in concert, and it seems unlikely that they will change, even with economic development.

RESEARCH IN SOCIAL PSYCHOLOGY — INTERPERSONAL PROCESSES

Interpersonal Attraction

In exploring the antecedent conditions for determining an individual's interpersonal attractiveness in Chinese society, it is generally found that most models of interpersonal attraction proposed by Western psychologists are also applicable to Chinese people. For instance, Chang systematically investigated the relationships between interpersonal attraction and such variables as similarity of opinion (Chang, 1976; 1977) and social desirability of opinion (Chang, 1977), by taking Chinese female college students in Taipei as subjects. His results generally supported Western findings that positive linear relationships exist between interpersonal attraction and similarity of attitude (Byrne, 1971), and between attraction and social desirability of opinion (Hewitt, 1972).

It is noteworthy, however, that the results of research studying the relationship between affiliation tendency and interpersonal attraction in Chinese society contradict those found in the West. Chang (1980) administered Mehrabian's scale of affiliation tendency (Mehrabian, 1970) to boys and girls from two junior high schools in Taipei. He found that affiliation tendency was positively and linearly related to sociometric status as perceived by others (interpersonal attraction) for boys but not for girls. For both sexes affiliation tendency was positively related to self-perceived sociometric status and to self-evaluation. The results are very different from findings of research conducted in the West. The latter generally revealed a significant negative relationship between the affiliative motive and interpersonal attraction (see, for example, Atkinson, Heynes, and Veroff, 1954).

The difference between East and West can be interpreted in terms of their divergence on cultural values surrounding affiliation. In Chinese culture, where collectivism and interpersonal 'dependency' are highly valued, an individual's concerns about establishing, maintaining, and improving interpersonal relationships can be viewed as desirable traits, which may make him attractive to others or to himself. On the contrary, in Western culture, which sets high values on individualism and independence, a strong affiliative tendency can be perceived as a weakness which consequently decreases an individual's interpersonal attractiveness.

Chang's other large-scale research study enables us to understand more about the determinants of interpersonal attraction in Chinese society (Chang, 1983). In order to examine the relative importance of affiliative tendency, desirable personal traits, physical attractiveness, similarity of attitudes, and intelligence as factors determining an individual's interpersonal attractiveness, Chang measured those variables in male and female students drawn from 20 classes of 19 junior high schools in Taipei. He also assessed the subjects' sociometric status in their class at two different times during the academic year. The results from regression analyses showed that, at the early stage of acquaintance (during the third to fourth week), the desirability of one's personal traits and self-rated physical attractiveness were the most important determinants of sociometric status for both males and females. At the later stage of acquaintance (about nine months later), the desirability of personal traits and subjective physical attractiveness were still the most important determinants of sociometric status for males; for females, the desirability of personal traits, subjective physical attractiveness, intelligence, and affiliative tendency were the most important determinants.

We may conceptualize physical attractiveness, intelligence, and affiliative tendency as 'desirable traits' in Chinese culture and summarize the research findings by Fishbein and Ajzen's (1975) expectancy-value model. This model asserts that the main reason that a person is liked is that he or she possesses desirable attributes. It can be described by the following equation:

$$A = \sum_{i=1}^{n} p_i e_i \ ,$$

where A is other's attitude towards an object O (this attitude may, for example, be attraction towards another person); p_i is the subjective probability that O possesses attribute i; e_i is the evaluation of the attribute i; and n is the number of beliefs about object O.

The expectancy-value model can be viewed as a universal model which can be applied to people of various cultures. The crucial question to be asked is what personal traits are perceived as 'desirable' by people in a given culture. Findings of previous research provide hints towards an answer. For example, Chien (1977) asked pupils in grade 4 in Taiwan to list the reasons for choosing certain people as their best friends. The traits cited most frequently were friendly, good at schoolwork, enthusiastic to serve others, and having similar interests. Likewise, Chang (1983) asked Taiwanese pupils in grade 7 to describe one of their most-liked peers and ranked the traits in terms of frequency of occurrence. The personal traits most frequently mentioned were, in order of magnitude: amiable, humble, altruistic, honest, hard-working, good at schoolwork, not slanderous, tidy and clean, good-looking, generous, and graceful in speech. In contrast, Kuhlen and Lee (1943) asked pupils in grades 6, 9, and 12 in the United States to nominate their classmates on each of 20 personality-descriptive statements. They found that, regardless of sex and grade, the highly accepted students were more often nominated on such traits as: cheerful, enthusiastic, popular, friendly, sociable, initiates games, enjoys jokes, and good-looking.

The sharp contrast between the Chinese and American lists of attractive personal traits reflects the difference between Chinese and American dynamics of relationship management (Stover, 1974). The former emphasizes the importance of maintaining harmonious interpersonal relationships and acting in a manner appropriate to one's position in a hierarchical social situation; the major concern of an individual in the latter is establishing social relationships and gaining social status by joking, initiating games, and expressing one's talents and social skills.

Face

There are numerous common expressions and proverbs about face in Chinese culture. These are frequently mentioned by Chinese as guidelines for interpreting or regulating social behaviour. Forty years ago, Hu (1944) collected many of these sayings, explained their meaning and usage in Chinese culture, and made an important distinction between two Chinese concepts of face, *lien* and *mianzi*. *Mianzi* 'stands for the kind of prestige that is emphasized in this country [America]: a reputation achieved through getting on in life, through success and ostentation' (p. 45). *Lien*, on the other hand, 'represents the confidence of society in the integrity of ego's moral character, the loss of which makes it impossible for him to function properly within the community. *Lien* is both a social sanction for enforcing moral standards and an internalized sanction' (p. 45).

The prevalence of face-related explanations in Chinese society should not be misinterpreted to suggest that it is a culture-specific phenomenon. On the contrary, the concept of face has universal applicability (Ho, 1976). In his classic work, the Western sociologist Goffman (1955) defined the term 'face' as 'the positive social value a person effectively claims for himself by the line others assume he has taken during a particular contact. Face is an image of self delineated in terms of approved social attributes' (p. 213). Goffman described social interaction as a theatrical performance in which each individual has to choose a 'line' or coherent pattern or verbal acts to express himself or herself, to maintain an image appropriate to the current social situation, and to secure a favourable evaluation from others. Goffman's dramaturgical perspective is akin to Alexander's theory of situated identities. The latter proposes that, for each social setting or interpersonal context, there is a pattern of social behaviour that conveys an identity particularly appropriate to that setting (Alexander and Knight, 1971; Alexander and Lauderdale, 1977). This behavioural pattern, which is called situated identity, is tied to a specific situational context and will change from situation to situation.

Goffman's theory of self-presentation and Alexander's theory of situated identities were formulated in the individualistic culture of America. Both refer face and situated identity to the situationally defined self-image which a person deliberately acts out to obtain immediate respect from others in a given instance of social encounter. These theories and their associated research illustrate the process of face-work in anonymous and mobile societies of the Western world (for examples of research on face-work, see Brown, 1968; 1970; Brown and Garland, 1971; Modigliani, 1971).

The basic propositions of these theories and research findings seem plausible. However, in order to generalize them to an Oriental culture like that of the Chinese, the hierarchical structure of society with its permanency of statuses should be taken into consideration. Stover (1974) took the cocktail party as an example for illustrating the American game of one-upmanship, and compared it with the Chinese game of face. In the typical American cocktail party, everybody plays the game of one-upmanship using the polite boasting and free-floating expressions of sentiment that go with elevating oneself as a means of establishing a positive image. They joke about this and that, jostling for position while gradually revealing something of their personality and feelings. At the Chinese dinner party, on the other hand, rank is fixed by the seating plan.

Everybody invited knows his standing relative to everybody else. They are all expected to follow *li*, doing the proper things with the right people, bowing and gesturing in verbal ritual, and paying respect to others. Stated more explicitly, in American interaction patterns, the situation is roughly the same for all. Everyone has a free choice in the use of language and action. The limits of the game are set by one's ability and ambition. Once an individual masters the skills for performing the game, he or she may doff or don them at will. On the other hand, in Chinese games of face, situations are different for each of those who are playing the game. One has to speak in the language suited to one's station and display appropriate behaviour and status symbols. It is generally believed that the image of self presented to others has a lasting impact, so one has to be very careful about one's behaviour (Stover, 1974, pp. 244–5).

K.K. Hwang (1983a) further explicates the concept of face in his model of Chinese power games. In a static society where the major social resources are controlled by a few allocators who may distribute resources in accordance with their personal preferences, Chinese tend to play the game of face to strengthen the *guanxi* between them. Since the petitioner's power and social status as perceived by others can guarantee an allocator's help, many people like to make the best of the special qualities of the mixed tie by doing face-work and cutting a figure of power to impress others so that they will disburse their resources in a favourable way. Viewed from the perspective of Goffman's dramaturgical theory (1959; 1967), face-work in Chinese society is mainly a kind of 'frontstage behaviour' which an individual deliberately performs before others in the mixed tie; 'backstage behaviour' is authentic behaviour which can only be revealed to persons in the expressive tie. An important aspect of Chinese collectivism is that the family is usually perceived as a basic social unit. If there is any conflict inside the family, it is deliberately handled as a kind of backstage behaviour which should not be brought to the front of the stage where it could be exposed to 'outsiders' of the mixed tie. On the other hand, if any one of the family members attains great achievement, that performance should be publicized frontstage, because it will not only enhance the status of the family as a whole, but also glorify the forebears as well. Such accreditation (Rosenfeld, Giacalone, Tedeschi, and Bond, 1983) enhances access to resources from the mixed tie.

In a typical instance of Chinese social interaction, each person communicates his or her perception of the hierarchical structure of the situation through verbal and non-verbal acts. The interaction proceeds smoothly as long as everybody's claim to face is supported by the evidence conveyed via the other participants. Sometimes others may conspire to invalidate the actor's claim to face, as when a person's misconduct is publicized. In consequence he or she may believe that face has been lost and feel ashamed or embarrassed. At this point, the actor may engage in a wide variety of behaviours in order to restore face. Meanwhile, others may also take some compensatory actions to save the actor's face (Bond and Lee, 1981). Thus behaviour of enhancing and saving face in Chinese society can be further classified into six categories according to the target of the face behaviour.

The first type of face behaviour is enhancing one's own face. Knowing what kind of qualities are most cherished by others in one's social network, one may deliberately do face-work to enhance one's social or positional status by showing off these most appreciated qualities. One may carefully arrange the setting for interaction, take care with one's appearance, and behave in a specific manner in order to manage other people's impressions. For example, a person who 'wants face' (yao mianzi) will strive to show himself or herself to be better situated, more capable, possessing better social connections or a better character than actually is the case. He or she may also 'struggle for face' (cheng mianzi) with others by endeavouring to outdo the latter in all ways of attracting favourable attention from the public (Hu, 1944).

The second classification of face behaviour is enhancing other's face. In addition to enhancing his or her own power image, an individual may adopt some tactics of ingratiation to enhance the resource allocator's face so that the latter might reciprocate by allotting resources in a way to benefit the ingratiator. The tactics include presenting compliments of sufficient credibility and spontaneity, conforming with his or her opinions and behaviour, and giving gifts or doing other pleasant and rewarding things for others (Jones, 1964). In a society where everybody has had to consider his or her face (ku mianzi) in order to advance his or her prestige, a person with lower power usually has to play the role of ingratiator and strive to 'add to his or her superior's face' (tseng-chia mianzi). In this case, the superior may reciprocate and try to increase the subordinate's prestige in front of other people, so that both sides of an interaction will have a feeling that 'we all have face' (ta-chia yu mianzi) (Hu, 1944).

The third type of face behaviour is losing one's own face. In a stable society with a hierarchical order, like that in China, the losing of face (*tiu lien* or *tiu mianzi*) may bring serious consequences for an individual, especially when he or she loses the so-called 'moral face' (King and Myers, 1977). In a static society where interpersonal morality is highly valued, giving accord to the requirements of moral standards is essential in maintaining one's status and prestige. If a person is judged by others as somebody who is ready to obtain benefits in defiance of moral standards, he or she will be severely condemned as 'not wanting face' (*pu-yao lien*) or 'having no face' (*mei-yu lien*). Both terms imply that the actor has laid aside all claims to being a person. An individual in Chinese society always belongs to some groups which absorb and reflect that individual's glory or shame. Consequently, a person who does not want *lien* may also be accused of 'losing *lien*' for someone or some group with whom he or she is closely connected.

Hurting other's face is the fourth type of face behaviour. In a highly structured society, a necessary condition for an individual to function appropriately is that he or she should be sensitive to his or her relationships with those higher or lower on the social scale and be aware of the important and special resources they control. When a man wants to ask for a favour from a resource allocator of some prestige, he first assesses his position relative to the allocator and the likelihood that he may be successful. If his request is then made and accepted, it is said that the allocator 'gave him *mianzi*' and his face is thus increased. On the contrary, if his request is rejected and the allocator does not give him *mianzi*, he may think that the refusal reflects badly on his own *mianzi* and blame the allocator, especially when the allocator occupies a lower social position. Retaliation may well follow, in accordance with the dictates of *bao* (reciprocity).

The fifth classification of face behaviour is saving one's own face. Losing face may cause an individual to experience an uneasy feeling of emotional arousal which has been labelled embarrassment, shame, or shyness. Chu (1983) asked Chinese subjects in Taiwan to assess their responses to nine hypothetical situations involving loss of face. Her results showed that various patterns of emotional arousal, consisting of anger, embarrassment, shame, anxiety, and self-blame, were associated with different types of face-saving behaviour. Three main categories of reaction were identified.

(a) Compensatory actions: when the responsibility for losing face is attributed to the actor, he or she may take some compensatory actions to restore face. These actions may consist of terminating the face-losing behaviour, reinterpreting the situation as one in which he or she was unable to act freely and clarifying the situation to the other, apologizing and asking for pardon from the other, working hard to enhance his or her social status, and so on. In some extreme cases, when he or she is severely humiliated, the actor may retreat permanently from the face-losing situation or even commit suicide.

(b) Retaliatory actions: when the responsibility for losing face is attributed to the other, the actor may decide to retaliate. Since overt aggressive behaviour within the in-group is generally inhibited for Chinese (Bond and Wang, 1983), one usually has to express dissatisfaction in a subtle and indirect way. One may bear the grudge in mind and wait for a favourable moment to air one's complaints, perhaps indirectly. However, when the humiliation comes from a person outside the social network, one is more likely to quarrel or fight back immediately and directly.

(c) Self-defensive reactions: in cases when neither compensatory nor retaliatory actions are acceptable, an individual may take no overt action, but cope with the face-losing situation by such defensive mechanisms as cognitively devaluating the opponent, de-emphasizing the seriousness of the face-losing event, pretending that nothing happened, and so on.

The final category of face behaviour is saving other's face. In a static society where the importance of structural harmony within a group is emphasized, every person has to concern himself or herself with 'right conduct in maintaining one's place in a hierarchical order' (Stover, 1974, p. 246). He or she must pay attention to preserving other's face in social encounters, especially the face of superiors. Since exposing a person's mistake may provoke public reaction and create disharmony, Chinese usually show heightened reluctance to criticize others. If it is necessary to do so, they tend to use vague or moderate language to protect the face of those being criticized (Bond and Lee, 1981). Because rejection of another's request could be interpreted as 'a matter of *mianzi*', a resource allocator will hesitate to turn down the request for help from superiors or persons who have special *guanxi* with him. If it is necessary to do so, the allocator of the resource usually has 'to pad the latter's face' (*fu yen mianzi*) by taking some compensatory action such as apologizing, appealing to external constraints for his inability to help, giving suggestions for alternative solutions, and so forth.

As asserted in the early paragraphs of this section, concern about face is a universal phenomenon. What constitutes a desirable face, however, is culturally more specific. This review of Chinese considerations and the data surrounding face underlines the importance of societal collectivism and power distance in understanding the dynamics of impression management. One's face is more interconnected with that of others, and its protection and enhancement more disciplined by concerns about hierarchical order in Chinese culture than in more individualistic egalitarian cultures (see also Redding and Ng, 1982).

Communication Patterns and Self-disclosure

Yang and Hwang (1980) developed a Chinese version of a self-disclosure questionnaire for young people that covered various domains of the self which a teenager could disclose about himself or herself. They administered the questionnaire to male and female students in junior high school to measure their willingness to disclose themselves when interacting with father, mother, best friend, and friends in general. The subjects' responses to each of the four objects on the questionnaire were factor analysed, revealing three clusters of topics for conversation; these topics related to sex, to family, and to general affairs (including music, television programmes, religion, clothing, and so on). Arranged in order of intimacy value, these three areas for conversation can be depicted as an onion, with topics related to sex at its core, then topics related to family, and topics of general affairs which have the lowest intimacy value located on the surface.

The mean scores of the teenagers' willingness to disclose themselves on the three topics to different social targets were then examined. For topics related to general affairs and family, the most preferred target of self-disclosure was mother, followed by best friend, father, and ordinary friends. However, for topics related to sex, teenagers most preferred to disclose to their best friends. The findings can be explained by the fact that parents are expected to play the roles of 'a stern father' and 'an affectionate mother' in Chinese culture. The sternness of the father probably places him at a greater distance from best friends than would be the case in most Western cultures; the affection of the mother probably positions her closer to her child relative to best friends than would be the case in most Western cultures.

No systematic research on the self-disclosure of Chinese adults is known to the authors. Nevertheless, some preliminary observations suggest that the domains of self for which the Chinese adult could engage in self-disclosure might also be structured as an onion but with a greater number of stratified layers inside. When a Chinese interacts with people of the 'mixed tie' (K.K. Hwang, 1983a) he or she has to consider their relationship (*guanxi*) as well as the hierarchical structure of the situation. The content of communication between casual friends, teachers and students, business associates, and public officials would involve only topics on the surface of the onion. An individual would be willing to disclose what is hidden deep inside the onion only to a few people of the 'expressive tie'.

H.H. Lin's (1984) research on the adjustment of Chinese women after divorce supports this general position. She interviewed divorced women in Taiwan, all of whom were well-educated urbanites with middle socio-economic status. Her data showed that the group most consulted by these women were the parents, who provided support for the women during the divorce. The next most frequently consulted group were the siblings. It thus seems that the main source of assistance for an individual facing a life crisis in Chinese society is his or her immediate family. It should be noted that few women consulted their friends, as is most often done in Western society (Thompson, 1979); nor did they discuss their marriage problems with relatives outside their immediate families. Marital discord is generally considered shameful in Chinese society and is consequently assigned to the 'backstage', an area occupied, in Chinese society, only by one's family of origin.

Leadership

Given the values and traditions which support the hierarchical structuring of interpersonal relationships (*guanxi*), one would expect Chinese social groups to function smoothly with more authoritarian interaction patterns between superior and subordinate. Consistent with this reasoning, Meade (1970) showed that, in an experimental situation, Chinese (in fact, Chinese American) groups were much more cohesive under a controlling style of leadership than were American groups, and vice versa under a more democratic approach. Bennett (1977) conducted another cross-cultural study which showed that, for Filipinos who were more concerned with the value of democracy in relationships between leaders and members, the relationship-oriented leader had higher leadership effectiveness than the task-oriented leader. However, for Chinese in Hong Kong who set a relatively low value on democracy, the opposite was true. The crucial question to ask of course is whether this finding about temporary relationships between leaders and subordinates in laboratory situations can be generalized to real-life situations.

Students of psychology in Taiwan have studied leadership behaviour as perceived by subordinates and its relationship with the job satisfaction of female government employees (Hsu, 1981), elementary school teachers (Liao, 1978), junior high-school teachers (T.T. Tseng, 1978), labour workers (P.S. Cheng, 1977; Huang and Wong, 1980), or accountants (S.Y. Hwang, 1983). Results of these studies consistently revealed that the leader's behaviour along the dimensions of consideration and initiating structure, as measured by the Chinese version of the Leader Behaviour Description Questionnaire (LBDQ), the Supervisory Behaviour Description Questionnaire (SBDQ), or the Leader Opinion Questionnaire (LOQ), was positively correlated with the subordinates' job satisfaction. In other words, subordinates in Chinese groups prefer a leadership style in which the leader maintains a harmonious, considerate relationship with the followers and defines clear-cut tasks for each member of the group.

Hsu's (1982) research on the relationship between a leader's power base and subordinates' job satisfaction in Chinese groups was also suggestive. He showed that the subordinates' job satisfaction was negatively correlated with the coercive power exercised by the leader, but positively correlated with the leader's expert power and his referent power. Stated more explicitly, in real-life working situations, Chinese do not like a punitive leader, but they do like a leader with abundant expertise and ability who is esteemed by others.

It seems that Chinese prefer an authoritiarian leadership style in which a benevolent and respected leader is not only considerate of his followers, but also able to take skilled and decisive action. Of course, one may argue that the above-mentioned research studied the leadership style of an employee's *immediate* supervisor. What characteristics of leadership will be adopted by the leader who heads a typical Chinese organization? Hofstede's (1980) empirical research located three Chinese samples from Hong Kong, Singapore, and Taiwan at the high end of the power distance scale compared with Americans and most other industrialized Western countries. Other social scientists (K.K. Hwang, 1983b; Redding, 1983; Silin, 1976) also described the 'typical' authoritarian pattern of leadership in the so-called family business found in Hong Kong, Taiwan, and the South-east Asian region, in which the business leader can arrange management practices in the organization as he, or occasionally she, wishes. It is generally assumed that the 'typical' Chinese concepts of leadership evolved mainly from the traditional ways by which the head of a family manages his household. The boss of a Chinese family business is almost always a father or father-figure who plays the role of paternalistic owner/manager. Owing to his generalized mistrust towards people outside his family, he tends to be reluctant about broadening the base of ownership and management control to outsiders, and is inclined to assign members of his family to key positions in the organization. As the major decision-maker of the business, he usually analyses the information input and makes decisions on the basis of his knowledge, personal intuition, or past experience. Open debates about his leadership tend to be viewed as either a threat to his face or a challenge to his authority. So the decision-making process is generally not subject to open analysis, and subordinates have to assume that the leader has taken everything into account. Because there are typically no detailed job definitions or clear-cut organization charts, the rights and responsibilities of employees are often left ambiguous and unspecified, their performances are evaluated on a global and subjective basis rather than by objective standards, and the employees are expected to follow decisions and instructions from the top leaders of the organization.

Empirical studies of family businesses in Taiwan generally support the above analysis. Soong (1979) conducted a survey of the administration of 404 medium- and small-scale businesses with 10 to 600 employees; T.Y. Tseng (1978) studied 91 medium- and small-scale businesses; Chou (1983) investigated 43 large-scale businesses with more than 500 employees. All these studies revealed that a high percentage of the sampled organizations (from 50 to 70 per cent) had the characteristics of family businesses stated above; namely, nepotism, a centralized decision-making process, lack of a long-term and formal plan, informal organization structure, and minimal management control of individual performances.

There were many business organizations, however, which had adopted Western ways of management, including delegation of power, developing long-term and formal plans, specifying individual responsibilities for areas of work, measuring performance achieved by individuals in those areas, and rewarding or 'punishing' the individuals accordingly. The adoption of Western management practices seems to be dependent on the size of the organization and the level of technology employed: the larger the organization and the higher the level of technology, the more difficult it becomes for the top leaders of the organization to keep everything under their direct span of control. They thus come under pressure to set up rules and to delegate aspects of their authority to subordinates.

What are the consequences for organizational effectiveness and employees' job satisfaction of variations in these management practices? K.K. Hwang's (1983b) research provided a partial answer to this question. He compared job satisfaction, working morale, and organizational characteristics as perceived by employees in four types of enterprise in Taiwan: family businesses, state-owned enterprises, overseas-funded enterprises, and private enterprises with formal rules of management. The analysis took as indicators: clarity of regulations, reasonableness of regulations, fairness of the reward system, interpersonal harmony, breadth of interpersonal communication, positive group identity, openness of atmosphere, wide delegation of authority, strong sense of responsibility, and activeness in initiating tasks. Results showed that foreign-funded enterprises and private enterprises with formal rules of management were similar, being higher in the above organizational characteristics than family businesses, while the latter were in turn higher than state-owned enterprises. Thus it seems that the more Chinese the style of management in an organization, the more deficient the perceived organizational climate. A similar relationship also holds for the employees' job satisfaction and working morale.

In conclusion, there may exist a greater power distance between leader and subordinates in the hierarchical social structure of Chinese organizations. Nevertheless, the effect of leadership style on subordinates depends on the nature of the power exercised by the leader in the working situation. The greater the expert power and the referent power of the leader, the more satisfied the subordinates are. On the other hand, the more frequently a leader exercises coercive power, the less satisfied they are. With awareness of such factors, many Chinese leaders tend to adopt an authoritarian pattern of leadership, making all the important decisions, assigning tasks to subordinates, all the while striving to be kind and considerate towards those led. This pattern of leadership may work well in temporary leader-subordinate relationships and in small-scale organizations. In large-scale organizations which require more complex levels of technology and organization, however, it is difficult for the manager to keep everything within his span of control. In the latter case insistence on running the organization by traditional ways may result in chaos and decrease the satisfaction level of subordinates. Demands of scale and complexity thus push the Chinese manager towards a more Western style of management — delegating and formalizing. At any given level of functioning of an organization, however, we expect the leader in Chinese cultures to adopt a more authoritarian approach (see Redding and Wong, this volume). Subordinates will appreciate this approach to the extent that it is leavened with compassion (*renqing*).

Conformity

At the descriptive level, conformity refers to behaviour which moves the actor's response closer to the position advocated by a designated source of influence. The possible motives for such accommodating behaviour are manifold, including the desires to avoid conflict, to ingratiate oneself with the source of influence, to be correct, and so forth. Given this variety of potential explanations, it would seem short sighted simply to take a theoretical position like Solomon's (1971) dependency orientation and predict that Chinese persons generally conform more than a given group with a more independent orientation.

The hierarchy of the Confucian social structure, for example, suggests a contrary prediction. One would expect that, when higher-status Chinese targets are influenced by lower-status sources, they would show less, rather than more, conformity than would be shown by targets from less authoritarian cultures. Similarly, the importance of relationship discussed by K.K. Hwang (1983a) should also affect Chinese conformity in surprising ways. One might predict that a stranger would have less influence in Chinese society than in some cultures which place less emphasis on established associations.

The conformity studies to date have tended to adopt a Confucian perspective and to focus on the impact of status. As discussed above, the norm of filial piety required loyalty and submission by children to parental wishes. This dynamic is explicitly extended to younger brothers *vis-à-vis* elder brothers, wives *vis-à-vis* husbands, and subjects *vis-à-vis* rulers. One would expect this dynamic to generalize, covering any consensually defined situation of superordination and subordination, such as that between teacher and student or between employer and employee (Hsu, 1965).

Submission to control from a superior would thus be reinforced more strongly in cultures like the Chinese with high power distance. Consequently, there should be greater responsiveness to this status variable among Chinese samples than among samples from cultures characterized by lower power distance. Only one study has manipulated the variable of positional status cross-culturally. Surprisingly, however, Huang and Harris (1973) found that, contrary to prediction, Chinese in Taiwan were no more sensitive in general to their status manipulation than Americans. Regardless of culture, a higher-status person was imitated more than one of lower status.

In fact, a closer inspection of the results would have shown that their conclusions held only when the model explicitly disclaimed any competence about the target issue. When the model claimed competence about this target issue, the predicted interaction between culture and relative status was shown in the means, although not at significant levels.

Thus, relative status appears to have more impact with Chinese than American subjects, at least under certain conditions of model competence. We believe that this conclusion would be confirmed at significant levels and across more varied situations had subjects and models been drawn from intact groups with established dominance hierarchies. The Confucian dynamic is particularistic and relational (Hsu, 1971b); strangers are rarely discussed. Consequently, experiments involving strangers are not as likely to reveal the unique impact of the Chinese cultural experience.

Of course, some generalization from previous experience will come into play when authoritative strangers or impersonal authoritative agencies attempt to influence the subjects. So the Chinese subjects studied by Huang and Harris (1973) imitated a college professor to a greater extent than did American college students. Chu (1966) found that Chinese subjects from Taiwan were more affected by attempts to influence them by the mass media than were American subjects in a similar study performed earlier by Janis and Field (1959). Lai (1981) compared Chinese secondary-school students in Hong Kong with similar English students, obtaining results similar to Chu's. Likewise, Whittaker and Meade (1968) conducted a cross-cultural study in which student subjects were presented with opinions on controversial issues originating from sources of high and of low credibility. The largest immediate difference in the effect of this credibility manipulation was found for the Hong Kong sample. Of the other four cultural groups only Brazil, another country high in

Hofstede's (1980) power distance, showed a similar degree of impact. As before, however, we believe that the fullest impact of the status variable will be shown among persons already enmeshed within a dominance hierarchy. Impersonal studies involving unknown sources of authority are less sensitive in revealing unique Chinese patterns.

So far we have discussed only influence attempts from superior to subordinate. What about those from subordinate to superior? As argued elsewhere (Bond and Lee, 1981; Wilson, 1970, pp. 19–49), such attempts must be undertaken with great circumspection in Chinese culture. The superior's face must be protected sedulously in any society marked by high power distance. It would be most interesting to give subordinates in cultures of differing power distance the task of influencing a superior and to see how their procedures differ. Regardless of procedure, however, we expect that Chinese superiors would be relatively less affected by such attempts, given Confucian social philosophy. Indeed, the opportunity for such direct attempts would be institutionally lacking.

Why is it then that Huang and Harris (1973) found that Chinese were influenced more than Americans by a low- (and probably lower-) status model? In public situations involving strangers thrown together, we believe that the core concern of the Chinese to avoid conflict becomes a prepotent issue. As the interactants have no probable future together, the agenda becomes one of avoiding potentially disruptive differences. Imitation of the other's responses is the obvious solution, especially when the topic discussed is of no moment.

We believe this desire to avoid open conflict lies behind the results of studies comparing the response of Chinese and Americans to peer-group pressure. In these situations, the status variable is not engaged. Instead, the collectivist concern of the Chinese to avoid interpersonal disharmony (Ho, 1979b) becomes salient. The individual's actual position on an issue is subordinated to his or her desire to protect the group's integrity by side-stepping open disagreement (Wilson, 1974, p. 196). Consequently, we find that Chinese male and female students shifted towards the majority position more frequently than American students (Meade and Barnard, 1973; 1975). This finding has also been confirmed with children imitating a peer (Chu, 1979). Meade and Barnard (1973) argued that the higher reaction times of Chinese subjects probably indicate that disagreement with their peers was more emotionally charged and aversive for them than for their American counterparts. Consequently, the Chinese subjects were less likely to respond independently of the group (Chu, 1979). Their focus was on defusing the disagreement, not on evaluating the issue. The Americans, relatively freed from this collectivist concern, responded with more anticonforming choices in both Meade and Barnard studies, with either a larger (Meade and Barnard, 1973) or smaller (Meade and Barnard, 1975) average shift towards the majority, probably depending on their assessment of the issues involved and their importance (Jones and Kiesler, 1971).

An interesting question in this conformity research concerns the extent to which these acts of public compliance represent internalized attitude changes in the actors involved. Public compliance can obviously be an act of impression management (Tedeschi and Riess, 1981), carrying no necessary relation to the actor's belief. Given the Chinese norms concerning harmony maintenance, we believe that the discrepancy between public presentation and private belief will be greater for Chinese than for people from more individualistic cultures such as the United States. Only recently have experimenters begun to use this public/private variable in studies of Chinese social interaction (for example, Bond and Hui, 1982; Leung and Bond, 1984). It is hoped that this variable will also be incorporated into cross-cultural studies of conformity. We may then confirm the hypothesis that Chinese make more conforming shifts publicly but actually change their private beliefs less than American subjects.

At first, it would seem that such public/private discrepancies are bound to be larger in collectivist than in individualistic cultures. For the collectivist tension is that the individual's interests should be subordinated to those of the group. Consequently, normative pressures will be brought to bear upon the individual's behaviour when it is judged to be contrary to group needs. Such group needs are universal, of course, but in less group-oriented cultures their demands are strongly tempered by a respect for individual self-seeking. A consonance between private wishes and public performance is thus easier to achieve in more individualistic cultures.

It may be, however, that it is easier in collectivist societies to internalize and accept group- or other-serving values so that the public/private tension disappears. Consistent with this reasoning is Huang and Harris' (1974) finding that Chinese in Taiwan who accepted a letter for posting from a stranger were more likely to post that letter than were Americans. Perhaps the high American sociability and need for affiliation and support (Abbott, 1970; Huang, 1963;

Tarwater, 1966), coupled with an individualistic orientation, traps them into public commitments that they are privately more likely to dishonour. Lacking this individualistic value structure, the Chinese are more loyal to their social commitments. In support of this argument is Harding's (1980) finding that the distance between the ideal self and the social self on Kelly's (1955) construct test was significantly smaller for Chinese than for American subjects. Social acts thus appear to be freer of conflict for the Chinese.

Clearly, this issue is potentially rich for exploration. Increased use of the public/private variable will not only illuminate aspects of Chinese social functioning, but also link research to an expanding body of Western data (Baumeister, 1982).

Distributive Justice

This term refers to the strategies used by people to divide a given resource or set of resources among a given set of potential recipients. Such division is a problem of fundamental human importance (Deutsch, 1975). Three types of broad strategy have been identified, namely, equity, equality, and need. An equity solution relates output to input, maintaining a constant proportion among all those contributing their resource inputs to produce a specified output. An equality solution simply divides the given resource equally among all the relevant parties. Finally, a need solution divides the resource among the relevant parties in terms of their perceived need along some relevant dimensions.

Researchers have typically used the material resource of money in their studies, since it is easily quantified. As Foa (1971) has pointed out, however, there are many types of resource to be distributed, and some, like love and status, may be of greater long-term moment than money. In fact, a recent study at The Chinese University of Hong Kong (Bond, 1984b) indicated that different strategies of allocation may be adopted depending on the type of resource — status was distributed equitably and money equally, at least between relevant groups. Future studies should attend to this important issue of resource type.

The studies available which have involved Chinese subjects can be neatly integrated by referring to K.K. Hwang's (1983a) theory of Chinese power games. The critical issue from his perspective is for the resource allocator to decide on the type of relationship which exists between himself and the potential recipient. If this relationship is of the mixed type where the possibility of a long-term relationship exists, Chinese will adopt a more egalitarian solution than less collectivistic Americans (see, for example, Bond, Leung, and Wan, 1982b; Chu and Yang, 1976; Leung and Bond, 1982; Leung and Bond, 1984). When dividing resources with a stranger in an instrumental relationship, however, Chinese will be more equitable than Americans, whose motives will include a higher need for affiliation and sociability (Leung and Bond, 1984).

These results can also be explained from the perspective of cultural collectivism. If one is concerned about maintaining the integrity of one's group, one learns to adopt a more egalitarian style of dividing resources. This approach minimizes the tendency of other group members to make invidious and divisive comparisons. As friendship needs are adequately satisfied within these existing groupings, however, one tends to adopt a more equitable strategy when distributing between self and strangers who fall outside these groups (see Leung and Bond, 1984, for elaboration of this argument).

The above studies have required individual subjects to divide a given resource with another individual where no information is given about that other beyond his or her relative input. What of the distributive problem when the parties involved are from different groups and their respective group memberships are made salient? Interest in this critical social problem has been galvanized by Tajfel's (1974; 1978) social identity theory. In a recent empirical examination of this process using Hong Kong Chinese, Ng (1984) found that subjects showed in-group favouritism when dividing a resource. No cross-cultural studies have yet been run at the intergroup level, however. One might predict that group membership would be a more important consideration guiding resource allocations for the collectivistic Chinese than for persons from more individualistic cultures.

Ethnic Affirmation versus Cross-cultural Accommodation

Language is an important marker of ethnic identity (Fishman, 1977); indeed, it can be a carrier of ethnic identity (Bond, in press), so that intergroup relations can be studied by examining reactions to language variation. Yang and Bond (1980) first explored this phenomenon by presenting bilingual university students in Hong Kong with a questionnaire written either in English or Chinese. There were 20 items in the scale, each of which asked the respondents to endorse either a traditional Chinese or a modern Western alternative regarding a particular behaviour or attitude. Chinese respondents selected more of the Chinese alternatives when the scale was written in English than in Chinese. Yang and Bond (1980) speculated that this shift towards one's cultural position was an act of self-presentation towards an out-group member (the English reader); they labelled the process 'ethnic affirmation'.

This same shift has occurred in two replications in Hong Kong (Bond and Yang, 1982; Kong, 1980) and in Malaysia (Ismail and Dyal, 1983). It thus appears to be a reliable phenomenon with the forced-choice questionnaire. However, an opposite shift has been observed on rating scales such as the modified Rokeach Value Survey (see Ng, Akhtar-Hoosain, Ball, Bond, Hayashi, Lim, O'Driscoll, Sinha, and Yang, 1982). Here, the respondent's self-ratings shift towards the out-group's position on the English language version, a process labelled 'cross-cultural accommodation'.

What determines whether the responses to the English language version show ethnic affirmation or cross-cultural accommodation? The critical issue seems to depend on where the subject's self-rating on a given item falls with respect to the perceived in-group and out-group position (Bond, 1983b). The closer the subject's self-rating lies to the out-group's position, the greater the tendency to affirm one's ethnicity (that is, shift back towards the in-group position) when responding to the English language instrument. Conversely, the closer the subject's self-rating lies to the in-group's position, the greater the amount of cross-cultural accommodation (that is, shift towards the out-group position). It appears that one affirms if one's ethnic group identity is questionable, but accommodates when one's ethnicity is more secure by being more closely aligned with the in-group.

The process of ethnic affirmation has also been demonstrated in response to variations in *spoken* language (Bond and Cheung, 1984). Here, Hong Kong university students gave more typically Western ratings to Chinese experimenters who addressed them in the Mandarin language than to those who used English or their native Cantonese. This repudiation of the traditional Chinese position reflects the perceived threat to Hong Kong's future which is posed by the People's Republic of China where, of course, Mandarin is the official language.

What is unclear in this line of language research is how the observed reactions are culturally influenced. Processes similar to ethnic affirmation and cross-cultural accommodation have been observed in research with other cultural groups (by, for example, Bourhis, Giles, Leyens, and Tajfel, 1979; Marin, Triandis, Betancourt, and Kashima, 1983). These shifts clearly reflect universal features of intergroup relations such as perception of shared fate or political threat. Given the Chinese concern for conflict avoidance, however, it is probable that they are less likely to show the same degree of ethnic affirmation than are other less collectivist cultural groups.

Aggression and Conflict

Surprisingly few studies have focused on Chinese behaviour whose object is to administer pain to another (see Bond and Wang, 1983, for an overview). Those that exist in the literature tend to be descriptive and lack a theoretical framework which would make cross-cultural studies productive (for example, Niem and Collard, 1972; Sugg, 1975). So, for example, Su (1969) measured aggression in both fantasy and play situations by boys and girls in various age-groups. Aggression was found to increase with age and, as consistently found elsewhere (Maccoby and Jacklin, 1974), to be higher in boys than in girls.

The exception to this generalization about conceptual vacuums is a recent study by Bond, Wan, Leung, and Giacalone (1985). They adopted a social control perspective, construing aggression as a set of coercive tactics, often physical, for asserting power and authority (see Tedeschi, Gaes, and Rivera, 1977). A person emitting such 'aggressive' behaviour will be censured only if his or her acts transgress cultural norms guiding the exercise of authority in given social positions. Societies differ in the extent to which they restrain the exercise of coercive behaviour by those in authority, with cultures low in power distance being more restrictive in granting these prerogatives (Hofstede, 1980, Chapter 3). Consequently, verbal abuse of a subordinate by his or her superior should be less acceptable, and the abusive actor judged more negatively in cultures of low power distance than in cultures of high power distance. The opposite pattern of results should be found for a subordinate's verbal insult of a superior.

University students in Hong Kong and the United States reacted to a scenario study, confirming the above predictions for the insulting superior (Bond et al., 1985). It was also found that the Chinese were particularly critical of a leader presiding over a meeting at which a superior and his subordinate were involved in a heated exchange. Among Chinese, one of the responsibilities of those in positions of power is to anticipate and defuse potential confrontations. Once these occur, he (or occasionally she) should take immediate action to terminate the encounter and to smooth over the issue backstage before another meeting takes place. The overall leader is the master puppeteer carefully balancing contending parties. In Chinese culture, one uses position power to enforce order. Indeed, this is probably a feature of the superior's role in all cultures characterized by high power distance.

As argued in Bond and Wang (1983), Chinese people are preoccupied with a concern for maintaining social order. This order is created through the hierarchical structuring of relationships underlying Confucian social philosophy. Each party to a duality is bound by responsibilities but, in return, enjoys access to prerogatives proportionate to rank. Consensual acceptance of this differential access to resources prevents competition for resources from rending the social fabric asunder.

This is an ideal picture, of course; conflict over resources often arises. Chinese strategies for resolving these conflicts, however, are characterized by strategies geared to short-circuit open conflict — the use of indirect language, middlemen, face-saving ploys, a long-range view, flexibility, and so on (Chiao, 1981). Strategies such as open debate, which require direct confrontation, are avoided (Bond et al., 1985). Overall primacy is instead attached to the need for social order, as a precondition for enjoying the fruit of any resolved conflict.

This fundamental concern with maintaining interpersonal harmony is reinforced by the typical structure of Chinese discourse. As Young (1982) argues, Chinese discussants first present the common problems and contextual constraints which are binding on all the participants, before stating their own position. This strategy results in their appearing diffident and vague to most Westerners, but effectively prevents a polarization of positions and a resulting conflict among the participants.

The importance attached to conflict avoidance by Chinese manifests itself clearly when American research paradigms are imported. So, for example, Li, Cheung, and Kau (1979) presented their subjects with Madsen's (1971) game board, but unexpectedly found that schoolchildren in Hong Kong and Taiwan continued to cooperate even when the reward structure was changed to be competitive. Bond (1979) found to his surprise that a future opponent in a face-to-face contest was rated more positively than a neutral stimulus person. At the interpersonal level, then, it appears to be 'Friendship first, competition second', as the Chinese proverb so neatly puts the issue.

Some indigenous research on strategies for dealing with conflict has produced richly suggestive findings. Hwang (1978) examined the socio-cultural stress, coping strategies, and psychopathological symptoms of 180 married men who were household heads of families residing in urban Taipei, Taiwan. The age of the subjects ranged from 30 to 60 years and their socio-economic status from low to high. He analysed his three sets of data separately, then tried to find the associations among these three sets of factors by using second-order factor analysis. On the basis of the results of this analysis, he developed a model to illustrate the dynamic process of coping with interpersonal conflicts in Chinese culture. The model indicates that, when facing an interpersonal conflict situation, an individual may adopt an active or passive coping strategy. The active coping strategy includes two alternatives: the mechanism of facing reality (*mien tuihsien-shih*) or the mechanism of self-assertion (*kau tzu-chi* and *tu-tuan tu-hsing*); the passive coping strategy is mainly characterized by perseverance (*ren-nai*).

The perception of interpersonal conflict situations is associated with the particular coping strategy used by an individual. Those who adopt the strategy of facing reality tend to attribute the responsibility for introducing interpersonal conflicts to themselves as well as others. Those who emphasize the importance of self-assertion, however, tend to attribute the fault to others. No matter how an individual perceives the locus of responsibility which leads to interpersonal conflicts, coping with the conflict situation by either active mechanism is accompanied by psychosomatic disorders in the oral-gastro-intestinal system and by sleep disturbances. As with the pattern of self-assertion, those who prefer to meet conflict situations passively with perseverance tend to attribute the fault to others. This pattern of coping is accompanied, however, by disturbance and retardation in cognitive functioning and withdrawal from interpersonal situations.

Clearly, there are individual differences among Chinese in their coping strategies and psychosomatic responses. These personality syndromes will undoubtedly interact with the social variables discussed in this section on aggression and conflict. So, for example, those who use self-assertion should respond to the company president in the Bond *et al.* (1985) scenario very differently from those who cope passively. They should likewise approach competitive zero-sum interactions with different responses. Further research using coping strategies as a moderator variable will help to articulate our understanding of Chinese responses to conflict situations.

FUTURE RESEARCH DIRECTIONS

In developing the field of cross-cultural psychology, it has been important to enhance the confidence of researchers from various countries that their cultural heritage and uniqueness would be respected. The need to foster this assurance is one factor underlying the continued currency of the much-touted 'emic/etic' issue (Berry, 1969). Of course, cultures have unique (emic) features, as do individuals; they also share comparable (etic) features, as do individuals. An overemphasis on their unique aspects, however, has resulted in the perceived need to replicate the wealth of American and European studies before generalizing them to other cultures. This is an impossible undertaking.

One alternative is to develop indigenous psychologies. Typically, the forum for this response is journals confined to local readership, often printed in the local language. Unfortunately, links with other traditions are usually not fostered and intellectual cross-fertilization is then discouraged. While this process enhances each culture's sense of positive distinctiveness (Tajfel, 1974), it defeats the larger purpose of constructing a universal science of psychology.

What is needed is a theory of cultural variation which can be incorporated into the theories of psychological functioning. In this way, one can begin predicting how persons from cultures differing in known ways should differ from one another in relevant behaviour (see, for example, Bond *et al.*, 1985; Detweiler, 1978; Gabrenya, Wang, and Latane, in press). Information about a person's culture would then function like information about his or her personality in generating predictions from theories of social behaviour.

For this reason, some attention has been paid in this overview to the cultural dimensions of collectivism and power distance. These constructs enable psychologists to locate the Chinese in a broader cultural network, linking their results in more understandable ways to those from other cultural traditions. Through this scientific 'bricklaying' we may begin building a more complex edifice in place of the disjointed pockets of settlement we have so far scattered about. Theory-guided data collection is a necessary condition in this undertaking. Theories of culture should be based upon a wide reading of the social science literature and should locate a variety of cultures empirically along their various dimensions (see, for example, Hofstede, 1980). With such theories, explanations of results will assume a much less *ad hoc* flavour and will create the potential for scientific growth.

To give more stringent tests to our reasoning, multicultural studies are required, so that one can assess whether the obtained results match the predicted pattern. Two-culture comparisons almost always produce differences, but are susceptible to a host of plausible rival hypotheses (Brislin *et al.*, 1973). Expansion beyond the typical two-culture contrast is possible because the international community of psychologists has reached a stage of sufficient maturity where such networking is now feasible (see, for example, Hofstede and Bond, 1984).

This review has necessarily focused on research areas where there has been some sustained activity. It has thus ignored 'one-shot' studies involving Chinese subjects where these studies cannot be easily integrated into the topics covered above. Some of this research can, however, be tied to the cultural constructs of collectivism and power distance discussed, and it is hoped that follow-up experiments will attempt such a linkage. Some of these studies would include, for instance, Whitney's (1971) on the perception of balance in interpersonal relations, Castell and Goldstein's (1977) and Smith and Vinacke's (1951) on humour, Chen's (n.d.) on group problem solving, and Hiniker's (1969) on cognitive dissonance.

Established areas of research in social psychology need to be expanded in promising directions. Many of these potential topics have been mentioned under their respective headings above. In general, it now seems important to incorporate the intergroup dimension into our studies more frequently (see Taylor and Brown, 1979), to examine the links between judgements of perception on the one hand and behaviour on the other, and to place more reliance on indigenous instruments and concepts in order to help 'decentre' the psychological enterprise from its Western centre of gravity (see Brislin *et al.*, 1973, pp. 37–9 and 130–1).

The purpose of this review is to stimulate such future studies in

Chinese social psychology. The undertaking is daunting and the present manpower is limited. Perhaps it would be appropriate, however, to remind those who will carry this torch of the Chinese proverb: 'A journey of a thousand miles begins with a single step'.

7 The Psychology of Chinese Organizational Behaviour

GORDON REDDING AND GILBERT Y.Y. WONG

INTRODUCTION

Chinese organizational behaviour is a field of immense variety, as its context ranges from the politically dominated organizations of the People's Republic of China (PRC) to the extremely *laissez-faire* capitalist institutions of Hong Kong, with all varieties of organizational purpose, forms of ownership, technologies, products, and services represented.

With such a background, it will be necessary to focus on only part of this set, otherwise there is a danger that too broad generalization will devalue what may be said. In the following discussion we have chosen to focus on the organizations of the Overseas Chinese, rather than on those of China.

The reasons for this choice are, firstly, that organizations in China are currently changing at such speed that most of our received knowledge of them is out of date and a review of it could be misleading. Reporting current research could also mislead if evolution continues at its present rate. The changing political ideology of China has a particularly strong influence on life in organizations since they have been, to some extent, designed with ideological purposes in mind. The second reason is that the Overseas Chinese form of organization, visible as the Chinese family business, is economically very significant in world terms. Thirdly, this form of organization is very little understood, and clearly deserves wider understanding. We shall therefore concentrate our attention on the Overseas Chinese, while acknowledging a fascination with the PRC which we are currently unable to indulge.

The psychological aspects of the organizational behaviour of the Overseas Chinese are of great interest from both theoretical and practical points of view. The understanding of organizational effectiveness commonly comes to rest in the intractable area of human feelings, no less so in the West than in the Orient, but such matters have been the subject of far deeper and more extensive study in the

West, where they may be claimed to be fairly well understood. In the Overseas Chinese case, one sees the intriguing paradox of a little-understood organizational form developing to a level of efficiency which offers a serious threat to Western bureaucratic forms of organization. Yet it is only recently, and still with only sporadic empirical evidence, that the sources of Chinese business success have begun to be sought out and described.

THE REGIONAL CONTEXT

Taking for the moment a wider regional perspective, one might suggest the existence of three culturally determined organizational forms of significance in East Asia: the Japanese, the South Korean, and that of the Overseas Chinese. The Japanese form, in consequence of its massive international impact, has been subjected to intensive study. The other two, somewhat later in establishing their international impact, remain little studied but are predictably due for much closer attention.

Some indication of success at the national level will serve to illustrate what many observers see as an economic miracle taking place in East Asia, an area where management practices have borrowed only selectively from Western precedents and where the retention of traditional forms has affirmed a subtle form of cultural confidence.

In 1950 (in 1973 US dollars), Taiwan's per capita income was 224, South Korea's was 146, and Hong Kong's was 470. Countries at a comparable stage of economic development were African countries with per capita incomes of 150 for Nigeria, 129 for Kenya, and 203 for Egypt. Economically the Latin American countries were clearly ahead, with per capita incomes of 373 in Brazil, 562 in Mexico, and 907 in Argentina. Thirty years later, the situation is utterly different. In 1982 South Korea, with a per capita Gross National Product (GNP) of 1,910, had left Nigeria at 860 far behind, despite the latter's oil. Kenya had improved only to 390 and Egypt to 690. Clearly even the success stories of Africa are no longer in the same league. Taiwan, from being a long way behind the big Latin American countries, had clearly outstripped them by 1982 with a per capita GNP of 2,720, compared to Brazil's 2,240, Mexico's 2,270, and Argentina's 2,520. By 1982 Hong Kong with 5,340 and Singapore with 5,910 had not only overtaken the Latin American countries but also passed Greece at 4,290, Israel at 5,090, Spain at 5,430, and Ireland at 5,150 (World Bank, 1984).

PROBLEMS OF EXPLANATION

Explanation of this phenomenon by economists suffers from their widespread refusal to acknowledge the influence of human factors at the micro level (Redding and Hicks, 1983b), but there is an occasional acceptance by perhaps the more broadminded among them of the fact that the element of people has a role to play in the explanation of economic growth. A sophisticated treatment, for instance, by Little (1981) concludes that the success rests on 'good policies and the people', and parallel cases have been made by Morawetz (1980) and Oshima (1981).

One of the more obvious causal issues emerges from the homogeneity of the Oriental cultures in which post-war growth has flourished so dramatically. This homogeneity does of course break down on closer inspection, but nevertheless, in world terms, Japan, Korea, and the non-Communist outliers of China have much in common, and certainly have a very strong set of roots with a common heritage in ancient Chinese civilization.

This shared heritage of the East Asian countries has provided strong prima-facie evidence to suggest that culture may be an important contributor to economic growth. The cultural origins of Japan and Korea owe much to Chinese civilization; and Hong Kong, Taiwan, and Singapore have overwhelming majorities of Overseas Chinese who arrived from mainland China following southward migration dating from as far back as the Ming Dynasty. The majority of the present-day Overseas Chinese, however, migrated to their host countries during the early part of the twentieth century, with an upsurge after the Chinese revolution in the late 1940s. Besides those in Hong Kong, Taiwan, and Singapore, there are substantial populations of Overseas Chinese in Malaysia. A minority of ethnic Chinese who play a crucial role in the business sector are also present in the Philippines, Thailand, and Indonesia (Hicks and Redding, 1982).

Intrigued by the close correlation between successful economic performance and common cultural heritage, Kahn (1979) proposed what has become known as the post-Confucian hypothesis. This suggests that the economic success of Japan, South Korea, Taiwan, Hong

Kong, and Singapore is due in large part to certain key traits common to cultures which, although they may now vary in the expression of it, derive their main social ideals from Confucian tradition. Recent research from sociological and psychological viewpoints has provided substantial support for Kahn's idea and will provide a main component of this chapter. At the same time, in considering the effect of culture, we would not wish to claim that it is the *only* cause of success but that it is one of the important causes that contribute to the new economic power of East Asian countries. We hope here to identify the distinctive cultural characteristics of the Overseas Chinese and explicate their effect on organizational behaviour.

BUILDING CULTURE INTO AN EXPLANATION

The question of the influence of culture on organizational effectiveness remains problematic in the literature. In part this is due to a lack of research and the fact that comparative management has only recently re-emerged after a period of being out of fashion. In part it is due to an endemic problem in the core discipline of anthropology over the nature and definition of culture.

Progress, however, may now be observed on both fronts. The shock of Japanese incursions into the American and European economies, and the quite sudden realization that there exist viable alternatives to the Western organizational model, have caused a reappraisal of the value of comparative management studies and one which gives alternatives much greater attention and support (Lammers and Hickson, 1979; Weinshall, 1977; Ouchi, 1981). Progress may also be detected in the development of the concept of culture itself. Anthropologists generally view culture as a complex system which embraces all of a society's 'folkways'. This is reflected in Tayor's definition (Child, 1981, p. 323) of culture as 'that complex whole which includes knowledge, belief, art, morals, law, custom and any capabilities and habits acquired by man as a member of society'. Such an all-embracing concept has not been fruitful in identifying the basic differences between cultures, nor for studying their impact on organizational structure and behaviour.

Recognizing this definitional confusion, and in an attempt to reduce the meaning of culture in such a way as to make it include less but explain more, recent thinking on culture has tended to confine the concept within the cognitive domain (Geertz, 1984; Hofstede, 1980; Kaplan and Manners, 1972; Keesing, 1974).

In this context, it may be useful to follow an early suggestion of Kroeber and Parsons which distinguishes between the concept of 'culture' and the term 'social system'. They confined the concept of 'culture' to the transmitted and created content of values, ideas, and other symbolic meaningful systems which are factors in the shaping of 'human behaviour', and used the term 'social system' to designate 'the specifically relational system of interaction among individuals and collectivities' (Kroeber and Parsons, 1958, p. 583). The distinction thus allows for the recognition that social actions and relationships can be conditioned by 'culture', the latter being the set of normative and preferential conditions for action, as well as by non-cultural variables such as technology and economic factors.

Confining culture to the cognitive domain, within Keesing's (1974) 'rules of the game' or Hofstede's (1980) 'collective programming of the mind', allows for theoretical progress in that it may sponsor more focusing of research. At the same time, the connections between the way in which people perceive society's rules and the way in which they behave in organizations should not simply be left as a series of black boxes. A simple approach is proposed, which leaves cognition as the base layer, as it were the foundation for other aspects, namely the interpersonal and the societal. All three are seen as interacting mutually with organizational behaviour.

In proposing connections between culture and organizational behaviour, care must of course be taken to acknowledge other parallel influences. These issues have been treated elsewhere (Redding and Hicks, 1983a; Redding, in press) and suffice it to say that the influences of historic, economic, technological, and political factors, although only acknowledged briefly here, are seen as essential parts of any full understanding.

The Post-Confucian Hypothesis

The over-arching idea provided by Kahn (1979), in the form of the post-Confucian hypothesis, should be noted before we consider one of its manifestations in greater detail via the case of the Overseas Chinese. This contribution to the understanding of the sources of economic growth rests on the notion of a common cultural heritage for Japan, Korea, and the Overseas Chinese, reaching back thousands of years. Variations in its modern manifestation are allowed for, in the same way that European countries display a wide variety of interpretations today of their Graeco-Roman heritage. Kahn proposes four traits consistent with Confucian ideology which have remained constant, and which have significant impact on present-day organizations in Japan, Korea, and among the Overseas Chinese. These are:

(a) socialization within the family unit in such a way as to promote sobriety, education, the acquisition of skills, and seriousness about tasks, job, family, and obligations;

(b) a tendency to help the group (however it might be identified);

(c) a sense of hierarchy and of its naturalness and rightness;

(d) a sense of complementarity in relationships which, combined with the sense of hierarchy, enhances perceptions of fairness and equity in institutions. For example, a boss's paternalistic concern for subordinates will be complemented by their willingness to cooperate without excessive resentment of (or perhaps even perception of) their relative subordination.

These traits will be woven into our account and we shall return to them when considering the final question of organizational effectiveness.

A FRAMEWORK FOR ANALYSIS

The understanding of Chinese organizations involves knowledge of organization structures, managerial processes, and organization members. In the background is the notion that such components will form a coherent and culturally acceptable whole. As adaptive social systems they will have accommodated themselves to their environment.

This analysis will thus subdivide its subject matter into three interconnected layers, namely: organization structures, management processes, and organizational members (and by extension the culture conveyed in the beliefs, values, and attitudes of members).

By organization structure we refer to the relatively enduring pattern of relationship among units and individuals inside an organization. It is the framework within which organizational behaviour takes place. While there are certain 'logics' of relations among structural parts, especially the 'logic' of technological and environmental factors, the relationships are nevertheless man-made and will still vary according to the company's preferences and the strategic choices of key decision-makers (Child, 1972).

By management processes, we refer to activities such as leadership, decision making, and the communication methods through which organization goals are achieved. The way in which the processes are carried out is the result of the interaction between the characteristics of the individuals and the structural characteristics of the organization.

The individual level of analysis will take account of certain ideas and ideals brought into the organization in the heads of individuals. These will be largely derived from their culture, but only those which may be considered to have an impact on the way the organization works will be considered here.

ORGANIZATION STRUCTURE

For the layman, the structure of an organization may be seen most easily in terms of its organization chart. Structuring is about the apportionment of authority, roles, and status, and it provides the skeleton framework for the organization's behaviour and processes. Its dimensions are commonly seen as specialization, standardization, and formalization (which represent the structuring of activities); and centralization and configuration (which represent the distribution of power).

The reasons that structures vary are twofold. Firstly, there are universal imperatives which appear valid for all organizations. Some examples would be the beliefs that greater size inevitably leads to more formalized activities, that greater dependence on other organizations leads to more centralization of decisions, and that certain kinds of technology will demand certain systems of management control.

Secondly, an authority system will also have to take account of what is locally perceived as an appropriate way of handling authority, and evidence has accumulated to indicate that this changes from one part of the world to another. For example, Crozier (1964) in his study of French factories suggested a French preference for impersonal bureaucracy, which has grown out of the French cultural aversion to personal dependence. Lincoln, Hanada, and Olson (1981, p. 95) argued that the low horizontal differentiation and high vertical differentiation in Japanese organizations was due to 'the desire to maximise consonance with the cultural expectation of their members'. Hofstede (1980, p. 384) came to much the same conclusion when he argued that

The combination of power distance and uncertainty avoidance typical for a country's culture affects the structure of organizations that will work best in that country — next to the demands of technology and the traditions of the kind of activity that the organization exercises: whether it be a shoe factory, a municipal administration, a school, or a hospital.

Uncertainty avoidance refers to the extent to which a society feels threatened by uncertain and ambiguous situations and tries to avoid these situations by providing greater career stability, establishing more formal rules, not tolerating deviant ideas, and so on. Power distance is the perception by members of substantial and natural hierarchical distances in the social order, or, at the other extreme, of egalitarianism.

Hofstede's argument is partially supported by a recent study of transnational banks in Hong Kong (Wong, 1985). Using the short form of the Aston questionnaire (Inkson, Pugh, and Hickson, 1970) to measure the organization structure dimensions of formalization and centralization, Wong found that banks from high power distance countries exhibit a much higher level of centralization of decision making than those from low power distance countries. The level of formalization, however, does not vary significantly with the uncertainty avoidance indices of the banks' countries of origin, when the factor of size is controlled.

Before considering the organization structures of Chinese companies, it is necessary to set the scene with a few words on their social and industrial context. They may thus be better understood as responses to a distinct set of forces. The key contextual variables are ownership, size, and technology.

Ownership

Writing of Hong Kong society, Lau (1982, p. 72) describes the dominant cultural code as 'utilitarianistic familism'. This is seen as a response to an environment offering little long-term stability and support, and the idea contains the following elements: (a) family interests are placed above those of society and other groups within it; (b) material interests take priority over non-material interests, this being manifest, for instance, in economic interdependence and the way in which peripheral members may be induced into or barred from the familial group. Lau also distinguishes four subgroups within the family, which he terms the core group, close relatives, distant relatives, and non-relatives, with different and flexible kinds of membership for each.

This combination of familism and materialism produces a logical next step which is the serving of both interests by a family company. The retention of ownership rights by a chosen few allows in turn the retention of profits by the same group. As long as capital may still be generated internally, or from sympathetic institutions, the growth of the company may still proceed without the need to surrender proprietorial rights over its resources. In the event, Overseas Chinese organizations are virtually all family businesses, and even the largest of them, although technically public companies, have rarely become professionally managed bureaucracies of the Western kind, and still commonly display heavy family influence if not absolute dominance.

An extension of this tendency for family and company to overlap is nepotism. Relatives are employed in key positions (Lai, 1978; Low, 1973; Yong, 1973). The same principle is often also evident in the employment of long-serving and loyal affiliates who become almost honorary family members, tied in by bonds of obligation in which patronage downwards and loyalty upwards are exchanged.

Size

Chinese companies are small and, contrary to normal expectations about the influence of national economic growth, are, on average, decreasing in size in Hong Kong. In 1951, of all manufacturing establishments in Hong Kong, 79 per cent employed fewer than 50 people. In 1971 this figure had become 88 per cent and by 1981 it was 92 per cent. Over the same period the small-company sector accounted for a proportion of the work-force which grew from 26 per cent to 41 per cent. Medium-size companies employing 50 to 500 employees declined in number from 19 per cent to 8 per cent of the total. They also accounted for fewer of the work-force, the figure dropping from 47 per cent to 43 per cent. In 1981 only 0.4 per cent of companies employed over 500 people, and they accounted for only 16 per cent of the work-force, with a steadily decreasing trend on each count.

Reasons for these tendencies are complex and are outside the scope of this chapter, but an important implication for organization structure must be noted. This is the fact that structuring will remain simple in the majority of companies. In itself this is of less import than is the resulting lack of examples in the business community of highly sophisticated company structures. This may well have an influence on the dispersal of managerial know-how and may serve as a brake on the development of advanced techniques and systems. Data on structure, to be presented shortly, will reflect this tendency.

Technology and Structure

It is not valid to generalize about the impact of technology on Chinese organizations except to say that there is a tendency for companies to act as manufacturers or providers of a specific service within a larger chain of operations, but not to manage the whole chain by vertical integration. This results in a restriction of the company's range of activities, very few manufacturers, for instance, having a fully fledged marketing function. This leads to a tendency within the organization to concentrate on one main line of activity or work-flow, and this in turn leads to a tendency for the technology of that process to influence the organization's structure in a way not found elsewhere (Pugh and Redding, 1985).

The results in Chinese organizations of the forces just noted are reflected in Table 7.1, which gives data from a survey of organization structures in 53 Hong Kong and 34 British companies, using the Aston instrument. This clearly indicates a lower level of structuring in Chinese companies: roles are less precisely defined; standard procedures are less prevalent; 'staff' as opposed to 'line' personnel are far less evident. As a compensating factor, centralization of decision making is higher. Only in formalization, that is, formal paperwork procedures, is there true similarity.

Such findings are consistent with those of King and Leung's (1975) study of Kwun Tong small factories, where they found that 40 per cent had no internal division into departments, 73.3 per cent of all internal communications were totally verbal, and 40 per cent of owners controlled their production workers in a direct way without passing through any intermediaries at all.

A picture thus emerges of an organizational type which is quite distinct and characterized by the following structural elements.

(a) Centralization of the power of decision making, usually to a

Table 7.1 Structural Variables for Hong Kong Chinese and British
Organizations with Fewer than 2,600 Employees

	Mean	Standard Deviation	Range
Role specialization			
HK organizations	18.5	14.4	0–69
UK organizations	26.2	13.8	0–62
Standardization			
HK organizations	59.8	23.0	11–111
UK organizations	74.4	20.4	30–117
Formalization			
HK organizations	19.7	10.0	1–41
UK organizations	19.8	9.9	4–41
Centralization			
HK organizations	109.9	15.2	70–139
UK organizations	80.9	13.9	57–116
Percentage of 'staff' personnel			
HK organizations	13.5	12.5	0–75
UK organizations	29.7	17.2	6–72

Note: HK organizations, n = 53; UK organizations, n = 34.

Source: Pugh and Redding (1985).

single dominant owner, manager, entrepreneur, founder, or father
figure.

(b) Small scale as a basic tendency (and even when large-scale exceptions do occur they tend to remain highly centralized).

(c) A low level of specialization, with fewer and/or less detailed
job specifications, less breaking up of the organization into
specialized departments, and with more people responsible for a
spread of activities across a number of fields.

(d) Less standardization of activities and thus fewer routine
procedures.

(e) A relative lack of ancillary departments such as research and
development, labour relations, public relations, market research,
and a tendency instead for all employees to deal with the main
product or service of the company.

(f) A strong overlap between ownership and control, the private family business being vastly predominant.

This, then, is the context in which organizational behaviour takes place. Before we consider possible psychological determinants, the managerial processes themselves should be noted; in other words, we look at *how* the structure works, before proceeding to consider *why*.

MANAGEMENT PROCESSES

Organizational 'process' is still a highly contentious research area, and one for which much conceptual work needs to be done within the central discipline of organization theory. The comparative branch of that theory is even less likely to provide a tidy set of accepted categories within which the managerial processes of concern to us may be discussed.

In consequence, we shall resort to two simple categories commonly used elsewhere, accepting that they contain some overlap. They are leadership behaviour and decision-making processes; and management control.

Leadership and Decision Making

Silin (1976) provides an unusual metaphor in describing Chinese leadership style as 'didactic', but the idea contains rich meaning. The implication is that the leader holds information, and thus power, and doles it out in small pieces to subordinates, who thus remain more or less dependent. The leader's role has some overtones of that of the teacher. At the same time, the leader does not normally commit himself openly to a line of action, but rather keeps his options open, leaving the direction of his organization or department to follow the lines detected by a somewhat nebulous but nevertheless powerful set of personal intuitions. The latter àre the responsibility of the leader, and his reputation, and to some extent his authority, rest on his capacity to intuit the right strategy. The low structuring scores noted earlier, and the commonly accepted lack in Chinese firms of the more obvious Western trappings in the form of such devices as corporate planning, lend prima-facie support to this notion.

In the event, leadership style within Chinese companies is directive and authoritarian. Research by Redding and Casey (1976) provided comparisons of beliefs about management behaviour which clearly indicated a distinctly more autocratic approach than that found in the West, especially in the contexts of sharing information with subordinates and allowing them to participate in decision making. This finding is supported in the data from studies in Taiwan reported by Bond and Hwang (Chapter 6 in this book).

Silin (1976, p. 63) also remarked on the concern of the leader with the retention of power, saying that the leader tends to be clearly and unequivocally predominant and 'tends to prevent executives from making highly visible personal contributions which might suggest that they possess leadership quality'. The consonance of such an approach with high power distance scores in Hofstede's (1980) research lends support to the idea that it is an appropriate adaptation within the organization to norms of the wider society.

Management Control

Management control, as it is normally understood, embraces the processes of defining organizational goals to the point where they can be turned into action; monitoring the results across a spectrum of activities; comparing results against expectations enshrined in, for example, a budget; and, finally, taking action to correct deviations from plan. It is in principle a rational process, and, as practised in Western bureaucracies, a largely open one with much of the information used for control being easily available to many people.

In the Chinese context, these clear principles run into two barriers, each with psychological components. Firstly, the establishment of corporate goals is usually an internal family matter and is not for discussion among a wider body of executives. It is not easy for a wide range of personnel to assume responsibility for corporate goals. Secondly, there is much secrecy about performance, and particularly over information bearing on finance and profitability. These are seen as private (that is, family) preserves. It is therefore difficult to operate completely open control systems except in non-controversial areas such as production management.

Alternative means of achieving predictable organizational behaviour come into play, and might be categorized as nepotism and obligation networks; non-objective performance assessment; and paternalism.

Evidence concerning nepotism and obligation networks is derived from a number of studies. In a study of factory managers in Kwun

Tong, Mok (1973) reported that in 69 per cent of the Chinese-owned factories decisions were made solely by proprietors, whereas in only 39 per cent of the non-Chinese-owned factories were decisions made by proprietors. In the absence of the proprietors, 35 per cent of the Chinese-owned factories relied on kinfolk for decision making while only 5 per cent of the non-Chinese-owned factories reported that they would rely on kinfolk for decision making.

Because of the importance of the family, and the tendency in a 'collectivist' society for the attachment of the individual to a group, relationships at all levels of Chinese business organizations tend to be modelled on familial relationships. This does not imply that individual family members are necessarily treated with benevolence. Indeed, the less powerful ones are often ruthlessly exploited (Wilson and Pusey, 1982). Superiors tend to be condescending to their subordinates, public humiliation of subordinates is not uncommon and may even be socially tolerated. This may explain why Redding and Ng (1982) found that 'face' is less important in the personnel area than in other management areas.

Nepotism does provide the organization with certain advantages, in that the personal and corporate goals of key executives from the family can be said to overlap, and this in turn provides for very strong motivation as well as cohesion in policy. It does, however, create the disadvantage that such an organization must remain small enough to prevent the need for outside professional managers. The small scale of most Chinese organizations is indicative of these limitations at work. The number of family members who can be trusted with responsibilities is a major determinant of organizational size.

When personal relationships displace performance as a basis for building a co-operative human system, there is a strong likelihood that obligation networks will extend beyond the boundary of the family itself. This leads to the development of cliques, usually based on clan or regional affiliations (Leeming, 1977). The cultural preference for harmony, at least on the surface, means that dissatisfaction among the subordinates and conflict between cliques are unlikely to be brought into the open. Hence, as in Imperial Chinese bureaucracies, there may come to exist considerable 'deceit, obfuscation, chicanery, collusion and selective performance of assigned tasks' (Sterba, 1978). To the outsider the Chinese organization may appear to be 'one large family'; underneath it may be seething with hostility between cliques and tense interpersonal relations based on differences in obligation nets. The individual's reaction to this situation is often one of frustration, but the response is usually to leave the organization rather than to attempt a reform of an element so informal as to be beyond managerial reach or interest. Ironically, subgroup solidarity under the paterfamilias is likely to fracture any larger solidarity of the working group as a whole, and we would argue that this is part of the reason that trade unionism has not been successful in the Chinese business context.

Reliance on personal relations extends also to external business relations. Leeming's (1977) study of trading companies in the Sheung Wan district of Hong Kong found that 'Overseas contacts are usually based on uncles and cousins living overseas. Business contacts are friends, and virtually all business is based on personal contacts' (p. 51). Here the relations are largely informal and great importance is placed on trust.

The salience of this element of trustworthiness is conveyed in Silin's (1972) study of market behaviour and in Barton's (1983) study of Chinese businessmen in Vietnam. In its Cantonese version the word expressing this crucial component in business relations is *sun yung* and Barton's description of its power (1983, p. 50) is as follows:

In a community almost totally oriented toward business transactions, *sun yung* was the most important aspect of a person's character and not merely a quality to be considered in economic affairs.

Sun yung referred not only to credit, in the sense of goods or services lent without immediate return against the promise of a future repayment, or to 'credit rating', which is an assessment made by a lender of the risks involved in extending credit to a specific individual; it further carried the connotation of a person's total reputation for trustworthiness and in this sense was a statement of a person's social and psychological characteristics as well as strictly economic reliability.

Reinforcing such tendencies is the background element of sensitivity to 'face', which acts to foster trustworthiness, in that the loss of face in the community can lead to ostracism of a kind felt particularly keenly by Chinese people (Redding and Ng, 1982), as indeed it may for any people brought up in such personalized social networks.

The second means of achieving predictable organizational behaviour is by non-objective performance assessment. The lack of a structured system of performance measurement is inevitable with a lower structuring of organizational procedures, and leads to a lack of data on which individual performance can be assessed. At the same time, the definition of responsibilities is often loose and changeable, and formal organization charts are rare. In these circumstances, a person's contribution to the organization is viewed by his superiors more in terms of loyalty and 'followership' than in terms of his objectively measured achievements. This, of course, produces a high level of upwards dependence in the relationship, and removes power from the subordinate, as his value to the organization is not determined objectively.

Paternalism is the third means by which predictable organizational behaviour may be achieved. An organization in which power and decision making are concentrated in family hands at the top of the organization, and where the majority of employees accept the status quo as normal, may be termed paternalistic. Such paternalism will not be entirely dysfunctional and it could be argued that in some ways it is a suitable adaptation to the expectations of employees, being in harmony with the values of respect for authority, conformism, and deference. Many employees do appear to be seeking a familistic context and to be willing to exchange loyalty for protection. At the same time, not all aspects of paternalism are positive.

The overconcentration of power at the top often leads to tension in vertical relationships at the lower levels. In a comparative study of supervisory roles in industrial firms in Singapore, Deyo (1978) found that supervisors in Chinese firms did not feel that they had sufficient authority to meet their responsibilities, and felt that they were often bypassed by their superiors who went straight to their subordinates. In examining this process of bypassing, Deyo (1983) makes a distinction between operating decisions, which are commonly delegated to supervisors, and finance and personnel decisions, which are made by top managers. The workings of paternalism are then as follows (Deyo, 1983, p. 216):

Recruitment decisions in Chinese firms emphasise trustworthiness and loyalty to a far greater degree than in Western firms. Well known is the tendency to hire kinsmen or closely trusted persons for top-level positions, rather than to search more widely for persons of the best qualifications. Lower and middle-level managers tend to be internally recruited, while lower-level persons are often hired on the basis of recommendations by supervisors or trusted persons.

In addition, top managers retain personal power over workers through retention of control over decisions relating to bonuses, pay increases, and employee discipline, as well as through personal loans to employees and joint involvement in formal social activities off the job (for example, festivities, weddings, and so on). In other words, while operating responsibility has been delegated to lower-level managers, effective power over workers is retained at higher levels. One consequence of the resulting disjuncture between supervisory operating responsibility and effective power is a lack of effective supervisory authority among lower management, and a frequent bypassing of persons at this level in disputes and other personnel questions.

ORGANIZATIONAL MEMBERS

We now consider Chinese organizational behaviour at the individual level of analysis, and in particular the values which are imported from the wider culture, carried in peoples' heads. Organizations are bounded expressions of a collection of acts of co-operation, and the elements of Chinese psychology which may be taken as salient for our present purposes are those which have some bearing on co-operativeness. The latter may be seen simply as both vertical and horizontal, in other words as going along (or otherwise) with bosses, and getting along (or otherwise) with fellow workers.

We shall elaborate on two main themes in the psychological make-up of organizational members, namely social stability and materialism, and observe the way in which the various elements within each theme affect the achievement of co-operation within organizations. We shall conclude that co-operation can flourish within certain limits but that its full potential is restricted.

These two major categories of values emerge consistently from a number of studies of Overseas Chinese societies. Social stability, usually seen as being based on familism, is given as a key Chinese value by Silin (1976), Salaff (1981), Lau (1982), Ryan (1961), Baker (1979), and Freedman (1979). Materialism and its ramifications are noted as central by Lau (1982), Ryan (1961), and Freedman (1979).

Social Stability

The first aspect of social stability which we shall consider is familism. The importance of family has already been noted in the context of company ownership, but there are aspects of it which affect the attitudes and behaviour of more junior employees which must now be considered.

In Salaff's (1981) study of female factory workers in Hong Kong, the perspective that she found essential in explaining behaviour was that of the centripetal family, which in turn is related to a sociological element which she termed factionalism. Such factionalism does not refer to political allegiances but occurs when kinship, ethnicity, and culture are used by people in the attempt to gain scarce resources.

Groups become internally cohesive via bonds of friendship, kinship, and language, but may well be in conflict, or at least in a state of non-co-operation, with other groups, as they attempt to accumulate group wealth.

In the centripetal form the family becomes a power base to manipulate other institutions. Families consequently stratify the community while endeavoring to develop their own power and wealth. A centripetal family gathers in its forces by demanding the primary loyalty of its members and mobilizing their labor power, political, and psychological allegiances on behalf of kinsmen. The centripetal norms and values aid families in their competition against other kin groups for scarce resources. (Salaff, 1981, p. 8.)

The power of such a system to survive is based partly on ancestor worship and partly on the perception of wealth as family wealth, to which all contribute and from which all may benefit. Although traditions of partible inheritance mean that wealth is passed on to sons equally, daughters are also supported by dowries and education. Circles of kin may also participate in this process of bounded mutal aid. For organizations there are two significant outcomes. Firstly, wages paid to workers are likely to pass directly to the family purse, thus breaking to some degree the link between individual effort and reward. Secondly, for most employees, emotional affiliation with, and loyalty to, the employing organization will inevitably take second place.

The second aspect of social stability for discussion is wider collectivism. The idea of a person's belonging to a set of different and overlapping social networks is implicit in Hofstede's (1980) description of collectivism/individualism as one of the primary dimensions of culture. His research results indicate high levels of collectivism for Chinese people. Although we have already indicated that the family is the most central of the collectivities, the idea of concentric circles of other allegiances (including work groups) must now be entertained.

With this notion goes the concept proposed by Fei (1948) of differential order. In this view, individuals do not perceive themselves as related to each other on some fundamentally equal basis. Instead the individual is at the centre of a series of concentric circles, the closest having the strongest blood ties. What is significant is that rights and obligations differ according to the relative positions of people in such circles. In such a context, multiple standards of morality may well operate and be seen as perfectly acceptable. Duty to the community at large, based on some universally agreed moral principle, is replaced by ethics based on taking each situation and interpreting it according to loosely formulated principles of *jen* (or human-heartedness). As Hsieh (1967, p. 321) has observed, 'For Confucian ethics, there is no abstract standard by which to resolve the conflict of values. The only solution is that every man should decide by his own conscience or *jen*.' Thus the application of multiple standards in dealing with people is not morally repugnant where the standards are set according to relative positions in the concentric circles.

In a society with such strong perceptions of collectivism, social needs take on great significance as part of the individual's psychological composition. In contrast to Westerners, for whom ego-centred needs such as self-actualization tend to dominate, both Chinese managers and Chinese employees are reported as giving a higher rank to social needs than to ego needs (Chau and Chan, 1984; Lui 1985; Redding and Casey, 1976).

Hsu's (1971b) concept of the Chinese perception of the person as inseparable from his or her networks adds further to our understanding. He argues, for instance, that basic perceptions by the individual about himself or herself are at opposite ends of a continuum between East and West. The Chinese word *jen*, with all its overtones of connectedness and reciprocal relations, does not coincide in meaning with the English word 'man', with all its overtones of separateness, free will, and individualism.

There are two implications for organizational behaviour here. Firstly, many Western managerial techniques in the human area of management carry with them unstated assumptions which may not transfer to the Chinese context. An example might be management by objectives, which rests on ideals of individual competitiveness, personal achievement, personal accountability, and open confrontation. All of these ideals clash with many of the perceptions and feelings about relationships in a society such as the Chinese, which is sensitive to collectivity. Chinese management control, in the event, becomes more a matter of the subtle tying up of obligation networks. Individually measured performance is rarely taken into account except in mechanical production systems and in the control of piecework operations. Secondly, the sensitivity to membership of networks and factions is likely to strengthen the influence of the informal organization, and the office which appears to run smoothly may in reality consist of rival cliques and obligation networks with strong influences on individual behaviour.

Thirdly, we examine 'face' and interpersonal harmony. A great deal of ritual behaviour takes place in a Chinese organization in an effort to maintain the social harmony which is so highly prized. Although ritual politeness and deference may break down in close relationships, there is nevertheless an almost visible tendency to be wary of others' sensitivities.

Many societies, and especially those of the Orient, have developed levels of sensitivity in interpersonal matters which are difficult for outsiders to comprehend or attain. It is as if the more collectivized a society becomes, the more sensitive must be the social mechanisms which maintain harmony, as escape from the network is not an option, and the network must stay intact. The central concept is common: in Japan, the *omoiyari* (or empathy) culture; in Korea, *kibun*, and in Thailand, *krengchai* (considerate behaviour); in the Philippines, *pakikisama* (the avoidance of interpersonal conflict at all costs); in Malay and Indonesian culture, the respect for the considerate person. All are crucial to an understanding of behaviour. In the Chinese case, the social lubricant is 'face'.

It has been rightly pointed out (Ho, 1976; Goffman, 1955) that face is a human universal. What is of interest in the present discussion is the degree to which people are concerned about it. For the Chinese the degree of concern is high.

The distinction proposed by Hu (1944) between *lien* and *mien-tzu* allowed an understanding of two distinct aspects of face. *Lien* is moral worth and contains the idea of being a 'decent' human being. It is ascribed rather than achieved and loss of it is serious. *Mien-tzu* carries with it the idea of reputation based on one's own efforts. It is more achieved than ascribed and although useful in life, it is not essential. Its absence is not a cause for condemnation.

The development of face sensitivity derives from the process of socialization (see Ho, this volume), but two aspects of such socialization are worthy of note for their relevance to co-operation in organizations. From studies of child-rearing practices in Taiwan, Wilson has described how face sensitivity enhances the stability of both *vertical* and *horizontal* relationships. He notes a strong connection between face and values which support a predominantly vertical group structure and a centralized authority pattern. Individuals invest in groups via the face they claim, and the emphasis on shaming techniques and group consciousness in child-rearing reinforces compliance.

Loyalty to other members of one's group is the society's most outstanding value and this loyalty requires that friends and relatives go to extreme lengths to honour their obligations to each other. The disloyal person is a person without face ... The strictures of face apply to all groups of which one is a member, but the most stringent implications are always in primary groups with those individuals one knows personally, and where affective ties are generally strongest. (Wilson, 1970, p. 127.)

In a study of face as perceived by 102 middle-level Chinese executives in Hong Kong, including the content analysis of 91 face episodes described from real life in organizations, it became apparent that social and or psychological transactions in which face was involved were common. This was especially so in relations between leaders and subordinates, in sales and negotiating, in management control, and even as an element in financial decision making (Redding and Ng, 1982).

The search for interpersonal harmony thus produces a person psychologically attuned to deference, compliance, and cooperativeness within delimited groups. Strength of identity with a group, however, introduces the risk of apathy about or even hostility towards other groups, and the question of the organization's internal effectiveness may well rest on whether the group to which a person belongs has aims which are in line with those of the organization. This is the rationale behind the power of paternalism, and one of the more subtle reasons for there being limits to growth. The emotional ties of paternalism cannot be stretched very widely.

Finally, we examine vertical relations. It was observed above that Chinese socialization teaches a person acceptance of hierarchy. It is noticeable, for instance, that in the *wu lun*, or Five Cardinal Relations on which centuries of impressive social stability have been built, four relationships are explicitly vertical, and training in accepting them creates an individual who understands the two-way obligations which they entail. Even relationships of friendship may be transformed in this way (King and Bond, 1985). The exchange of obligations is a matter of Confucian duty and the expression of such duty serves to stabilize the family unit which is the framework for all the relationships.

Leadership behaviour in the organizational context was discussed earlier, but not from the viewpoint of the subordinate, and an examination now of what we might term 'followership' reveals an important aspect of Chinese organizations which separates them from both Japanese and Western equivalents and which may well delimit their size and effectiveness. Within the directive and authoritarian tone of the relationship between Chinese leaders and subordinates described earlier lie elements of suspicion by each party of the other. These prevent the development of the emotional bonds so commonly described for Japanese as a source of organizational strength and worker commitment (Morishima, 1982; Nakane, 1973; Rohlen, 1974; Vogel, 1979).

Instead, the vertical relationship in the Chinese case remains more formal, more aloof, more reserved, as if to acknowledge tacitly that true loyalties are likely to be directed elsewhere. The remaining bonds which do keep this relationship operating are the traditional Confucian respect for authority and the utilitarian perception that it is rational for authority to be exercised for the common good. The tone is thus more calculating than emotional, when seen from below.

Silin (1976, p. 11) notes that 'The formal rejection of the affective component in creating solidarities is striking and has direct implications for leadership'. He proposes two tensions which may result from this: firstly, the potential withdrawal of support by subordinates, against which a leader must be constantly on guard; secondly, the danger of a subordinate's challenging the leader's position. To counteract the latter, Silin argues that superiors regularly play down or deny the contributions of subordinates.

A further significant contrast with Japan appears when one analyses the element of dependence. Dependence upwards and a degree of solicitude downwards in the relationship between leader and subordinate may be seen as keys to Japanese character (Doi, 1973). As such, they explain much of the solidarity of Japanese groups and explain also something of the capacity of organizations to grow extremely large. Japanese managers expend much effort on cultivating co-operation from workers by making constant and active expressions of respect for them as individuals. The manager is then able to obtain high levels of commitment from workers who appear to have strong needs for identification with company aims and pride in company achievements. Such a management system may well reduce the need for elaborate and costly alternative systems of management control.

The Chinese vertical relationship is more complex, and Silin's (1976) findings might be summarized as follows.

(a) The individual has an unavoidable responsibility for his own actions;

(b) the top-down tradition of authority at the same time leaves little room for subordinate initiative;

(c) subordinate behaviour which is not in tune with the leader's intentions is likely to have serious repercussions for the subordinate;

(d) goals will normally be derived from the leader's intentions and may not be openly and clearly defined;

(e) a test of loyalty is the capacity to understand and espouse these intentions.

The organizational limitations of the system are shown in its reliance on key personalities, and the related constraint that in one organization there is room for only one key personality to control the strategic processes. Subdivision of the policy-making role becomes problematic, and a limit to growth is immediately apparent.

Materialism

The first aspect of materialism to be considered is the pursuit of wealth. The use of phrases such as 'money as religion' exemplifies the danger that a Western perspective may distort the view of this facet of Chinese psychology.

Lau (1982) regards 'emphasis on material values' as the first of the major normative orientations of Hong Kong, and provides reasons for the infatuation with money which ensues. In his view, the main determinants are:

(a) a historic tradition of commercialization and business shrewdness in Kwangtung province, which antedates exposure to the West;

(b) the freedom of a migrant class from traditional moral constraints on acquisitiveness, and the related absence of a gentry class to set alternative values;

(c) the blocking of upward mobility through political channels in a colonial society, and the use of economic mobility as the only viable alternative;

(d) the stimuli of visible inequality and conspicuous consumption;

(e) the openness of the economy and the resulting inability of any élite to monopolize economic opportunities.

Such materialism is not, however, restricted to Hong Kong and suggests a further deeper reason connected with human needs for security in a potentially threatening environment. The Chinese throughout the Asian region suffer degrees of repression, discrimination, uncertainty, and occasional physical violence. It is perhaps not surprising that the shelter of money in a hostile world should be a matter for idealism.

In a study of a Chinese trading community in Indonesia, Ryan (1961, p. 16) discussed the 'focal value of wealth', saying, 'In the day to day course of events, it is around this value that energies are mobilized, interest centred, the very life and household organized, and in the service of which social relations are patterned'.

That such a value is typical of the Overseas Chinese generally is suggested also by Freedman (1979, p. 25), when he says:

Shrewdness in handling money was an important part of the equipment which ordinary Chinese took with them when they went overseas in search of a livelihood. Their financial skill rested above all on three characteristics of the society in which they were raised: the respectability of the pursuit of riches, the relative immunity of surplus wealth from confiscation by political superiors, and the legitimacy of careful and interested financial dealings between neighbours and even close kinsmen. The Chinese were economically successful in Southeast Asia not simply because they were energetic immigrants, but more fundamentally because in their quest for riches they knew how to handle money, and organize men in relation to money.

Attitude surveys among Chinese workers regularly find that monetary rewards are high on the list of priorities (Chau and Chan, 1984; Lui, 1985). It is, however, worth noting the finding from a large sample survey reported by Turner (1980), that those most concerned with pay were the less skilled workers, casual employees, those in smaller private firms, and those in manufacturing industry.

The second aspect of materialism for discussion is entrepreneurialism. Familism, materialism, and the pursuit of wealth must have a vehicle, and entrepreneurial skill is, in consequence, held in high regard. Ryan's (1961) study of Chinese values suggested that, as an outcome of the importance accorded to the search for wealth, a cluster of values emerge which sponsor respect for cleverness, nerve, and skill, especially in the commercial or industrial context. Equipped with these, a young man can go out and earn — not his fortune, but a family fortune. The respect due to him within the family for such endeavours may well be as important as the material advantages themselves.

Such respect is also societal, and reveals an important aspect of the search for fulfilment which motivates the entrepreneur and causes such a proliferation of entrepreneurs. In discussing this phenomenon, Ryan (1961, p. 20) makes an important distinction between 'individualism' and 'self-reliance', indicating that the former is not appropriate but that the latter is.

The crucial requirement of this value is that each adult male should have his own business in which the responsibility for risks of loss and the possibilities for profit are borne by the individual. This value is of tremendous importance in shaping the form of the economic units which make up the economy ... As a result small business units multiply and there is a considerable barrier to expansion beyond a family operation ... Persons who work for others and who do not have the capital to operate as independent business men fall into the lower rungs of the prestige scale and have, in actuality, little voice in community affairs. There is no element in the value system giving support to the role of wage earner.

The outcome of such pressures is visible in Hong Kong organizations. In a study of the Hong Kong economy, T.Y. Cheng (1977, p. 57) noted that of the 280,000 establishments 'all but a small fraction ... are very small in scale and owned by a single person or a few partners'. He also pointed out that there is one business unit for every 18 people, compared with one for every 36 people in the United States, noting that the high Hong Kong figure 'may be seen to reflect the strong pecuniary drive of the local inhabitants as well as the relatively lenient laws governing the formation of business'.

Entrepreneurial drive of course is not the same as entrepreneurial skill, and the distinction is made evident in the high mortality rate of such ventures. Although 52,000 new firms come into being each year, another 35,000 disappear, and of the 438,600 registered between 1945 and 1977, only two-thirds remain.

The implication of this drive for independence and for the garnering of family wealth is that many managers in large companies are accumulating knowledge, skills, and contacts with a view to starting their own businesses whenever the opportunity arises. Although such individuals comprise only 5.5 per cent of the population, they are nevertheless the more dynamic and ambitious people in an average group, and there must be a high likelihood of their assuming positions of responsibility, at least within the lower supervisory and managerial ranks of any large company. It could thus be argued that in any large company, the relationship between many key personnel and the organization is likely to be utilitarian. One might further speculate that corporate growth will inevitably be constrained by the lack of commitment of such personnel to the organization and its goals, and the inability of the owner or manager to trust personnel who have not been won over by patronage of one form or another.

Reflections on organizational problems arising from this attitude are provided in Wong's (1979) study of management in the Hong Kong textile industry. For the industry as a whole, the proliferation of independent companies provides the flexibility which gives vitality and dynamism. For the individual firm, however, the internal strains can be threatening. The urge of workers to start their own businesses undermines teamwork and, according to a Shanghainese manager quoted by Wong (1979, p. 213), results in 'the atrocious downgrading of standard and quality'.

The centralization of decision making in Chinese companies noted earlier, the autocratic flavour of the decision-making process, and the tight control of operations are seen by Wong (1979) as part of a defensive strategy to counteract low motivation, threats of desertion, and mistrust. Autocracy is, of course, only one of a number of strategies which could be used, but its prevalence is clearly widespread. Two other approaches, patronage and bureaucratization, may be said to be equally valid. Of these, patronage appears to fit more closely with local expectations as an alternative to autocracy, but these are of course two sides of the same coin in the end.

Finally, in our examination of materialism, we consider the work ethic. In discussing the post-Confucian hypothesis as an explanation for the dramatic economic progress of East Asia, Kahn (1979) indicated that seriousness of purpose and diligence were important components of East Asian cultures. It is a common observation that the Overseas Chinese work hard, but the fact that one cannot confidently generalize the same statement to the PRC suggests that institutions and ideological factors in the environment have a part to play in shaping a work ethic. An extension of this reasoning is that culture alone is not the only cause of the high levels of diligence observed; necessary, perhaps, but not of itself sufficient.

The reasons for the development of such a strong work ethic have much to do with the particular circumstances of life for the Overseas Chinese and especially the surrounding element of insecurity which tends to affect them. In Hong Kong, the shadow of 1997 looms; in Taiwan, the shadow of the PRC; while in the Philippines, Indonesia, Thailand, and Malaysia, the Chinese are an economically successful minority whose acceptance by host cultures cannot always be taken for granted. Occasional outbreaks of racial violence and a long tradition of anti-Chinese legal discrimination cause them to see themselves as a besieged minority, surviving by their wits, and especially by their hard work.

The tendency to work hard may thus be attributed to the following factors:

(a) the importance of wealth as a surrogate for security and the clear connection seen between effort and reward;

(b) the long tradition of obligation to the family, which sponsors seriousness of purpose;

(c) the acceptance of discipline in a high power distance and status-conscious culture;

(d) the demonstration, in many of their environments, of the success attributable to work;

(e) the relative lack of other universally valued attributes used in the ascription of status;

(f) highly sensitive social networks and forms of group pressure which are able to influence the individual to conform to the general ethic, and to avoid the odium and the loss of belonging which are caused by being considered lazy.

THE SPECIAL NATURE OF CHINESE ORGANIZATIONAL PSYCHOLOGY

We have noted that Chinese organizations contribute to some of the most impressive national growth records ever achieved. If this sum of their efforts is notably successful, it is reasonable to suppose that the general level of the organization's internal efficiency is high. In reaching this efficiency they tend to adopt a remarkably consistent form as organizations, being normally small, loosely structured, family dominated, and paternalistic structures.

The leadership process is generally didactic and the management control process relies heavily on nepotism, obligation networks, subjective performance assessment, and paternalism or patronage. Members of the organization enter it with a set of values stressing familism, a wider collectivism, a sensitivity to interpersonal harmony, and a sense of social hierarchy. They act with a strong interest in wealth, a respect for entrepreneurialism, and much diligence.

In consequence, the balancing of forces which produces high levels of vertical and horizontal co-operation and which allows productive effort to serve equally sets of personal and organizational goals, is a matter of some delicacy. If the organization becomes too large, it is beyond the reach of the personal ties which bind people in effectively. Too much protective paternalism will reduce the level of effort by subordinates. Too much nepotism may weaken effectiveness in key positions; too little may raise problems of trust. Too much delegation may risk misuse and a high turnover of supervisors and lower-level managers; too little will place a heavy burden on the owner/manager.

In the tightrope walk which all organizations negotiate, the Chinese organization tends to find one particular point of balance. It is a matter of small being beautiful, and it is a lesson being relearnt elsewhere.

As indicated at the outset, this chapter has concerned itself with the Overseas Chinese on the grounds that their forms of organization are especially deserving of study, because of, firstly, the great economic power of the business systems composed of such units, and secondly, the gap in our knowledge which requires to be filled.

The literature and research which have been cited are eclectic and leave many areas still to be understood. Detailed descriptions of the workings of organization structures can still only be anecdotal. There has been little research into managerial thinking and ideology. We still lack detailed ethnographic studies of working life and worker attitudes, although the beginnings of such research are discernible. Thus the picture is still only visible in outline form, and much more research into the social psychology of Chinese organization is called for.

In the background lies China, which is moving inexorably towards the foreground in the thinking of both the theoreticians and the practitioners of organizational knowledge in Asia. Managers want to know what it is like to run a factory there. Joint-venture partners want to know what business dealings will be like. Marketers want to know how to adapt their skills to the new context.

As we noted earlier, the scene in China is changing quickly. Changes in reward and incentive systems will inevitably affect motivation as well as attitudes to work and to the institution where work takes place. Changes in political ideology will perhaps suggest new reasons for organizations to exist. Changes in technology will affect not just production processes and efficiency but also job satisfaction for the individual.

A shortage of empirical data, together with a conviction that the changes will continue to cause any research to become 'dated' quickly, has led us to leave China out of our account. This does not, however, remove the urgency of understanding it, and we would conclude with an expression of hope that, in time, we will be in a position to gather together a parallel description of people and organizations in the other Chinese world than the one we have just been observing.

References

Aaron, P. G., and Handley, A. C. (1975). 'Directional scanning and cerebral asymmetrics in processing visual stimuli', *Perceptual and Motor Skills, 40*, 719–25.

Abbott, K. A. (1970). *Harmony and Individualism*. Taipei: Oriental Cultural Service.

____(1974). 'Psychological functioning, delinquency, and family in San Francisco and Taipei'. In W. P. Lebra (Ed.), *Mental Health Research in Asia and the Pacific: Vol. 1. Youth, Socialization, and Mental Health* (pp. 121–52). Honolulu: University of Hawaii Press.

____(1976). 'Culture change and the persistence of the Chinese'. In G. A. De Vos (Ed.), *Response to Change: Society, Culture, and Personality* (pp. 74–103). New York: van Nostrand.

Abel, T. M., and Hsu, F. L. K. (1949). 'Some aspects of personality of Chinese as revealed by the Rorschach Test', *Rorschach Research Exchange and Journal of Projective Techniques, 13*, 285–301.

Adorno, T. W., Frenkel-Brunswik, E., Levinson, D., and Sanford, R. (1950). *The Authoritarian Personality*. New York: Harper and Row.

Aeroff, J. (1977). 'Process vs. impact in men's and women's achievement motivation', *Psychology of Women Quarterly, 1*, 228–93.

Ai, W. (1949). *A Study of Chinese Characters*. Shanghai: Zhonghua.

Alexander, A. A., Workneh, F., Klein, N. H., and Miller, M. H. (1976). 'Psychotherapy and the foreign student'. In P. Pederson, W. J. Lonner, and J. G. Draguns (Eds.), *Counseling across Cultures* (pp. 227–43). Honolulu: University of Hawaii Press.

Alexander, C. N., and Knight, G. W. (1971). 'Situated identities and social psychological experimentation', *Sociometry, 34*, 65–82.

Alexander, C. N., and Lauderdale, P. (1977). 'Situated identities and social influence', *Sociometry, 40*, 225–33.

Allport, G. W., Vernon, P. E., and Lindzey, G. (Eds.) (1951). *Study of Values: a Scale for Measuring the Dominant Interests in Personality* (third edition). Boston: Houghton Mifflin.

Altrocchi, K., Parsons, O. A., and Dickoff, H. (1960). 'Changes in self-ideal discrepancy in repressors and sensitizers', *Journal of Abnormal and Social Psychology, 61*, 67–72.

Ando, N. (1965). 'A cross-cultural study on value pattern of seven cultural samples', *Psychologia, 8*, 177–86.

Anthony, E. J. (1970). 'Behavior disorders'. In E. H. Mussen (Ed.), *Carmichael's Manual of Child Psychology* (third edition, Vol. 2, pp. 667–764). New York: Wiley.

Appleton, S. (1970). 'Surveying the values of Chinese college students', *Asian Forum*, April–June, 75–88.

——(1979). 'Sex, values, and change in Taiwan'. In R. W. Wilson, A. A. Wilson, and S. L. Greenblatt (Eds.), *Value Change in Chinese Society* (pp. 185–202). New York: Praeger.

Argyle, M., Henderson, M., Bond, M.H., Iizuka, Y., and Contarello, A. (1984). 'Cross-cultural variations in relationship rules'. Unpublished manuscript, Oxford University.

Atkinson, J. W., Heynes, R. W., and Veroff, J. (1954). 'the effect of experimental arousal of the affiliation motive on thematic apperception', *Journal of Abnormal and Social Psychology, 49*, 405–10.

Au, T. K.-F. (1983). 'Chinese and English counterfactuals: the Sapir–Whorf hypothesis revisited', *Cognition, 15*, 155–87.

Baddeley, A. D., Thomson, N., and Buchanan, M. (1975). 'Word length and the structure of short-term memory', *Journal of Verbal Learning and Verbal Behavior, 14*, 575–89.

Baker, H. R. D. (1979). *Chinese Family and Kinship*. London: Macmillan.

Bandura, A. (1969). *Principles of Behavior Modification*. New York: Holt, Rinehart and Winston.

Barry, H., Child, I., and Bacon, M. (1959). 'Relationship between child training to subsistence economy', *American Anthropologist, 61*, 61–3.

Barton, C. A. (1983). 'Trust and credit: some observations regarding business strategies of overseas Chinese traders in South Vietnam'. In L. Y. C. Lim and L. A. P. Gosling (Eds.), *The Chinese in Southeast Asia: Vol. 1: Ethnicity and Economic Activity* (pp. 46–64). Singapore: Maruzen Asia.

Battig, W. F., and Montague, W. E. (1969). 'Category norms for verbal items in 56 categories: a replication and extension of the Connecticut category norms', *Journal of Experimental Psychology Monograph, 80*, No. 3.

Baum, C. L., and Baum, R. (1979). 'Creating the new communist child: continuity and change in Chinese styles of early childhood socialization'. In R. W. Wilson, A. A. Wilson, and S. L. Greenblatt (Eds.), *Value Change in Chinese Society* (pp. 98–121). New York: Praeger.

Baumeister, R. F. (1982). 'A self-presentational view of social phenomena', *Psychological Bulletin, 91*, 3–26.

Belmont, L., and Marolla, F. A. (1973). 'Birth order, family size, and intelligence', *Science, 182*, 1096–1101.

Benedict, R. (1947). *The Chrysanthemum and the Sword*. London: Secker and Warburg.

Bennett, M. (1977). 'Testing management theories cross-culturally', *Journal of Applied Psychology, 62*, 578–81.

Berlin, B., and Kay, P. (1969). *Basic Color Terms: Their Universality and Evolution*. Berkeley and Los Angeles: University of California Press.

Berry, J. W. (1966). 'Temne and Eskimo perceptual skills', *International Journal of Psychology, 1*, 207–29.

——(1967). 'Independence and conformity in subsistence-level societies', *Journal of Personality and Social Psychology, 7*, 415–18.

——(1969). 'On cross-cultural comparability', *International Journal of Psychology, 4*, 119–28.

——(1971). 'Ecological and cultural factors in spatial perceptual development', *Canadian Journal of Behavioural Science, 3*, 324–36.

——(1972). 'Muller–Lyer susceptibility: culture, ecology or race', *International Journal of Psychology, 6*, 193–7.

——(1976). *Human Ecology and Cognitive Style*. New York: Sage-Halsted.

——(1979). 'A cultural ecology of social behavior'. In L. Berkowitz (Ed.), *Advances in Experimental Social Psychology* (Vol. 12, pp. 177–206). New York: Academic Press.

Bezooijen, R. V., Otto, S. A., and Heenan, T. A. (1983). 'Recognition of vocal expressions of emotion: a three-nation study to identify universal characteristics', *Journal of Cross-Cultural Psychology, 14*, 387–406.

Biederman, I., and Tsao, Y. C. (1979). 'On processing Chinese ideographs and English words: some implications from Stroop-test results', *Cognitive Psychology, 11*, 125–32.

Bloom, A. H. (1977a). 'A cognitive dimension of social control: the Hong Kong Chinese in cross-cultural perspective'. In A. A. Wilson, S. L. Greenblatt, and R. W. Wilson (Eds.), *Deviance and Social Control in Chinese Society* (pp. 67–81). New York: Praeger.

——(1977b). 'Two dimensions of moral reasoning: social principledness and social humanism in cross-cultural perspective', *Journal of Social Psychology, 101*, 29–44.

——(1981). *The Linguistic Shaping of Thought: a Study in the Impact of Language on Thinking in China and the West*. Hillsdale, New Jersey: Erlbaum.

Blumenthal, E. P. (1977). 'Models in Chinese moral education: perspectives from children's books'. *Dissertation Abstracts International, 37*, 6357A–6358A. (University Microfilms No. 77-7876, 250pp.)

Body, M. K. (1955). 'Patterns of aggression in the nursery school', *Child Development, 26*, 3–11.

Boey, K. W. (1976). 'Rigidity and cognitive complexity: an empirical investigation in the interpersonal, physical, and numerical domains under task-oriented and ego-involved conditions'. Unpublished doctoral thesis, University of Hong Kong.

Bond, M. H. (1979a). 'Dimensions of personality used in perceiving peers: cross-cultural comparisons of Hong Kong, Japanese, American, and Filipino university students', *International Journal of Psychology, 14*, 47–56.

——(1979b). 'Winning either way: the effect of anticipating a competitive interaction on person perception', *Personality and Social Psychology Bulletin, 5*, 316–19.

_____(1980). 'Cultural influence on perception and cognition: a review and interpretation of the Chinese case'. Unpublished manuscript, The Chinese University of Hong Kong.

_____(1983a). 'A proposal for cross-cultural studies of attribution processes'. In M. Hewstone (Ed.), *Attribution Theory: Social and Applied Extensions* (pp. 144–57). Oxford: Blackwell.

_____(1983b). 'How language variation affects inter-cultural differentiation of values by Hong Kong bilinguals', *Journal of Language and Social Psychology, 2*, 57–66.

_____(1984a). 'Mutual stereotypes of two interacting cultural groups in Hong Kong'. Unpublished manuscript, The Chinese University of Hong Kong.

_____(1984b). 'Type of reward as a factor affecting distributive strategies in Hong Kong'. Unpublished manuscript, The Chinese University of Hong Kong.

_____(in press). 'Language as a carrier of ethnic stereotypes in Hong Kong', *Journal of Social Psychology*.

_____and Cheung, M. K. (1984). 'Experimenter language choice and ethnic affirmation by Chinese trilinguals in Hong Kong', *International Journal of Intercultural Relations, 8*, 347–56.

_____and Cheung, T. S. (1983). 'The spontaneous self-concept of college students in Hong Kong, Japan, and the United States', *Journal of Cross-Cultural Psychology, 14*, 153–71.

_____, Chiu, C. K., and Wan, K. C. (1984). 'When modesty fails: the social impact of group-effacing attributions following success or failure', *European Journal of Social Psychology, 14*, 335–8.

_____and Forgas, J. P. (1984). 'Linking person perception to behavioural intention across cultures: the role of cultural collectivism', *Journal of Cross-Cultural Psychology, 15*, 337–52.

_____, Hewstone, M., Wan, K. C., and Chiu, C. K. (1984). 'Group-serving attributions across intergroup contexts: cultural differences in the explanation of sex-typed behaviors'. Unpublished manuscript, The Chinese University of Hong Kong.

_____and Hui, H. C. C. (1982). 'Rater competitiveness and the experimenter's influence on ratings of a future opponent', *Psychologia, 25*, 91–9.

_____and Lee, P. W. H. (1981). 'Face-saving in Chinese culture: a discussion and experimental study of Hong Kong students'. In A. Y. C. King and R. P. L. Lee (Eds.), *Social Life and Development in Hong Kong* (pp. 288–305). Hong Kong: The Chinese University Press.

_____, Leung, K., and Wan, K. C. (1982a). 'The social impact of self-effacing attributions: the Chinese case', *Journal of Social Psychology, 118*, 157–66.

_____, Leung, K., and Wan, K. C. (1982b). 'How does cultural collectivism operate? The impact of task and maintenance contributions on reward allocation', *Journal of Cross-Cultural Psychology, 13*, 186–200.

———, Wan, K. C., Leung, K., and Giacalone, R. (1985). 'How are responses to verbal insult related to cultural collectivism and power distance?', *Journal of Cross-Cultural Psychology, 16*, 111–27.

———and Wang, S. H. (1983). 'Aggressive behavior in Chinese society: the problem of maintaining order and harmony'. In A. P. Goldstein and M. Segall (Eds.), *Global Perspectives on Aggression* (pp. 58–74). New York: Pergamon Press.

———and Yang, K. S. (1982). 'Ethnic affirmation versus cross-cultural accommodation: the variable impact of questionnaire language on Chinese bilinguals in Hong Kong', *Journal of Cross-Cultural Psychology, 13*, 169–85.

Borke, H., and Su, S. (1972). 'Perception of emotional responses to social interaction by Chinese and American children', *Journal of Cross-Cultural Psychology, 3*, 309–14.

Bourhis, R. Y., Giles, H., Leyens, J. P., and Tajfel, H. (1979). 'Psycholinguistic distinctiveness: language divergence in Belgium'. In H. Giles and R. N. St. Clair (Eds.), *Language and Social Psychology* (pp. 158–85). Baltimore: University Park Press.

Boys' and Girls' Clubs Association, The (1980). *A Study of Children's Perception of Parental Roles*. Hong Kong: The Boys' and Girls' Clubs Association. (In Chinese.)

Bradburn, N. M. (1963). 'Need achievement and father dominance in Turkey', *Journal of Abnormal and Social Psychology, 67*, 464–8.

Braine, L. G. (1968). 'Asymmetries of pattern perception observed in Israelis', *Neuropsychologia, 6*, 73–88.

Bransford, J.D., and Franks, J. J. (1971). 'The abstraction of linguistic ideas', *Cognitive Psychology, 2*, 331–50.

Braun, J. S., and Chao, H. M. (1978). 'Attitudes towards women: a comparison of Asian-born Chinese and American Caucasians', *Psychology of Women Quarterly, 2*, 195–201.

Brickman, P., Rabinowitz, V. C., Karuza, J., jun., Coates, D., Cohn, E., and Kidder, L. (1982). 'Models of helping and coping', *American Psychologist, 37*, 368–84.

Brigham, J. C. (1971). 'Ethnic stereotypes', *Psychological Bulletin, 76*, 15–38.

Brislin, R. W. (Ed.) (1976). *Translation: Applications and Research*. New York: Wiley.

———(1980). 'Translation and content analysis of oral and written material'. In H. C. Triandis and J. W. Berry (Eds.), *Handbook of Cross-cultural Psychology: Methodology* (Volume 2, pp. 389–444). London: Allyn and Bacon.

———, Lonner, W. J., and Thorndike, R. W. (1973). *Cross-cultural Research Methods*. New York: Wiley.

Bronson, G. W. (1972). 'Infants' reactions to unfamiliar persons and novel objects', *Monographs of the Society for Research in Child Development*, *37*(3), Serial No. 148.

Broverman, I. K., Broverman, D. M., Clarkson, F. E., Rosenkrantz, P. S., and Vogel, S. R. (1970). 'Sex-role stereotypes and clinical judgments of mental health', *Journal of Consulting and Clinical Psychology, 34*, 1–7.

Brown, B. R. (1968). 'The effects of need to maintain face on interpersonal bargaining', *Journal of Experimental Social Psychology, 4*, 107–22.

_____ (1970). 'Face-saving following experimentally induced embarrassment', *Journal of Experimental Social Psychology, 6*, 255–71.

_____and Garland, H. (1971). 'The effects of incompetency, audience acquaintanceship, and anticipated evaluative feedback on face-saving behavior', *Journal of Experimental Social Psychology, 7*, 490–502.

Brown, L. B. (1981). *Psychology in Contemporary China*. Oxford: Pergamon Press.

Bryden, M. P. (1965). 'Tachistoscopic recognition, handedness, and cerebral dominance', *Neuropsychologia, 3*, 1–8.

Bunzel, R. (1950). 'Explorations in Chinese culture'. Unpublished manuscript. New York: Columbia University Research in Contemporary Cultures.

Bureau of Social Welfare (1980). *Survey Report on the Current Status of the Life of Youth in Taiwan*. Taichung, Taiwan: Bureau of Social Welfare, Taiwan Provincial Government. (In Chinese.)

Buss, A. H. (1980). *Self-consciousness and Social Anxiety*. San Francisco: W. H. Freeman.

_____and Plomin, R. (1975). *A Temperament Theory of Personality Development*. New York: Wiley.

Byrne, D. (1961). 'The Repression–Sensitization Scale: rationale, reliability, and validity', *Journal of Personality, 29*, 334–49.

_____(1971). *The Attraction Paradigm*. New York: Academic Press.

_____, Barry, J., and Nelson, D. (1963). 'Relation of the revised Repression–Sensitization Scale to measures of self-description', *Psychological Reports, 13*, 323–34.

California Department of Public Health, Bureau of Maternal and Child Health (1962–7). *Epidemiology of Childhood Accidents Project*. Berkeley, Calif.: California Department of Public Health.

Campbell, D. T., and Fiske, D. W. (1959). 'Convergent and discriminant validation by the multitrait-multimethod matrix', *Psychological Bulletin, 56*, 81–105.

Carlson, E. R. (1962). 'Generality of order of concept attainment', *Psychological Reports, 10*, 375–80.

Castell, P. J., and Goldstein, J. H. (1977). 'Social occasions for joking: a cross-cultural study'. In A. J. Chapman and H. C. Foot (Eds.), *It's a Funny Thing, Humour* (pp. 193–7). Oxford: Pergamon Press.

302   REFERENCES

Cattell, R. B. (1963). *IPAT Self Analysis Form*. Champaign, Illinois: Institute for Personality and Ability Testing.

Caudill, W. (1972). 'Tiny dramas: vocal communication between mother and infant in Japanese and American families'. In W. P. Lebra (Ed.), *Transcultural Research in Mental Health* (pp. 25–48). Honolulu, Hawaii: University of Hawaii Press.

Cerny, J. (1965). 'Chinese psychiatry', *International Journal of Psychiatry, 1*, 229–47.

Chan, D. W. (in press). 'Perception and judgment of facial expressions among the Chinese', *International Journal of Psychology*.

___and Chan-Ho, M. W. (1983). 'Stressful life events: overview and lessons from a Chinese context', *Journal of the Hong Kong Psychiatric Association, 3*, 3–7.

___, Chan-Ho, M. W., and Chan, T. (1984). 'Life event scaling: the Chinese experience', *Social Science and Medicine, 18*, 441–6.

Chan, J. (1976a). 'Is Raven's Progressive Matrices test culture-free or culture-fair? Some research findings in Hong Kong context'. Paper presented at the Third International Association for Cross-Cultural Psychology Congress, Tilburg, Netherlands.

___(1976b). 'Parent-child interaction and education: a cross-cultural comparative study', *New Horizons, 17*, 69–81.

___(1979). 'Effects of parent-child interaction on verbal and other intellectual abilities: an empirical study', *New Horizons, 20*, 19–30.

___(1981a). 'A crossroads in language instruction', *Journal of Reading, 22*, 411–15.

___(1981b). 'Correlates of parent-child interaction and certain psychological variables among adolescents in Hong Kong'. In J. L. M. Dawson, G. H. Blowers, and R. Hoosain (Eds.), *Perspectives in Asian Cross-cultural Psychology* (pp. 112–31). Lisse, Netherlands: Swets and Zeitlinger.

___and Eysenck, S. B. G. (1981). 'National differences in personality: Hong Kong and England'. Paper presented at the joint IACCP-ICP Asian Regional Meeting, National Taiwan University, Taipei, Taiwan, August.

Chan, S. L. (1983). 'Social support and mental health of youths in Chaiwan district'. Unpublished master's thesis, The Chinese University of Hong Kong. (In Chinese.)

Chang, C. F. (1982). 'Interpersonal relations and self concept, attribution traits in college freshmen', *Journal of Education and Psychology, 5*, 1–46. (In Chinese.)

Chang, P. H. (1979). 'Children's literature and political socialization'. In G. C. Chu and F. L. K. Hsu (Eds.), *Moving a Mountain: Cultural Change in China* (pp.237–56). Honolulu: University of Hawaii Press.

Chang, S. S. (1959). 'Value orientations of American and Chinese students'. Unpublished master's thesis, Ohio State University.

Chang, S. S., and Lu, C. Y. (1969). 'A report on the Guilford–

Zimmerman Temperamental Survey', *Acta Psychologica Taiwanica,* *11*, 13–23. (In Chinese.)

Chang, W. C. (1984). 'A cross-cultural study of depressive symptomatology'. Paper presented at the VIIth International Congress of Cross-cultural Psychology, Acapulco, Mexico, August–September.

Chang, W. H. (1975). 'A study on the personal preferences of Tunghai University students', *Psychological Testing* (Taipei), *22*, 59–63. (In Chinese.)

Chang, W. J. (1976). 'Interpersonal attraction as a function of opinion similarity and opinion presentation sequence', *Bulletin of Educational Psychology, 9*, 73–84. (In Chinese.)

——(1977). 'Effects of opinion similarity and opinion social desirability on interpersonal attraction and interaction intention', *Bulletin of Educational Psychology, 10*, 61–74. (In Chinese.)

——(1980). 'Affiliation tendency and sociometric status', *Bulletin of Educational Psychology, 13*, 153–78. (In Chinese.)

——(1983). 'The prediction of junior high-school student sociometric status from some psycho-social variables'. Unpublished doctoral thesis, University of Oregon.

Chao, Y. R. (1970). *Language and Symbolic Systems.* Cambridge: Cambridge University Press.

Chau, W. L., and Chan, W. K. (1984). 'A study of job satisfaction of workers in local factories of Chinese, Western and Japanese ownership', *The Hongkong Manager, 20*, 9–14.

Chen, A. K., Zhang, B. Y., Shih, H. Y., Xu, E. T., Chen, Z. L., and Hu, X. F. (1980). 'A preliminary research in the arousal level of paranoid and nonparanoid schizophrenics', *Acta Psychologica Sinica, 1*, 68–74. (In Chinese.)

Chen, C. I. B. (n.d.). 'Chinese and American differences in group performance and strategies in problem solving groups'. Unpublished manuscript, National Chengchi University. (In Chinese.)

Chen, C. N. (1984). 'The aims and scope of the Psychiatric Epidemiology Research Unit'. Paper given at the Symposium on Cross-cultural Psychiatric Epidemiology, Hong Kong.

Chen, H. N., and Su, C. W. (1977). 'The perception of parent-child relationship and its relation to adjustment of adolescence', *Bulletin of Educational Psychology* (Taiwan Normal University), *10*, 91–106. (In Chinese.)

Chen, M. J. (1981). 'Direction scanning of visual displays: a study with Chinese subjects', *Journal of Cross-Cultural Psychology, 12*, 252–71.

——and Huang, J. T. (1982). 'Attributes of intelligent behaviour: perceived relevance and difficulty by Australian and Chinese students', *Journal of Cross-Cultural Psychology, 13*, 139–56.

Chen, Y., and Wu, Y. (1981). 'The operational level of Chinese elementary and secondary school students on test of cognitive development'. Paper presented at the Joint IACCP-ICP Asian Regional Meeting, Taipei, Taiwan, August.

Chen, Y. Y. (1977). 'Political socialization of Chinese university students in Taiwan'. Unpublished doctoral thesis, National Chengchi University. (In Chinese.)

Chen, Z. K. (1964). 'Psychogalvanic reflex and the subjective states of neurasthenics', *Hsin-li hsueh-pao, 1*, 103–8. (In Chinese.)

Cheng, C., and Huang, H. (1980). 'The process of verifying affirmative and negative sentences against pictures', *Memory and Cognition, 8*, 573–83.

Cheng, C. C. (1982). 'The Chinese concepts of face: a conceptual and empirical study'. Unpublished master's thesis, National Taiwan University. (In Chinese.)

Cheng, C. K. (1946). 'Characteristic traits of the Chinese people', *Social Forces, 25*, 146–55.

Cheng, H. H., and Fan, C. M. (1976). 'Comparisons of directive and non-directive counseling methods in vocational counseling'. In H. H. Cheng (Ed.), *Counseling Studies in the Republic of China* (pp. 129–63). Taipei: Young Lion Publishing Co. (In Chinese.)

Cheng, H. H., and Lui, S. E. (1976). 'Effectiveness of non-directive counseling techniques among high school students'. In H. H. Cheng (Ed.), *Counseling Studies in the Republic of China* (pp. 59–78). Taipei: Young Lion Publishing Co. (In Chinese.)

Cheng, H. H., and Wu, E. C. (1977). 'Effectiveness of counseling in terms of method and frequency with high school students', *Mental Health Bulletin, 21*, 35–46. (In Chinese.)

Cheng, H. L., and Yang, K. S. (1977). 'The effects of attributional process on achievement motivation and scholastic achievement', *Bulletin of the Institute of Ethnology, Academia Sinica, 43*, 85–127. (In Chinese.)

Cheng, P. S. (1977). 'Research on leading behavior: the effects of leadership, situation factors and personality attributes on the job satisfaction of workers'. Unpublished master's thesis, National Taiwan University. (In Chinese.)

Cheng, S. W., and Lei, T. (1981). 'Performance of Taiwanese students on Kohlberg's moral judgement inventory'. Paper presented at the IACCP-ICP Joint Asian Regional Conference, Taipei, Taiwan, August.

Cheng, T. Y. (1977). *The Economy of Hong Kong*. Hong Kong: Far East Publications.

Chern, Y. H. (1978). 'Moral judgement development in Chinese adolescents', *Journal of Education* (Kaoshung Normal College), 98–159. (In Chinese.)

Cheung, F. M. (1981a). 'Mental health and recreational activities in a Chinese commune'. In R. P. L. Lee and S. K. Lau (Eds.), *The People's*

Commune and Rural Development (pp. 95–113). Hong Kong: The Chinese University Press. (In Chinese.)

———(1981b). 'Opening Pandora's box on counselling: comments on Norman Brier's article "The emperor's new clothes" ', *Hong Kong Journal of Mental Health, 10*, 10–12.

———(1982). 'Psychological symptoms among Chinese in urban Hong Kong', *Social Science and Medicine, 16*, 1339–44.

———(1984). 'Preferences in help-seeking among Chinese students', *Culture, Medicine and Psychiatry, 8*, 371–80.

———(1985a). 'Cross-cultural considerations for the translation and adaptation of the Chinese MMPI in Hong Kong'. In J. N. Butcher and C. D. Spielberger (Eds.), *Advances in Personality Assessment* (Vol. 4, pp. 131–58). Hillsdale, New Jersey: Lawrence Erlbaum Associates.

———(1985b). 'An overview of psychopathology in Hong Kong with special reference to somatic presentation'. In W. S. Tseng and D. Wu (Eds.), *Chinese Culture and Mental Health* (pp. 287–304). New York: Academic Press.

———(in press). 'The indigenization of neurasthenia in Hong Kong', *Culture, Medicine and Psychiatry*.

———and Lau, B. W. K. (1982). 'Situational variations of help-seeking behavior among Chinese patients', *Comprehensive Psychiatry, 23*, 252–62.

———, Lau, B. W. K., and Waldmann, E. (1980–1). 'Somatization among Chinese depressives in general practice', *International Journal of Psychiatry in Medicine, 10*, 361–74.

———, Lau, B. W. K., and Wong, S. W. (1984). 'Paths to psychiatric care in Hong Kong', *Culture, Medicine and Psychiatry, 8*, 207–28.

———and Lee, P. L. M. (1984). 'Anxiety among secondary school students in Hong Kong and its relationship with academic performance', *The Chinese University of Hong Kong Education Journal, 12*, 56–63.

———, Lee, S. Y., and Chan, Y. Y. (1983). 'Variations in problem conceptualizations and intended solutions among Hong Kong students', *Culture, Medicine and Psychiatry, 7*, 263–78.

Chiang, L. Y. H. (1982). 'Women, work and the family in a developing society: Taiwan'. Paper presented at the Conference on Women in the Urban and Industrial Workforce: Southeast and East Asia, Manila.

Chiang, Y. (1940). *A Chinese Childhood*. London: Methuen. (Republished New York: John Day, 1952; New York: Norton, 1963.)

Chiao, C. (1981). 'Chinese strategic behavior: some general principles'. Paper presented at a conference in honour of Professor John M. Roberts, Claremont, Calif., U.S.A., November–December.

Chien, M. (1977). 'Factors related to peer interaction among school children in urban and rural areas', *Psychological Testing, 24*, 32–40. (In Chinese.)

Chien, M. (1979). *Chinese National Character and Chinese Culture: a Perspective from Chinese History*. Taipei: Liang Ching Co. (In Chinese.)

Child, J. (1972). 'Organization structure, environment and performance: the role of strategic choice', *Sociology, 6*, 1–22.

_____(1981). 'Culture, contingency, and capitalism in the cross-national study of organizations'. In L. L. Cummings and B. M. Staw (Eds.), *Research in Organizational Behaviour* (Vol. 3). Greenwich: JAI Press.

Chin, A. S. (1964). 'The ideal local party secretary and the "model" man', *The China Quarterly, 17*, 229–40.

Chin, R., and Chin, A. S. (1969). *Psychological Research in Communist China: 1949–1966*. Cambridge, Mass.: MIT Press.

Chinese Psychological Association (1979). *Attitudes Towards the Environment of Life among College and University Students in Taiwan*. Taipei, Taiwan: Chinese Psychological Association. (In Chinese.)

Chiu, C. O. (1963). 'A comparative study on the personality of Chinese and American students'. Unpublished bachelor's thesis, National Taiwan University. (In Chinese.)

Chiu, E., and Tan, E. S. (1985). 'Psychiatric morbidity among Chinese immigrants in Victoria, Australia'. In W. S. Tseng and D. Wu (Eds.), *Chinese Culture and Mental Health* (pp. 251–64). New York: Academic Press.

Chiu, L. H. (1971). 'Manifested anxiety in Chinese and American children', *Journal of Psychology, 79*, 237–84.

_____(1972). 'A cross-cultural comparison of cognitive styles in Chinese and American children', *International Journal of Psychology, 7*, 235–42.

Chiu, W. C. (1967). 'Survey of social interests: a preliminary report'. *Psychological Testing* (Taipei), *14*, 45–50. (In Chinese.)

Chong, L. E., Cragin, J. P., and Scherling, S. A. (1983). 'Manager work-related values in a Chinese corporation'. Paper presented to the annual meeting of the Academy of International Business, San Francisco, U.S.A., April.

Chou, S. K., and Mi, C. Y. (1937). 'Relative neurotic tendency of Chinese and American students', *Journal of Social Psychology, 8*, 155–84.

Chou, Y. M. (1983). 'Value systems and administrative behaviours in large-scale Taiwanese businesses'. Unpublished doctoral thesis, Cheng-chi University. (In Chinese.)

Christie, R., and Geis, F. (1970). *Studies in Machiavellianism*. New York: Academic Press.

Chu, C. L. (1973). 'On the shame orientation of the Chinese'. In Y. Y. Li and K. S. Yang (Eds.), *Symposium on the Character of the Chinese: An Interdisciplinary Approach* (pp. 85–117). Taipei: Institute of Ethnology, Academia Sinica. (In Chinese.)

Chu, C. P. (1973). 'Parental attitudes in relation to young children's creativity', *Acta Psychologica Taiwanica, 15*, 10–24.

____(1974). 'Parental attitudes in relation to young children's creativity: cross-cultural comparison', *Acta Psychologica Taiwanica, 16,* 53–72.

____(1975). 'The development of differential cognitive abilities in relation to children's perceptions of their parents', *Acta Psychologica Taiwanica, 17,* 47–62.

Chu, G. C. (1966). 'Culture, personality, and persuasibility', *Sociometry, 29,* 167–74.

____(1967). 'Sex differences in persuasibility factors among Chinese', *International Journal of Psychology, 2,* 283–8.

Chu, J. L., and Yang, K. S. (1976). 'The effects of relative performance and individual modernity on distributive behavior among Chinese college students', *Bulletin of the Institute of Ethnology, Academia Sinica, 41,* 79–95. (In Chinese.)

Chu, L. (1979). 'The sensitivity of Chinese and American children to social influences', *Journal of Social Psychology, 109,* 175–86.

Chu, R. L. (1983). 'Empirical research on the psychology of face'. Unpublished doctoral thesis, National Taiwan University. (In Chinese.)

Chung, Y. C., and Hwang, K. K. (1981). 'Attribution of performance and characteristics of learned helplessness in junior high school students', *Acta Psychologica Taiwanica, 23,* 155–64. (In Chinese.)

Clark, H. H., and Chase, W. G. (1972). 'On the process of comparing sentences against pictures', *Cognitive Psychology, 3,* 472–517.

Cohen, B. H., Bousfield, W. A., and Whitmarsh, G. A. (1957). *Cultural Norms for Verbal Items in 43 Categories* (Technical Report No. 22). Storrs, Conn.: University of Connecticut.

Colby, A., Gibbs, J., and Kohlberg, L. (1978). *Standard Form Scoring Manual I and II.* Cambridge, Mass.: Center for Moral Education, Harvard University.

Cole, M., and Scribner, S. (1974). *Culture and Thought: a Psychological Introduction.* New York: Wiley.

'Columbia University research in contemporary cultures — Chinese series' (1950). Unpublished. New York: American Museum of Natural History. (Sent to the Library of Congress for archiving.)

Committee for Education Planning, Ministry of Education, Republic of China (1983). *Values and their Correlates among Chinese Adolescents.* Taipei, Taiwan: Ministry of Education. (In Chinese.)

Crandall, V. J., Dewey, R., Katkovsky, W., and Preston, A. (1964). 'Parents' attitudes and behaviors and grade-school children's academic achievement', *Journal of Genetic Psychology, 104,* 53–66.

Crozier, M. (1964). *The Bureaucratic Phenomenon.* Chicago: The University of Chicago Press.

Cunningham, S. (1984). 'Cross-cultural study of achievements calls for changes in home', *APA Monitor, 15,* Nos. 9, 10.

Curran, H. V. (1980). 'Cross-cultural perspectives on cognition'. In G.

Claxton (Ed.), *Cognitive Psychology: New Directions* (pp. 300–34). London: Routledge and Kegan Paul.

Davis, F. B., Lesser, G. S., and French, E. G. (1960). 'Identification and classroom behavior of gifted elementary school children', *Cooperative Research Monograph, 2*.

Dawson, J. L. M. (1963). 'Psychological effects of social change in West Africa'. Unpublished doctoral thesis, University of Oxford.

___(1967a). 'Cultural and physiological influences on spatial-perceptual processes in West Africa, Part I', *International Journal of Psychology, 2*, 115–28.

___(1967b). 'Cultural and physiological influences on spatial-perceptual processes in West Africa, Part II', *International Journal of Psychology, 2*, 171–85.

___(1977a). 'Theory and method in bio-social psychology'. In L. L. Adler (Ed.), *Issues in Cross-cultural Research* (pp. 46–65). New York: The New York Academy of Sciences.

___(1977b). 'Alaskan Eskimo hand, eye, auditory dominance and cognitive style', *Psychologia, 20*, 121–35.

___(1981a). 'The cross-cultural aspects of the development of spatial ability: a bio-social approach'. Paper presented at the VIth ISSBD Conference, Toronto.

___(1981b). 'The bio-social adaptation of the boatpeople (Tanka) and the Hakka agriculturalists of Hong Kong, on cognitive style, illusion susceptibility, and modernization'. Unpublished manuscript, University of Hong Kong.

___, Law, H., Leung, A., and Whitney, R. E. (1971). 'Scaling Chinese Traditional-Modern attitudes and the GSR measurement of "important" versus "unimportant" Chinese concepts', *Journal of Cross-Cultural Psychology, 2*, 1–27.

___, Young, B. M., and Choi, P. P. C. (1973). 'Developmental influences on geometric illusion susceptibility among Hong Kong Chinese children', *Journal of Cross-Cultural Psychology, 4*, 49–74.

Detweiler, R. A. (1978). 'Culture, category width, and attributions: a model-building approach to the reasons for cultural effects', *Journal of Cross-Cultural Psychology, 9*, 259–84.

Deutsch, M. (1975). 'Equity, equality, and need: what determines which value will be used as the basis of distributive justice?', *Journal of Social Issues, 31*, 137–49.

De Vos, G. A. (1966). *A Comparison of the Personality Differences in Two Generations of Japanese Americans by Means of the Rorschach Test*. SSRI Reprint No. 14, Social Science Research Institute, University of Hawaii, Honolulu.

___(1973). *Socialization for Achievement: Essays on the Cultural Psychology of the Japanese*. Berkeley: University of California Press.

Deyo, F. C. (1978). 'Local foremen in multinational enterprise: a comparative case study of supervisory role-tensions in Western and Chinese factories of Singapore', *Journal of Management Studies, 15*, 308–17.

———(1983). 'Chinese management practices and work commitment in comparative perspective'. In L. A. P. Gosling and L. Y. C. Lim (Eds.), *The Chinese in Southeast Asia: Vol. II. Identity, Culture and Politics* (pp. 215–30). Singapore: Maruzen Asia.

Dimitriou, E. C., and Eysenck, S. B. G. (1978). 'National differences in personality: Greece and England', *International Journal of Intercultural Relations, 2*, 266–82.

Doi, T. (1973). *The Anatomy of Dependence*. Tokyo: Kodansha International Ltd.

Douglas, J. D., and Wong, A. C. (1977). 'Formal operations: age and sex differences in Chinese and American children', *Child Development, 48*, 689–92.

Dube, E. F. (1977). 'A cross-cultural study of the relationship between "intelligence" level and story recall'. Unpublished doctoral thesis, Cornell University.

Earle, M. J. (1969). 'A cross-cultural and cross-language comparison on dogmatism scores', *Journal of Social Psychology, 79*, 19–24.

Eberhard, W. (1967). *Guilt and Sin*. Berkeley and Los Angeles: University of California Press.

Edwards, A. L. (1959). *Manual for the Personal Preference Schedule*. New York: Psychological Corp.

Ekman, P. (1971). 'Universals and cultural differences in the facial expression of emotion'. In J. Cole (Ed.), *Nebraska Symposium on Motivation* (Vol. 19, pp. 207–84). Lincoln, Nebraska: University of Nebraska Press.

———and Oster, H. (1979). 'Facial expression of emotion', *Annual Review of Psychology, 30*, 527–54.

Ellis, N. C., and Hennelly, R. A. (1980). 'A bilingual word-length effect: implications for intelligence testing and the relative ease of mental calculation in Welsh and English', *British Journal of Psychology, 71*, 43–51.

Erickson, D., Mattingly, I., and Turvey, M. (1977). 'Phonetic activity and reading: an experiment with kanji', *Language and Speech, 20*, 384–403.

Ewing, J. A., Rouse, B. A., and Pellizzari, E. D. (1974). 'Alcohol sensitivity and ethnic background', *American Journal of Psychiatry, 131*, 206–10.

Fairbank, J. K. (1966). 'How to deal with the Chinese revolution', *The New York Review of Books, 6*, 12.

———and Reischauer, E. O. (1973). *China: Tradition and Transformation*. New York: Houghton Mifflin.

Fei, X. T. (1948). *Rural China*. Shanghai: Guancha She.

Fenz, W. D., and Arkoff, A. (1962). 'Comparative need patterns of five ancestry groups in Hawaii', *Journal of Social Psychology, 58*, 67–89.

Fishbein, M., and Ajzen, I. (1975). *Belief, Attitude, Intention, and Behavior: an Introduction to Theory and Research*. Reading, Mass.: Addison-Wesley.

Fishman, J. A. (1977). 'Ethnicity and language'. In H. Giles (Ed.), *Language, Ethnicity, and Intergroup Relations* (pp. 15–57). London: Academic Press.

Foa, U. G. (1971). 'Interpersonal and economic resources', *Science, 171*, 345–51.

Freedman, D. G. (1971). 'An evolutionary approach to research on the life cycle', *Human Development, 14*, 87–99.

———(1974). *Human Infancy: an Evolutionary Perspective*. Hillsdale, New Jersey: Erlbaum.

———and Freedman, N. C. (1969). 'Behavioural differences between Chinese-American and European-American newborns', *Nature, 224*, 1227.

Freedman, M. (1979). *The Study of Chinese Society*. Stanford: Stanford University Press.

Freeman, R. D. (1980). 'Visual acuity is better for letters in rows than in columns', *Nature, 286*, 62–4.

Fried, M. H. (Ed.) (1958). *Colloquium on Overseas Chinese*. New York: Institute of Pacific Relations.

———(1969). *The Fabric of Chinese Society: a Study of the Social Life of a Chinese County Seat*. New York: Octagon Books.

———(1976). 'Chinese culture, society, and personality in transition'. In G. A. De Vos (Ed.), *Response to Change: Society, Culture, and Personality* (pp. 45–73). New York: van Nostrand.

Frostig, M., Maslow, P., Lefever, D.W., and Whittlesey, J. R. B. (1963). *The Marianne Frostig Developmental Test of Visual Perception*. Palo Alto: Consulting Psychologists' Press.

Fung, Y. L. (1948). *A Short History of Chinese Philosophy*. New York: Macmillan.

Furth, H. G. (1964). 'Research with the deaf: implications for language and cognition', *Psychological Bulletin, 62*, 145–64.

Fuster, J. M. (1962). 'A study of the Edwards Personal Preference Schedule on Indian college students', *Journal of Social Psychology, 57*, 309–14.

Gabrenya, W. K., and Wang, Y. E. (1983). 'Cultural differences in self-schemata: China and the United States'. Paper presented at the meeting of the Southeast Psychological Association, Atlanta, Georgia, U.S.A., March.

Gabrenya, W. K. jun., Wang, Y. E., and Latane, B. (in press). 'Cultural differences in social loafing', *Journal of Cross-Cultural Psychology*.

Gallin, R. S. (1982). 'The impact of development on women's work and status: a case study from Taiwan'. Working papers on women in international development, Michigan State University, East Lansing, Michigan, U.S.A.

Geertz, C. (1984). *Local Knowledge: Further Essays in Interpretive Anthropology.* New York: Basic Books.

Gergen, K. J. (1973). 'Social psychology as history', *Journal of Personality and Social Psychology, 26,* 309–20.

Ginsburg, G. P., McGinn, N. F., and Harburg, E. (1970). 'Recalled parent-child interaction of Mexican and United States males', *Journal of Cross-Cultural Psychology, 1,* 139–52.

Goffman, E. (1955). 'On face-work: an analysis of ritual elements in social interaction', *Psychiatry, 18,* 213–31.

____(1956). 'Embarrassment and social organization', *American Journal of Sociology, 62,* 264–71.

____(1959). *The Presentation of Self in Everyday Life.* New York: Doubleday.

____(1967). *Interaction Ritual.* New York: Doubleday.

Goldberg, D. P. (1978). *Manual of the General Health Questionnaire.* Windsor, U.K.: NFER Publishing Co.

Goldberg, L. R. (1980). 'Some ruminations about the structure of individual differences: developing a common lexicon for the major characteristics of human personality'. Paper presented at the meeting of the Western Psychological Association, Honolulu, Hawaii, U.S.A., May.

Golin, S., Herron, E. W., Lakota, R., and Reineck, L. (1967). 'Factor analytic study of the manifest anxiety, extraversion, and repression-sensitization scales', *Journal of Consulting Psychology, 31,* 564–9.

Gong, Y. (1984). 'Use of the Eysenck Personality Questionnaire in China', *Personality and Individual Differences, 5,* 431–8.

Gordon, L. V. (1960). *Survey of Interpersonal Values.* Chicago: Science Research Associates.

Gough, H. G. (1960). *Manual for the California Psychological Inventory* (revised edition). Palo Alto, Calif.: Consulting Psychologists Press.

Green, L. (1979). 'Rural high school students' perceptions of the basic values and educational philosophies of significant secondary school role models', *Personnel and Guidance Journal, 57,* 392–7.

Green, N. (1969). 'An exploratory study of aggressive behavior in two preschool nurseries'. Unpublished master's thesis, University of Chicago, Committee on Human Development, Chicago.

Grichting, W. (1971). *The Value System on Taiwan, 1970.* Taipei, Taiwan: privately printed.

Guilford, J. P. (1934). 'Introversion-extroversion', *Psychological Bulletin, 31,* 331–54.

____(1959). *Personality.* New York: McGraw-Hill.

____and Zimmerman, W. S. (1949). *The Guilford–Zimmerman Temperament Survey: Manual of Instructions and Interpretations.* Beverly Hills, Calif.: Sheridan Supply Co.

Guo, N. F. (1984). 'Studies of lateralization in Chinese language functions'. In H. S. R. Kao and R. Hoosain (Eds.), *Psychological Studies of the Chinese Language* (pp. 1–9). Hong Kong: Chinese Language Society of Hong Kong.

Gwee, A. L. (1963). 'Koro — a cultural disease', *Singapore Medical Journal, 4*, 119–22.

____(1968). 'Koro — its origin and nature as a disease entity', *Singapore Medical Journal, 9*, 3–6.

Han, E. Y. H. (1974). 'Responses of Chinese university students to the Thematic Apperception Test', *Journal of Social Psychology, 92*, 315–16.

Hang, T. C. (1966). *Chinese National Character*. Taipei: Shang Wu Co. (In Chinese.)

Hanno, M.S., and Jones, L. E. (1973). 'Effects of a change in reference person on the multidimensional structure and evaluations of trait adjectives', *Journal of Personality and Social Psychology, 28*, 368–75.

Harding, C. (1980). 'East meets West: a conflict of values', *Hong Kong Psychological Society Bulletin, 5*, 35–43.

Hardyck, C., and Petrinovich, L. F. (1977). 'Left-handedness', *Psychological Bulletin, 84*, 385–404.

Harrell, S. (1981). 'Normal and deviant drinking in rural Taiwan'. In A. Kleinman and T. Y. Lin (Eds.), *Normal and Abnormal Behavior in Chinese Culture* (pp. 49–59). Dordrecht, Holland: D. Reidel.

Harvey, J. H., Yarkin, K. L., Lightner, J. M., and Town, J. P. (1980). 'Unsolicited interpretation and recall of interpersonal events', *Journal of Personality and Social Psychology, 38*, 551–68.

Hatta, T. (1977). 'Recognition of Japanese Kanji in the left and right visual field', *Neuropsychologia, 15*, 685–8.

Hchu, H. Y. (1971). 'Chinese individual modernity and personality'. Unpublished master's thesis, National Taiwan University. (In Chinese.)

____and Yang, K. S. (1972). 'Individual modernity and psychogenic needs'. In Y. Y. Li and K. S. Yang (Eds.), *Symposium on the Character of the Chinese: an Interdisciplinary Approach* (pp. 381–410). Taipei: Institute of Ethnology, Academia Sinica. (In Chinese.)

Heider, E. R. (1972). 'Universals in color naming and memory', *Journal of Experimental Psychology, 93*, 10–20.

____and Olivier, D. (1972). 'The structure of the color space in naming and memory for two languages', *Cognitive Psychology, 3*, 337–54.

Heider, F. (1958). *The Psychology of Interpersonal Relations*. New York: Wiley.

Hellersberg, E. F. (1953). 'Visual perception and spatial organization: a study of performance on the Horn–Hellersberg Test by Chinese subjects'. In M. Mead and R. Metraux (Eds.), *The Study of Culture at a Distance* (pp. 320–8). Chicago: University of Chicago Press.

Hewitt, J. (1972). 'Similarity vs social desirability as determinants of attraction', *Psychonomic Science, 26*, 219-21.

Hewstone, M., Bond, M. H., and Wan, K. C. (1983). 'Social facts and social attributions: the explanation of intergroup differences in Hong Kong', *Social Cognition, 2*, 142-57.

Hewstone, M., and Ward, C. (in press). 'Intergroup attributions for positive and negative behaviors: a field study with ethnic Chinese and Malays in Malaysia', *Journal of Personality and Social Psychology*.

Heyer, V. (1953). 'Relations between men and women in Chinese stories'. In M. Mead and R. Metraux (Eds.), *The Study of Culture at a Distance* (pp. 221-34). Chicago: University of Chicago Press.

Hicks, G. L., and Redding, S. G. (1982). 'Culture and corporate performance in the Philippines: the Chinese puzzle', *Philippines Review Of Economics And Business* (Special Issue of Essays in Development Economics in Honor of Harry T. Oshima), *19*, 199-215.

Higginbotham, H. N. (1984). *Third World Challenge to Psychiatry: Cultural Accommodation and Mental Health Care*. Honolulu: East-West Center Press.

Hiniker, P. J. (1969). 'Chinese reactions to forced compliance: dissonance reduction or national character?', *Journal of Social Psychology, 77*, 157-76.

Hinkle, L. (1974). 'The effect of exposure to culture change, social change, and changes in interpersonal relationships on health'. In B. S. Dohrenwend and B. P. Dohrenwend (Eds.), *Stressful Life Events: Their Nature and Effects* (pp. 9-44). New York: Wiley.

Ho, D. Y. F. (1974a). 'Early socialization in contemporary China' (Abstract). In Science Council of Japan, *Proceedings of the Twentieth International Congress of Psychology* (p. 442). Tokyo: University of Tokyo Press.

____(1974b). 'Prevention and treatment of mental illness in the People's Republic of China', *American Journal of Orthopsychiatry, 44*, 620-36.

____(1976). 'On the concept of face', *American Journal of Sociology, 81*, 867-84.

____(1979a). 'Parental education is not correlated with verbal intelligence or academic performance in Hong Kong pupils', *Genetic Psychology Monographs, 100*, 3-19.

____(1979b). 'Psychological implications of collectivism: with special reference to the Chinese case and Maoist dialectics'. In L. H. Eckensberger, W. J. Lonner, and Y. H. Poortinga (Eds.), *Cross-cultural Contributions to Psychology* (pp. 143-50). Lisse, Netherlands: Swets and Zeitlinger.

____(1979c). 'Sibship variables as determinants of intellectual-academic ability in Hong Kong pupils', *Genetic Psychology Monographs, 100*, 21-39.

_____(1979d). 'Therapeutic intervention for parents and children in Hong Kong: problems, frustrations, and reflections from a cross-cultural perspective', *The Hong Kong Journal of Social Work, 13*, 15–22. (Republished in C. H. Hwang and E. K. Yeh, (Eds.), *Family, Child and Mental Health: Proceedings of the Western Pacific Regional Workshop on Mental Health* (pp. 162–74). Taipei: Chinese National Association for Mental Hygiene, 1979.)

_____(1981a). 'Traditional patterns of socialization in Chinese society', *Acta Psychologica Taiwanica, 23*, 81–95.

_____(1981b). 'Childhood psychopathology: a dialogue with special reference to Chinese and American cultures'. In A. Kleinman and T. Y. Lin (Eds.), *Normal and Abnormal Behavior in Chinese Culture* (pp. 137–55). Dordrecht, Netherlands: D. Reidel.

_____and Kang, T. K. (1984). 'Intergenerational comparisons of child-rearing attitudes and practices in Hong Kong', *Developmental Psychology, 20*, 1004–16.

_____and Lee, L. Y. (1974). 'Authoritarianism and attitudes toward filial piety in Chinese teachers', *Journal of Social Psychology, 92*, 305–6.

Ho, S. K., and Hoosain, R. (1984). 'Hemisphere differences in the perception of Chinese opposites'. In H. S. R. Kao and R. Hoosain (Eds.), *Psychological Studies of the Chinese Language* (pp. 11–22). Hong Kong: Chinese Language Society of Hong Kong.

Hofstede, G. (1980). *Culture's Consequences: International Differences in Work-related Values*. London and Beverly Hills: Sage.

_____(1983). 'Dimensions of national cultures in fifty countries and three regions'. In J. B. Deregowski, S. Dziurawiec, and R. C. Annis (Eds.), *Expiscations in Cross-cultural Psychology* (pp. 335–55). Lisse, Netherlands: Swets and Zeitlinger.

_____and Bond, M. H. (1984). 'An independent validation of Hofstede's culture dimensions using Rokeach's value survey', *Journal of Cross-Cultural Psychology, 15*, 417–33.

Hogan, R. T. (1975). 'Theoretical egocentrism', *American Psychologist, 30*, 535–40.

_____and Emler, R. T. (1978). 'The biases in contemporary social psychology', *Social Research, 45*, 478–534.

Holmes, T., and Rahe, R. (1967). 'The social readjustment rating scale', *Journal of Psychosomatic Research, 11*, 213–18.

Hong Kong Young Women's Christian Association and Hong Kong Shue Yan College (1982). *Report on Working Mothers in Family Functioning*. Hong Kong: Hong Kong Young Women's Christian Association and Hong Kong Shue Yan College.

Hoosain, R. (1979). 'Forward and backward digit span in the languages of the bilingual', *Journal of Genetic Psychology, 135*, 263–8.

_____(1984a). 'Asymmetry between the lexicons of the bilingual'. Paper presented at the International Symposium on Psychological Aspects of the Chinese Language, Hong Kong.

_____(1984b). 'Experiments on digit spans in the Chinese and English languages'. In H. S. R. Kao and R. Hoosain (Eds.), *Psychological Studies of the Chinese Language* (pp.23–38). Hong Kong: Chinese Language Society of Hong Kong.

_____and Osgood, C. E. (1983). 'Information processing times for English and Chinese words', *Perception and Psychophysics, 34*, 573–7.

Howarth, E., and Browne, J. A. (1972). 'An item-factor-analysis of the Eysenck Personality Inventory', *British Journal of Social and Clinical Psychology, 11*, 162–74.

Hsiao, H. H. (1941). 'Hsiao's revision of Personal Data Sheet', *Educational Bulletin, 4*, No. 6. (In Chinese.)

Hsiao, K. C. (1954). 'A history of Chinese political thought'. Taipei: Chung-Hua Wen-Hua Chu-Pan She. (In Chinese.)

Hsieh, T., Shybut, J., and Lotsof, E. (1969). 'Internal versus external control and ethnic group membership: a cross-cultural comparison', *Journal of Consulting and Clinical Psychology, 33*, 122–4.

Hsieh, Y. W. (1967). 'The status of the individual in Chinese ethics'. In C. A. Moore (Ed.), *The Chinese Mind* (pp. 307–22). Honolulu: University of Hawaii Press.

Hsiung, S. L. (1965). 'Ethnic stereotypes and prejudice: a cross-cultural comparison'. Unpublished manuscript, Cheng-chi University. (In Chinese.)

Hsu, C. C. (1966). 'A study on "problem children" reported by teachers', *Japanese Journal of Child Psychiatry, 7*, 91–108.

_____(1973). 'A comparative study of well-adjusted and maladjusted junior high school students', *Journal of the Formosan Medical Association, 72*, 167–83.

Hsu, E. H. (1951). 'The neurotic score as a function of culture', *Journal of Social Psychology, 34*, 3–30.

Hsu, F. L. K. (1948). *Under the Ancestors' Shadow*. New York: Columbia University Press.

_____(1949). 'Suppression versus repression: a limited psychological interpretation of four cultures', *Psychiatry, 12*, 223–42.

_____(1953). *Americans and Chinese: Two Ways of Life*. New York: Abelard-Schuman.

_____(1961). 'Kinship and ways of life: an exploration'. In F. L. K. Hsu (Ed.), *Psychological Anthropology: Approaches to Culture and Personality* (pp. 509–67). Homewood, Ill.: Dorsey.

_____(1963). *Clan, Caste and Club*. New York: van Nostrand.

_____(1965). 'The effect of dominant kinship relationship on kin and non-kin behaviour: a hypothesis', *American Anthropologist, 67*, 638–61.

_____(1967). *Under the Ancestors' Shadow: Kinship, Personality, and Social*

Mobility in Village China (revised and expanded edition). New York: Doubleday.

———(1971a). 'A hypothesis on kinship and culture'. In F. L. K. Hsu (Ed.), *Kinship and Culture* (pp. 3–30). Chicago: Aldine.

———(1971b). 'Psychological homeostasis and jen: conceptual tools for advancing psychological anthropology', *American Anthropologist, 73*, 23–44.

———(1971c). 'Filial piety in Japan and China: borrowing, variation and significance', *Journal of Comparative Family Studies, 2*, 67–74.

———, Watrous, B. G., and Lord, E. M. (1961). 'Culture pattern and adolescent behaviour', *International Journal of Social Psychiatry, 7*, 33–53.

Hsu, J. (1972). 'Chinese parent-child relationships as revealed in popular stories for children'. In Y. Y. Li and K. S. Yang (Eds.), *The Character of the Chinese: an Interdisciplinary Approach* (Monograph Series B, No. 4, pp. 201–18). Taipei: Institute of Ethnology, Academia Sinica. (In Chinese.)

———and Tseng, W. S. (1974). 'Family relations in classic Chinese opera', *International Journal of Social Psychiatry, 20*, 159–72.

Hsu, T. O. (1981). 'Leadership style, characteristics of work and satisfaction of government female employees in Taiwan'. Unpublished master's thesis, National Chengchi University. (In Chinese.)

Hsu, Y. S. (1982). 'Leader's power basis, leadership, and employees' job satisfaction'. Unpublished master's thesis, National Chengchi University. (In Chinese.)

Hu, F. (1977). 'Personality traits and political value orientations'. Unpublished manuscript, National Taiwan University. (In Chinese.)

———(1982). 'Yu-Chuan (有權) and Wu-Chuan (無權): a conceptual and empirical analysis of political value orientations'. In K. S. Yang and C. I. Wen (Eds.), *The Sinicization of Social and Behavioural Science Research in China* (pp. 381–416). Taipei: Institute of Ethnology, Academia Sinica. (In Chinese.)

Hu, H. C. (1944). 'The Chinese concepts of "face" ', *American Anthropologist, 46*, 45–64.

———(1950). 'Chinese folk literature and the Chinese child'. Unpublished manuscript. New York: Columbia University Research in Contemporary Cultures.

———(1951). 'Sex experiences of children'. Unpublished document (RCC-CH-PR4). New York: Columbia University Research in Contemporary Cultures.

Huang, H. C., Hwang, K. K., and Ko, Y. H. (1983). 'Life stress, attribution style, social support and depression among university students'. *Acta Psychologica Taiwanica, 25*, 31–47. (In Chinese.)

Huang, J., and Liu, I. (1978). 'Paired-associate learning proficiency as a function of frequency count, meaningfulness, and imagery value in Chinese two-character ideograms', *Acta Psychologica Taiwanica, 20*, 5–17.

Huang, K. L., and Lin, C. H. (1979). 'The change in Chinese stereotypes about Americans after U.S. decognition of the Republic of China'. Unpublished manuscript, Cheng-chi University. (In Chinese.)

Huang, K. Y., and Wong, I.F. (1980). 'The influence of leadership style and personality traits on the job satisfaction of workers', *National Chengchi University Journal, 41*, 45–60. (In Chinese.)

Huang, L. C., and Harris, M. B. (1973). 'Conformity in Chinese and Americans: a field experiment', *Journal of Cross-Cultural Psychology, 4*, 427–34.

____(1974). 'Altruism and imitation in Chinese and Americans: a cross-cultural experiment', *Journal of Social Psychology, 93*, 193–5.

Huang, L. J. (1971). 'Sex role stereotypes and self-concepts among Chinese and American students', *Journal of Comparative Family Studies, 2*, 215–34.

Huang, L. L., and Hwang, K. K. (1979). 'Influence of authoritarian and dogmatic personality upon the perception of the U.S. decognition of the Republic of China', *Bulletin of the Institute of Ethnology, Academia Sinica, 48*, 155–96. (In Chinese.)

Huang, S. C. (1963). 'A comparison of selected values among Formosan and American adolescents'. Doctoral thesis, Ohio State University, 1962. *Dissertation Abstracts International, 24*, 381.

Huang, W. Y. (1976). 'A research on the relation between parental discipline and personality traits of public junior high school students', *Thought and Word* (Taipei), *14*(2), 54–65, *14*(3), 41–60. (In Chinese.)

Huang, Y. L., and Jones, B. (1980). 'Naming and discrimination of Chinese ideograms presented in the right and left visual fields', *Neuropsychologia, 18*, 703–6.

Hulse, S. H., Deese, J., and Egeth, H. (1975). *The Psychology of Learning.* New York: McGraw-Hill.

Hummel, A. W. (1960). 'The art of social relations in China', *Philosophy East and West, 10*, 13–22.

Hung, D. L., and Tzeng, O. J. L. (1981). 'Orthographic variations and visual information processing', *Psychological Bulletin, 90*, 377–414.

Hung, K. Y., and Yang, K. S. (1979). 'Attributional variables as cognitive traits: measurement and validation', *Bulletin of The Institute of Ethnology, Academia Sinica, 48*, 89–154. (In Chinese.)

Hurvich, L. M., and Jameson, D. (1974). 'Opponent processes as a model of neural organization', *American Psychologist, 29*, 88–102.

Hwang, C. H. (1955). 'Popular Rorschach responses of Chinese subjects', *Psychological Testing* (Taipei), *3*, 63–70. (In Chinese.)

____(1967). 'A study of the personal preferences of Chinese university students by Edwards' Personal Preference Schedule', *Psychology and Education* (Taipei), *1*, 52–68.

——(1968). 'Reactions of Chinese university students to Rosenzweig's Picture Frustration Study', *Psychology and Education, 2*, 37–48.

——(1974a). *A Comparative Study on Social Attitudes of Adolescents in Glasgow and in Taipei.* Taipei: Oriental Cultural Service.

——(1974b). 'The use of a semantic differential in studying social attitudes of Chinese and Scottish adolescents', *Psychological Testing* (Taipei), *21*, 39–46. (In Chinese.)

——(1975). 'A follow-up study on social attitudes of Chinese and Scottish adolescents', *Bulletin of Educational Psychology* (Taipei), *8*, 95–106.

——(1976). 'Change of psychological needs over thirteen years', *Bulletin of Educational Psychology* (Taipei), *9*, 85–94.

——(1982). 'Studies in Chinese personality: a critical review', *Bulletin of Educational Psychology, 15*, 227–40.

Hwang, K. K. (1977). 'The patterns of coping strategies in a Chinese society', *Acta Psychologica Taiwanica, 19*, 61–73. (In Chinese.)

——(1978). 'The dynamic processes of coping with interpersonal conflicts in a Chinese society', *Proceedings of the National Science Council, 2*, 198–208.

——(1979). 'Coping with residential crowding in a Chinese urban society: the interplay of high-density dwelling and interpersonal values', *Acta Psychologica Taiwanica, 21*(2), 117–33.

——(1981). 'Perception of life events: the application of non-metric multidimensional scaling', *Acta Psychologica Taiwanica, 22*(2), 22–32. (In Chinese.)

——(1983a). 'Face and favour: Chinese power games'. Unpublished manuscript, National Taiwan University.

——(1983b). 'Business organizational patterns and employee's working morale in Taiwan', *Bulletin of the Institute of Ethnology, Academia Sinica, 56*, 85–133.

——(1984). 'The organization pattern of family business in Taiwan'. In C. T. Wei and H. H. Lee (Eds.), *Tides of Thought* (pp. 327–71). Taipei: Linking Publishing.

——and Marsella, A. J. (1977). 'The meaning and measurement of Machiavellianism in Chinese and American college students', *Journal of Social Psychology, 101*, 165–73.

——and Yang, K. S. (1972). 'Chinese individual modernity and social orientation', *Bulletin of the Institute of Ethnology, Academia Sinica 32*, 245–78. (In Chinese.)

Hwang, S. Y. (1983). 'A study of the job satisfaction of accounting officers in the local government of Taiwan'. Unpublished master's thesis, National Chengchi University. (In Chinese.)

Hwang, W. C. (1980). *America as Perceived by Chinese High School Students.* Taipei: Dai-yen Publishing Co.

Inkeles, A., Hanfmann, E., and Beier, H. (1958). 'Modal personality and adjustment to the Soviet socio-political system', *Human Relations, 11*, 3–22.

Inkeles, A., and Levinson, D. J. (1954). 'National character: the study of modal personality and sociocultural systems'. In G. Lindzey (Ed.), *Handbook of Social Psychology* (pp. 977–1020). Cambridge, Mass.: Addison-Wesley.

____(1969). 'National character: the study of modal personality and sociocultural systems'. In G. Lindzey and E. Aronson (Eds.), *Handbook of Social Psychology* (second edition) (Vol. 4, pp. 418–506). Reading, Mass.: Addison-Wesley.

Inkson, J. H. K., Pugh, D. S., and Hickson, D. J. (1970). 'Organization context and structure: an abbreviated replication', *Administrative Science Quarterly, 15*, 318–29.

Irvine, S. H., and Carroll, W. K. (1980). 'Testing and assessment across cultures: issues in methodology and theory'. In H. C. Triandis and J. W. Berry (Eds.), *Handbook of Cross-cultural Psychology: Methodology* (Vol. 2, pp. 181–244). London: Allyn and Bacon.

Ismail, B., and Dyal, J. (1983). 'Language variation and ethnic affirmation by Chinese and Malays in Malaysia'. Paper presented at the Third Asian meeting of the International Association of Cross-cultural Psychology, Bangi, Malaysia, May.

Jacobs, J. B. (1979). 'A preliminary model of particularistic ties in Chinese political alliances: *Kan-ch'ing* and *kuan-hsi* in a rural Taiwanese township', *China Quarterly, 78*, 232–73.

Jahoda, G. (1971). 'Retinal pigmentation, illusion susceptibility and space perception', *International Journal of Psychology, 6*, 199–208.

____(1979). 'A cross-cultural perspective on experimental social psychology', *Personality and Social Psychology Bulletin, 5*, 142–8.

Janis, I. L., and Field, P. (1959). 'Sex difference and personality factors related to persuasibility'. In C. I. Hovland and I. L. Janis (Eds.), *Personality and Persuasibility* (pp. 55–68). New Haven: Yale University Press.

Jaquish, G. A., Ripple, R. E., and Arndt, S. (under review). 'Perceptions of life-span development: a cross-cultural developmental approach'. Manuscript submitted for publication.

Jeng, C., Lai, M., and Liu, I. (1973). 'Category norms in Chinese and English from bilingual subjects', *Acta Psychologica Taiwanica, 15*, 81–153.

Jones, C. E., and Davis, K. K. (1965). 'From acts to dispositions: the attribution process in person perception'. In L. Berkowitz (Ed.), *Advances in Experimental Social Psychology* (Vol. 2, pp. 219–65). New York: Academic Press.

Jones, E. E. (1964). *Ingratiation: a Social Psychological Analysis*. New York: Appleton-Century-Crofts.

Jones, J. M., and Kiesler, C. A. (1971). 'The interactive effects of commitment and forewarning: three experiments'. In C. A. Kiesler (Ed.), *The Psychology of Commitment* (pp. 90–108). New York: Academic Press.

Jones, L. V., and Bock, R. D. (1960). 'Multiple discriminant analysis applied to "Ways to Live" ratings from six cultural groups', *Sociometry, 23*, 162–76.

Just, M. A., and Carpenter, P. A. (1971). 'Comprehension of negation with quantification', *Journal of Verbal Learning and Verbal Behavior, 10*, 244–53.

Kagan, J. (1966). 'Reflection-impulsivity: the generality and dynamics of conceptual tempo', *Journal of Abnormal Psychology, 71*, 17–24.

———, Kearsley, R. B., and Zelazo, P. R. (1978). *Infancy: its Place in Human Development*. Cambridge, Mass.: Harvard University Press.

———and Moss, H. A. (1962). *Birth to Maturity*. New York. Wiley.

Kahn, H. (1979). *World Development: 1979 and Beyond*. London: Croom Helm.

Kao, L. Y. (1962). 'The standardization of a Chinese version of the Thurstone Temperament Schedule', *Psychological Testing* (Taipei), *9*, 35–48. (In Chinese.)

Kaplan, D., and Manners, R. A. (1972). *Culture Theory*. Englewood Cliffs, New Jersey: Prentice-Hall.

Katz, D., and Braly, K. (1933). 'Racial stereotypes of one hundred college students', *Journal of Abnormal and Social Psychology, 28*, 288–90.

Keesing, R. M. (1974). 'Theories of culture', *Annual Review of Anthropology*, 73–97.

Kelley, H. H. (1967). 'Attribution theory in social psychology'. In D. Levine (Ed.), *Nebraska Symposium on Motivation* (pp. 192–238). Lincoln, Neb.: University of Nebraska Press.

Kelly, G. A. (1955). *The Psychology of Personal Constructs* (Vol. 1). New York: Norton.

Kerlinger, F., and Rokeach, M. (1966). 'The factorial nature of the F and D scales', *Journal of Personality and Social Psychology, 4*, 391–9.

Kessen, W. (Ed.) (1975). *Childhood in China*. New Haven, Conn.: Yale University Press.

Keyes, S. (1979). 'The development of spatial ability in Hong Kong adolescents', *Hong Kong Psychological Society Bulletin, 2*, 21–6.

Khoo, O. T., and Fernandez, P. (1971). 'The problem of alcoholism in Singapore', *Singapore Medical Journal, 12*, 154–60.

King, A. Y. C. (1981). 'The individual and group in Confucianism: a relational perspective'. Paper presented at the Conference on Individualism and Wholism, York, Maine, June.

———and Bond, M. H. (1985). 'The Confucian paradigm of man: a sociological view'. In W. S. Tseng and D. Y. H. Wu (Eds.), *Chinese Culture and Mental Health* (pp. 29–46). New York: Academic Press.

_____and Leung, D. H. K. (1975). 'The Chinese touch in small industrial organizations'. Occasional Paper, Social Research Centre, The Chinese University of Hong Kong.

_____and Myers, J. T. (1977). 'Shame as an incomplete conception of Chinese culture: a study of face'. Unpublished manuscript, Social Research Centre, The Chinese University of Hong Kong.

Kintsch, W., and Monk, D. (1972). 'Storage of complex information in memory: some implications of the speed with which inferences can be made', *Journal of Experimental Psychology, 94*, 25–32.

Kirk, S. A., McCarthy, J. J., and Kirk, W. D. (1968). *The Illinois Test of Psycholinguistic Abilities.* Urbana, Ill.: University of Illinois Press.

Klein, M. H., Miller, M. H., and Alexander, A. A. (1981). 'The American experience of the Chinese student: on being normal in an abnormal world'. In A. Kleinman and T. Y. Lin (Eds.) *Normal and Abnormal Behavior in Chinese Culture* (pp. 311–30). Dordrecht, Netherlands: D. Reidel.

Kleinman, A. M. (1977). 'Depression, somatization and the "new cross-cultural" psychiatry', *Social Science and Medicine, 11*, 3–10.

_____(1980). *Patients and Healers in the Context of Culture.* Berkeley, Calif.: University of California Press.

_____(1982). 'Neurasthenia and depression: a study of somatization and culture in China', *Culture, Medicine and Psychiatry, 6*, 117–90.

_____and Gale, J. L. (1982). 'Patients treated by physicians and folk healers: a comparative outcome study in Taiwan', *Culture, Medicine and Psychiatry, 6*, 405–23.

_____, Kunstadter, P., Alexander, E. R., and Gale, J. L. (Eds.) (1975). *Medicine in Chinese Cultures: Comparative Studies of Health Care in Chinese and Other Societies.* Washington, DC: U.S. Department of Health, Education, and Welfare.

_____and Lin, T. Y. (1981). 'Introduction'. In A. Kleinman and T. Y. Lin (Eds.), *Normal and Abnormal Behavior in Chinese Culture* (pp. *xiii–xxiii*). Dordrecht, Netherlands: D. Reidel.

_____and Mechanic, D. (1979). 'Some observations of mental illness and its treatment in the People's Republic of China', *Journal of Nervous and Mental Disease, 167*, 267–74.

Klineberg, O. (1938). 'Emotional expression in Chinese literature', *Journal of Abnormal and Social Psychology, 33*, 517–20.

Kluckhohn, F. R., and Strodtbeck, F. L. (1961). *Variations in Value Orientations.* Evanston, Ill.: Row, Peterson.

Ko, Y. H. (1980). *Mental Health, Vol. 1 — Theory.* Taipei: Tai Yang Publishers. (In Chinese.)

Kocel, K. M. (1977). 'Cognitive abilities: handedness, familial sinistrality, and sex'. In S. J. Diamond and D. A. Blizard (Eds.), *Evolution and Lateralization of the Brain* (pp. 233–43). New York: New York Academy of Sciences.

Kohlberg, L. (1958). 'The development of modes of moral thinking and choice in the years 10 to 16'. Unpublished doctoral thesis, University of Chicago.

——(1969). 'Stage and sequence: the cognitive-developmental approach to socialization'. In D. Goslin (Ed.), *Handbook of Socialization Theory and Research* (pp. 347–475). Chicago: Rand McNally.

——(1976). *Moral Development and Behaviour.* New York: Holt, Rinehart and Winston.

——and Tappan, M. (1983). *Substage Scoring Manual.* Cambridge, Mass.: Center for Moral Education, Harvard University.

Kolers, P. A. (1972). 'Experiments in reading', *Scientific American, 227,* 84–91.

Kong, F. (1980). 'Ethnic identity of the Chinese following an English secondary education: factors influencing affirmation or accommodation'. Unpublished manuscript, University of Hong Kong.

Koran, L. M. (1972). 'Psychiatry in mainland China: history and recent status', *American Journal of Psychiatry, 128,* 84–92.

Kriger, S. F., and Kroes, W. H. (1972). 'Child-rearing attitudes of Chinese, Jewish, and Protestant mothers', *Journal of Social Psychology, 86,* 205–10.

Kroeber, A. L., and Parsons, T. (1958). 'The concept of culture and social systems', *American Sociological Review, 23,* 583–94.

Kubany, E. S., Gallimore, R., and Buell, J. (1970). 'The effects of extrinsic factors on achievement-oriented behaviour: a non-Western case', *Journal of Cross-Cultural Psychology, 1,* 77–84.

Kugelmass, S., and Lieblich, A. (1970). 'Perceptual exploration in Israeli children', *Child Development, 41,* 1125–31.

Kuhlen, R. G., and Lee, R. J. (1943). 'Personality characteristics and social acceptability in adolescence', *Journal of Educational Psychology, 34,* 321–40.

Kuhn, M. H., and McPartland, T. S. (1954). 'An empirical investigation of self-attitudes', *American Sociological Review, 19,* 68–76.

Kung, Y. H. (1963). 'An EEG and clinical study of the cortical function of neurasthenics', *Hsin-li hsueh-pao, 1,* 65–74. (In Chinese.)

Kuo, S. Y. (1984). 'The relationships of causal attributions for success or failure and achievement-related behavior', *Bulletin of Educational Psychology, 17,* 1–22. (In Chinese.)

Kuo, W. H., Gray, R., and Lin, N. (1979). 'Locus of control and symptoms of psychological distress among Chinese-Americans', *International Journal of Social Psychiatry, 25*(3), 176–87.

Kuo, Y. Y. (1971). 'Psychology in communist China', *Psychological Record, 21,* 95–105.

Kurokawa, M. (1969). 'Acculturation and childhood accidents among Chinese and Japanese Americans', *Genetic Psychology Monographs, 79,* 89–159.

Kvan, E. (1969). 'Problems of bilingual milieu in Hong Kong: strain of the two-language system'. In I. C. Jarvie (Ed.), *Hong Kong: a Society in Transition* (pp. 327–43). London: Routledge and Kegan Paul.

Kwan, S. S. (1984). 'A study of the determinants of organization and managerial control in Chinese companies'. Unpublished master's thesis, University of Hong Kong.

La Barre, W. (1945). 'Some observations on character structure in the Orient: the Japanese', *Psychiatry, 8*, 319–42.

_____(1946). 'Some observations on character structure in the Orient: the Chinese, part one', *Psychiatry, 9*, 215–37.

Lai, P. W. H. (1978). 'Nepotism and management in Hong Kong'. Unpublished diploma thesis, University of Hong Kong.

Lai, P. Y. (1981). 'Persuasibility in Chinese and English secondary students'. Unpublished master's thesis, University of London.

Lammers, C. J., and Hickson, D. J. (Eds.) (1979). *Organizations Alike and Unlike*. London: Routledge and Kegan Paul.

Landis, C. (1929). 'The interpretation of facial expression of emotion', *Journal of Genetic Psychology, 2*, 59–72.

Lang, O. (1946). *Chinese Family and Society*. New Haven, Conn.: Yale University Press.

Langner, T. S. (1966). 'A twenty-two item screening score of psychiatric symptoms indicating impairment', *Journal of Health and Human Behavior, 3*, 269–76.

Lao, R. C. (1977). 'Levinson's IPC (internal-external control) scale: a comparison of Chinese and American students', *Journal of Cross-Cultural Psychology, 9*, 113–24.

_____, Chuang, C. J., and Yang, K. S. (1977). 'Locus of control and Chinese college students', *Journal of Cross-Cultural Psychology, 8*, 299–313.

Lau, S. K. (1982). *Society and Politics in Hong Kong*. Hong Kong: The Chinese University Press.

Law, S. K. (1978). 'Urban-rural differences in student mental health: the Hong Kong scene', *Australian and New Zealand Journal of Psychiatry, 12*, 277–81.

_____(1979). 'Common child psychiatric problems in the school setting', *Hong Kong Journal of Mental Health, 8*(1), 25–7.

Lazure, D. (1962). 'The family and youth in New China: psychiatric observations', *Canadian Medical Association Journal, 86*, 179–83.

Lee, P. H. (1973). 'Personality correlates of Chinese individual modernity', *Acta Psychologica Taiwanica, 15*, 46–53. (In Chinese.)

Lee, R. P. L. (1975). 'Interaction between Chinese and western medicine in Hong Kong: modernization and professional inequality'. In A. Kleinman, P. Kunstadter, E. R. Alexander, and J. L. Gale (Eds.), *Medicine in Chinese Culture: Comparative Studies of Health Care in Chinese and Other Societies* (pp. 219–40). Washington, DC: U.S. Department of Health, Education, and Welfare.

——(1976). 'Sex and social class differences in mental illness: the case of Hong Kong'. Occasional Paper, Social Research Centre, The Chinese University of Hong Kong.

——(1980). 'Perceptions and uses of Chinese medicine among the Chinese in Hong Kong', *Culture, Medicine and Psychiatry, 4*, 345–75.

——(1981). 'Sex roles, social status, and psychiatric symptoms in urban Hong Kong'. In A. Kleinman and T. Y. Lin (Eds.), *Normal and Abnormal Behavior in Chinese Culture* (pp. 273–89). Dordrecht, Netherlands: D. Reidel.

——(1982). 'Social science and indigenous concepts: with "yuan" in medical care as an example'. In K. S. Yang and C. I. Wen (Eds.), *The Sinicization of Social and Behavioral Science Research in China* (pp. 361–80). Taipei: Institute of Ethnology, Academia Sinica. (In Chinese.)

——(1985). 'Social stress and coping behavior in Hong Kong'. In W. S. Tseng and D. Wu (Eds.), *Chinese Culture and Mental Health* (pp. 193–214). New York: Academic Press.

Leeming, F. (1977). *Street Studies in Hong Kong*. Hong Kong: Oxford University Press.

Lei, C. T., Kuo, T. C., and Chen, Y. C. (1945). *The Mental Health of Chinese College and Secondary School Students in War Time*. Public Health Section, Medical Research Institute, Central University, Nanking, Report No. 3. (In Chinese.)

Lei, T., and Cheng, S. W. (1984). 'A little but special light on the universality of moral judgement'. Unpublished manuscript, National Taiwan University. (In Chinese.)

Lei, T., and Yang, K. S. (1984). 'The change of basic values of Chinese university students in Taiwan: twenty years later'. Paper read at the Interdisciplinary Conference on Social and Cultural Change in Taiwan held in the Institute of Ethnology, Academia Sinica, Taipei, September. (In Chinese.)

Leifer, A. (1972). 'Ethnic patterns in cognitive tasks', *Dissertation Abstracts International, 33*, 1270–1.

Leighton, D., and Kluckhohn, C. (1947). *Children of the People*. Cambridge, Mass.: Harvard University Press.

Lesser, G. S. (1976). 'Cultural differences in learning and thinking styles'. In S. Messick (Ed.), *Individuality in Learning* (pp. 137–60). San Francisco: Jossey-Bass.

——, Fifer, G., and Clark, D. H. (1965). 'Mental abilities of children from different social class and cultural groups', *Monograph of the Society for Research in Child Development, 30* (4).

Leung, H. F. (1984). 'An impression of the first Reagan–Mondale debate', *Min-Pao*, 18 October, p. 25.

Leung, K., and Bond, M. H. (1982). 'How Americans and Chinese reward task-related contributions: a preliminary study', *Psychologia, 25*, 2–9.

____(1984). 'The impact of cultural collectivism on reward allocation', *Journal of Personality and Social Psychology, 47*, 793–804.

Levinson, H. (1974). 'Activism and powerful others: distinctions within the concept of internal-external control', *Journal of Personality Assessment, 38*, 377–83.

Levy, M. (1949). *The Family Revolution in Modern China.* Cambridge, Mass.: Harvard University Press.

Lew, W. J. F. (1979). 'A Chinese woman intellectual: family, education, and personality', *Education Journal* (Hong Kong), *7*, 166–97.

____(1983). 'Personality traits of Hong Kong secondary school teachers', *Chinese University Education Journal, 11*, 36–46.

Lewis, J. W. (1965). 'Education and political development: a study of pre-school training programs in Mainland China'. In J. S. Coleman (Ed.), *Education and Political Development* (pp. 423–9). Princeton, New Jersey: Princeton University Press.

Li, A. K. F. (1974). 'Parental attitudes, test anxiety, and achievement motivation: a Hong Kong study', *Journal of Social Psychology, 93*, 3–11.

Li, F. L. (1970). 'A case study of child training and education in rural Taiwan', *Bulletin of The Institute of Ethnology, Academia Sinica, 29*, 151–98. (In Chinese.)

Li, M. C., Cheung, S. F., and Kau, S. M. (1979). 'Competitive and cooperative behavior of Chinese children in Taiwan and Hong Kong', *Acta Psychologica Taiwanica, 21*, 27–33. (In Chinese.)

Li, M. C., and Yang, K. S. (1972). 'A study of values among Chinese college students'. In Y. Y. Li and K. S. Yang (Eds.), *Symposium on the Character of the Chinese: an Interdisciplinary Approach* (pp. 313–32). Taipei: Institute of Ethnology, Academia Sinica. (In Chinese.)

Li, S. Y., and Wong, S. Y. (1980). 'A cross-cultural study on sex-role stereotypes and social desirability', *Sex Roles, 8*, 481–91.

Li, X. T. (1985). 'The effect of family on the mental health of the Chinese people'. In W. S. Tseng and D. Wu (Eds.), *Chinese Culture and Mental Health* (pp. 83–94). New York: Academic Press.

Li, Y. Y. (1975). 'The modernization of the traditional man and his traditional attitudes', *Man and Society* (Taipei), *3*, 62–5. (In Chinese.)

Liang, S. L. (1984). 'The organizational identification of civil servants of central government organizations'. Unpublished doctoral thesis, National Taiwan University. (In Chinese.)

Liao, S. H. (1978). 'The relationship among principals' leadership style, teachers' personality traits and job satisfaction of teachers in elementary schools of Taiwan'. Unpublished master's thesis, National Chengchi University. (In Chinese.)

Liberman, I. Y., Shankweiler, D., Fischer, F. W., and Carter, B. (1974). 'Explicit syllable and phoneme segmentation in the young child', *Journal of Experimental Child Psychology, 18*, 201–12.

Lim, L. Y. C. (1983). 'Multinationals and the state: manufacturing for export in Malaysia and Singapore'. In L. Y. C. Lim and L. A. P. Gosling (Eds.), *The Chinese in Southeast Asia* (pp. 245–74). Singapore: Maruzen Asia.

Lin, C. I. (1978). 'The influence of leadership on job satisfaction'. Unpublished master's thesis, National Chengchi University. (In Chinese.)

Lin, F. S. (1978). 'Stereotypes, personality traits, and the utilization of mass media: the effects of the TV series "Roots" '. Unpublished master's thesis, Cheng-chi University. (In Chinese.)

Lin, H. H. (1984). 'Post-divorce adjustment and post-divorce counselling: a study of counselling effectiveness with divorced women in Taiwan'. Unpublished doctoral thesis, University of Toronto.

Lin, K. M. (1981). 'Traditional Chinese medical beliefs and their relevance for mental illness and psychiatry'. In A. Kleinman and T. Y. Lin (Eds.), *Normal and Abnormal Behavior in Chinese Culture* (pp. 95–111). Dordrecht, Netherlands: D. Reidel.

_____and Kleinman, A. (1981). 'Recent development of psychiatric epidemiology in China', *Culture, Medicine and Psychiatry, 5*, 135–43.

_____, Kleinman, A., and Lin, T. Y. (1981). 'Overview of mental disorders in Chinese cultures: review of epidemiological and clinical studies'. In A. Kleinman and T. Y. Lin (Eds.), *Normal and Abnormal Behavior in Chinese Culture* (pp. 237–72). Dordrecht, Netherlands: D. Reidel.

Lin, N., Dean, A., and Ensel, W. M. (1981). 'Social support scales: a methodological note', *Schizophrenia Bulletin, 7*, 73–88.

Lin, N., Simeone, R. S., Ensel, W. M., and Kuo, W. (1979). 'Social support, stressful life events, and illness: a model and an empirical test', *Journal of Health and Social Behavior, 20*, 108–19.

Lin, R. Y. (1983). 'General situation of juvenile delinquency in Taiwan, the Republic of China, and national programs for its prevention and treatment'. In *Proceedings of the Second Asian-Pacific Conference on Juvenile Delinquency* (pp. 70–95). Seoul, Korea: Cultural and Social Centre for the Asia and Pacific Region.

Lin, T. Y. (1953). 'A study of the incidence of mental disorder in Chinese and other cultures', *Psychiatry, 16*, 313–36.

_____(1982). 'Culture and psychiatry: a Chinese perspective', *Australian and New Zealand Journal of Psychiatry, 16*, 235–45.

_____(1983). 'Psychiatry and Chinese culture', *The Western Journal of Medicine, 139*, 862–7.

_____(1984). 'Mental health and family values'. Public lecture delivered at Chung Chi College, The Chinese University of Hong Kong, 1 March.

_____(1985). 'Mental disorders and psychiatry in Chinese culture: characteristic features and major issues'. In W. S. Tseng and D. Wu (Eds.), *Chinese Culture and Mental Health* (pp. 367–93). New York: Academic Press.

___and Lin, D. T. C. (1982). 'Alcoholism among the Chinese: further observations of a low-risk population', *Culture, Medicine and Psychiatry, 6*, 109–16.

___and Lin, M. C. (1978). 'Service delivery issues in Asian-North American communities', *American Journal of Psychiatry, 135*, 454–6.

___and Lin, M. C. (1981). 'Love, denial and rejection: responses of Chinese family to mental illness'. In A. Kleinman and T. Y. Lin (Eds.), *Normal and Abnormal Behavior in Chinese Culture* (pp. 387–401). Dordrecht, Netherlands: D. Reidel.

___, Rin, H., Yeh, E. K., Hsu, C. C., and Chu, H. M. (1969). 'Mental disorders in Taiwan, fifteen years later'. In W. Caudill and T. Y. Lin (Eds.), *Mental Health Research in Asia and the Pacific* (pp. 66–91). Honolulu: East-West Center Press.

___, Tardiff, K., Donetz, G., and Goresky, W. (1978). 'Ethnicity and patterns of help-seeking', *Culture, Medicine and Psychiatry, 2*, 3–13.

Lin, Y. H. L. (1939). 'Confucius on interpersonal relations', *Psychiatry, 2*, 475–81.

Lin, Y. N. (1978). 'A study of the value orientations of junior high school students in the Republic of China', *Guidance Journal* (Changhua, Taiwan), *1*, 291–344. (In Chinese.)

Lin, Y. T. (1935). *My Country and my People.* New York: Reynal and Hitchcock.

Lincoln, J. R., Hanada, M., and Olson, J. (1981). 'Cultural orientation and individual reactions to organizations: a study of employees of Japanese-owned firms', *Administrative Science Quarterly, 26*, 93–115.

Lindsay, P. H., and Norman, D. A. (1977). *Human Information Processing.* New York: Academic Press.

Little, I. M. D. (1981). 'The experience and causes of rapid labour-intensive development in Korea, Taiwan Province, Hong Kong and Singapore; and the possibilities of emulation'. In Eddy Lee (Ed.), *Export-led Industrialization and Development* (pp. 23–46). Geneva: International Labour Office.

Liu, C. H. (1950). 'The influence of cultural background on the moral judgment of children'. Doctoral thesis, Columbia University, 1950. *Dissertation Abstracts, 10*, 319–21. (University Microfilms No. 1869, 104pp.)

Liu, C. Y., Chen, C. H., Chen, Y. H., and Yang, K. S. (1973). 'A survey of the every-day behaviour of National Taiwan University students', *Thought and Word* (Taipei), *10*(5), 6–9; *10*(6), 1–19. (In Chinese.)

Liu, I. M. (1973). 'Cross-cultural comparison of association patterns'. Paper presented at the conference of The Interface between Culture and Learning at the Culture Learning Institute, East-West Center, Honolulu.

___(1978). 'Methods of acquiring Chinese vocabulary', *Bulletin of the Sun Yat-sen Cultural Foundation, 22*, 159–87.

___(1984a). 'Sentence comprehension in Chinese and English'. In

H. S. R. Kao and R. Hoosain (Eds.), *Psychological Studies of the Chinese Language* (pp. 181–217). Hong Kong: Chinese Language Society of Hong Kong.

____(1984b). 'A survey of memorization requirement in Taipei primary and secondary schools'. Unpublished manuscript, National Taiwan University.

____(1985). 'Categorization time as independent of the number of condition-action rules', *Perception and Psychophysics, 37*, 8–16.

____, Chuang, C., and Wang, S. (1975). *Frequency Count of 40,000 Chinese Words*. Taipei: Lucky Books.

____and Hsu, M. (1974). 'Measuring creative thinking in Taiwan by the Torrance test', *Testing and Guidance, 2*, 108–9.

____and Liang, K. (1977). 'Verifying affirmative and negative sentences', *National Science Council Monthly, 5*, 432–41.

____and Ma, H. (1970). 'On the nature of a training trial in verbal learning', *Journal of Experimental Psychology, 86*, 126–7.

____, Yeh, J. S., Wang, L. H., and Chang, Y. K. (1974). 'Effects of arranging Chinese words as units on reading efficiency', *Acta Psychologica Taiwanica, 16*, 25–32.

Liu, K. S., and Shen, H. M. (1977). 'Effects of language structure and intertrial interval on the speed of silent reading', *Acta Psychologica Taiwanica, 19*, 57–9.

Liu, W. T. (1966). 'Chinese value orientations in Hong Kong', *Sociological Analysis, 27*, 55–66.

Liu, X. (1981). 'Psychiatry in traditional Chinese medicine', *British Journal of Psychiatry, 138*, 429–33.

Lo, W. H. (1967). 'A follow-up study of obsessional neurotics in Hong Kong Chinese', *British Journal of Psychiatry, 113*, 823–32.

____(1981). 'Culture and depression — with special reference to treatment'. Paper presented at the Symposium on Transcultural Psychiatry, Macau, September.

____and Lo, T. (1977). 'A ten-year follow-up study of Chinese schizophrenics in Hong Kong', *British Journal of Psychiatry, 131*, 63–6.

Loftus, G. R., and Loftus, B. F. (1976). *Human Memory. The Processing of Information*. New York: Wiley.

Low, N. K. (1973). 'Nepotism in industries: a comparative study of sixty Chinese modern and traditional industrial enterprises'. Unpublished bachelor's thesis, University of Singapore.

Lu, C. M. (1978). 'A report on the revision of the Gordon Personal Inventory', *Psychological Testing* (Taipei), *25*, 54–63.

Lu, C. Y. (1970). 'A study on the personality traits of freshmen at the National Taiwan University', *Acta Psychologica Taiwanica, 12*, 1–6. (In Chinese.)

Lu, Y. C. (1978). 'The collective approach to psychiatric practice in the People's Republic of China', *Social Problems, 26,* 2–14.

Lu, Y. H. (1980). 'Women's attitudes toward career role and family role in Taiwan's social change', *Bulletin of the Institute of Ethnology, Academia Sinica, 50,* 25–66. (In Chinese.)

____(1982). 'Value stretch of women's role attitude in Taiwan', *Journal of the Humanities and Social Science, 20*(2), 135–50. (In Chinese.)

Lui, M. (1985). 'Work-related needs among Hong Kong commercial employees'. Unpublished master's thesis, University of Hong Kong.

Ma, C. C. (1984). 'The problem of juvenile delinquency'. In K. S. Yang and C. C. Yeh (Eds.), *Social Problems in Taiwan* (revised edition, pp. 489–521). Taipei: Chu Liu Book Co. (In Chinese.)

McArthur, L. Z., and Baron, R. M. (1983). 'Toward an ecological theory of social perception', *Psychological Review, 90,* 215–38.

MacArthur, R. (1967). 'Sex differences in field-dependence for the Eskimo: replication of Berry's findings', *International Journal of Psychology, 2,* 139–40.

McClelland, D. C. (1958). 'Methods of measuring human motivation'. In J. W. Atkinson (Ed.), *Motives in Fantasy, Action, and Society* (pp. 7–42). Princeton, New Jersey: van Nostrand.

____(1961). *The Achieving Society.* Princeton, New Jersey: van Nostrand.

____(1963). 'Motivational patterns in Southeast Asia with special reference to the Chinese case', *Social Issues, 19,* 6–19.

____, Atkinson, J. W., Clark, R. A., and Lowell, E. L. (1953). *The Achievement Motive.* New York: Appleton-Century-Crofts.

Maccoby, E. E., and Jacklin, C. N. (1974). *The Psychology of Sex Differences.* Stanford, Calif.: Stanford University Press.

McConkie, G. W., and Rayner, K. (1975). 'The span of the effective stimulus during a fixation in reading', *Perception and Psychophysics, 17,* 578–86.

McCusker, L. X., Hillinger, M. L., and Bias, R. G. (1981). 'Phonological recoding and reading', *Psychological Bulletin, 89,* 214–45.

McGuigan, F. J. (1984). 'How is linguistic meaning accessed? A psychophysiological approach', *The Pavlovian Journal of Biological Science, 19,* 119–36.

Madsen, M. C. (1971). 'Developmental and cross-cultural differences in the cooperative and competitive behavior of young children', *Journal of Cross-Cultural Psychology, 2,* 365–71.

Magnusson, D., and Endler, N. S. (1977). 'Interactional psychology: present status and future prospects'. In D. Magnusson and N. S. Endler (Eds.), *Personality at the Crossroads: Current Issues in Interactional Psychology* (pp. 3–36). Hillsdale, New Jersey: Lawrence Erlbaum.

Marin, G., Triandis, H. C., Betancourt, H., and Kashima, Y. (1983). 'Ethnic affirmation versus social desirability: explaining discrepancies in bilinguals' responses to a questionnaire', *Journal of Cross-Cultural Psychology, 14,* 173–86.

Marlowe, D., and Crowne, D. P. (1964). *The Approval Motive: Studies in Evaluational Dependence.* New York: Wiley.

Marsella, A. (1980). 'Depressive affect and disorder across cultures'. In H. Triandis and J. Draguns (Eds.), *Handbook of Cross-Cultural Psychology, Vol. V, Psychopathology* (pp. 30–72). Boston: Allyn and Bacon.

——, Kinzie, J., and Gordon, P. (1973). 'Ethnocultural variations in the expression of depression', *Journal of Cross-Cultural Psychology, 4,* 453–8.

Martin, R. (1975). 'The socialization of children in China and on Taiwan: an analysis of elementary school textbooks', *China Quarterly, 62,* 242–62.

Maykovich, M. K. (1980). 'Social distance between the Chinese and Americans', *Acta Psychologica Taiwanica, 22,* 1–12.

Mead, M. (1937). *Cooperation and Competition among Primitive Peoples.* New York: McGraw-Hill.

——and Metraux, R. (Eds.) (1953). *The Study of Culture at a Distance.* Chicago: University of Chicago Press.

——and Wolfenstein, M. (Eds.) (1955). *Childhood in Contemporary Cultures.* Chicago: University of Chicago Press.

Meade, R. D. (1970). 'Leadership studies of Chinese and Chinese-Americans', *Journal of Cross-Cultural Psychology, 1,* 325–32.

——and Barnard, W. A. (1973). 'Conformity and anti-conformity among Americans and Chinese', *Journal of Social Psychology, 89,* 15–24.

——and Barnard, W. A. (1975). 'Group pressure on American and Chinese females', *Journal of Social Psychology, 96,* 137–8.

——and Whittaker, J. O. (1967). 'A cross-cultural study of authoritarianism', *Journal of Social Psychology, 72,* 3–7.

Mechanic, D. (1972). 'Social psychological factors affecting the presentation of bodily complaints', *New England Journal of Medicine, 286,* 1132–9.

——(1977). 'Illness behavior, social adaptation and the management of illness', *Journal of Nervous and Mental Disease, 165,* 79–87.

Mehrabian, A. (1970). 'The development and validation of measures of affiliative tendency and sensitivity to rejection', *Educational and Psychological Measurement, 30,* 417–28.

Metzger, T. A. (1981a). 'Selfhood and authority in neo-Confucian political culture'. In A. Kleinman and T. Y. Lin (Eds.), *Normal and Abnormal Behavior in Chinese Culture* (pp. 7–27). Dordrecht, Netherlands: D. Reidel.

——(1981b). 'Foreword'. In R. W. Wilson, S. L. Greenblatt, and A. A. Wilson (Eds.), *Moral Behavior in Chinese Society* (pp. 9–25). New York: Praeger.

Millar, S. E. (1976). 'Health and well-being in relation to high density living in Hong Kong'. Doctoral thesis, Australian National University.

___(1979). *The Biosocial Survey in Hong Kong*. Canberra: Centre for Resource and Environmental Studies, Australian National University.

Mischel, W. (1968). *Personality and Assessment*. New York: Wiley.

Mitchell, R. E. (1972a). *Family Life in Urban Hong Kong*. Taipei: Oriental Cultural Service.

___(1972b). *Pupil, Parent, and School: a Hong Kong Study*. Taipei: Oriental Cultural Service.

___and Lo, I. (1968). 'Implications of changes in family authority relations for the development of independence and assertiveness in Hong Kong children', *Asian Survey, 8*, 309–22.

Modigliani, A. (1971). 'Embarrassment, face-work, and eye contact', *Journal of Personality and Social Psychology, 17*, 15–24.

Mok, K. P. (1984). *Mental Health Thoughts in Ancient China*. Hong Kong: Hong Kong Mental Health Association. (In Chinese.)

Mok, V. (1973). 'The organization and management of factories in Kwun Tong'. Occasional Paper, Social Research Centre, The Chinese University of Hong Kong.

Mooney, R. L., and Gordon, L. V. (1950). *Mooney Problem Check List*. New York: Psychological Corporation.

Moore, C. A. (1967). 'Introduction: the humanistic Chinese mind'. In C. A. Moore (Ed.), *The Chinese Mind: Essentials of Chinese Philosophy and Culture* (pp. 1–10). Honolulu: University of Hawaii Press.

Morawetz, D. (1980). 'Why the emperor's new clothes are not made in Colombia'. Staff Working Paper, No. 368. Washington, DC: World Bank.

Morishima, M. (1982). *Why has Japan Succeeded?* Cambridge: Cambridge University Press.

Morris, C., and Jones, L. V. (1955). 'Value scales and dimensions', *Journal of Abnormal and Social Psychology, 51*, 523–35.

Morris, C. W. (1956). *Varieties of Human Value*. Chicago: University of Chicago Press.

Morris, L. W. (1979). *Extraversion and Introversion: an Interactive Perspective*. New York: Wiley.

Muensterberger, W. (1951). 'Orality and dependence: characteristics of southern Chinese'. In G. Roheim *et al.* (Eds.), *Psychoanalysis and the Social Sciences* (Vol. 3, pp. 37–69). New York: International Universities Press.

Murdock, B. B., jun. (1961). 'The retention of individual items', *Journal of Experimental Psychology, 62*, 618–25.

Muste, M. J., and Sharpe, D. F. (1947). 'Some influential factors in the determination of aggressive behavior in preschool children', *Child Development, 18*, 11–28.

Nakamura, H. (1964). *Ways of Thinking of Eastern Peoples: India, China, Tibet, and Japan.* Honolulu: University of Hawaii Press.

Nakane, C. (1973). *Japanese Society.* London: Penguin.

Nanjing Child Mental Health Research Center (1984). *Brief Introduction.* (Introductory) Pamphlet of the Research Center.) (In Chinese.)

Neisser, U. (1967). *Cognitive Psychology.* New York: Appleton-Century-Crofts.

Ng, S. H. (1984). 'Equity and social categorization effects on intergroup allocation of rewards', *British Journal of Social Psychology, 23,* 165–72.

——, Akhtar-Hoosain, A. B. M., Ball, P., Bond, M. H., Hayashi, K., Lim, S. P., O'Driscoll, M. P., Sinha, D., and Yang, K. S. (1982). 'Human values in nine countries'. In P. Rath, H. S. Asthana, D. Sinha, and J. B. P. Sinha (Eds.), *Diversity and Unity in Cross-cultural Psychology* (pp. 196–205). Lisse, Netherlands: Swets and Zeitlinger.

Ngui, P. W. (1969). 'The Koro epidemic in Singapore', *Australian and New Zealand Journal of Psychiatry, 3,* 263–6.

Niem, T. I., and Collard, R. R. (1972). 'Parental discipline of aggressive behaviors in four-year-old Chinese and American children', *Proceedings of the 80th Annual Convention of the American Psychological Association, 7,* 95–6.

Nih, L., Cheng, F. Y., and Chang, H. H. (1954). 'Rorschach Test: its application to Chinese high school students', *Psychological Testing* (Taipei), *2,* 33–9. (In Chinese.)

Nordlie, P. G. (1968). 'The role of values in psychological operations'. In *HSR Conference on Psychological Operations and Communications with Foreign Nationals, Research Report* 68/9-CR. McLean, Va.: Human Sciences Research, Inc., June.

Norman, W. T. (1963). 'Toward an adequate taxonomy of personality attributes: replicated factor structure in peer nomination personality ratings', *Journal of Abnormal and Social Psychology, 66,* 574–83.

Northrop, F. S. C. (1946). *The Meeting of East and West.* New York: Macmillan.

Oksenberg, L. (1970). 'Machiavellianism in traditional and Westernized Chinese students'. In W. Lambert and R. Weisbrod (Eds.), *Comparative Perspectives in Social Psychology* (pp. 92–9). Boston: Little, Brown.

Olsen, N. J. (1971). 'Sex differences in child training antecedents of achievement motivation among Chinese children', *Journal of Social Psychology, 83,* 303–4.

——(1975). 'Social class and rural-urban patterning of socialization in Taiwan', *Journal of Asian Studies, 34,* 659–74.

Osgood, C. (1975). *The Chinese: a Study of a Hong Kong Community* (Vols. 1–3). Tucson, Arizona: University of Arizona Press.

Osgood, C. E., and Hoosain, R. (1974). 'Salience of the word as a unit in the perception of language', *Perception and Psychophysics, 15*, 168–92.

Osgood, C. E., May, W. H., and Miron, M. S. (1975). *Cross-cultural Universals of Affective Meaning*. Urbana, Ill.: University of Illinois Press.

Oshima, H. T. (1981). 'Manpower quality and the differential economic growth between East and Southeast Asia'. Working Paper, School of Economics, University of Philippines, Manila.

Ouchi, W. G. (1981). *Theory Z*. Reading, Mass.: Addison-Wesley.

Pai, T., Sung, S. M., and Hsu, E. H. (1937). 'The application of Thurstone's Personality Schedule to Chinese subjects', *Journal of Social Psychology, 8*, 47–72.

Paivio, A. (1965). 'Abstractness, imagery, and meaningfulness in paired-associate learning', *Journal of Verbal Learning and Verbal Behavior, 4*, 32–8.

Parish, W. L., and Whyte, M. K. (1978). *Village and Family in Contemporary China*. Chicago: University of Chicago Press.

Paschal, B. J., and Kuo, Y. Y. (1973). 'Anxiety and self-concept among American and Chinese college students', *College Student Journal, 7*, 7–13.

____, and Schurr, K. T. (1980–1). 'Creative thinking in Indiana and Taiwan college students'. Paper presented at the Fifth Conference of the International Association of Cross-Cultural Psychology, Bhubaneshwar, India, December 1980–January 1981.

Paykel, E. S., Prusoff, B. A., and Uhlenhuth, E. H. (1971). 'Scaling of life events', *Archives of General Psychiatry, 25*, 340–7.

Pedersen, P. B. (1983). 'Asian personality theory'. In R. J. Corsini and A. J. Marsella (Eds.), *Personality Theories, Research and Assessment* (pp. 367–97). Itasca, Ill.: F. E. Peacock.

Peng, J. J. (1963). 'A study of Edwards Personal Preference Schedule among Chinese college students'. Unpublished bachelor's thesis, National Taiwan University.

Peng, O. L., Orchard, L. N., and Stern, J. A. (1983). 'Evaluation of eye movement variables of Chinese and American readers', *The Pavlovian Journal of Biological Science, 18*, 94–102.

Pepitone, A. (1976). 'Toward a normative and comparative biocultural social psychology', *Journal of Personality and Social Psychology, 34*, 641–53.

Peterson, L. R., and Peterson, M. J. (1959). 'Short-term retention of individual items', *Journal of Experimental Psychology, 58*, 193–8.

Piaget, J. (1932). *The Moral Judgement of the Child*. New York: Free Press.

____(1952). *The Origin of Intelligence in Children*. New York: International Universities Press.

____(1964). *Judgment and Reasoning in the Child*. Patterson, New Jersey: Littlefield, Adams, and Co.

Pierce, J. V. (1961). *Sex Differences in Achievement Motivation*. Quincy, Ill.: Quincy Youth Development Project.

Pilkonis, P. A., and Zimbardo, P. G. (1979). 'The personal and social dynamics of shyness'. In C. E. Izard (Ed.), *Emotions in Personality and Psychopathology* (pp. 133–60). New York: Plenum.

Plummer, J. P. (1982). 'An analysis of some exercises, therapies and techniques capable of correcting posture and muscle imbalance'. In D. Garlick (Ed.), *Proprioception, Posture and Emotion* (pp. 195–213). Sydney: Committee in Postgraduate Medical Education, University of New South Wales.

Post, E. L. (1943). 'Formal reductions of the general combinatorial decision problem', *American Journal of Mathematics, 65*, 197–268.

Prince, R., and Mombour, W. (1967). 'A technique for improving linguistic equivalence in cross-cultural surveys', *International Journal of Social Psychiatry, 13*, 229–37.

Pruitt, I. (1945). *A Daughter of Han: the Autobiography of a Chinese Working Woman*. New Haven, Conn.: Yale University Press. (Republished Stanford, Calif.: Stanford University Press, 1967.)

Psychological Corporation (1981). *Hong Kong Wechsler Intelligence Scale for Children Manual*. New York: Psychological Corporation.

Pugh, D. S., and Hickson, D. J. (1976). *Organizational Structure in its Context*. Farnborough: Saxon House.

Pugh, D. S., and Redding, S. G. (1985). 'A comparative study of the structure and context of Chinese businesses in Hong Kong'. Paper presented at the Association of Teachers of Management Research Conference, Ashridge, England, January.

Redding, S. G. (1980). 'Cognition as an aspect of culture and its relation to management processes: an exploratory view of the Chinese case', *Journal of Management Studies, 17*, 127–48.

——(1983). 'Management styles East and West'. Paper presented at the Orient Airlines Association Conference, Manila, Philippines, May.

——(in press). 'Operationalizing the post-Confucian hypothesis: the overseas Chinese case'. In K. C. Mun (Ed.), *Chinese Style Enterprise Management*. Hong Kong: The Chinese University Press.

——and Casey, T. W. (1976). 'Managerial beliefs among Asian managers'. In R. L. Taylor, M. J. O'Connell, R. A. Zawacki, and D. D. Warwick (Eds.), *Proceedings of the Academy of Management 36th Annual Meeting* (pp. 351–6). Kansas City: Academy of Management.

——and Hicks, G. L. (1983a). 'Culture, causation and Chinese management', Mong Kwok Ping Management Data Bank Working Paper, Department of Management Studies, University of Hong Kong.

——and Hicks, G. L. (1983b). 'The story of the East Asia economic miracle; part II: the culture connection', *Euro-Asia Business Review, 2*(4), 18–22.

____and Ng, M. (1982). 'The role of face in the organizational perceptions of Chinese managers', *Organization Studies, 3*, 201–19.

Reynolds, D. K. (1980). *The Quiet Therapies: Japanese Pathways to Personal Growth*. Honolulu: University of Hawaii Press.

Richards, T. W. (1954). 'The Chinese in Hawaii: a Rorschach report'. In F. L. K. Hsu (Ed.), *Aspects of Culture and Personality* (pp. 67–89). New York: Abelard-Schuman.

Ridley, C. P., Godwin, P. H. B., and Doolin, D. G. (1971). *The Making of a Model Citizen in Communist China*. Stanford, Calif.: Hoover Institution.

Rin, H., Chu, H. M., and Lin, T. Y. (1966). 'Psychophysiological reactions of a rural and suburban population in Taiwan', *Acta Psychiatrica Scandinavica, 42*, 410–73.

Rin, H., and Lin, T. Y. (1962). 'Mental illness among Formosan Aborigines as compared with Chinese in Taiwan', *Journal of Mental Science, 108*, 133–46.

Rin, H., Schooler, C., and Caudill, W. (1973). 'Symptomatology and hospitalization: culture, social structure and psychopathology in Taiwan and Japan', *Journal of Nervous and Mental Disease, 157*, 296–312.

Ripple, R. E., Jaquish, G. A., Lee, H. W., and Spinks, J. A. (1983). 'Intergenerational differences in descriptions of life-span stages among Hong Kong Chinese', *International Journal of Intercultural Relations, 7*, 425–37.

Robins, L. N., Helzer, J., Croughan, J., Williams, J. B. W., and Spitzer, R. L. (1979). *National Institute of Mental Health Diagnostic Interview Schedule*. Washington, DC: Government Printing Office.

Rodd, W. G. (1959). 'Cross-cultural use of "The Study of Values" ', *Psychologia, 2*, 157–64.

Roe, A., and Siegelman, M. (1963). 'A parent-child relations questionnaire', *Child Development, 34*, 355–69.

Rohlen, T. P. (1974). *For Harmony and Strength*. Berkeley: University of California Press.

Rohrl, V. J. (1979). 'Culture, cognition, and intellect: towards a cross-cultural view of "intelligence" ', *Journal of Psychological Anthropology, 2*, 337–64.

Rokeach, M. (1960). *The Open and Closed Mind*. New York: Basic Books.

____(1967). *Value Survey*. Sunnyvale, Calif.: Halgren Press.

Rosen, B. C., and D'Andrade, R. G. (1959). 'The psychological origins of achievement motivation', *Sociometry, 22*, 185–218.

Rosen, B. M., Bahn, A. K., and Kramer, M. (1964). 'Demographic and diagnostic characteristics of psychiatric clinic outpatients in the U.S.A., 1961', *American Journal of Orthopsychiatry, 34*, 445–68.

Rosenfeld, P., Giacalone, R. A., Tedeschi, J. T., and Bond, M. H. (1983). 'The cross-cultural efficacy of entitlements in American and Hong Kong

Chinese students'. In J. B. Deregowski, S. Dziurawiek, and R. C. Annis (Eds.), *Expiscations in Cross-cultural Psychology* (pp. 266–9). Lisse, Netherlands: Swets and Zeitlinger.

Rosenkrantz, P. S., Vogel, S. R., Bee, H., Broverman, I. K., and Broverman, D. M. (1968). 'Sex-role stereotypes and self-concepts in college students', *Journal of Consulting and Clinical Psychology, 32*, 287–95.

Rosenzweig, S., Fleming, E. E., and Clarke, H. J. (1947). 'Revised scoring manual for the Rosenzweig Picture-Frustration Study', *Journal of Psychology, 24*, 165–208.

Rothbaum, F., Weisz, J. R., and Snyder, S. S. (1982). 'Changing the world and changing the self: a two-process model of perceived control', *Journal of Personality and Social Psychology, 42*, 5–37.

Rotter, J. B. (1966). 'Generalized expectancies for internal versus external control of reinforcement', *Psychological Monographs, 80* (Whole No. 609).

____and Mulry, R. C. (1965). 'Internal vs external control of reinforcement and decision time', *Journal of Personality and Social Psychology, 2*, 598–604.

Rozin, P., Poritsky, S., and Sotsky, R. (1971). 'American children with reading problems can easily learn to read English represented by Chinese characters', *Science, 171*, 1264–7.

Ryan, E. J. (1961). 'The value system of a Chinese community in Java'. Unpublished doctoral thesis, Harvard University.

Ryback, D., Sanders, A. L., Lorentz, J., and Koestenblatt, M. (1980). 'Child-rearing practices reported by students in six cultures', *Journal of Social Psychology, 110*, 153–62.

Ryle, G. (1949). *The Concept of Mind*. London: Hutchinson.

Salaff, J. (1981). *Working Daughters of Hong Kong*. Cambridge: Cambridge University Press.

Salili, R., and Hoosain, R. (1985). 'Hyperactivity among Hong Kong Chinese children', *International Journal of Intercultural Relations, 9*, 177–85.

Sampson, E. E. (1977). 'Psychology and the American ideal', *Journal of Personality and Social Psychology, 35*, 767–82.

Sanford, F. H., and Older, H. J. (1950). *A Short Authoritarian–Equalitarian Scale*. Philadelphia: Institute for Research in Human Relations. Report No. 16, Series A, June.

Sarason, S. B., Davidson, K. S., Lighthall, F. F., Waite, R. R., and Ruebush, B. K. (1960). *Anxiety in Elementary School Children: a Report of Research*. New York: Wiley.

Sasanuma, S., Itoh, M. K., Mori, K., and Kobayashi, Y. (1977). 'Tachistoscopic recognition of Kana and Kanji words', *Neuropsychologia, 15*, 547–53.

Schaefer, E., Bell, R., and Bayley, N. (1959). 'Development of a maternal behavior research instrument', *Journal of Genetic Psychology, 95,* 83–104.

Schiffman, H. R. (1976). *Sensation and Perception: an Integrated Approach.* New York: Wiley.

Schlosberg, H. (1954). 'Three dimensions of emotion', *Psychological Review, 61,* 81–8.

Schneider, D. W., Hastorf, A. H., and Ellsworth, P. E. (1979). *Person Perception* (second edition). Reading, Mass.: Addison-Wesley.

Schwartz, G. E. (1980). 'Testing the biopsychosocial model: the ultimate challenge facing behavioral medicine?', *Journal of Consulting and Clinical Psychology, 50*(6), 1040–53.

Scofield, R. W., and Sun, C. W. (1960). 'A comparative study of the differential effect upon personality of Chinese and American child training practices', *Journal of Social Psychology, 52,* 221–4.

Sears, P. S. (1951). 'Doll play aggression in normal young children: influence of sex, age, sibling status, father's absence', *Psychological Monographs, 65*(6).

Sears, R. R., Maccoby, E. E., and Levin, H. (1957). *Patterns of Child Rearing.* New York: Harper and Row.

Segall, M. H., Campbell, D. T., and Herskovits, M. J. (1966). *The Influence of Culture on Visual Perception.* Indianapolis: Bobbs-Merrill.

Selby, H. A. (1977). 'Semantics and causality in the study of deviance'. In M. Sanches and B. G. Blount (Eds.), *Sociocultural Dimensions of Language Change* (pp. 11–24). New York: Academic Press.

Seligman, M. E. P. (1975). *Helplessness: on Depression, Development, and Death.* San Francisco: Freeman.

_____(1978). 'Comment and integration', *Journal of Abnormal Psychology, 87,* 165–79.

_____, Abramson, L. V., Semmel, A., and Von Baeyer, C. (1979). 'Depressive attributional style', *Journal of Abnormal Psychology, 88,* 242–7.

Serpell, R. (1976). *Culture's Influence on Behaviour.* London: Methuen.

Shanghai Mental Hospital (1981). *Study on MBD Children in Shanghai.* Nanjing: WHO/Nanjing Workshop on Child Psychiatry.

Shen, E. C. (1927). 'An analysis of eye movements in the reading of Chinese', *Journal of Experimental Psychology, 10,* 158–83.

_____(1936). 'Differences between Chinese and American reactions to the Bernreuter Personality Inventory', *Journal of Social Psychology, 7,* 471–4.

_____and Liu, C. C. (1935). 'The norms for Bernreuter's Personality Inventory in China', *Education and Vocation, 161,* 11–13. (In Chinese.)

Shen, Y. C. (1985). 'The mental health home care program: Beijing's rural Haidian district'. In W. S. Tseng and D. Wu (Eds.), *Chinese Culture and Mental Health* (pp. 357–66). New York: Academic Press.

Shweder, R. A., and Bourne, E. J. (1982). 'Does the concept of the person vary cross-culturally?'. In A. J. Marsella and G. M. White (Eds.), *Cultural Conceptions of Mental Health and Therapy* (pp. 97–137). Dordrecht, Netherlands: D. Reidel.

Sidel, R. (1972). *Women and Child Care in China: a Firsthand Report*. New York: Hill and Wang.

——(1973). 'The role of revolutionary optimism in the treatment of mental illness in the People's Republic of China', *American Journal of Orthopsychiatry, 43*, 732–6.

——and Sidel, V. (1972). 'The human services in China', *Social Policy, 3*, 25–30.

Sidel, V., and Sidel, R. (1973). *Serve the People: Observations on Medicine in the People's Republic of China*. New York: Josiah Macy jun. Foundation.

Silin, R. (1972). 'Marketing and credit in a Hong Kong wholesale market'. In W. E. Willmott (Ed.), *Economic Organization in Chinese Society* (pp. 327–52). Stanford: Stanford University Press.

——(1976). *Leadership and Values*. Cambridge, Mass.: Harvard University Press.

Silver, S. D., and Pollack, R. H. (1967). 'Racial difference in pigmentation of the Fundus oculi', *Psychonomic Science, 7*, 159–60.

Silverman, A. J., Adevai, G., and McGough, E. W. (1966). 'Some relationships between handedness and perception', *Journal of Psychosomatic Research, 10*, 151–8.

Singer, K. (1972). 'Drinking pattern and alcoholism in the Chinese', *British Journal of Addiction, 67*, 3–14.

——(1974). 'The choice of intoxicant among the Chinese', *British Journal of Addiction, 69*, 257–68.

——(1976a). 'Culture and mental health: II, childhood and family'. In W. H. Lo, W. Chan, K. S. Ma, A. Wong, and K. K. Yeung (Eds.), *Perspectives in Mental Health, Hong Kong, 1976* (pp. 45–8). Hong Kong: Mental Health Association of Hong Kong.

——(1976b). 'Culture and mental health: III, psychodynamics'. In W. H. Lo, W. Chan, K. S. Ma, A. Wong, and K. K. Yeung (Eds.), *Perspectives in Mental Health, Hong Kong, 1976* (pp. 49–54). Hong Kong: Mental Health Association of Hong Kong.

——(1977). 'Somatization and new cross-cultural psychiatry — reply', *Social Science and Medicine, 11*(1), 11–12.

——, Chang, P. T., and Hsu, G. L. K. (1972). 'Physique, personality and mental illness in the southern Chinese', *British Journal of Psychiatry, 121*, 315–19.

——, Lieh-Mak, F., and Ng, M. L. (1976). 'Physique, personality and mental illness in southern Chinese women', *British Journal of Psychiatry, 129*, 243–7.

____, Ney, P. G., and Lieh-Mak, F. (1978). 'A cultural perspective on child psychiatric disorders', *Comprehensive Psychiatry, 19*, 533–40.

Singh, P. N., Huang, S., and Thompson, G. C. (1962). 'A comparative study of selected attitudes, values, and personality characteristics of American, Chinese, and Indian students', *Journal of Social Psychology, 57*, 123–32.

Smith, A. H. (1894). *Chinese Characteristics*. New York: Fleming H. Revell. (Reprinted 1972 by Oliphont, Anderson and Ferrier, London.)

Smith, M. E. (1938). 'A comparison of the neurotic tendencies of students of different racial ancestry in Hawaii', *Journal of Social Psychology, 9*, 395–417.

Smith, N. V. O., and Vinacke, W. E. (1951). 'Reactions to humorous stimuli of different generations of Japanese, Chinese and Caucasians in Hawaii', *Journal of Social Psychology, 34*, 69–96.

Snyder, M. (1979). 'Self-monitoring processes'. In L. Berkowitz (Ed.), *Advances in Experimental Social Psychology, 12* (pp. 85–128). New York: Academic Press.

____(1982). 'When believing means doing: creating links between attitudes and behavior'. In M. P. Zanna, E. T. Higgins, and C. P. Herman (Eds.), *Consistency in Social Behavior: the Ontario Symposium* (vol. 2, pp. 90–122). Hillsdale, New Jersey: Erlbaum.

Sollenberger, R. T. (1968). 'Chinese-American child-rearing practices and juvenile delinquency', *Journal of Social Psychology, 74*, 13–23.

Solomon, R. H. (1965). 'Educational themes in China's changing culture', *China Quarterly, 22*, 154–70.

____(1969). 'Mao's effort to reintegrate the Chinese polity: problems of authority and conflict in Chinese social processes'. In A. D. Barnett (Ed.), *Chinese Communist Politics in Action* (pp. 271–361). Seattle: University of Washington Press.

____(1971). *Mao's Revolution and the Chinese Political Culture*. Berkeley, Calif.: University of California Press.

Song, W. Z. (1981). 'Application of the Minnesota Multiphasic Personality Inventory in some areas of the People's Republic of China'. Paper presented at the 7th International Conference on Personality Assessment, Honolulu, Hawaii, February.

Soong, Y. S. (1979). 'A comparative research on the administrative behavior of medium- and small-scale businesses in Taiwan'. Unpublished master's thesis, National Taiwan University. (In Chinese.)

Sterba, R. L. A. (1978). 'Clandestine management in the Imperial Chinese bureaucracy', *Academy of Management Review, 3*, 69–78.

Stern, J. A. (1978). 'Eye movements, reading, and cognition'. In J. W. Senders, D. F. Fisher, and R. A. Monty (Eds.), *Eye Movements and the Higher Psychological Functions* (pp. 145–55). Hillsdale, New Jersey: Erlbaum.

Stevenson, H. W., Stigler, J. W., Lucker, G. W., Lee, S.-Y., Hsu, C. C., and Kitamura, S. (1982). 'Reading disabilities: the case of Chinese, Japanese, and English', *Child Development*, *53*, 1164–81.

Stover, L. E. (1974). *The Cultural Ecology of Chinese Civilization*. New York: New American Library.

Su, C. W. (1968). 'The child's perception of parent's role', *Psychology and Education* (Taiwan Normal University), *2*, 87–109. (In Chinese.)

——(1969). 'A study of aggressive behavior in preschool children', *Psychology and Education* (Taiwan Normal University), *3*, 11–28. (In Chinese.)

——(1975a). 'Maternal child rearing attitudes and practices in relation to aggressive behavior of school children', *Bulletin of Educational Psychology* (Taiwan Normal University), *8*, 25–44. (In Chinese.)

——(1975b). 'Parental child-rearing practices as related to moral behavior in adolescence', *Acta Psychologica Taiwanica*, *17*, 109–24. (In Chinese.)

——(1976). 'The perceived parental attitudes of high-achieving and under-achieving junior high school students', *Bulletin of Educational Psychology* (Taiwan Normal University), *9*, 22–32. (In Chinese.)

——, Hwang, C. H., Lu, C. M., and Chen, S. M. (1979). 'Parent-child relationship and personality development of Chinese school children', *Bulletin of Educational Psychology* (Taiwan Normal University), *12*, 195–212. (In Chinese.)

Sue, D., Ino, S., and Sue, D. M. (1983). 'Nonassertiveness of Asian Americans: an inaccurate assumption?', *Journal of Counseling Psychology*, *30*(4), 581–8.

Sue, D. W. (1978). 'Eliminating cultural oppression in counseling: toward a general theory', *Journal of Counseling Psychology*, *25*, 419–28.

——and Kirk, B. A. (1972). 'Psychological characteristics of Chinese-American students', *Journal of Counseling Psychology*, *19*, 471–8.

——and Kirk, B. A. (1975). 'Asian Americans: use of counseling services on a college campus', *Journal of Counseling Psychology*, *22*, 84–6.

——and Sue, D. (1973). 'Understanding Asian-Americans: the neglected minority', *Personnel and Guidance Journal*, *51*, 386–9.

——and Sue, D. (1977). 'Barriers to effective cross-cultural counseling', *Journal of Counseling Psychology*, *24*, 420–9.

——and Sue, S. (1972). 'Counseling Chinese-Americans', *Personnel and Guidance Journal*, *50*, 637–44.

Sue, S., and Nakamura, C. Y. (1984). 'An integrative model of physiological and social/psychological factors in alcohol consumption among Chinese and Japanese Americans', *Journal of Drug Issues*, *2*, 349–64.

Sue, S., and Sue, D. W. (1971). 'Chinese American personality and mental health', *Amerasia Journal*, *1*(2), 36–49.

——(1974). 'MMPI comparisons between Asian-American and non-Asian students utilizing a student health psychiatric clinic', *Journal of Counseling Psychology, 21,* 423–7.

Sugg, M. L. (1975). 'Adolescent aggression in Hong Kong'. Unpublished manuscript, Social Research Centre, The Chinese University of Hong Kong.

Sun, C. W. (1968). 'A comparative study of Chinese and American college students on the Cattell Sixteen Personality Factor Questionnaire', *Psychological Testing* (Taipei), *8,* 33–7. (In Chinese.)

Szalay, L. B., and Deese, J. (1978). *Subjective Meaning and Culture: an Assessment through Word Association.* Hillsdale, New Jersey: Erlbaum.

Tajfel, H. (1974). 'Social identity and inter-group behavior', *Social Science Information, 13,* 65–93.

___(Ed.) (1978). *Differentiation between Social Groups: Studies in Intergroup Behaviour.* London: Academic Press.

Tan, E. S. (1981). 'Culture-bound syndromes among overseas Chinese'. In A. Kleinman and T. Y. Lin (Eds.), *Normal and Abnormal Behavior in Chinese Culture* (pp. 371–86). Dordrecht, Netherlands: D. Reidel.

Tan, H. (1967). 'Intercultural study of counseling expectancies', *Journal of Counseling Psychology, 41,* 122–30.

Tarwater, J. W. (1966). 'Chinese and American students' interpersonal values: a cross-cultural comparison', *Journal of College Student Personnel, 7,* 351–4.

Taylor, D. M., and Brown, R. J. (1979). 'Towards a more social social psychology?', *British Journal of Social and Clinical Psychology, 18,* 173–80.

Taylor, I. (1981). 'Writing systems and reading'. In G. E. MacKinnon and T. G. Waller (Eds.), *Reading Research: Advances in Theory and Practice* (Vol. 2, pp. 1–51). New York: Academic Press.

___and Taylor, M. M. (1983). *The Psychology of Reading.* New York: Academic Press.

Taylor, S. E., and Fiske, S. T. (1975). 'Point of view and perception of causality', *Journal of Personality and Social Psychology, 32,* 439–45.

Tedeschi, J. T., Gaes, G. G., and Rivera, A. N. (1977). 'Aggression and the use of coercive power', *Journal of Social Issues, 33,* 101–25.

Tedeschi, J. T., and Riess, M. (1981). 'Verbal strategies in impression management'. In C. Antaki (Ed.), *Ordinary Language Explanations of Social Behaviour* (pp. 272–310). London: Academic Press.

Thomas, A., and Chess, S. (1977). *Temperament and Development.* New York: Brunner/Mazel.

Thompson, C. M. (1979). 'Single-parent women'. Unpublished master's thesis, Wilfred Laurier University.

Thorndike, E. L., and Lorge, I. (1944). *The Teacher's Word Book of 30,000 Words.* New York: Bureau of Publications, Teachers College.

Thumb, A., and Marbe, K. (1901). *Experimentelle Untersuchungen über die psychologischen Grundlagen der sprachlichen Analogiebildung.* Leipzig: Engelmann.

Topley, M. (1970). *Chinese Traditional Ideas and the Treatment of Disease: Two Examples from Hong Kong.* Hong Kong: Centre of Asian Studies Reprint Series no. 24, University of Hong Kong.

Torrance, E. P. (1966). *Torrance Tests of Creative Thinking: Norms—Technical Manual.* Princeton, New Jersey: Personnel Press.

Treiman, R. A., Baron, J., and Luk, K. (1981). 'Speech recoding in silent reading: a comparison of Chinese and English', *Journal of Chinese Linguistics, 9,* 116–25.

Triandis, H. C. (1972). *The Analysis of Subjective Culture.* New York: Wiley.

――(in press). 'Collectivism vs individualism: a reconceptualization of a basic concept in cross-cultural psychology'. In C. Bagley and G. K. Verma (Eds.), *Personality, Cognition and Values: Cross-cultural Perspectives of Childhood and Adolescence.* London: Macmillan.

――and Vassiliou, V. (1967). 'Frequency of contact and stereotyping', *Journal of Personality and Social Psychology, 7,* 316–28.

――, Vassiliou, V., and Nassiakou, M. (1968). 'Three cross-cultural studies of subjective culture', *Journal of Personality and Social Psychology Monograph Suppl., 8,* 1–42.

Tsai, T., Teng, L. N., and Sue, S. (1981). 'Mental health status of Chinese in the United States'. In A. Kleinman and T. Y. Lin (Eds.), *Normal and Abnormal Behavior in Chinese Culture* (pp. 291–310). Dordrecht, Netherlands: D. Reidel.

Tsai, W. F. (1966). 'A study of interpersonal relationships in the family', *Thought and Word, 4*(2), 25–7. (In Chinese.)

Tsao, K. S. (1981). 'Generation gap among Taipei high school students', *Acta Psychologica Taiwanica, 23,* 9–16. (In Chinese.)

Tsao, Y. C. (1973). 'Comprehension processes in bilinguals'. Unpublished doctoral thesis, State University of New York, Buffalo.

Tseng, M. S. (1972). 'Attitudes towards the disabled: a cross-cultural study', *Journal of Social Psychology, 87,* 311–12.

Tseng, T. T. (1978). 'The relationship between principals' leadership style and the working morale of teachers in junior high schools of Taiwan'. Unpublished master's thesis, National Taiwan Normal University. (In Chinese.)

Tseng, T. Y. (1978). 'The administrative system of medium- and small-scale businesses in Taiwan'. Unpublished master's thesis, National Chengchi University (In Chinese.)

Tseng, W. S. (1972). 'On Chinese national character from the viewpoint of personality development'. In Y. Y. Li and K. S. Yang (Eds.), *The Character of the Chinese: an Interdisciplinary Approach* (Monograph Series B, No. 4, pp. 227–50). Taipei: Institute of Ethnology, Academia Sinica. (In Chinese.)

____(1973a). 'The concept of personality in Confucian thought', *Psychiatry, 36*, 191–202.

____(1973b). 'The development of psychiatric concepts in traditional Chinese medicine', *Archives of General Psychiatry, 29*, 569–75.

____(1975a). 'The nature of somatic complaints among psychiatric patients: the Chinese case', *Comprehensive Psychiatry, 16*, 237–45.

____(1975b). 'Traditional and modern psychiatric care in Taiwan'. In A. Kleinman, P. Kunstadter, E. R. Alexander, and J. L. Gale (Eds.), *Medicine in Chinese Culture: Comparative Studies of Health Care in Chinese and Other Societies* (pp. 177–94). Washington, DC: United States Department of Health, Education, and Welfare.

____and Hsu, J. (1969–70). 'Chinese culture, personality formation and mental illness', *International Journal of Social Psychiatry, 16*, 5–14.

____and Hsu, J. (1972). 'The Chinese attitude toward parental authority as expressed in Chinese children's stories', *Archives of General Psychiatry, 26*, 28–34.

Tsoi, W. F. (1985). 'Mental health in Singapore and its relation to Chinese culture'. In W. S. Tseng and D. Wu (Eds.), *Chinese Culture and Mental Health* (pp. 229–50). New York: Academic Press.

____and Chen, A. J. (1979). 'New admissions to Woodridge Hospital, 1975 with special reference to schizophrenia', *Annals of the Academy of Medicine, 8*(3), 275–9.

Turner, H. A. (1980). *The Last Colony: But Whose?* Cambridge: Cambridge University Press.

Tzeng, O. J. L., and Hung, D. L. (1981). 'Linguistic determinism: a written language perspective'. In C. J. L. Tzeng and H. Singer (Eds.), *Perception of Print: Reading Research in Experimental Psychology* (pp.237–55). Hillsdale, New Jersey: Erlbaum.

____, Cotton, B., and Wang, W. S.-Y. (1979). 'Visual lateralization effect in reading Chinese characters', *Nature, 282*, 488–501.

____, and Wang, W. S.-Y. (1977). 'Speech recoding in reading Chinese characters', *Journal of Experimental Psychology: Human Learning and Memory, 3*, 621–30.

Tzeng, O. J. L., and Wang, W. S.-Y. (1983). 'The first two R's', *American Scientist, 71*, 238–43.

Vagg, P. R., and Hammond, S. B. (1976). 'The number and kind of invariant personality (Q) factors: a partial replication of Eysenck and Eysenck', *British Journal of Social and Clinical Psychology, 15*, 121–9.

Vernon, P. E. (1982). *The Abilities and Achievements of Orientals in North America*. New York: Academic Press.

Vinacke, W. E. (1949). 'The judgment of facial expressions by three national-racial groups in Hawaii: I. Caucasian faces', *Journal of Personality, 17*, 407–29.

____and Fong, R. W. (1955). 'The judgment of facial expressions by three national-racial groups in Hawaii: II. Oriental faces', *Journal of Social Psychology, 41,* 185–95.

Vogel, E. F. (1979). *Japan as Number One.* Cambridge, Mass.: Harvard University Press.

Walder, A. G. (1983). 'Organized dependency and cultures of authority in Chinese industry', *Journal of Asian Studies, 63,* 51–75.

Walters, J., Pearce, D., and Dahms, L. (1957). 'Affectional and aggressive behavior of preschool children', *Child Development, 28,* 15–26.

Wan, K. C., and Bond, M. H. (1982). 'Chinese attributions for success and failure under public and anonymous conditions of rating', *Acta Psychologica Taiwanica, 24,* 23–31.

Wang, L. W. (1981). 'Values and the alienation attitudes towards the school: the case of junior high school students'. Unpublished master's thesis, National Taiwan University. (In Chinese.)

Ward, B. E. (1970). 'Temper tantrums in Kau Sai: some speculations upon their effects'. In P. Mayer (Ed.), *Socialization: the Approach from Social Anthropology* (pp. 109–25). London: Tavistock.

Wason, P. C. (1959). 'The processing of positive and negative information', *Quarterly Journal of Experimental Psychology, 11,* 92–107.

Waterman, A. S. (1981). 'Individualism and interdependence', *American Psychologist, 36,* 762–73.

Watrous, B. G., and Hsu, F. L. K. (1963). 'A thematic apperception test study of Chinese, Hindu, and American college students'. In F. L. K. Hsu, *Clan, Caste, and Club* (pp. 263–311). New York: van Nostrand.

Weakland, J. (1950). 'The organization of action in Chinese culture', *Psychiatry, 13,* 361–70.

——(1956). 'Orality in Chinese conceptions of male genital sexuality', *Psychiatry, 19,* 237–47.

Wegner, D. M., and Vallacher, R. R. (Eds.) (1980). *The Self in Social Psychology.* Oxford: Oxford University Press.

Wei, C. T. (1972). 'The ideal character of the traditional Chinese'. In Y. Y. Li and K. S. Yang (Eds.), *Symposium on the Character of the Chinese: an Interdisciplinary Approach* (pp. 1–45). Taipei: Institute of Ethnology, Academia Sinica. (In Chinese.)

Weiner, B., Heckhausen, H., Meyer, W., and Cook, R. E. (1972). 'Causal ascriptions and achievement behavior: the conceptual analysis of effort', *Journal of Personality and Social Psychology, 21,* 239–48.

Weinreich, H. (1970). 'Some consequences of replicating Kohlberg's original moral development study on a British sample', *Journal of Moral Education, 7,* 32–9.

Weinshall, T. D. (Ed.) (1977). *Culture and Management.* London: Penguin.

Weinstein, M. S. (1969). 'Achievement motivation and risk preference', *Journal of Personality and Social Psychology, 13,* 153–72.

Wen, C. I. (1972a). 'Chinese national character as revealed in value orientations'. In Y. Y. Li and K. S. Yang (Eds.), *Symposium on the*

Character of the Chinese: an Interdisciplinary Approach (pp. 47–84). Nankang, Taipei: Institute of Ethnology, Academia Sinica. (In Chinese.)

_____(1972b). 'Stability and change of traditional Chinese values', *Bulletin of the Institute of Ethnology, Academia Sinica, 33,* 287–301. (In Chinese.)

_____(1979). 'Community differences in values: a comparison of four Chinese communities'. In *Collection of Papers for the Celebration of Professor H. S. Tao's Eightieth Birth Anniversary.* Taipei: Shih Huo Publishing Co. (In Chinese.)

Wen, J. K., and Wang, C. L. (1981). '*Shen-k'uei* syndrome: a culture-specific sexual neurosis in Taiwan'. In A. Kleinman and T. Y. Lin (Eds.), *Normal and Abnormal Behavior in Chinese Culture* (pp. 357–69). Dordrecht, Netherlands: D. Reidel.

Werner, O., and Campbell, D. T. (1970). 'Translating, working through interpreters, and the problem of decentering'. In R. N. Naroll and R. Cohen (Eds.), *A Handbook of Methods in Cultural Anthropology* (pp. 398–422). New York: Columbia University Press.

Westbrook, C. H., and Yao, H. H. (1937). 'Emotional stability of Chinese adolescents as measured by the Woodworth–Cady–Mathews Questionnaire', *Journal of Social Psychology, 8,* 401–9.

White, G. M. (1982). 'The role of cultural explanations in "somatization" and "psychologization" ', *Social Science and Medicine, 16,* 1519–30.

Whitney, R. E. (1971). 'Agreement and positivity in pleasantness ratings of balanced and unbalanced social situations: a cross-cultural study', *Journal of Personality and Social Psychology, 17,* 11–14.

Whittaker, J. O., and Meade, R. D. (1968). 'Retention of opinion change as a function of differential source credibility: a cross-cultural study', *International Journal of Psychology, 3,* 103–8.

Whorf, B. (1956). *Language, Thought, and Reality.* Cambridge, Mass.: Massachusetts Institute of Technology Press.

Wilson, R. W. (1970). *Learning to be Chinese: the Political Socialization of Children in Taiwan.* Cambridge, Mass.: Massachusetts Institute of Technology Press.

_____(1973). 'Shame and behaviour in Chinese society', *Asian Profile, 1,* 431–47.

_____(1974). *The Moral State: a Study of the Political Socialization of Chinese and American Children.* New York: The Free Press.

_____(1977). 'Perceptions of group structure and leadership position as an aspect of deviance and social control'. In A. A. Wilson, S. L. Greenblatt, and R. W. Wilson (Eds.), *Deviance and Social Control in Chinese Society* (pp. 52–66). New York: Praeger.

_____(1981). 'Moral behavior in Chinese society: a theoretical perspective'. In R. W. Wilson, S. L. Greenblatt, and A. A. Wilson (Eds.), *Moral Behavior in Chinese Society* (pp. 1–37). New York: Praeger.

_____and Pusey, A. W. (1982). 'Achievement motivation and small business relationship patterns in Chinese society'. In S. L. Greenblatt, R. W. Wilson, and A. A. Wilson (Eds.), *Social Interaction in Chinese Society*. New York: Praeger.

Wing, J. K., Cooper, J. E., and Sartorius, N. (1974). *The Description and Classification of Psychiatric Symptoms: an Instruction Manual for the PSE and CATEGO System*. London: Cambridge University Press.

Witkin, H. A. (1967). 'Cognitive styles across cultures: a cognitive style approach to cross-cultural research', *International Journal of Psychology, 2*, 233–50.

―――and Berry, J. W. (1975). 'Psychological differentiation in cross-cultural perspective', *Journal of Cross-Cultural Psychology, 6*, 4–87.

―――, Dyk, R. B., Paterson, H. F., Goodenough, D. R., and Karp, S. A. (1962). *Psychological Differentiation*. New York: Wiley.

―――, Goodenough, D. R., and Oltman, P. K. (1979). 'Psychological differentiation: current status', *Journal of Personality and Social Psychology, 32*, 1127–45.

―――, Lewis, H. B., Hertzman, M., Machover, K., Meissner, P. B., and Wapner, S. (1954). *Personality through Perception*. New York: Harper and Row.

Wolf, A. P. (1964). 'Aggression in a Hokkien village: a preliminary description'. Paper presented at a seminar on Personality and Motivation in Chinese Society, Bermuda, January.

Wolf, M. (1970). 'Child training and the Chinese family'. In M. Freedman (Ed.), *Family and Kinship in Chinese Society* (pp. 37–62). Stanford, Calif.: Stanford University Press. (Republished in A. P. Wolf (Ed.), *Studies in Chinese Society* (pp. 221–46). Stanford, Calif.: Stanford University Press, 1978.)

Wolfenstein, M. (1955). 'Some variants in moral training of children'. In M. Mead and M. Wolfenstein (Eds.), *Childhood in Contemporary Cultures* (pp. 349–68). Chicago: University of Chicago Press.

Wolff, P. (1972). 'Ethnic differences in alcohol sensitivity', *Science, 125*, 449–51.

Wong, C. K., and Chan, T. S. C. (1984). 'Somatic symptoms among Chinese psychiatric patients', *Hong Kong Journal of Mental Health, 13*, 5–21.

Wong, G. Y. Y. (1985). 'Organisation structure and culture: a study of transnational banks in Hong Kong', Mong Kwok Ping Management Data Bank Working Paper, Department of Management Studies, University of Hong Kong.

Wong, J. C. H., Lai, P. M. Y., Wong, C. K., Hong, K. W., and Chen, C. N. (1984). 'The preliminary findings of work carried out with psychiatric patients and normal controls'. Paper given at the Symposium on Cross-Cultural Psychiatric Epidemiology, Hong Kong, May.

Wong, J. S. (1950). *Fifth Chinese Daughter*. New York: Harper and Row. (Republished London: Hurst and Blackett, 1952.)

Wong, S. L. (1979). 'Industrial entrepreneurship and ethnicity: a study of the Shanghainese cotton spinners in Hong Kong'. Unpublished doctoral thesis, University of Oxford.

Wong, T. (1982). 'Aggression, personality and political culture', *Bulletin of the Hong Kong Psychological Society, 9*, 5–17.

Woo, E. Y. C., and Hoosain, R. (1984). 'Visual and auditory functions of Chinese dyslexics', *Psychologia, 27*, 164–70.

World Bank (1984). *World Development Report 1984*. New York: Oxford University Press.

World Health Organization (1973). *Pilot Study of Schizophrenia*. Geneva: WHO.

Wright, A. F. (1962). 'Values, roles and personalities'. In A. F. Wright and D. Twitchett (Eds.), *Confucian Personalities* (pp. 3–23). Stanford: Stanford University Press.

Wright, G. N., Phillips, L. D., Whalley, P. C., Choo, G. T., Ng, K. O., Tan, I., and Wishuda, A. (1978). 'Cultural differences in probabilistic thinking', *Journal of Cross-Cultural Psychology, 9*, 285–99.

Wu, D. (1982). 'Psychotherapy and emotion in traditional Chinese medicine'. In A. J. Marsella and G. M. White (Eds.), *Cultural Conceptions of Mental Health and Therapy* (pp. 285–301). Dordrecht, Netherlands: D. Reidel.

Wu, D. Y. H. (1981). 'Child abuse in Taiwan'. In J. E. Korbin (Ed.), *Child Abuse and Neglect: Cross-cultural Perspectives* (pp. 139–65). Berkeley: University of California Press.

Wu, H. Y. (1984). *A Comparative Study of Value Patterns of Medical and non-Medical Students in Taiwan*. Taipei, Taiwan: Chung-Shung Publishing Co. (In Chinese.)

Wu, Y. H. (1966). 'An anthropologist looks at Chinese child training method', *Thought and Word, 3*(6), 3–7. (In Chinese.)

Xia, Z. Y. (1985). 'The mental health delivery system in Shanghai'. In W. S. Tseng and D. Wu (Eds.), *Chinese Culture and Mental Health* (pp.341–56). New York: Academic Press.

_____, Yan, H. Q., and Wang, C. H. (1980). 'Mental health work in Shanghai', *Chinese Medical Journal, 93*, 127–9.

Yang, C. F. (1982). 'The "pao" of Chinese consumer behavior'. Unpublished manuscript, The Chinese University of Hong Kong.

Yang, K. S. (1965). 'Psychological studies on Chinese national character: a literature review', *Thought and Word* (Taipei), *2*, 3–19. (In Chinese.)

_____(1967a). 'A comparative study on the motivational and temperamental characteristics of Malaya and Singapore overseas Chinese students in Taiwan', *Bulletin of the Institute of Ethnology, Academia Sinica, 22*, 139–68.

_____(1967b). 'Need patterns of overseas Chinese students in Taiwan from different Southeast Asian countries', *Acta Psychologica Taiwanica, 9*, 1–23. (In Chinese.)

___(1970). 'Authoritarianism and evaluation of appropriateness of role behaviour', *Journal of Social Psychology, 80*, 171–81.

___(1972). 'Expressed values of Chinese college students'. In Y. Y. Li and K. S. Yang (Eds.), *Symposium on the Character of the Chinese: an Interdisciplinary Approach* (pp. 257–312). Taipei: Institute of Ethnology, Academia Sinica. (In Chinese.)

___(1974). 'Individual modernity and reactions to frustration'. Unpublished manuscript, National Taiwan University. (In Chinese.)

___(1976). 'Psychological correlates of family size, son preference, and birth control', *Acta Psychologica Taiwanica, 18*, 67–94. (In Chinese.)

___(1981a). 'Social orientation and individual modernity among Chinese students in Taiwan', *Journal of Social Psychology, 113*, 159–70.

___(1981b). 'The formation and change of Chinese personality: a cultural-ecological perspective', *Acta Psychologica Taiwanica, 23*, 39–56. (In Chinese.)

___(1982a). 'Sinicization of psychological research in a Chinese society: directions and issues'. In K. S. Yang and C. I. Wen (Eds.), *The Sinicization of Social and Behavioural Science Research in China* (pp. 153–87). Taipei: Institute of Ethnology, Academia Sinica. (In Chinese.)

___(1982b). '*Yuan* (緣) and its functions in modern Chinese life'. In *Proceedings of the Conference on Traditional Culture and Modern Life* (pp. 103–28). Taipei: Committee on the Renaissance of Chinese Culture. (In Chinese.)

___and Bond, M. H. (1980). 'Ethnic affirmation in Chinese bilinguals', *Journal of Cross-Cultural Psychology, 11*, 411–25.

___and Bond, M. H. (1983). 'The Chinese orientation towards the description of personality'. Paper presented at the Conference on Modernization and Chinese Culture, The Chinese University of Hong Kong, Hong Kong, March.

___and Chang, F. L. (1975). 'Chinese value orientations and their change: the case of university students'. Unpublished manuscript, National Taiwan University. (In Chinese.)

___, Chen, W. Y., and Hsu, C. Y. (1965). 'Rorschach responses of normal adults: IV. The speed of production', *Acta Psychologica Taiwanica, 7*, 34–51.

___and Hchu, H. Y. (1974). 'Determinants, correlates, and consequences of Chinese individual modernity', *Bulletin of the Institute of Ethnology, Academia Sinica, 37*, 1–38. (In Chinese.)

___and Hwang, L. L. (1984). 'The change of preferences for ways to live of Chinese students in Taiwan: twenty years later'. Paper read at the Interdisciplinary Conference on Social and Cultural Change in Taiwan held in the Institute of Ethnology, Academia Sinica, Taipei, September. (In Chinese.)

___and Lee, P. H. (1971). 'Likeability, meaningfulness, and familiarity of 557 Chinese adjectives for personality trait description', *Acta Psychologica Taiwanica, 13*, 36–57. (In Chinese.)

___and Liang, W. H. (1973). 'Some correlates of achievement motivation among Chinese high school boys', *Acta Psychologica Taiwanica, 15*, 59–67. (In Chinese.)

___, Tsai, S. G., and Hwang, M. L. (1963). 'Rorschach responses of normal Chinese adults: III. Number of responses and number of refusals', *Psychological Testing* (Taipei), *10*, 127–36. (In Chinese.)

___ and Yang, P. H. L. (1974). 'Relationship of repression-sensitization to self-evaluation, neuroticism, and extraversion among Chinese senior high school boys', *Acta Psychologica Taiwanica, 16*, 111–18. (In Chinese.)

Yang, L. S. (1957). 'The concept of *pao* as a basis for social relations in China'. In J. K. Fairbank (Ed.), *Chinese Thought and Institutions* (pp. 291–309). Chicago: University of Chicago Press.

___(1968). 'Historical notes on the Chinese world order'. In J. K. Fairbank (Ed.), *The Chinese World Order* (pp. 20–33). Cambridge, Mass.: Harvard University Press.

Yang, M. C. (1945). *A Chinese Village*. New York: Columbia University Press.

___(1967). 'Child training and child behavior in varying family patterns in a changing Chinese society', *Journal of Sociology* (National Taiwan University), *3*, 77–83. (In Chinese.)

Yang, M. J., and Hwang, K. K. (1980). 'The wedge model of self-disclosure and its correlates', *Acta Psychologica Taiwanica, 22*, 51–70. (In Chinese.)

Yang, P. H. L., and Yang, K. S. (1970). 'National-ethnic stereotypes of 240 Chinese students at the National Taiwan University', *Acta Psychologica Taiwanica, 12*, 7–32. (In Chinese.)

___(1972). 'Change in the stereotypes of National Taiwan University students towards different national and ethnic groups', *Acta Psychologica Taiwanica, 14*, 137–56. (In Chinese.)

Yang, X. L. (1985). 'An investigation of minimal brain disorders among primary school students in the Beijing area'. In W. S. Tseng and D. Wu (Eds.), *Chinese Culture and Mental Health* (pp. 315–24). New York: Academic Press.

Yap, P. M. (1965a). 'Koro — a culture-bound depersonalization syndrome', *British Journal of Psychiatry, 111*, 43–50.

___(1965b). 'Phenomenology of affective disorder in Chinese and other cultures'. In A. V. S. de Reuck and R. Porter (Eds.), *Transcultural Psychiatry, CIBA Foundation Symposium* (pp. 84–114). London: J. and A. Churchill.

___(1967). 'Ideas of mental health and disorders in Hong Kong and their practical influence'. In M. Topley (Ed.), *Some Traditional Chinese Ideas and Conceptions in Hong Kong Social Life Today* (pp. 73–85). Hong Kong: Hong Kong Branch of the Royal Asiatic Society.

——(1971). 'Guilt and shame, depression and culture: a psychiatric cliché re-examined', *Community Contemporary Psychiatry, 1*(2), 35.

Yee, D. H., and Yang, K. S. (1977). 'Differences in attributional and coping responses between the actor and the observer under cheating situations', *Acta Psychologica Taiwanica, 19*, 111–24.

Yeh, E. K. (1985). 'Sociocultural changes and prevalence of mental disorders in Taiwan'. In W. S. Tseng and D. Wu (Eds.), *Chinese Culture and Mental Health* (pp. 265–86). New York: Academic Press.

——and Chu, H. M. (1974). 'The images of Chinese and American character: cross-cultural adaptation by Chinese students'. In W. P. Lebra (Ed.), *Youth, Socialization, and Mental Health Research in Asia and the Pacific* (pp. 200–16). Honolulu: University of Hawaii Press.

——, Chu, H. M., Ko, Y. H., Lin, T. Y., and Lee, S. P. (1972). 'Student mental health: an epidemiology study in Taiwan', *Acta Psychologica Taiwanica, 14*, 1–26 (In Chinese).

——, Fan, B. Y., and Tien, S. J. (1979). 'A statistical study of the discharged patients from the Taipei City Psychiatric Center during 1969–1978', *Ten Years Report of the Taipei City Psychiatric Center* (pp. 209–40). Taipei: Taipei City Psychiatric Center. (In Chinese.)

Yeh, M. H. (1981). 'The relationship of life stress, ego strength, and individual modernity to mental health'. Unpublished master's thesis, National Taiwan University. (In Chinese.)

Yong, H. L. (1973). 'The practice of nepotism: a study of sixty Chinese commercial firms in Singapore'. Unpublished bachelor's thesis, University of Singapore.

Young, L. W. L. (1982). 'Inscrutability revisited'. In J. J. Gumperz (Ed.), *Language and Social Identity* (pp. 72–84). Cambridge: Cambridge University Press.

Young, R. L. (1980). 'Social images and interpersonal interaction among Hong Kong and American students'. Unpublished master's thesis, University of Hawaii, Honolulu.

Yu, B., and Liu, I. (1982). 'Applicability of the model of Chinese sentence comprehension to English sentences', *Acta Psychologica Taiwanica, 24*, 59–63. (In Chinese.)

Yu, E. S. H. (1974). 'Achievement motive, familism, and *hsiao*: a replication of McClelland–Winterbottom studies', *Dissertation Abstracts International, 35*, 593A (University Microfilms No. 74-14, 942).

Yu, G. J. (1981). 'Report on the investigation and management of MBD children in a primary school in Beijing'. Paper presented at the First National Workshop on the Health of Children and Juveniles, Beijing, China.

Yu, L. (1985). 'An epidemiological study of child mental health problems in Nanjing district'. In W. S. Tseng and D. Wu (Eds.), *Chinese Culture and Mental Health* (pp. 305–14). New York: Academic Press.

Yuan, S. S. (1972). 'Family authority patterns, rearing practices and children's sense of political efficacy', *Thought and Word, 10*(4), 35–55. (In Chinese.)

Yuen, R. K. W., and Tinsley, H. E. A. (1981). 'International and American students' expectancies about counseling', *Journal of Counseling Psychology, 28*, 66–9.

Zhang, C. X. (1980). *Chinese Medical Treatment of Psychiatric Illness.* Hupei, China: Hupei People's Publishers. (In Chinese.)

Zimbardo, P. G. (1980). 'Cognitive and cultural contributions to shyness and loneliness'. Paper presented at the American Pyschological Association annual meeting, Montreal, Quebec, September.

Index